D0760954

Introduction to
Transportation
Security

Introduction to
Transportation
Security

Frances L. Edwards and Daniel C. Goodrich

CRC Press
Taylor & Francis Group
Boca Raton London New York

CRC Press is an imprint of the
Taylor & Francis Group, an **informa** business

CRC Press
Taylor & Francis Group
6000 Broken Sound Parkway NW, Suite 300
Boca Raton, FL 33487-2742

Printed in the United States of America on acid-free paper
Version Date: 20120618

International Standard Book Number: 978-1-4398-4576-9 (Hardback)

Library of Congress Cataloging-in-Publication Data

Edwards, Frances L.
    Introduction to transportation security / Frances L. Edwards, Daniel C. Goodrich.
        p. cm.
    Includes bibliographical references and index.
    ISBN 978-1-4398-4576-9 (alk. paper)
    1. Transportation--Security measures--United States. 2. Terrorism--Prevention--United States. I. Goodrich, Daniel C. II. Title.

HE194.5.U6E39 2013
363.28'70973--dc23   2012016178

Visit the Taylor & Francis Web site at
http://www.taylorandfrancis.com

and the CRC Press Web site at
http://www.crcpress.com

To

Colonel Horace E. Knapp, USMC (ret.)

Mentor, role model, and consummate public administrator

Contents

SECTION I   Safety, Security, and Emergency Management

SECTION II Multimodal Surface Transportation Security: Threats and Strategies

CHAPTER 6 — Road-Based Busses, Livery, Paratransit, Ambulances, and Delivery Vehicles 153

CHAPTER 7 — Mass Transit on Fixed Rails and Guideways 179

SECTION III Putting It All Together

Foreword

My long interest and connection with the world of transportation spans decades. That time has provided many memories, but none more vivid than September 11, 2001, when the airplanes crashed into the World Trade Center, the Pentagon, and a Pennsylvania field. As United States Secretary of Transportation, I stopped all flights in the country, grounding all the planes. That decision, a necessary and reasonable response, had consequences for millions of individuals and businesses. The economic costs both public and private were enormous, as were the emotional and actual losses. The use of planes as instruments for terrorism was a nightmare come true. We are still living with the consequences of that seminal event to this day.

As central as that series of attacks is to the American experience, there are many other incidents both here and abroad which make clear that the safety and security of all our transportation systems must be a priority. Whether it is the ability of a pipeline to carry a lifeline of fuel to market or the confidence that a bridge will not fail or a train leave the tracks, the proper functioning of these systems is the backbone of our economy and the connection we have to each other. Whether the cause of a disaster is natural or man-made, we must be prepared. We should use our knowledge to reduce the risk of disaster from the beginning concept and design all the way through operation and maintenance.

Considerable research in recent years and the need for trained professionals who will protect us by using that research require a focused effort to convey it and to organize it for study and use in the field. This book serves that purpose well. The authors are faculty members in the master's degree in transportation security program at San José State University, a program of the Mineta Transportation Institute. The original research and their experience in both professional work and the classroom combine to make this book practical, reliable, and comprehensive. I take great pride in the work of the Institute, its researchers, and its faculty for the contributions they have made and continue to make in the field of transportation safety and security.

The reader or student will find here the full spectrum of issues associated with the field, from threat analysis to response and recovery. The work moves from theory to practice, crosses all transportation modes, covers the wide range of agencies with interest and responsibility in the field, and includes the role of the private sector and support systems such as electricity supply. In a word, it is comprehensive.

There are reasons that terrorists so often choose a transportation setting for their attacks. They can and often do disrupt the economy of the locale, or in the case of 9-11, even the economy of a nation. Transportation represents about one-sixth of the United States economy, a vital link for businesses and individuals in just about everything they do. Damage to this sector can have widespread economic effects. Terrorists can also strike victims on a grand scale in a transportation setting, spreading terror and fear with all their consequences.

Because terrorists find these targets attractive for those reasons and more, we need to find the means to counter their efforts. Considering how to build, operate, and maintain our system with an eye toward safety and security is just common sense.

We all know that it is impossible to have one-hundred percent safety, but we can improve the odds by applying knowledge and training. Safety and security personnel can be equipped with that knowledge and training, and this book makes a solid contribution to the effort. For those who aspire to or hold these positions and also for those responsible for planning, building, operating, or using transportation systems, this book serves as a resource that is both scholarly and readable. I commend Dr. Edwards and Mr. Goodrich for their accomplishment in providing such a comprehensive approach to the research that now underpins a robust and necessary field of study.

In a world with so many competing needs for our resources and attention, I reflect on the years when my work was to provide those resources and attention. Whether as a councilmember or mayor of San José, California, a leader on transportation issues in the U.S. Congress, or Secretary of Commerce (Clinton administration)—and especially in my role as U.S. Secretary of Transportation (George W. Bush administration), I have faced the challenges of planning, building, operating, and securing transportation systems of all kinds. I cannot emphasize enough the satisfaction my work has provided me, and I am delighted that new generations are making transportation their life's work as well.

The American people have a precious resource in our many and varied transportation systems. We need to protect, maintain, and continue to build, all the while keeping an eye on the destruction that nature or man can do.

Norman Y. Mineta
Secretary of Transportation, 2001–2006
Secretary of Commerce, 2000–2001

Preface

On 9/11 the world watched while transportation became a weapon. Always previously considered a means of connecting people and creating commerce, transportation suddenly became a weapon of war, with civilian aircraft loaded with passengers used as missiles. Personal freedom and privacy have become a trade-off with secure transportation, as airline passengers remove their shoes and submit to full-body scanners to enhance security.

In 2005 Hurricane Katrina flooded New Orleans, made roads along the Gulf Coast inaccessible, destroyed bridges and ports, and closed pipelines. The effects were felt not only by the stranded Gulf Coast residents, but also by Midwestern farmers who could not export their harvested corn and East Coast drivers whose source of gasoline was stopped.

In 2011 the cascading disaster of the Great East Japan Earthquake generated the largest recorded tsunami in Japanese history, sweeping away the coastal fishing ports and the roads and railroads that served the disaster area. The railroad company has no plans to rebuild the coastal rail line, meaning that the small villages cannot be rebuilt. Without the railroad to carry the area's maritime and agricultural products to large city markets, there is no way to restore the local economy.

Transportation is a critical infrastructure in any community, yet this fact is often unrecognized until the residents experience a disruption in the services that they depend on. The creation of transportation systems allows people to live in areas that would not be reachable on foot and that could not sustain human societies without the importation of food and raw materials from other places. Diversified transportation systems from camel caravans to jumbo jets have enabled humans to move away from the rivers; to develop economic activity in Alaska, on the Great Plains of America, and on the steppes of Eurasia; and to exploit more natural resources and land area.

Transportation is the backbone of the economy. The movement of goods across the city and across the globe enables people to buy the necessities of life and luxury goods. Just-in-time management concepts have led to goods being moved on tight and easily disrupted schedules. A disaster in a far away city can lead to economic losses locally when damage to working ports and roads makes parts unavailable to feed local assembly lines, at the loss of thousands of dollars a day, or to stock store shelves or to fill gas station tanks, costing local residents money and inconvenience.

The ability to provide a reliable transportation system is a reflection of the sovereignty of a nation-state. Roads allowed the Romans to project their power across Europe, trade routes secured by local rulers connected Asia and Europe along the Silk Road, and for centuries Britannia ruled the waves. Rousseau reflected on humanity's movement from the natural dispersed state into organized societies, noting that people formed governments and gave up liberty for protection. A government's ability to protect its trade routes and the cargo owned by its merchants wherever they trade is a demonstration of the power of the ruler and central government.

Since the terrorist attacks of 9/11, the United States government has placed an emphasis on "homeland security." While the term has been embodied in legislation and a federal department, there is no consensus on what "security" means in practice. Similarly, "safety" and "emergency management" are related terms used by the transportation sector and other industries—often interchangeably—leading to uncertainty about what services and responsibilities belong to each. This book was developed with the goal of creating an understanding of the relationships between transportation and security, safety, and emergency management.

The tension between transportation and security has cost kings and counselors nights of insomnia since the establishment of the trade routes of the Grand Trunk Road and the Silk Road. Perfect security is impossible, yet raids by thieves had to be prevented, requiring a balance between the cost and benefit of protection. Modern transportation managers are equally challenged by twenty-first century threats, including theft, piracy, and the introduction of destructive devices—requiring not only a cost/benefit calculation, but also a passenger acceptance calculation for security design. It is hoped that the information in this book will offer insights into transportation security that will help to flatten the learning curve for transportation professionals who manage this critical infrastructure.

The authors are grateful to a number of colleagues who have provided support, insights, and information as this book was being developed and during its creation. The Mineta Transportation Institute provided support for a number of research projects whose products enriched this book and gave the authors an intellectual base. Executive Director Rod Diridon, Sr. and Research Director Dr. Karen Philbrick nurtured relationships across the transportation industry and governmental agencies that created access to essential knowledge of transportation's role in the community and economy. Research colleagues Brian Jenkins and Bill Medigovich provided insights into transportation security's role in society, from a knowledge base developed during their distinguished careers in public service. Herby Lissade and Randy Iwasaki of the California Department of Transportation (Caltrans) shared their knowledge of the role of transportation in the economy and society of the nation's most populous state. Our colleagues in the American Society for Public Administration's Section on Emergency and Crisis Management, especially professors Beverly Cigler, Louise Comfort, Rick Sylves, and Bill Waugh, provided essential basic research on emergency management's critical function in maintaining civil society. Finally, the United States Marine Corps contributed years of hard-won knowledge about the security function in a maritime and high threat level environment.

About the Authors

Frances L. Edwards, MUP, PhD, CEM, is the director of the master of public administration program and professor of political science at San Jose State University. She is deputy director of the National Transportation Security Center of the Mineta Transportation Institute at SJSU, where she is also a research associate and teaches emergency management in the master of science in transportation management program. Her current research is focused on the continuity of the operations process and its relationship to emergency management in transportation organizations; climate change and transportation; and transportation security. She is a member of the National Academy of Sciences Transportation Research Board's ABE40 Committee, focused on critical infrastructure security, and past chair of the American Society for Public Administration's Section on Emergency and Crisis Management.

Dr. Edwards's publications include two books on terrorism in the NATO Science Series, coauthored with Dr. Friedrich Steinhausler of the University of Salzburg; numerous journal articles and professional papers; and numerous chapters in textbooks and professional books, many coauthored with Daniel Goodrich, including a chapter on global supply chain security in *Supply Chain Security: International Innovations and Practices for Moving Goods Safely and Efficiently.* She has written eight reports on aspects of transportation security for the Mineta Transportation Institute, five with Professor Goodrich. Most recently she was an invited speaker for the U.S. Department of Homeland Security's Transportation

Security Roundtable in 2011 and the U.S. Department of Agriculture-funded workshop on *Building Disaster Resiliency and Sustainability* in 2012.

Dr. Edwards was the U.S. chair for the European Union CAST Project for the development of unified training for first responders, an invited presenter at the Second Istanbul Conference on Democracy and Global Security, and a 2006 Fellow of the Foundation for Defense of Democracies. She chaired the 2006 NATO STS-CNAD meeting on terrorism response for 20 nations in Portugal, and cochaired the 2004 NATO Advanced Research Workshop on technology to support first responders to terrorism in Germany.

Previously, Dr. Edwards was director of the Office of Emergency Services in San Jose, California for 14 years, including 1 year as acting assistant chief, San Jose Fire Department. She was director of San Jose's Metropolitan Medical Task Force (MMTF), a CBRNE terrorism response unit, and head of the four-county DHS-funded San Jose Urban Area Security Initiative (UASI). In October 2001, while Dr. Edwards was director of the Office of Emergency Services, the *Wall Street Journal* called San Jose the "best prepared city in the United States" for disasters. She represented emergency management on the five-night "Bio-War" series on ABC's *Nightline With Ted Koppel* in October 1999.

Dr. Edwards has been a member of the Stanford University Working Group on Chemical and Biological Warfare, the Department of Justice's Executive Session on Domestic Preparedness at the Kennedy School of Government at Harvard University, the National Academy of Sciences Institute of Medicine MMRS Review Committee, and the California Seismic Safety Commission. She was named Public Official of the Year 2002 by *Governing* magazine, and one of the "Power 100 of Silicon Valley" by *San Jose Magazine*. She has a PhD in public administration and a master of urban planning from New York University, an MA in political science (international relations) from Drew University, and a certificate in hazardous materials management from the University of California at Irvine. She is a certified emergency manager.

Daniel C. Goodrich, MPA, CEM, is a research associate with the Mineta Transportation Institute; an instructor in the master of science in transportation management program, where he teaches the security for transportation managers course; and a lecturer in the San Jose State University master of public administration program. His current research is focused on the continuity of the operations process and its relationship to emergency management in transportation organizations and on transportation security issues, especially related to critical infrastructure protection.

Professor Goodrich's publications include five transportation security reports for the Mineta Transportation Institute, coauthored with Dr. Edwards, and numerous coauthored chapters in textbooks and professional books, including a chapter on global supply chain security in *Supply Chain Security: International*

Innovations and Practices for Moving Goods Safely and Efficiently. He has coauthored a chapter, "Organizing for Emergency Management," in the ICMA textbook *Emergency Management* with Dr. Edwards, and has three entries on nuclear topics in *The WMD Encyclopedia.* He has delivered papers at numerous professional conferences, including invited papers on maritime security for the American Society for Public Administration, and employee emergency management training and exercises at the Natural Hazards Conference. Other recent work includes forthcoming chapters with Dr. Edwards in *Natural Hazard Mitigation: A Handbook for Practitioners and Academics.*

Professor Goodrich was appointed U.S. security documents reviewer for the European Union's CAST Project. In June 2007 he was a guest of the Turkish government at the Second Istanbul Conference on Democracy and Global Security, and his paper on policing after disasters was published in Turkey. He was a 2006 fellow of the Foundation for Defense of Democracies, studying Middle Eastern terrorism in Israel at Tel Aviv University. He delivered a paper on fourth generation warfare at the 2006 NATO STS-CNAD meeting for 20 nations in Portugal, which was included in *NATO and Terrorism: On Scene!,* the book developed from the workshop by Drs. Edwards and Steinhausler. In 2004 he chaired a session on "first responders" at the NATO Advanced Research Workshop in Germany that focused on the research needs to support first responders to CBRNE terrorism. He also served as a member of the NATO Expert Session on Nuclear Transportation Security in 2003 and 2004.

Mr. Goodrich has been an active member of the San Jose Metropolitan Medical Task Force, a CBRNE response unit, since 1999, where he has served as exercise director for eight facilitated exercises, a model of exercise that he developed. Harvard University's Kennedy School of Government has selected the creation of this exercise style for a case study in its executive management series.

Mr. Goodrich's civilian career has included emergency management positions for the city of San Jose, the Santa Clara County Public Health Department, and Lockheed Martin Space Systems Company. He currently serves as a consultant to the California Department of Transportation on emergency management and continuity of operations planning and training, and he has provided training services for NASA/Ames Research Center staff in emergency management.

Mr. Goodrich served in the United States Marine Corps for 10 years, including leadership positions in Security Forces. He is distinguished with both rifle and pistol, and a member of the President's Hundred. He also served for 6 years in the Army Reserve Military Police as a small arms instructor and a member of the U.S. Army Reserve shooting team. He was recalled to active duty in 2003 to train reservists being deployed to Iraq and Iraqi civilian officials.

Mr. Goodrich has a master of public administration degree from San Jose State University and is a certified emergency manager and a FEMA professional continuity practitioner.

Section I

Safety, Security, and Emergency Management

Chapter **1**

Security Theory and Practice

Keywords: security, safety, emergency management, protection, prevention, detect, deter, deny, mitigate, threat, threat analysis intermodal, risk, hazard, business continuity, continuity of operations critical infrastructure, NIMS, National Infrastructure Protection Plan, Urban Area Security Initiative, IED, HAZMAT, HSPD-7, National Asset Database, BZPP, Transit Security Grant Program (TSGP)

Learning Objectives

After reading this chapter you should be able to

- Understand the differences among safety, security, and emergency management
- Understand the theoretical bases for transportation security
- Understand the threats to surface transportation and intermodal transportation nodes
- Perform a risk analysis for transportation considering threats from natural hazards, technological hazards and human-caused hazards

FIGURE 1.1 Diridon Station, San Jose, California.

Introduction

Transportation is the lifeline of any nation, connecting people, goods and services, supporting the economy and facilitating the delivery of public safety response services. Designated by Congress as a "critical infrastructure" (Department of Homeland Security [DHS], 2007), the importance of transportation security has been underscored by the number of federal grants—five separate programs in 2010—offered to various transportation entities to enhance their security through physical and planning strategies. (The grant programs will be discussed in detail later in the chapter.) Technological accidents like the Baltimore Tunnel fire—a rail accident involving a 60-car freight train in downtown Baltimore on July 18, 2001—and human-caused attacks on surface transportation assets—like the bombings in Madrid, London, Moscow, and Mumbai (described in more detail in Chapter 7)—demonstrate the vulnerability of the open systems to disruption and the consequences of attacks in damage to people, property, and the economy (Figure 1.1).

Safety, Security, and Emergency Management

Security can be defined as the effort to protect assets—physical, human, or intellectual—from criminal interference, removal, or destruction, whether by terrorists or domestic criminals, or incidental to technological failures or even natural hazards events. The Transportation Research Board defines the objectives of security as to deter, detect, deny, and mitigate. These objectives may be accomplished by direct intervention by human or canine assets or through physical barriers and the application of technology.

Surface transportation, in order to be efficient and effective, must be open to all potential users, readily accessible, and focused on timeliness in the delivery of the service or public good. These characteristics make it very difficult to include a high level of security. Unlike air transportation—where the use of the air space is controlled by the government and there are controlled gateways and lead time before flights—surface transportation relies on enabling individuals to make a travel decision at a moment's notice and on enabling motor carriers to reroute and change schedules to enhance profitability and customer satisfaction. While each of these factors works toward business success, they unfortunately work against security.

Safety, security, and emergency management are terms that are often used interchangeably. While closely related, each term represents a distinct domain. At times, the distinct effort represented by each term may be at odds with the other efforts, making the understanding of each term and its related functions crucial to successful transportation security.

Security

Security defines the domain of protecting something valuable from any form of deliberate interference. It is the oldest of the domains, going back to the earliest human civilizations. Security requires a physical response to an external conscious threat, normally meaning that this is a human versus human issue.

In transportation, security involves both the items being transported and the machinery used to transport the items, and the owners of each have differing priorities for security. The owner of the goods wants them protected at any cost for safe delivery to the destination. The owner of the transportation assets wants to protect them—rolling stock, rails, bridges and tunnels, ships, ports—in order to stay in business, even at the cost of losing the cargo. When the "cargo" is human beings, the transporter is responsible for the transportation assets' performance for a successful delivery to the intended destination, but there is a societal debate about who is responsible for the security of the individual passenger on the asset. Was the London Underground responsible for the deaths at the hands of the suicide bombers in 2005? Was the Moscow subway system responsible for the deaths on their system as a result of the Chechen attack?

While a debate over responsibility for passenger security is outside the scope of this book, the distinction between the management of assets and the management of passengers must be made. Local law enforcement will focus on the passengers first in a disaster, while private security services may have equal responsibility for the human and materiel assets. Historically, private security has patrolled the physical assets of the transportation sector, such as rail yards, docks, and freight warehouses, using civilian personnel (Fischer & Green, 2004, p. 26).

Security is benchmarked against best practices rather than formal standards in the transportation domain. An individual set of circumstances exists for each type of cargo and for each transportation route, necessitating a separate security analysis for each. For example, a cargo of coal does not have the security requirements of a cargo of depleted nuclear fuel rods, even though they may use the same route and the same engines.

Safety

Safety is the next oldest domain. It developed out of the need to prevent accidental deaths and injuries due to natural or inadvertent man-made activities. It is an effort to mitigate the damage inflicted by unconscious forces that humans encounter that can usually be avoided by thinking through the environmental issues and creating barriers or procedures to help prevent unsafe events from occurring. Safety developed into a workplace focus during the Industrial Revolution with the recognition that employees were susceptible to injury around machinery unless precautions in operation were observed and, in some cases, protective equipment was used.

Safety in transportation includes agency worker and operator safety on the job, as well as passenger safety while on the asset. For example, a driver's license is required to operate motorized transport to ensure that all drivers know the vehicle codes and "rules of the road" to avoid accidents. Different classes of licenses are required for more complex transportation equipment. Mass transit work rules are focused on enhancing safety for crew and passengers, limiting the length of shifts worked and outlawing unsafe behaviors like texting while driving. Physical barriers are also used, such as divided highways, and traffic controls, like lights and signals, to enhance safety (Figure 1.2).

Safety has a more formal basis. While it relies on best practices, it also has clear legal mandates and case law governing its practice in the United States. Groups like NIOSH (National Institute for Occupational Safety and Health) and OSHA (Occupational Safety and Health Administration) dictate safety rules for workers in transportation, including mandates for respiratory protection and eye protection in specific applications.

Emergency Management

Emergency management is the newest of the three domains and becomes necessary when either safety or security fails. It became critical as urbanization progressed and people became dependent on technology and shared

FIGURE 1.2   Street crossing.

systems of infrastructure for their day-to-day activities. While flooding fields added nutrients and fresh top soil in an agricultural era, flooding that same land after urbanization has led to catastrophic damage to infrastructure and loss of life, as in Grand Forks when the Red River flooded. While early settlers in California withstood the Fort Tejon earthquake in 1864 with little long-term social disruption, today in California emergency management systems for earthquake preparedness and response are critical because bridges and mass transit infrastructure are subject to catastrophic destruction by shaking.

Historically, emergency management was also guided principally by best practices as developed by the Federal Emergency Management Agency (FEMA). However, in 1997 the National Emergency Management Association, the professional association of state-level emergency services directors, convened stakeholders who created the Emergency Management Standard. The Emergency Management Accreditation Program (EMAP) evaluates state and local emergency management programs for conformance with the standard, awarding certifications for agencies in compliance with all the EMAP standards. In the next chapter this domain will be discussed in more detail.

Deter, Detect, Deny, Mitigate

Surface transportation assets provide an attractive target to terrorists and criminals because of the value of their contents—both material and human—and the openness of the systems. To be successful, security measures have to impact the adversary's view of a target's attractiveness while enhancing the passenger's or shipper's view of the asset's functionality. Jenkins, Butterworth, and Gerston note that "Americans' preference [is] for security that is passive and egalitarian" (2010, p. 6)—that is, a plan that does not interfere with anyone's ability to use public transit. This openness further limits the measures available to transportation operators and owners to prevent security breaches that could cause damage to their systems and customers.

The Transportation Research Board has identified four objectives in transportation security: deter, detect, deny, and mitigate (Transportation Research Board, 2006b, p. 9). Security plans are developed and evaluated based on the four objectives in securing a transportation asset. Not all four objectives can be achieved for each transportation asset, so priorities for each activity are set for each asset and system, based on financial and physical capability and evaluated cost benefit of the proposed program.

The effort to deter activity that would breach the security of a transportation asset has two elements. Some measures deter unwanted activity by making the planning and execution of an attack too difficult, causing the adversary to seek an easier target. Such deterrence measures might include active surveillance of stations and platforms with staffed cameras that result in an immediate response to a perceived threat, or selective passenger screening using personnel and dogs (Figure 1.3), for example. The goal is to make the adversary's surveillance and planning efforts fruitless or very difficult while posing little inconvenience to customers. Because the best time to stop a terrorist attack is during the target selection and reconnaissance phase (New Mexico Tech, 2005, slide 3-6), systems that demonstrate randomness and iniquitousness may frustrate the efforts to develop a workable plan for an attack.

The other deterrence strategy is devaluing the target by protecting the principal assets. This can be accomplished by fencing or walls, guarded entrances, or alarms. Such security measures prevent the possibility of reaching any mission-critical elements of the transportation asset undetected. For example, protecting the anchor points of a suspension bridge may prove an adequate deterrence because attacking other elements of the bridge would not result in newsworthy damage that would have a negative impact on functionality. The Israelis have long employed this kind of deterrence in bus attacks by cleaning up the bombing site immediately, leaving no indications of the attacks for subsequent news coverage.

Detection is the second objective: to discover evidence of a planned event before it occurs. This may be through either discovering the planning effort in progress or finding the actual device before detonation.

Detection of planning for an attack on transportation infrastructure may be prospective, accomplished through intelligence gathering and analysis, or through observed behavior at stations and assets. For example, people

FIGURE 1.3 Istanbul K-9 unit.

taking photos of critical infrastructure elements that are not tourist attractions or inherently interesting may indicate target surveillance. Rumors of attack plans, reports of purchases of large amounts of bomb-making materials by actors outside the normal user industries, or discovery of communications among bombing planners may provide information that leads to the detection of an attack plan against a transportation infrastructure asset or site.

Detection may also occur in the early stages of attack plan implementation. Monitored cameras may detect suspicious behavior on a platform or attempts to enter restricted spaces by unauthorized personnel. Passengers may report the presence of a suspicious package, or canines may sniff out an explosive device before it detonates. In these cases, protective actions like evacuation are rendered safe by explosive ordinance specialists, and arrests may prevent a successful attack against transportation infrastructure.

Sometimes security may achieve the objective of denying access to the target, even after an attack plan has been made. Barriers may be reinforced, access points may be changed, and security system hardware and access methods (codes, keys, scanners, and cards) may be rotated randomly. In some cases, high-value or targeted assets may be moved to an alternate location temporarily during high-threat periods, such as during political conventions or events likely to create civil unrest.

Finally, mitigation of an attack—lessening its impact or severity—may be possible, even when it cannot be prevented through achieving the other objectives. For example, rail cars can be designed with unreinforced roofs to allow an explosion to dissipate upward rapidly, limiting the blast and over-pressure damage. Shatter-resistant glass may be used to limit shrapnel creation during a detonation. Potential hiding places for explosive devices like refuse containers and vending machines can be redesigned or repositioned to limit their usefulness. For example, a refuse container made of wire mesh with a plastic liner would provide inadequate containment to amplify the explosive capacity of an improvised explosive device (IED). Sprinkler systems could dilute a toxic aerosol release.

Through the implementation of these four objectives, the security of transportation assets and infrastructure may be greatly enhanced, although perfect security is impossible in an open environment. To keep mass transit accessible to commuters and roads available for constant use by a variety of drivers, these security objectives have to be applied in ways that do not interfere with the operation of systems and assets, while at the same time providing reasonable attainment of the objectives of deterrence, detection, denial, and mitigation.

Risk Assessment

Risk assessment is the systematic analysis of the potential sources of damage or disruption to a valuable asset, with the goal of instituting mitigation or protective measures that would prevent or lessen the impact of such an event. Risk assessment for transportation infrastructure has four segments: understanding what natural and technological hazards and human-caused threats exist in the target community, determination of the likelihood of a hazard or threat event occurring, defining the elements of a system that are vulnerable to the hazards or threat, and evaluating the consequence of such an occurrence.

Hazards and threats are normally categorized in three segments, as shown in Table 1.1: natural, technological, and human caused (Transportation Research Board, 2006a, p. 7). Kathleen Tierney, of the Natural Hazards Center, has often pointed out that there are no natural disasters, only natural hazards. Disasters are caused by the interaction of sensitive human receptors and the hazard or threat (Tierney, 2010). For example, hurricanes hitting uninhabited islands are events, not disasters, while hurricanes hitting populated areas may become catastrophes.

A comprehensive security plan has to consider what kinds of hazards exist in the area of the asset to be protected and what threats could impact the asset. Second, the likelihood of the occurrence has to be considered. Some hazards are seasonal or cyclical, while others occur in geologic time.

TABLE 1.1 Classes of Hazards That May Affect Transportation Systems and Assets

Hazard	Frequency	Scope of impact
Natural		
Biological		
Disease outbreak—natural	Seasonal, irregular	Localized to international
Geological		
Earthquake[a]	Cyclical, 100 years or more	Regional
Landslides	Tied to seismic, volcanic, or hydrologic events	Localized
Sinkhole	Tied to groundwater draw down	Localized
Volcanic eruption	Cyclical, over 100 years or more	Multistate, worldwide
Hydrological/Meteorological		
Flood	Seasonal, often annual	Localized through regional
Heat wave	Seasonal	Localized through multistate
Hurricane[a]	Seasonal, often annual	Regional, multistate
Ice storm	Seasonal	Localized to regional
Lightning	Seasonal	Localized to regional
Mudslide	Tied to wildfire aftermath, severe weather events	
Tornado	Cyclical, often annual	Localized through multistate
Tsunami	Intermittent, generally tied to volcanic eruption or earthquake	Localized through international
Wildland urban interface fire	Seasonal, cyclical	Localized through multistate
Technological		
Hazardous materials accident	Irregular	Localized, regional; tied to transportation or industrial locations
Pipeline	Irregular	Localized, regional; often located along rail transportation routes
Power outage	Irregular	Localized to international; often tied to aging infrastructure, high heat, or ice storms

continued

TABLE 1.1 (continued) Classes of Hazards That May Affect Transportation Systems and Assets

Hazard	Frequency	Scope of Impact
Structural collapse	Irregular	Localized to regional; often tied to aging infrastructure, exceeding design standards, or natural hazard
Human Caused		
Arson	Irregular	Localized to regional
Biological attack—animal[b]	Irregular	Localized to international
Biological attack—crop[b]	Irregular	Localized to international
Biological attack—human[b]	Irregular	Localized to international
Chemical weapon attack[b]	Irregular	Localized
Civil unrest/riot	Irregular	Localized to regional
Cyber attack[b]	Irregular	Localized to international
"Dirty bomb" (radiological)[b]	Irregular	Localized
Explosion—bomb	Irregular	Localized
Explosion—IED[b]	Irregular	Localized
Explosion—vehicle-borne IED (VBIED)	Irregular	Localized to regional
Incendiary	Irregular	Localized to regional
Nuclear weapon attack[b]	Irregular	Localized to regional
Sabotage	Irregular	Localized to international
Theft	Irregular	Localized to international
Transportation operation accident	Irregular	Localized to regional; international if at border
Workplace violence	Irregular	Localized

[a] Earthquake in Los Angeles and hurricane in Miami are included in the 15 planning scenarios in the *National Preparedness Guidelines*.

[b] Included in the 15 scenarios in the *National Preparedness Guidelines*.

Some threats are continuous, like arson or sabotage, while others may be tied to certain groups or triggers. For example, introduction of bombs onto transit systems is more likely during periods of tension; extremist groups are known to use this strategy to gain attention. The Madrid bombing was designed to deter Spain from continuing to participate in the Iraq War, for example.

Third, the plan must contain an evaluation of the elements of the transportation asset that are vulnerable to each of the hazards and threats. A vulnerability is a gap or exposure in the protection of an asset that can lead to damage or destruction that takes the transportation system out of service for a period of time that is economically or socially damaging.

Different hazards and threats will impact different vulnerable elements of a transportation system, requiring different types of protection or mitigation. For example, a suspension bridge is most vulnerable to catastrophic attack at the pier ends of the cables, where the cables are tied down. Trying to destroy a bridge by destroying the road surface would result in a denial of service, but the road could be replaced relatively quickly. This means that security technology must be concentrated at the vulnerable piers, while the road surface is less vulnerable and therefore requires less concentrated surveillance as a protective measure. Similarly, the ties in rail service are a vulnerability because they can be pulled up with a hook attached to a train, a technique used by retreating German troops in World War II. Destroying the ties in a rail system would cause the rails to be unstable, creating a temporary denial of service.

Fourth, the consequences of the hazard when it becomes an event have to be added to the analysis. Some elements of a transportation system are crucial to its operation, while others have readily available substitutes or work-arounds. Some of the consequences are denial of service, undermining the credibility of the operator, and longer term destruction of the asset.

For example, a railroad tunnel is vulnerable to damage at the tunnel entrance as well as along its length. One consequence of blowing up a tunnel could be a catastrophic bottleneck in the system that could require years of redesign and reconstruction for service restoration. The hazardous materials fire in the Howard Street CSX tunnel in Baltimore blocked the only north–south rail access along the East Coast. While the fire caused no fatalities, the smoke escaped through manholes into the city of Baltimore, resulting in off-site consequences including significant economic disruption, and lawsuits against CSX, the owner (Transportation Research Board, 2006a, p. 23). This would suggest that because the tunnel is an essential link in the transportation system, monitoring the condition of cars both entering the tunnel and inside the tunnel is essential to avoid accidents and events that could destroy or significantly damage the tunnel.

Different hazards and threats will cause different types of damage to transportation infrastructure: direct and indirect.

Earthquakes may shake transportation infrastructure apart, and hurricanes can tear up tracks and signal systems, so these are direct impacts that are easy to understand. Other types of events may have a more indirect impact on transportation assets. For example, although a biological attack on crops might seem unrelated to rail transportation, if a train passes through areas where crops have been dusted with wheat rust in a biological attack, it would need to be cleaned thoroughly before proceeding on its route into an uninfected area. During an outbreak of exotic Newcastle disease, the California Department of Transportation (Caltrans) had to decontaminate trucks entering and leaving quarantined areas within California, as well as those entering and leaving the state, to prevent the disease from spreading.

Finally, an analysis of the types of damage caused by the various hazards needs to be conducted. Air quality in and around transportation systems may be affected by hazardous materials events or smoky fires, and chemical bombs or biological attacks could be inhalation hazards. Flooding may wash away or destroy transportation infrastructure and assets. Denial of service of the transportation asset may be caused by direct attacks like bombing or sabotage and by indirect events like power outages, cyber attacks against controller systems, or contamination in a natural disease outbreak. Table 1.2 demonstrates such an analysis.

The security plan takes into account the hazards most likely to occur within the community that will have the highest consequences. This list forms the guide for the investment of scarce resources. Appropriate planning, equipment acquisition, and personnel training must be provided to respond to the hazards with the highest frequency, as well as those with the highest community consequences, even if they are infrequent. For example, while it is possible that a sinkhole will occur under the mass transit station that serves the urban center, preconstruction geotechnical engineering studies make that most unlikely. Conversely, earthquakes occur with no notice, often on unmapped faults, so if a community is in a seismic hazard zone, the transportation infrastructure must be built to withstand earthquake shaking without collapsing.

Federal Grants for Transportation Security

The Department of Homeland Security and FEMA administer five grant programs designed to support the development of security systems and plans for transportation agencies. The overarching grant is the Transit Security Grant Program (TSGP), discussed later, which is multimodal. The other four grants are mode specific and will be described in the later chapters related to those modes of transportation. Table 1.3 shows the five grants and their 2010 allocations.

The TSGP began in 2006 as a grant to transit agencies based on a formula that uses risk, vulnerability, and consequences (GAO, 2009, p. 7). This grant program grew out of the events of 9/11, and the funding was included in the Implementing Recommendations of the 9/11 Commission Act of 2007 and the Department of Homeland Security appropriation for 2010 (DHS, 2010, p. 2). Eligibility to apply for funding is predicated on being compliant with the National Incident Management System (NIMS) requirements and having a DHS security assessment or an internally developed security plan

TABLE 1.2 Consequences of Hazards to Transportation Systems

Hazards	Damage to Physical Infrastructure	Denial of Use	Human Life/Health	Economy
Natural				
Biologic				
Disease outbreak— natural	None	Perhaps limited	Up to millions	Very damaging
Geological				
Earthquake	Severe	Extensive	Up to thousands	Damaging
Landslide	Localized, severe	Possible, localized	Possible	Possible if in urban area
Sinkhole	Localized, severe	Possible, localized	Possible	Possible if key resource
Volcanic eruption	Severe	Extensive	Up to thousands	Damaging
Hydrological/Meteorological				
Flood	Moderate to severe	Localized, severe	Possible, especially flash flooding	Damaging
Heat wave	Moderate to severe	Possible, localized	Up to millions	Possible if prolonged
Hurricane	Severe	Extensive	Up to thousands	Very damaging
Ice storm	Localized severe	Localized to regional	Yes, greater impact in high-density areas	Possible if prolonged
Lightning	Localized severe	Localized to regional	Localized	Possible if prolonged recovery
Mudslide	Localized severe	Localized to regional	Localized	Possible if prolonged recovery
Tornado	Localized severe	Localized to regional	Localized to regional; depends on warning	Damaging if regional
Tsunami	Localized to regional severe	Localized to regional severe	Up to thousands	Damaging

continued

TABLE 1.2 (continued) Consequences of Hazards to Transportation Systems

Hazards	Damage to Physical Infrastructure	Denial of Use	Human Life/Health	Economy
Wildland urban interface fire	Localized to regional severe	Localized to regional severe	Localized to regional, greater in high density	Damaging if regional
Technological				
Hazardous materials accidents	Possible	Yes, depending on location	Dozens to thousands	Possible if prolonged recovery
Pipeline	Severe	Yes	Possible	Possible if prolonged recovery
Power outage	Possible	Yes	Medically dependent, others possible	Possible if prolonged recovery
Structural collapse	Severe	Yes	Possible, extensive if in use	Possible if prolonged recovery
Human Caused				
Arson	Yes	Yes	Possible if in use	Possible if key resource
Biological attack—animal	Unlikely	Unlikely	Possible if zoonosis or food chain	Yes
Biological attack—crop	Unlikely	Unlikely	Possible	Yes
Biological attack—human	Unlikely	Unlikely	Severe	Yes
Chemical weapon attack	Possible	Possible	Yes	Possible if prolonged recovery
Civil unrest/riot	Yes	Yes	Yes	Possible if prolonged recovery
Cyber attack	Possible	Yes	Possible for medically dependent	Possible if prolonged recovery
"Dirty bomb" (radiological)	Possible	Possible	Possible blast effect, shrapnel	Probable

TABLE 1.2 (continued) Consequences of Hazards to Transportation Systems

Hazards	Damage to Physical Infrastructure	Denial of Use	Human Life/Health	Economy
Explosion— bomb	Yes	Yes	Blast effect and shrapnel in red zone	Possible if prolonged recovery
Explosion—IED	Yes	Yes	Blast effect and shrapnel in red zone	Possible if prolonged recovery
Explosion— VBIED	Yes	Yes	Blast effect and shrapnel in red zone	Possible if prolonged recovery
Incendiary	Yes	Yes	Blast effect, burns in red zone	Possible if key resource
Nuclear weapon attack	Yes	Yes	Thousands to millions	Yes
Sabotage	Depends on attack target and mechanism	Depends on attack target and mechanism	Depends on attack target and mechanism	Yes
Theft	Possible	Yes	Possible	Depends on target
Transportation operation accident	Yes	Yes	Dozens to hundreds if in vehicles	Depends on target
Workplace violence	No	Possibly	Yes	Possible

TABLE 1.3 Federal Transportation Grants, 2010

Name	Agency	FY10 Funding
Transit Security Grant Program	DHS, FEMA	$253 million
Freight Train Security Grant Program	DHS, FEMA	$15 million
Intercity Passenger Rail—Amtrak	DHS, FEMA	$20 million
Intercity Bus Security Grant Program	DHS, FEMA	$11.52
Port Security Grant Program	DHS, FEMA	$288 million

Source: Paddock, M. (2010). *Homeland Security Today, 7*(2), G11–G12.

(DHS, 2010, p. 9) leading to a risk-based Security Emergency Preparedness Plan for each agency.

DHS has made risk assessment the basis for participation in many of its grants, notably "core DHS State and local grant programs" (DHS, 2009, December, p. 9) and the Transportation Security Grant Program. Using a 100-point scale to rate the priority for funding for different communities, 20 points are allocated for the presence of hazards or threats, while 80 points are awarded for vulnerability/consequences (DHS, 2009, December, p. 10). The eight communities rated highest for risk share the noncompetitive cooperative agreement process and are categorized as Tier 1. All other eligible transit agencies participate in a competitive grant program (DHS, 2009, December, p. i).

In the first years of using risk-based eligibility determinations, the C.A.R.V.E.R. method was used for some grants. This acronym stands for criticality, accessibility, "recuperability," vulnerability, effect, and recognizability. The process is used by military Special Forces to select targets, so it provides a workable basis for selecting potential infrastructure to be targeted by the adversaries (U.S. Army, n.d.). When transportation infrastructure is evaluated, a score is developed that gives a measure of relative risk among various transportation assets.

The exact process used for rating each community for 2009 and 2010 DHS grant eligibility is defined only as "a comprehensive, empirically grounded risk analysis model" (DHS, 2009, December, p. 3). The TSGP Guidance notes that factors include "intelligence community assessments of threat, potentially affected passenger populations, and the economic impact of attack." Factors include "unlinked passenger trips for rail and bus systems, the number of underground track miles, the number of underwater tunnels, and the location-specific intelligence community risk analysis" (DHS, 2009, p. 10).

The funding provided through the grant is intended to enable transportation agencies to undertake projects that fulfill their obligation under the National Preparedness Guidelines, which includes the 15 scenario events deemed of greatest concern by the Department of Homeland Security noted in Table 1.2 and the National Infrastructure Protection Plan. Taken together, they are intended to achieve the four preparedness objectives: "to prevent, protect against, respond to, and recover from terrorist attacks and catastrophic natural disasters" (DHS, 2010, p. 2). Table 1.4 shows the priorities and activities eligible for funding under this grant.

The activities under the Transit Security Grant Program may be in one of six categories: planning, equipment acquisition, training, exercises, and two categories with limitations: management and administration that must be no more than 5% of the grant and "operational packages." The planning funding may be used to develop the required Security Emergency

TABLE 1.4 Transit Security Grant Program Eligible Categories and Examples

Priority Group No.	Project Effectiveness Group Score	Project Effectiveness Group Description	Project Types (Sample Only, Not Comprehensive)
A	5	Training, operational deterrence, drills, public awareness activities	• Developing security plans • Training (basic before follow-on): security awareness, DHS-approved behavior recognition detection courses, countersurveillance, immediate actions for security threats/incidents. • Operational deterrence: canine teams, mobile explosives screening teams, antiterrorism teams • Crowd assessment • Public awareness
B	4	Multiuser high-density key infrastructure protection	Antiterrorism security enhancement measures, such as intrusion detection, visual surveillance with live monitoring, alarms tied to visual surveillance system, recognition software, tunnel ventilation and drainage system protection, flood gates and plugs, portal lighting and similar "hardening" actions for: • Tunnel hardening • High-density elevated operations • Multiuser high-density stations • Hardening of SCADA systems

C	3	Single-user high-density key infrastructure protection	• Antiterrorism security enhancement measures for:
			  • High-density stations
			  • High-density bridges

D	2	Key operating asset protection	• Physical hardening/security control centers • Secure stored/parked trains, engines, and busses; bus/rail yards • Maintenance facilities
E	1	Other mitigation activities	• Interoperable communications[a] • Evacuation plans • Antiterrorism security enhancement measures for low-density stations

Source: DHS. (2009). *Fiscal Year 2010 Transit Security Grant Program Guidance and Application Kit,* p. 5, Table 1: Project Effectiveness Groups Listed in Priority Order.

[a] Additional information on interoperable communications is included in FY2009 SAFECOM Recommended Guidance for Federal Grant Programs, which can be found at http://www/safecomprogram.gov.SAFECOM_grant_default.htm

Management Plan. "Operational packages" obtained under the grant must support dedicated law enforcement personnel who work exclusively on transit security activities. These grant funds may cover no more than 36 months and must be used for new, dedicated, full-time law enforcement positions or to cover overtime costs to establish a new security position. Receiving jurisdictions must demonstrate a sustainment program for the personnel and related assets once the grant period expires (DHS, 2010, p. 20).

Regional cooperation among transit agencies is also a requirement of the Transit Security Grant Program. Earlier grants supported the development of a Regional Security Strategy and Regional Transit Security Working Groups. The regional plan was compiled based on the elements in the individual Security Emergency Preparedness Plan, and the annual review and updating of the regional plan as the agency plans evolve. All transit security-related plans must be in harmony with the relevant Urban Area Security Initiative's overall strategy. All grant funding requests must include only projects that support the regional security strategy. Funding preference is given to projects that address "risk specific to the region, regional security priorities to mitigate that risk, and the identification of projects with significant risk mitigation potential" (DHS, 2010, p. 3).

By 2010 the annual grant had risen to $253 million, focused on transportation infrastructure security activities, with an emphasis on regional cooperation among owners and operators of transit assets. For the purposes of the Transportation Security Grant Program, the definition of mass transit includes "heavy rail, commuter rail, light rail and bus" systems (GAO, 2009, p. 6) and ferry systems (DHS, 2010, p. 2), which share the funding. Eligible agencies are located in the Urban Area Security Initiative communities and are part of the National Transit Database of unlinked passenger trips (Paddock, 2010, p. G11).

Funding for 2010 projects reflected a shift to capital project orientation and the application of new technologies for the eligible agencies, but challenges include the difference between the period of the award, which is 5 years at the most, and the actual cost for a design-build remediation project for a capital asset. Currently, the cost to the agency of managing the design phase of the capital project is not reimbursable through federal funds, and the states will only reimburse for approved projects, putting the transportation agency at some financial risk in proposing a design (DHS, 2010, p. 14).

For 2011 the available funds will be divided, with 10% of the funding to support the Vulnerability Assessment/Security Plan, public awareness programs, and drills and exercises. Ninety percent of the funds are for capital projects that are based on the Approved Remediation Design developed in previous years or approved in 2010. The funding for these programs is based on risk (DHS, 2010, p. 5).

Critical Infrastructure/Key Resources

The 9/11 attacks on the World Trade Center in New York City damaged not just the buildings, but also the infrastructure that was housed within, below, and adjacent to them. Subway lines running under the towers were flooded and out of use for months. The Port Authority Trans-Hudson (PATH) train station was destroyed, only reopening in 2004 (Figure 1.4). The television towers on the top of Tower One served the entire metropolitan area, resulting in a denial of service for television stations throughout the metropolitan area and thus making public outreach and information sharing to the affected community very difficult. Debris projectiles damaged the telephone infrastructure in the adjacent Verizon Building, destroying telephone service to lower Manhattan (Jenkins & Edwards, 2002).

In October 2001 anthrax was delivered to a journalist in Florida and to elected officials on Capitol Hill in Washington, DC. In the process of mail sorting, a mail processing facility was also contaminated. In addition to the journalist and two postal workers, a woman in New York and a woman in Connecticut died of anthrax. The Capitol was closed down and decontaminated, resulting in a denial of use to its usual inhabitants and a denial of service to the public.

On December 17, 2003, President George W. Bush issued Homeland Security Presidential Directive 7 (HSPD-7), "Critical Infrastructure Identification, Prioritization, and Protection"—in large part to prepare for and counter any potential future incident such as these. This identified

FIGURE 1.4 Restored subway tunnels at World Trade Center site, 2004.

"critical infrastructure and key resources" of the United States that required protection to ensure continuity of service. Background 4 states:

> The Nation possesses numerous key resources, whose exploitation or destruction by terrorists could cause catastrophic health effects or mass casualties comparable to those from the use of a weapon of mass destruction, or could profoundly affect our national prestige and morale. In addition, there is critical infrastructure so vital that its incapacitation, exploitation, or destruction, through terrorist attack, could have a debilitating effect on security and economic well-being.

HSPD-7 identified areas of critical infrastructure that needed protection, including transportation systems composed of "mass transit, aviation, maritime, ground/surface, and rail and pipeline systems" (Bush, 2003, #16). Further, the Secretary of Homeland Security was mandated to create an "integrated National Plan for Critical Infrastructure and Key Resources Protection" (CI/KR) (Bush, 2003, #27) that involved government and private sector owners and operators of critical infrastructure assets. By July of 2004 all federal agencies had to submit reports to the Office of Management and Budget detailing their plans to protect their systems' physical and cyber assets.

The Department of Homeland Security developed a National Asset Database detailing the types of sites that would be included in the CI/KR definition. Eight types of infrastructure were included: banking and finance; chemical and HAZMAT; commercial assets, including shopping malls over one million square feet, stadiums and arenas with 10,000 or more seats; electricity; oil and natural gas; nuclear power plants; government facilities; and transportation assets including "mass transit systems and rail bridges over major waterways that, if destroyed, would cause significant economic loss" (DHS, 2005, March, p. 2). Because the information was considered "sensitive," the locations eligible for funding were provided only to the states, which then disseminated the information to each county or city for that community only.

On March 5, 2005, the Buffer Zone Protection Program (BZPP) grant was opened to enhance safety zones around critical infrastructure throughout the United States. The grant identified 10 critical infrastructure sectors and five categories of key resources (DHS, 2005, March, p. 9). Table 1.5 lists the infrastructure and Table 1.6 lists the resources.

During the first year, the funding was distributed to the states using a base of $50,000, plus additional funding based on population, and distributed to local governments, permitting up to $50,000 for each identified site. The money could be spent "to reduce the vulnerabilities of CI/KR sites by extending the protected area around the site into the surrounding community" (DHS, 2005, March, Foreword).

TABLE 1.5 Critical Infrastructure Sectors

Agriculture and food

Water

Public health

Emergency services

Defense industrial base

Information and telecommunications

Energy

Transportation

Banking and finance

Chemical

Source: DHS. (2005). *Fiscal year 2005 Buffer Zone Protection Program.* www.fema.gov/pdf/government/grant/ bzpp/fy05_bzpp.shtm, p. 9.

TABLE 1.6 Key Resources

National monuments and icons

Nuclear power plants and radioactive material

Dams

Government facilities

Commercial key assets

Source: DHS. (2005). *Fiscal year 2005 Buffer Zone Protection Program.* www.fema.gov/pdf/government/grant/ bzpp/fy05_bzpp.shtm, p. 9.

Preferred strategies for application of the BZPP funding were to make the target "too costly or unattractive" to attack; use physical barriers, cameras, and security guards as deterrence; and use technology to detect weapons and suspects as they moved toward the target outside the danger zone (DHS, 2005, March, p. 11). In most communities, the police department was in charge of evaluating the CI/KR within the community and setting priorities for the use of funding. In one large city, bollards were installed at the curb around the Internal Revenue Service building and the telephone exchange to prevent anyone from parking a vehicle-borne IED adjacent to the building, as had been done in Oklahoma City at the Murrah Building. Known as "hardening the target," such protective measures were taken to make a site unattractive to potential terrorists because, at that time, there were many other unprotected places that would make an attractive target that was easier to reach.

The security plan contains sensitive information that could be "read backwards" by a trained adversary, revealing protective strategies and technologies. This makes the exchange of information across professions and locations very difficult. Overarching elements like threat assessment and general statements of protective measures are the only portions that are normally released outside the security apparatus. Even within security there may be compartmentalized knowledge of the plan. It is impossible to protect all of the assets of any transportation agency all of the time, so security strategies are developed to provide the best overall protection from attack and interference with the assets. Detailed discussions of modal security plans will be covered in succeeding chapters.

Case Studies

Transportation and Disease Outbreaks: Exotic Newcastle Disease

In January 2003 Governor Gray Davis declared a state of emergency for an outbreak of exotic Newcastle disease (END) in Southern California, believed to be related to illegal cockfighting and the importation of diseased birds. It is a "fatal contagious virus that affects all species of birds, and is one of the most infectious diseases of poultry in the world" (CIDRAP, 2010). The outbreak, which began in October of 2002, resulted in a quarantine being placed on six Southern California counties: San Diego, Riverside, San Bernardino, Orange, Los Angeles, and Ventura (Hoover-Hardwick, 2003); later, Imperial and Santa Barbara were added (Fitzsimmons, 2003). A 1971 outbreak of the same disease in California had resulted in the destruction of 12 million birds and affected the egg supply in the nation. At that time, the eradication effort cost $56 million in public funds and took 3 years (CIDRAP, 2010).

Governor Gray Davis declared a state of emergency as a result of the potential economic damage from END on January 8, 2003, setting as a goal "stopping the spread of disease and eradicating it as quickly as possible." He placed responsibility for managing the disease on the secretary of agriculture and the emergency services director. This state of emergency opened the resources of all state agencies to assist with the eradication effort.

Transporting diseased birds was only one way that the disease spread. Guidance from state agricultural departments noted that the disease could be carried on truck tires (Arizona Department of Agriculture, n.d.). Under the state of emergency, Caltrans was part of the eradication effort, contracting for personnel to conduct the decontamination of trucks that had traveled through the quarantined counties, using Caltrans's wash racks (Lissade, personal communication, 2010). END was eradicated in California by September 2003, with 3.5 million birds destroyed at a cost of $160 million to control the outbreak.

Howard Street CSX Tunnel Fire, Baltimore, Maryland

On July 18, 2001, a 60-car CSX freight train derailed inside the Howard Street tunnel under Baltimore; eight cars, including some carrying hazardous materials, caught fire. While the crew escaped by uncoupling the engines and driving out of the tunnel, the single track was blocked for days as the fire was extinguished, the accident investigated, and the wreckage removed. Smoke from the fire blanketed areas of Baltimore, venting through manhole covers.

The Baltimore Fire Department feared that the train cars with hazardous materials might explode, so they closed streets, stopping traffic to the downtown and Inner Harbor tourist areas. Camden Yards baseball stadium was near the tunnel, so all personnel and fans were evacuated from the park and the second game of the double header was cancelled. No scheduled game was played again until July 21, causing $3 million in losses to the team.

A water main that ran above the tunnel in the public street ruptured due to "thermal expansion of the tunnel due to the fire." The break caused service disruption for the light rail line for 56 days. A Michigan Parks and Recreation department 800 number answered in Cumberland, Maryland, was also disrupted, delaying calls for campsite reservations.

The CSX line represents a portion of the main north–south freight corridor along the Atlantic seaboard. It took 5 days to put the fire out and remove the wrecked cars. It took another 55 days to complete the restoration of the tunnel. Freight from Chicago to East Coast cities was significantly disrupted and had to be rerouted through New Jersey; other CSX freight service had to use Norfolk Southern lines to bypass the damaged area of rail.

Tunnel operations resumed without additional security precautions. The National Transportation Safety Board recommended better coordination between the city and the railroad on managing hazardous materials in the tunnel. CSX paid $1.3 million to the city of Baltimore for its emergency response costs (Transportation Research Board, 2006a, pp. 22–26).

Summary

Communications across disciplines require that security, safety, and emergency management are defined in consistent ways. The various strategies for coping with risk include deterrence, detection, responding to an event, and mitigating. A risk assessment must be constructed, leading to an acknowledgment of the hazards and threats, vulnerabilities, and consequences that must be addressed. Federal funding is available through transportation-specific grants and critical infrastructure-oriented grants. Together, these comprise the security environment for transportation.

Discussion Questions

1. Explain the differences among safety, security and emergency management in the management of transportation's critical infrastructure.

2. Transportation security focuses on four functions: deter, detect, deny, and mitigate. How would you create a security plan using these functions for a specific type of transportation infrastructure?

3. Describe the major types of threats to the transportation infrastructure. How does each type impact the operation of transportation services?

4. How does the USAI program interact with transportation grant programs and the National Infrastructure Protection Plan? How could an eligible community harmonize these programs to get the greatest benefit from their support?

5. You are the security director for an urban mass transit organization that has busses, surface light rail, and subway services. What steps would you take to create a security plan for your agency?

References

Arizona Department of Agriculture (n.d.). Exotic Newcastle Disease. http://www.azda.gov/main/end.htm.

Bush, G. W. (2003, December 13). Homeland Security Presidential Directive 7: Critical infrastructure identification, prioritization, and protection. Washington, DC: The White House.

CIDRAP. (2010). *Exotic Newcastle disease.* University of Minnesota. http://www.cidrap.umn.edu/cidrap/content/biosecurity/ag-biosec/anim-disease/exnewcastle.html

DHS (U.S. Department of Homeland Security). (2005). *Fiscal year 2005 Buffer Zone Protection Program.* www.fema.gov/pdf/government/grant/bzpp/fy05_bzpp.shtm

DHS (U.S. Department of Homeland Security). (2007). *Critical infrastructure and key resources.* www.dhs.gov/xprevprot/programs/gc_1189168948944.shtm

DHS (U.S. Department of Homeland Security). (2009, December). *Fiscal year 2010 Transit Security Grant Program guidance and application kit.* http://www.fema.gov/pdf/government/grant/2010/fy10_tsgp_guidance.pdf

DHS (U.S. Department of Homeland Security). FEMA/TSA. (2010, August). *Transit Security Grant Program stakeholder input: FY 2011 look ahead, FY 2010 look back.* http://www.tsa.gov/assets/pdf/fy_2010_tsgp_aac_stakeholder_feedback.pdf

Fischer, R. J., & Green, G. (2004). *Introduction to security.* Amsterdam, the Netherlands: Elsevier, Butterworth, Heineman.

Fitzsimmons, E. (2003, January 10). Poultry quarantine now covers 8 counties in region, officials declare state of emergency. *Union Tribune.* http://legacy.signonsandiego.com/news/metro/20030110-9999_1m10emer.html

GAO (Government Accountability Office). (2009, June). *Transit Security Grant Program: DHS allocates grants based on risk, but its risk methodology, management controls, and grant oversight can be strengthened.* Report GAO 09-491. Report to the Chairman, Committee on Homeland Security, U.S. House of Representatives. Washington, DC: GAO.

Hoover-Hardwick, M. (2003). Exotic Newcastle disease state of emergency. http://www.calrecycle.ca.gov/LEA/Mail/

Jenkins, B. M., Butterworth, B., & Gerston, L. (2010). *Supplement to MTI study on selective passenger screening in the mass transit rail environment.* San Jose, CA: Mineta Transportation Institute.

Jenkins, B. M., & Edwards-Winslow. (2002). *Saving city lifelines.* San Jose, CA: Mineta Trasnportation Institute.

New Mexico Tech (New Mexico Institute of Mining and Technology). (2005). *Prevention and response to suicide bombing incidents.* Socorro, NM: EMRTC.

Paddock, M. (2010, February). The Homeland Security funding landscape. *Homeland Security Today, 7*(2), G11–G12.

Tierney, K. (2010, July 11). Opening plenary. *Natural Hazards Center Annual Conference.*

Transportation Research Board. (2006a). *Making transportation tunnels safe and secure.* TCRP Report 86, Vol. 12. Washington, DC: Transportation Research Board of the National Academies.

Transportation Research Board. (2006b). *Security measures for ferry systems.* TCRP Report 86. Public Transportation Security, Vol. 11. Washington, DC: Transportation Research Board of the National Academies.

U.S. Army. (n.d.). *C.A.R.V.E.R. target analysis tool.* Tab 3. http://www.amc.army.mil/G3/ops/fp/threat/FP%20Chris%20Carver1%20Assessment.doc

Chapter **2**

Emergency Management Theory and Practice

Keywords: emergency management, event, emergency, disaster, catastrophe, risk management, crisis management, continuity of operations, business continuity, mitigation, planning, preparedness, response, recovery

Learning Objectives

After reading this chapter you should be able to

- Distinguish the differences between event, emergency, disaster, and catastrophe
- Understand the distinction between emergency management and continuity of operations
- Understand the theoretical basis for, and underpinnings of, emergency management

Introduction

Transportation is both a government service and a business enterprise. While mass transportation systems in most parts of the United States started as private business ventures (Figure 2.1), the advent of the automobile damaged the profitability of most urban mass transit systems. In the middle of the twentieth century, many of these systems were taken over by special

FIGURE 2.1   Historic Charleston horse-drawn street car.

purpose governments, such as the Port Authority of New York and New Jersey or the Southeast Pennsylvania Transportation Authority (SEPTA).

Mass transit is viewed as an appropriate government service because it is an essential element of the urban economy, enabling workers to commute from home to work in areas of dense population. Other forms of transportation remain as private sector businesses, such as intercity busses, trucking, freight rail, and maritime and air transportation. Whether a transportation system is government owned or privately owned, it has to balance its revenues against its expenditures and manage emergencies that impact the system. The risk to the system can be managed through a variety of strategies including internal planning and insurance. Understanding the emergency management cycles and systems will make selecting the best strategies for managing various threat scenarios more accurate, thereby applying scarce resources appropriately to meet the system's greatest needs.

As mass transit systems across the United States suffer from inadequate revenue and growing demands for government subsidies, the demand for increased security and emergency management system development and implementation also grows. Aging infrastructure, climate change-induced operational problems, and crime against the systems—from graffiti to terrorism—challenge operators to provide day-to-day safety and security while preparing to manage emergencies. Increasing costs for fuel and insurance challenge private transportation system owners to prepare for emergencies as efficiently as possible.

Emergency Management, Safety, and Security

As was discussed in Chapter 1, security focuses on preventing events from occurring. However, not all events are preventable, and mitigation cannot prevent all forms of damage to a transportation system in the face of every type of disaster. Emergency management is the third prong of the systems approach to maintaining transportation functionality. Once security has been applied to the system and safety features have been appropriately implemented, the transportation owner and operator must use the risk analysis to determine what is not ultimately preventable and how such events will be managed once they occur.

Security, safety, and emergency management are each a part of a continuum. For example, a mass transit organization creates stations that have surveillance systems and limited entry points to protect the system from illegal intrusions and related system disruptions. It trains its operators and employees in safe practices and ensures that proper licenses are maintained. However, inevitably, an event occurs that interferes with system operation, such as a power outage or heat wave. The system operator has to be ready to deal with the event and to care for the passengers and employees until the disruption is over.

Despite being components of a continuum, security, safety, and emergency management may at times be at odds with each other. For example, the Port Authority of New York and New Jersey built the World Trade Center twin towers with a focus on security for this center of commerce and finance. To minimize the possibility of intrusions into sensitive work spaces, the building exit stairways only existed for runs of several stories, and then the user had to enter the elevator lobby area to transition to the next portion of the exit stairwell. While discontinuous, each stairwell had appropriate safety features such as lighting, reflective paint on the stairs, and handrails. However, when the 9/11 attacks occurred, the security system of discontinuous stairways interfered with the ability of occupants to exit the building rapidly. Burning diesel fuel that poured from the roof through elevator shafts made some elevator lobby areas impassable, possibly contributing to loss of life as occupants lost access to the next portion of the exit stairway system. Thus, the emergency management plan, which was to evacuate the building, was thwarted by the security plan to limit access to the exit stairwells.

Emergency management, safety, and security planners must understand each other's professional needs and work together to ensure that the three prongs indeed function as part of a system with the common focus of human life preservation and property protection, regardless of the threat or event.

Theoretical Bases for Emergency Management: Terms

Emergency management "is the quintessential government role…to provide support and assistance when resources of individuals and families are overwhelmed;…the management of risk so that societies can live with environmental and technical hazards and deal with the disasters that they cause" (Waugh, 2000, p. 3). The risks can lead to various levels of incidents that demand different levels of response. A lexicon of terminology has developed over the years to make the response levels clearer for planning, investment decision-making, and response purposes.

Event

An event is something that happens that triggers a response using day-to-day resources and that can be managed within the normal operational modes and tempo. For example, a passenger may trip on the stairs and fall down in a mass transit station. Station personnel can help the person to his feet, evaluate the need for medical screening, and complete appropriate reporting forms.

On a community level, a house fire can be an event for the mass transit agency. The fire department response may block the light rail tracks for several hours and require the mass transit company to create a bus bridge around the blocked area. This will result in the activation of the passenger notification systems managed by the public information officer, including posting signs at the blocked light rail stops. It may require bus driver callbacks and activation of the reserve fleet of busses to support the light rail system work-around.

In both cases, the successful management of the event is based on a previously completed risk analysis leading to a recognition that an event might occur. Plans, personnel, and systems are in place to deal with the event immediately. Their implementation has little direct impact on the operation of the system and poses little inconvenience to system riders. The cost to the impacted agency is minimal, unless the injury is severe or the bus bridge requires significant overtime. Accident insurance policies and an overtime budget based on past experience with events can both mitigate the financial impact on the system.

Emergency

An emergency requires a more robust response than an event, based on detailed planning. "Emergencies are unforeseen but predictable and narrow in scope, occur frequently and are dealt with by means of standard

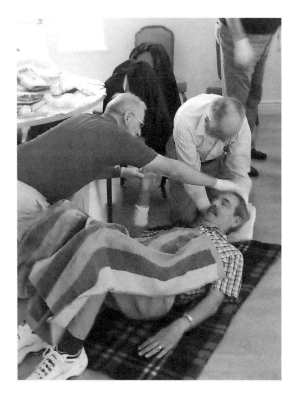

FIGURE 2.2 Employees practice cardiac care.

operating procedures" (Perry & Lindell, 2007, p. 160). Emergencies impact those immediately involved and may invoke public emergency response services, but have little impact on the community at large.

If a passenger has a heart attack in a transit station, the agency staff member present needs to call for emergency medical services and then begin delivering assistance (Figure 2.2). Depending on agency policy, planning, and training, the assistance may include using an automatic electronic defibrillator (AED), using first aid training including cardiopulmonary resuscitation (CPR), or just remaining with the patient until medical help arrives. The event may require closing an entrance to the station to facilitate the arrival of emergency medical personnel and limiting passenger access to parts of the station or platform.

A fire in an industrial building that houses hazardous materials may result in a neighborhood evacuation to the local high school and the closure of roads downwind and downhill of the fire for many hours. Commercial transportation uses may be curtailed, including detours that add distance and time to a delivery. Railroad rights of way may be within the exclusion zone, resulting in denial of service for freight and passenger trains. The local transit agency may be called on to provide busses for the evacuation and for use as temporary shelters while the high school is being opened, especially if it is cold or raining. Busses may be requested for use as command posts for first responders or as personnel staging areas if there is inclement weather. All bus services on the closed roads will have to be rerouted or stopped, triggering notification systems to the community. Multiple agencies such as the American Red Cross (ARC) and police and fire departments will respond to the scene, and city parks and recreation staff will coordinate with ARC and school district staff to open and staff the shelter for evacuees. Nongovernmental organizations may be activated to serve access- and mobility-needs population members who are evacuated and taken to the shelter. Services might include sign language interpreters or interpreters for non-English speakers (Edwards & Goodrich, 2007, pp. 50–51).

In both cases, the successful management of the event is based on standard operating procedures and, in some cases, mutual aid agreements that have been developed through the cooperation of the multiple agencies involved. Their implementation has a significant impact on the system users or even on the immediate community. The emergency response costs will most likely be borne by the agency and community without insurance reimbursements. Delays, lost work time for affected commuters, and personal disruption will become costs to affected organizations. Because few public entities maintain a budget line item for emergency response costs, the agency's budget may have to be changed to absorb the cost of the event, unless reimbursement can be obtained from a responsible party or a business interruption insurance policy.

Disaster

Response to a disaster involves an entire community. "Disasters…disrupt social interaction and interrupt the ability of major community systems to afford reasonable conditions of life…they require resources from outside the community [but] are confined to a sufficiently narrow geographic area that resources can come from nearby" (Perry & Lindell, 2007, p. 160). The response to a disaster will involve the whole emergency response system of the community and possibly invoke the activation of the mutual aid system on a statewide basis.

The Loma Prieta earthquake of 1989 was a disaster. Loss of life, property damage, and critical infrastructure disruption occurred across the San Francisco Bay area. The Bay Area Rapid Transit (BART) system was closed for hours while infrastructure was checked for damage. The Bay Bridge top-deck portion collapsed onto the bottom deck, closing the bridge for months while repairs were completed. This loss of commuter access resulted in the restoration of historic ferry service from Oakland to San Francisco and, ultimately, in the creation of the Water Emergency Transportation Authority (WETA) for use in future disruptive events.

Deaths and destruction from the Loma Prieta earthquake occurred from Watsonville in Monterey County to Santa Cruz, Santa Clara, San Francisco, and Alameda Counties. Mutual aid came from all over the state, and federal financial assistance was required for restoration of infrastructure and public facilities. Yet even with this regional impact, there were areas that suffered little damage and were able to assist with response to the most damaged areas. For example, the San Jose Fire Department provided search and rescue mutual aid to the collapse of the Cypress structure of the I-880 freeway in Oakland, just 35 miles away. Functioning utility services enabled restaurants in Fremont, less than 20 miles away, to provide food for the first responders. The California Department of Transportation (Caltrans) had to close and repair the bridge and the Cypress structure and take down the Embarcadero Freeway in San Francisco, but after they inspected their other infrastructure, the Bay Area's major circulation patterns were restored.

Response to a disaster requires not only well-developed plans and standard operating procedures, but also regional coordination and outside financial assistance for recovery. California's mutual aid system, begun in the wake of World War II and the beginning of the Cold War, encompasses 24 professions, such as law enforcement, fire service, emergency medical service, ambulance service, building officials, and coroners organized along regional lines to respond to disasters (Integrated Waste Management Plan, 2010). A disaster also demands significant financial support, sometimes from available insurance, but most often through state and federal government emergency assistance programs. In a presidentially declared disaster, the federal government pays at least 75% of the emergency response costs under the Stafford Act, and additional public assistance funds are available for the restoration of public facilities (Edwards & Afawubo, 2009).

Although federal and state funds may assist with local recovery and reconstruction, the impacted community still bears part of the financial burden, and if the local destruction is significant, the lack of local funds may result in long-term economic slowing. For example, even though the Northridge Earthquake of 1994 was localized within Los Angeles, those neighborhoods with significant damage to residential structures had a slow recovery as owners, already with highly leveraged mortgages, could not find loans or grants to repair or rebuild. The loss of residents in turn bankrupted neighborhood businesses, resulting in the abandonment of areas, called "ghost-towning" (California OES, 1995). The impact of disasters may be localized but is long term and multidimensional.

Catastrophe

A catastrophe is an event that causes widespread, multisector damage to multiple communities at the same time. Quarantelli (2006) notes that a catastrophe is characterized by wholesale damage to infrastructure and the built environment, including significant damage to the disaster response assets and deaths or injuries to emergency response personnel. This results in large numbers of outside responders assuming responsibility for local response efforts, which may not be conducted according to local emergency plans unless there are local leaders available to coordinate with the outside resources. Because of the widespread damage, outside assistance may have to come from a distance, exacerbating the challenges of immediate response. National and international media coverage of the event continues for weeks to months, politicizing the event on many levels.

While Hurricane Katrina is the latest U.S. catastrophe, the 1900 Galveston hurricane, 1906 San Francisco earthquake, and 1947 Texas City maritime explosion are also examples of catastrophes. In each case, the entire community was devastated by the event, resulting in loss of local response capabilities and a distance-generated delay in response from first responders. In each case, aid came from other states and the military, and rebuilding was politicized.

The magnitude of a catastrophe is difficult to predict in advance because it usually involves a "perfect storm" of factors: an unusually large or impactful disaster event, notification failures, poor immediate response, failure of the residents to act on the information available to them, and poor pre-event physical planning and construction. Because the infrastructure is significantly damaged, outside response is delayed, leading to increases in loss of life and suffering for survivors.

Emergency Management

One approach to dealing with emergencies, disasters, and catastrophes is emergency management. Sylves (2008) calls emergency management "the discipline and profession of applying science, technology, planning and management to deal with extreme events,…limit[ing] losses and costs" (p. 5). It includes the recognition of the need to estimate risks to a community, plan for lessening potential damage through physical and educational methods, plan the response, and estimate the steps needed to restore the community to functionality.

Emergency management takes place at the organizational, community, state, and national levels and through multinational frameworks like non-governmental organizations, regional governmental collaboratives (e.g., Organization of America States or Pan American Health Organization), and United Nations commissions and organizations.

Tools available to emergency managers include government-based codes, regulations, and laws, like building codes and zoning regulations. Community organization and education for emergency planning and response can be accomplished through government-sponsored activities, like the community emergency response team (CERT) programs of FEMA, and through nongovernmental organizations like the American Red Cross.

Risk Management

Risk is the recognition of the existence of a hazard that has the potential to impact a community where people and systems will be vulnerable, resulting in significant damage and leading to an emergency, disaster, or catastrophe. Risk management is the profession of estimating risks to an organization or community, determining what level of risk is "acceptable," and taking action to mitigate the remaining risks.

Risk managers have a variety of tools to assist with risk-related decisions. Specialist organizations like the U.S. Geological Survey or the National Weather Service can provide data on the likelihood, frequency, and severity of hazard events for a given jurisdiction (Edwards, 2009). Geographical information system (GIS) maps can be used to plot the location of natural hazards, hazardous materials, floodplains, and other potential threats overlaid on a community map that shows concentrations of vulnerable populations, high-occupancy structures, and critical infrastructure. Such maps can assist in evaluating the risk to a community and determining the investment that should be made in managing, mitigating, or eliminating the threat to human populations. Insurance can be used to mitigate the financial impact of risks on an organization or community, provided that the premiums for the policy are affordable.

Risk management takes place at the individual level, impacting decisions on where to live; the organizational level, impacting decisions on where and how to conduct business; and on the community level, impacting decisions on what can be used, built, or developed and where. At the state and national levels, the same types of analyses occur for organizational activities and regulatory functions (Figure 2.3). For example, a family might decide to live in a floodplain to have ready access to a creek for wading and fishing and recognize that they will have to take steps to protect valuable property by elevating structures and carrying insurance. A business might choose to locate in seismically active Silicon Valley for the intellectual synergy, but define its level of acceptable risk and undertake mitigation actions such as tying down its equipment and insuring its physical assets against earthquake losses.

Crisis Management

A crisis is the sudden onset of an event of any scale that may have an immediate and negative impact on the individual, organization, community, or government. Howitt and Leonard (2009, pp. 5, 278) suggest that there is also

FIGURE 2.3 Urban planners map community hazards.

an aspect of novelty to a crisis, or a unique combination of features, or a significantly larger scale than seen in more routine emergencies. It is often the novelty, combination, or scale, rather than the scope alone, that makes a crisis—such as the discovery of tampering with a company's primary product like the Tylenol case in 1982 or the recognition of the presence of a hazardous materials fire of unknown origin in a railroad tunnel, as happened on the CSX line in Baltimore in 2001.

Emergency managers have a variety of tools for dealing with crisis. Planning done for more routine emergencies will provide the basis for a rapid response to a crisis. For example, when the plane crashed into the Pentagon on 9/11, the Arlington Fire Department was able to coordinate with Pentagon staff, work with the FBI, and successfully manage the complex event because they had conducted fire drills at the Pentagon before, using the flexible and expandable Incident Command System (ICS). The emergency operations plan (EOP) and emergency operations center (EOC) are designed for the "worst case" scenario for a given community, but when a crisis occurs that has a greater and more rapid impact, the EOP and EOC provide the backbone for the immediate response, bringing together in an organized fashion the appropriate experts who can design the crisis response as the crisis unfolds.

Crisis management takes place at all levels, from individual response to a house fire to community response to a terrorist attack. Because by definition a crisis was not part of the risk evaluation outcome, mitigation through insurance or physical construction changes may be impossible, but steps taken to prepare for expected emergencies may also assist with the management of a crisis. For example, the implementation of the coastal evacuation plan in Mississippi before Hurricane Katrina made landfall followed the pattern for a "normal" hurricane, but it saved lives as the tidal surge carried gambling barges and yachts miles inland, destroying houses and infrastructure in its path.

Continuity of Operations

Continuity of operations (COOP), also known as business continuity, refers to the need to continue to provide essential services to customers or the community in the face of any adversity. While continuity of operations is most closely related to emergency management and emergency operations planning, there are security elements incorporated into the continuity of operations plan. Events listed in Table 1.2 of Chapter 1 all have the potential to impact the security of a business or government agency. When a natural hazard event impacts a community, an emergency, disaster, or catastrophe may ensue, resulting in damage to assets that may include a loss of security. Hurricanes can breach building security by destroying walls. Floods can carry file cabinets of sensitive material far downstream. Tornadoes can uproot protective fencing. However, natural hazards have no element of intent or planning, and damage to the security of an individual agency or facility is incidental to the community-wide damage that encompasses a wide variety of impacts.

Continuity of operations planning recognizes that intentional threats to the security of transportation assets are possible. These threats may occur as part of a planned attack on a facility—conventional or cyber—or be incidental to an attack, sometimes for the purpose of frightening an opponent, which is known as "counting coo." (For a complete description of the historical practice see Plenty Coups & Linderman, 2002.)

Continuity of operations plans is designed to ensure that a business or government agency can continue to provide services to its normal customers. To ensure this continuity of service, the organization has to evaluate its services and determine what assets are crucial to the continuation of service delivery. As with security plan development, the first step in continuity planning is an evaluation of threat to the organization. The organization then determines its essential functions—what it must do even in a disaster—and what activities are necessary to be able to deliver those services. These are designated as "essential services" (FEMA, n.d., a). Activities that support the essential services are also defined and made a priority for continuity and rapid recovery. For example, Caltrans has determined that the maintenance of California's road infrastructure is essential under all emergency circumstances. In order to continue to operate the state's road system, Caltrans needs access to the "as-builts" (detailed final plans) for roads, bridges, and tunnels.

This collection of plans and supporting documents is then designated a "vital record," and extra steps are taken to ensure its security and availability when needed. A strategy such as cloud computing, off-site storage, or redundant copies may be selected based on what will ensure access, even in the most austere conditions. Because earthquakes are the highest consequence events in California that occur within reasonably short periods of time (on average, a significant earthquake on a specific fault happens every 150 years), the plan must take into account loss of power and phone lines, making reliance on the "cloud" or even electronic copies inadequate for true emergency response purposes. Thus, hard copies must be stored in safe locations for ready access after a disaster.

In order to ensure that services continue, a pre-established alternate site may be needed for specific activities, such as maintaining payroll or providing supporting information about transportation assets to other agencies. Alternate locations must have the equipment and functionalities of the normal business center, but be located out of the immediate disaster area and supplied with "work-around" equipment like backup generators and satellite telephones with fax and e-mail capability.

Lines of succession must be established for each essential function to ensure that if the primary authorities are unavailable or otherwise incapacitated, others are trained to take over the management of the essential functions and coordination with higher levels of government or other business partners. Legal delegations of authority must be in place to ensure that the person filling a position has the clear authority to conduct specific business and make specific decisions.

There is also a security element to every continuity of operations plan. Vital records must be stored in a protected environment, both to prevent deterioration or tampering and to ensure ready access when needed. Alternate facilities must be able to be locked and protected from intruders. However, such buildings must also be built for safety, using seismic or wind building codes to ensure that the building can withstand the disaster so that essential services, using vital records, can be delivered from that safe, disaster-resistant alternate location.

The Four Phases of Emergency Management

In 1979 the National Governors' Association issued a report on the nation's emergency management. This report described four "phases" of emergency management that are part of a cycle: mitigation, preparedness/planning,

FIGURE 2.4   Cycle of emergency management.

response, and recovery (Figure 2.4). While the phases are described as separate, for the purpose of making their functions clear, the phases actually flow into each other, often with several occurring at the same time.

Mitigation

The term *mitigation* means to minimize the damage from an unwanted event. It encompasses physical activities, such as the construction of levees to prevent flooding, and regulatory activity, such as the adoption of a building code that is designed to provide life safety performance levels for buildings in a seismic event. Mitigation begins with a risk assessment to determine "the most severe, likely, and frequent threats" that the organization or community must expect to "protect critical infrastructure and improve the overall safety of the community" (Edwards & Goodrich, 2007, p. 49). Appropriate responses are designed to protect lives, lessen damage to the environment and property, and facilitate economic recovery.

Studies have demonstrated the value of mitigation to the economy, as well as to the avoidance of misery for potential victims. In 2005 the Multihazard Mitigation Council of the National Institute of Building Sciences released a study that showed that "each dollar spent on mitigation saves an average of four dollars" in damages (FEMA, 2009b).

Zoning is also a form of mitigation, preventing the construction of built environment and infrastructure in especially dangerous areas. For example, the Alquist-Priolo zoning in California prevents the construction of high-occupancy buildings within 1,000 feet of an active fault line. Floodplain zoning may require that buildings for human occupancy be elevated to a certain height, be built on pilings, or have no occupancy on the first floor of the building.

Nonstructural hazard mitigation focuses on the contents and architectural features of a building that do not contribute to its strength. Nonstructural elements of buildings may be strengthened or tied down to resist wind damage or seismic shaking. Nonstructural actions might include bolting tall furniture to the building's studs in an earthquake-prone area or tying the corners of the roof to the building's framing in hurricane-prone or tornado-prone areas.

Mitigation may also lack physical attributes. A public education campaign on nonstructural hazard mitigation, strengthening foundations, or improving roof connections is a mitigation action. The purchase of hazard insurance is a form of financial mitigation—lessening the economic impact of a disaster on a community or organization.

Preparedness/Planning

The risk analysis forms the basis for the planning process within the organization. The risks must be reevaluated on a regular basis and plans updated accordingly (Edwards & Goodrich, 2007). For example, development of formerly agricultural areas of a community may lead to changes in the flooding profile, as absorbent areas of grass and dirt are paved and roofed, generating increases in runoff. An EOP is created with checklists that cover the standard operating procedures for responding to the worst-case scenario for the organization or community (Edwards & Goodrich, 2010b). Additional plan sections are developed that cover other frequently occurring emergencies requiring organization-wide or community-wide response. (The EOP will be discussed in detail later.) The planning process includes the creation of an EOC, which is in a secure location and designed to meet organizational needs, based on the threats detailed in the EOP. (The EOC will be discussed in detail later.)

Employee education regarding the threats to the organization and their role in responding to them is an essential part of the preparedness activity. For example, in California all public employees are disaster service workers and required to stay at work in a disaster. Employees must be encouraged to prepare personal support supplies—a car or desk kit (Figure 2.5)—to remain at work during an emergency response. Those who have a field response role must also have appropriate personal protective equipment, clothing, and professional equipment readily available to fulfill that role.

In order to ensure that employees will remain at work, it is important for them to make an emergency plan with their families (Figure 2.6). The family should assemble a "get away" kit with vital documents, medications, and other essential supplies that is ready for a rapid departure. FEMA provides a comprehensive family kit list at http://www.fema.gov/plan/prepare/supplykit.shtm (Figure 2.7).

WATER. *This is your most important item.* You will need water to drink, for first aid, and to take medicine. In your kit, have at least 1 gallon of water per person, based on who usually rides in your car. You could purchase a box of foil packets or cans of water at a camping store, or 1-liter bottles at COSTCO in a 20-bottle flat.

PRESCRIPTION MEDICATIONS. *This is the second most important item.* If you take medications on which your health depends, you must carry a 3-day supply at all times. This would include heart, blood pressure, and diabetes medications. If you regularly take other prescription drugs for allergies or other health concerns, it is also wise to carry these. Keep this supply fresh by rotating it every week. Also include any nonprescription medications you often use: nose drops, antihistamines, allergy remedies, diarrhea medication, or indigestion medications. In times of stress such as an emergency, health problems can become worse. Having proper medications and keeping to the prescribed schedule is very important.

FOOD. Food is important for psychological reasons and to keep your blood sugar level up to avoid dizzy or shaky feelings. People with diabetes, heart disease, or other health problems should consult their physicians for advice about the foods for their kits. The healthy general public should select foods like crackers; peanut butter; snack packs of fruit, pudding, granola bars, and dried fruit; and single-serving cans of juice. Plan on four light meals per day. Avoid high-sugar foods like candy and soft drinks as they make you very thirsty. Avoid alcoholic beverages.

LIGHT SOURCE. A chemical light stick provides long shelf life and a sparkless source of light. A flashlight with a special long-life battery or a long-burning candle may be used after you have checked the area to be sure that there is no leaking gas or petroleum in the area. Do not rely on a regular flashlight as ordinary batteries lose their power quickly in the heat of a car. You might consider an electric light with an attachment to your car cigarette lighter, available at camping stores.

RADIO. Your car radio is your source for emergency broadcast information. Get a list of all-news stations for the area where you live and work, and areas you drive to or through. Keep this list in your glove compartment and in your emergency kit. A hand-cranked emergency radio is also useful and eliminates the need for batteries. These often come with flashlights that run on the same power source.

EMERGENCY BLANKET. Mylar emergency blankets are available at camping-goods stores. They can be used as a blanket or a heat shield against the sun. They fold into a small package. A thermal blanket may be substituted when storage space permits.

FIRST AID SUPPLIES. Include 4 × 4 gauze, cloth that can be torn into strips to hold a bandage in place, Kerlex, antibacterial ointment (Neosporin, Bacitracin, etc.), burn cream, rolls of gauze, large gauze pads, rolls of first aid tape, scissors, a large cloth square for a sling or tourniquet, safety pins, needles and heavy thread, matches, eye wash, and a chemical ice pack. Rotate these supplies every 6 months.

FIGURE 2.5   Emergency kit for the car.

PERSONAL CARE AND HYGIENE ITEMS. Include alcohol-based hand sanitizer, small plastic bottle of pine oil or other disinfectant, six large heavy-duty garbage bags with ties for sanitation and waste disposal, box of tissues, roll of toilet paper, and a plastic bucket to use as a toilet after lining it with a plastic garbage bag. (Your smaller kit items can be stored in your bucket inside a sealed trash bag.)

ADDITIONAL ITEMS TO CONSIDER. Have sturdy shoes (especially if your work shoes are not good for walking), sweater or jacket, hat/sun visor, mouthwash, feminine hygiene supplies, whistle (to attract attention and call for help), rope or string, pencil and tablet, and change for a pay phone.

DO NOT LET YOUR GAS TANK FALL BELOW HALF FULL! The radio and heater in your car may save your life, but you cannot run the car's accessories long without the gas to start the engine and recharge the battery. If you travel in isolated areas, on the freeway, or far from home, an adequate gasoline supply is crucial. Fill up often. After the quake, the gas pumps may not work for several days while electrical power is restored, and once the pumps work, the supplies will quickly be depleted through panic buying. NEVER CARRY CANS OF GAS IN YOUR TRUNK! A can of gas is a bomb!

FIGURE 2.5 (continued) **Emergency kit for the car.**

Employees also need training in emergency functions. For example, EOC staff members need to be trained in their roles. Field staff members need safety training for working in emergency conditions. All staff members should be familiar with the Incident Command System (ICS) and National Incident Management System (NIMS), which will be discussed later.

Response

When an emergency occurs, the EOP will guide the response, based on ICS and NIMS, as required by federal regulations. Transit agency and passenger rail resources may be needed for evacuations, temporary shelters, or staging areas. Transportation departments will be tasked with debris removal, critical infrastructure inspections, and repairs to transportation assets. Security systems may be damaged or without power, requiring the presence of more employees for surveillance and property protection. Passengers may need assistance with evacuation. Transit and transportation agencies may be asked to provide liaisons to government EOCs at the local or state government levels to coordinate evacuation, movement of people without cars, and road openings. After safety inspections are completed, railroads may be used to carry supplies and equipment to the damaged community. Maritime assets may be used in novel ways, such as the cruise ships that provided emergency housing for first responders during the response to Hurricane Katrina in New Orleans.

Family Emergency Plan
Fire • Police • Medical
Dial 9-1-1

Places to meet if family members become separated:

1. _____
2. _____
3. _____

Out-of-town relative for relaying messages to family members:

Name: _____

Address: _____

Phone: _____

Family Information:

Father's work address/phone; mother's work address/phone

_____   _____

_____   _____

_____   _____

Child's school address/phone; school policy is to:

_____ _____ Hold children

_____ _____ Release children

Child's school address/phone; school policy is to:

_____ _____ Hold children

_____ _____ Release children

Utilities:

Gas shutoff: _____

Water shutoff: _____

Electric shutoff: _____

Emergency supplies: (type and location)

_____

Doctor: _____   Dentist: _____

Hospital: _____   Ambulance:_____

Medical insurance number: _____

Nearest medical center; nearest fire station:

_____

Poison Control Center: 1-800-876-4766

FIGURE 2.6   Family emergency plan template.

During a disaster, like an earthquake or flood, you may need to evacuate your home rapidly. You will want to have some important legal documents with you and others in a safe place. Take steps now to ensure that you safeguard your legal documents and have appropriate access to them for disaster recovery!

1. **Open a bank safe deposit box, or buy a fireproof safe** for essential, irreplaceable, original documents. These include
   - Family birth certificates
   - Marriage certificates and divorce papers
   - Citizenship papers
   - Military records and discharge papers, copies of the face of military ID cards
   - Copies of insurance policies with agent contact information
   - A list of bank accounts with the bank address
   - A list of credit card numbers and addresses
   - Accountant's copy of your income tax filings for 7 years
   - Securities, U.S. savings bonds, certificates of deposit, and similar financial instruments
   - Original Social Security cards for all family members
   - Titles and deeds for property
   - Vehicle titles and a copy of the registration papers
2. **Make a GoKit document cache** to keep in your family emergency kit. Organize these records in a 1-inch ring binder with page protectors or in a waterproof container. You can use a 14-inch piece of 3-inch PVC pipe and two end caps. Use adhesive to attach one end cap permanently and use a threaded cap for the other end. Fill the book or tube with the following documents/copies and update it each spring and fall:
   - Copies of birth certificates and marriage/divorce papers
   - Emergency contact information for all family members: work address and phone, school address and phone, day care/after school care address and phone
   - Out-of-area contact person's name, address, and phone number
   - Copies of citizenship papers/green cards
   - Original passports for all family members
   - Military papers to prove veteran's benefits eligibility, copies of the face of military ID cards
   - Copies of medical information for each family member: physicians' names and numbers, prescription drug names and dosages, pharmacy name and number
   - Copies of insurance policies with 24-hour contact information for every policy
   - Copies of the tax bill, mortgage papers, or property deed to prove home ownership; copy of lease to prove legal right to alternate shelter
   - Copies of two utility bills less than 1 year old to prove residency (owners and renters)
   - Copies of the credit card list and emergency numbers to report lost cards
   - Copies of all family drivers' licenses and auto registrations
   - Copies of all Social Security cards
   - One pad of checks and one credit card for an account that you seldom use to use for emergency expenses: food, alternate lodging, replacement clothing
   - $50 in small bills in case cash registers and credit card machines do not work
   - $10 in quarters for the pay phone
   - A copy of the wills for each family member; make sure that an out-of-area family member has another copy in a safe place and that your legal adviser has a copy
   - Copies of funeral arrangements in place or last wishes for adults

DO NOT LEAVE YOUR FAMILY'S FINANCIAL SECURITY TO CHANCE...BE PREPARED!

FIGURE 2.7   Family vital records list.

Recovery

The recovery phase begins while the response phase is still underway. Organizing resources for debris removal and road repair must begin as soon as the damage assessment is completed. Contracts for emergency supplies and emergency repairs need to be negotiated as early as possible. As recovery and reconstruction measures are being developed, mitigation measures should be incorporated. Current federal doctrine focuses on resilience, or repairing damage so that future similar emergencies will cause less damage, with a focus on speeding restoration of service and economic recovery.

Public mass transit agencies may be eligible for financial assistance from FEMA, while transportation agencies that manage roads may be eligible for assistance from the Federal Highway Administration (FHWA) Emergency Relief Assistance Program (EA). Losses must be at least $700,000 for EA eligibility, with EA covering 90% for repairs to the interstate system highways and 80% for all other eligible highways. EA includes emergency work and permanent work, as shown in Figures 2.8 and 2.9. Emergency work may be reimbursed at 100% under some circumstances (Edwards & Goodrich, 2010b).

Recovery is crucial to restarting the community and its economy. This phase enables choices to be made that will enhance future livability, lessen risk, and encourage environmentally sensitive planning. FEMA has programs that even include the relocation of communities away from hazards to end the cycle of repetitive losses. For example, following the 1995 floods along the Mississippi River, the state of Missouri and FEMA began a systematic buyout of repetitive flooding areas that has resulted in federal purchase of 99 communities, including 4,045 properties (FEMA, 2008b).

Systems for Emergency Management: ICS, SEMS, NIMS

Following a season of large wildland interface fires in 1970, the California fire service leadership created the Incident Command System (ICS). Modeled on the military's command and general staff concept, ICS provides a flexible and hierarchical framework for use in managing emergencies. Today ICS is used by the fire service across the United States for its day-to-day emergency response, as well as for response to catastrophes. The ICS structure includes an incident commander in overall charge of the tactical response to the event. Four sections work for him, each headed by a section chief: operations, planning/intelligence, logistics, and finance/administration. The incident commander is supported by three staff officers: public information, safety, and liaison. This structure may expand, with each section developing branches, units, and groups to provide for specialized response and to ensure a span of control of 1:3 to 1:7 for both safety and efficiency

Section I	Public Assistance: Categories of Work	Description
		Emergency work
Category A	Debris removal	Trees; building wreckage; sand/mud/silt/gravel; vehicles from public property
Category B	Emergency protective measures	Before, during, and after a disaster—to save lives, protect public health and safety, and protect improved public and private property
		Permanent work
Category C	Roads and bridges	Repair of roads, bridges, shoulders, ditches, culverts, lighting, and signs
Category D	Water control facilities	Repair of irrigation systems, drainage channels, and pumping facilities. Repairs of levees, dams, and flood control channels fall under D, but eligibility is restricted
Category E	Buildings and equipment	Repair or replacement of buildings, including contents and systems; heavy equipment and vehicles
Category F	Utilities	Repair of water treatment and delivery systems, power generation facilities and distribution lines, and sewage collection and treatment facilities
Category G	Parks, recreational, and other	Repair and restoration of parks, playgrounds, pools, cemeteries, and beaches and other public facilities that do not fall under the other categories

Source: FEMA. (1999, October). *Public Assistance Guide*, 322, pp. 44–60.

FIGURE 2.8 FEMA public assistance.

(Figure 2.10). For a complete list of positions and responsibilities, review the ICS guide at http://www.firescope.org/ics-8x11-fog.htm.

Since 1994 all fire departments in California are mandated to use ICS. During Hurricane Katrina, in 2005, the most successful first responder agencies—urban search and rescue teams and disaster medical assistance teams—used ICS to organize their resources for rescue operations (Edwards, 2009). The Coast Guard adopted ICS for use in its response to hazardous materials events and used it in disaster responses. "By applying a common organizational structure and key management principles in a standardized way, ICS has evolved into an 'all-risk' system appropriate to all types of emergencies" (U.S. DOT, 2002, p. 36).

In 1991 California experienced two disasters just months apart: a hazardous materials spill into the upper Sacramento River in Dunsmuir and the Oakland Hills firestorm in Oakland and Berkeley. As a result of the response problems at both events, the fire service leadership asked State Senator Nicholas Petris, a victim of the fire, to sponsor a bill that would

Section II: Emergency Protective Measures

Before and after the event	After the event
Warning devices: barricades, signs, announcements	Search and rescue
Security: police and guards	Bracing/shoring damaged structures
Construction of temporary levees	Emergency repairs
Provision of shelter or emergency care	Emergency demolition
Sandbagging	Removal of health and safety hazards
Provision of food, water, ice, and essential supplies	

Source: FEMA. (2001, October). *Public Assistance Policy Digest,* 321, p. 42.

Section III: Eligible Applicants

Public facilities	Private nonprofit
Roads	Classrooms, supplies and equipment
Sewage treatment plants	Utilities (gas, water, power)
Airports	Fire stations, rescue squads
Irrigation channels	Hospitals and outpatient centers
Schools	Custodial care facilities
Buildings	Others: community centers, homeless shelters, libraries,
Bridges and culverts	museums, rehabilitation centers, senior citizen centers,
Utilities	sheltered workshops, zoos, health and safety services

Source: FEMA. (2001, October). *Public Assistance Policy Digest,* 321, pp. 37, 39.

FIGURE 2.8 (continued)   FEMA Public Assistance.

Emergency repairs: essential traffic, to minimize the extent of damage or to protect the remaining facilities

Emergency detours
Removing slides and debris
Temporary bridges or ferry services
Regrading of roadway embankments and surfaces
Placing rip-rap to prevent further scour

Permanent repairs: restoration to pre-disaster condition

Restoring pavement surfaces
Reconstructing damaged bridges and culverts
Replacing signs, guardrails, fences, and other highway appurtenances

Source: U.S. DOT, FHWA. (2009, February). *A Guide to the Federal-Aid Highway Emergency Relief Program,* http://fhwa.dot.gov/specialfunding/er/guide.cfm

---

FIGURE 2.9   Federal-Aid Highway Emergency Relief Program.

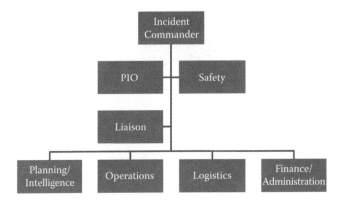

FIGURE 2.10   ICS structure.

mandate both the use of ICS by the fire service and the creation of a standardized emergency management system (SEMS) for use at all levels of emergency management. SEMS was mandated for all state agencies, but use of SEMS is optional for local governments and special districts. However, in order to be eligible to receive reimbursement for the state's share of emergency response costs, local agencies must use SEMS. As a result, SEMS, the indoor version of ICS, is used in most communities and special districts throughout the state.

SEMS is based on ICS. However, since the EOC application of SEMS is community-wide and strategic, the leadership position in the EOC is called management, but all the rest of the positions have the same names as ICS (Figure 2.11). The span of control under SEMS is more flexible, with 1:10 being acceptable.

ICS and SEMS are both based on unity of command in a hierarchical and flexible system that allows for staffing to be assigned as needed, while the five functions continue to be performed during the response. Both ICS and SEMS are based on management-by-objective principles that require specific achievable goals to be set and a specific time frame—action period—to be established for the achievement of the goals. This process is called action planning (incident action planning in the field) and is conducted by the five section chiefs. Half an hour before the end of each action period, the five section chiefs gather to review the goals that were set, the achievement of those goals, challenges facing the organization in achieving the goals, and direction that is needed for the next action planning period. The incident commander or management section chief reviews the information from the four sections and determines the goals and next action period time frame. The planning/intelligence section chief creates a written version of the management section chief's directions and distributes the plan to all five sections to guide their next operations.

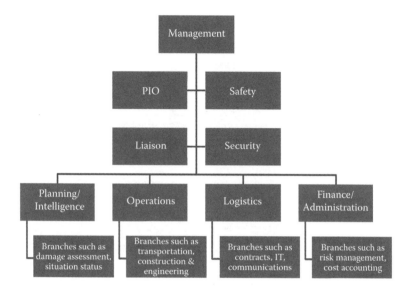

FIGURE 2.11   SEMS structure.

Following the attacks of 9/11, the value of ICS was demonstrated at the Pentagon, where the Arlington County Fire Department used ICS to coordinate the multiagency, interjurisdictional response to the fire and destruction caused by the airplane. President George W. Bush mandated the adoption of "a comprehensive national incident management system" in Homeland Security Presidential Directive-5 (Bush, 2003a). NIMS is largely based on ICS.

NIMS is mandated for all communities that wish to receive federal financial assistance under the Stafford Act by HSPD-8 (Bush, 2003b). It has six elements: "command and management, preparedness, resource management, communications and information management, supporting technologies, and ongoing management and maintenance" (Edwards & Goodrich, 2007, p. 40). When command is in the field, it follows ICS. When management is in the EOC, it may follow a model like SEMS, called the "ESF model" by FEMA—especially when community-wide or organization-wide management is being conducted. The 15 emergency support functions (ESFs) encompass most activities that are conducted to manage resources during a disaster. It is significant that ESF-1 is transportation—again indicating the importance of transportation in moving personnel and resources to relieve the suffering of the victims of an emergency (see Tables 2.1 and 2.2). When the management activity is only oriented toward resource management, it may follow the Multiagency Coordination Systems (MACS) model. Given the complex interactions required of transit and transportation agencies, the SEMS model provides a more flexible and coordinated framework for interaction with multiple jurisdictions and other levels of government (Edwards & Goodrich, 2010b).

TABLE 2.1 Roles and Responsibilities of the ESFs

ESF 1—Transportation	Aviation/airspace management and control Transportation safety Restoration/recovery of transportation infrastructure Movement restrictions Damage and impact assessment
ESF 2—Communications	Coordination with telecommunications and information technology industries Restoration and repair of telecommunications infrastructure Protection, restoration, and sustainment of national cyber and information technology resources Oversight of communications within the federal incident management and response structures
ESF 3—Public works and engineering	Infrastructure protection and emergency repair Infrastructure restoration Engineering services and construction management Emergency contracting support for lifesaving and life-sustaining services
ESF 4—Firefighting	Coordination of federal firefighting activities Support to wildland, rural, and urban firefighting operations
ESF 5—Emergency management	Coordination of incident management and response efforts Issuance of mission assignments Resource and human capital Incident action planning Financial management
ESF 6—Mass care, emergency assistance, housing, and human services	Mass care Emergency assistance Disaster housing Human services
ESF 7—Logistics management and resource support	Comprehensive, national incident logistics planning, management, and sustainment capability Resource support (facility space, office equipment and supplies, contracting services, etc.)
ESF 8—Public health and medical services	Public health Medical Mental health services Mass fatality management
ESF 9—Search and rescue	Lifesaving assistance Search and rescue operations
ESF 10—Oil and hazardous materials response	Oil and hazardous materials (chemical, biological, radiological, etc.) response Environmental short- and long-term cleanup
ESF 11—Agriculture and natural resources	Nutrition assistance Animal and plant disease and pest response Food safety and security Natural and cultural resources and historic properties protection and restoration Safety and well-being of household pets

TABLE 2.1 (continued) Roles and Responsibilities of the ESFs

ESF 12—Energy	Energy infrastructure assessment, repair, and restoration Energy industry utilities coordination Energy forecast
ESF 13—Public safety and security	Facility and resource security Security planning and technical resource assistance Public safety and security support Support to access, traffic, and crowd control
ESF 14—Long-term community recovery	Social and economic community impact assessment Long-term community recovery assistance to states, local governments, and the private sector Analysis and review of mitigation program implementation
ESF 15—External affairs	Emergency public information and protective action guidance Media and community relations Congressional and international affairs Tribal and insular affairs

Source: FEMA. (2008a, January). Emergency support function annexes: Introduction. P. ESF-i to ESF-ii. http://www.fema.gov/pdf/emergency/nrf/nrf-esf-intro.pdf

TABLE 2.2 SEMS and ESF Crosswalk

SEMS	ESF
Management	
PIO	ESF 15
Safety	
Security	ESF 13 (portions)
Liaison	
Emergency management coordinator	ESF 5 (portions)
Planning/intelligence	
Damage assessment	
Situation status	
Recovery	ESF 14, ESF 11 (portions)
Economic	
Environmental	ESF 10 (portions)
Public health	ESF 8 (portions)
Temporary housing	ESF 6 (portions)
Operations	
Law enforcement	ESF 13 (portions)
Coroner	ESF 8 (portions)
Movement/evacuation	ESF 1 (portions)

continued

TABLE 2.2 (continued) SEMS and ESF Crosswalk

SEMS	ESF
Fire operations	
Fire suppression	ESF 4
Hazardous materials management	ESF 10 (portions)
Search and rescue	ESF 9
Emergency medical services	ESF 8 (portions)
Care and shelter	
Mass care	ESF 6 (portions), ESF 11 (portions)
Mental health	ESF 8 (portions)
Pet issues	ESF 11 (portions)
Construction and engineering	ESF 3
Public facility damage assessment/repair	ESF 1 (portions)
Utilities	ESF 12
Transportation	ESF 1 (portions)
Communications	ESF 2 (portions)
Logistics	ESF 7
Communications	ESF 2 (portions)
Information technology	
Contracting	
Transportation	
Finance/administration	ESF 5 (portion)
Time keeping	
Risk management	
Cost accounting	

Emergency Operations Plan

As part of the planning and preparedness phase, every jurisdiction must develop an EOP. FEMA provides detailed guidance for the creation of the EOP through *Community Planning Guide 101* (FEMA, 2009a). The plan begins with a statement of the authorities and regulations that govern the development and implementation of the plan. Next there is a comprehensive threat review, a matrix of responsibility that shows the roles of the emergency management organization by hazard event, and a description of some continuity of governance elements, such as chain of succession for key roles, alternate locations for the emergency management function should the EOC be inaccessible, and a description of the methods for safeguarding the vital records of the organization. The last section is a comprehensive threat analysis for the community. This material is called the "basic plan."

The second part of the EOP is composed of descriptions and checklists for each emergency management organization position as it responds to the major threat to that jurisdiction. In California, for example, that would normally be earthquake, while in Miami it is hurricanes. Throughout most of the Midwest the principal threat is flooding, while ice storms and power outages are usually the focus of plans in the Northeast. For large cities, the focus might be terrorism. Generally called "annexes," these segments are each devoted to one focus area. The first five cover the five sections within the EOC: management, planning/intelligence, operations, logistics, and finance/administration. Each of these annexes begins with a brief description of the work of the section and then provides a one- to three-page checklist for each EOC position, starting with the section chief, then the director for each branch or leader for each unit, and finally for any group. A set of example annexes is available in *The Role of Transportation in Campus Emergency Management* (Edwards & Goodrich, 2009).

Following are a number of annexes devoted to individual threats that describe what different actions would be taken. Current FEMA guidance requires at least a terrorism annex, but communities and organizations may also create annexes for any significant threats to the entity for which the plan is written. For example, in a flood annex, the work would focus on monitoring the condition of reservoirs and water courses. Public information materials might focus on cleaning flood-damaged household goods and medical precautions for people exposed to flood waters. A heat wave annex would focus on establishing cooling centers for vulnerable populations.

Transit and transportation agencies would generally follow the same threat-based pattern as the community's EOP. They might plan to send a liaison to the local government EOC to coordinate the use of their rolling stock assets in the community response, such as for evacuations or sheltering. Transportation agencies would coordinate regarding debris removal, damage assessment of road assets, and management of inspections of critical infrastructure like highway bridges and tunnels. Because first responders rely on roads to reach victims, the role of the transportation organization is crucial in the overall emergency response (Edwards & Goodrich, 2009).

While ICS forms one method for organizing the annexes, some communities prefer to use the MACS format, especially if the principal role is managing resources rather than coordinating organization-wide response. A hybrid model can be developed that uses ICS, but provides a reference to the appropriate ESF in the relevant section, branch, unit or group. This system is best when organization-wide coordination is required as well as resource management, but the organization's focus is primarily on coordination with federal assets.

Emergency Operations Center

The emergency operations center is a location where the leadership of the organization's emergency management sector gathers to make joint decisions about the impending or existing emergency. The center is designed to be secure, to be able to operate on independent power and communications systems for the duration of the emergency, to provide the information support elements essential for the management of an emergency in that organization, and to be large enough to accommodate the assigned staff. The size, location, and assets of the EOC are all designed to support a response to the events evaluated in the threat assessment (Edwards & Goodrich, 2007, p. 41).

The EOC must be designed to support the implementation of the EOP. In a SEMS/ICS model EOC, there will be five section areas:

- Management
- Operations
- Planning/intelligence
- Logistics
- Finance/administration

These enable each section chief to coordinate with the members of the section throughout the emergency. There will usually be a side room where the five section chiefs can meet for action planning meetings, a time when goals are set and progress in managing the event is evaluated. In a MACS-based model, there may be a "boardroom" approach using a large horseshoe-shaped table set up with each unit in its own area. Because a MACS-oriented structure is focused on resource management, this model allows easy cross communication among the functions. Other designs, such as a "bull's-eye" model where the leadership sits together while workers are in different areas and the "mission control" model that is an amphitheater focused on TV and GIS screens, are used by some agencies (Botterell, 2002). The design of the center may vary in any configuration that best supports the EOP of that organization.

During the course of an event, the staffing in the various EOC sections will change. Initially, the Operations Section may have multiple branches and units to manage various aspects of the field support. The Planning/Intelligence Section will need staff for damage assessment and map making, while the Logistics Section may only be acquiring food for the field and EOC staff members and activating existing emergency contracts and open purchase orders. Once the immediate response—search and rescue, fire suppression, road opening—has been completed, the focus may shift to care and shelter of the victims and creating new contracts for repair and debris removal, including hazardous materials cleanup, creating work for the Logistics and Finance/Administration Sections, while the Operations Section has few field responders to support.

After the Northridge earthquake in Los Angeles, the city and county opened their EOCs

> ...to facilitate interagency decision making and information flow. They accommodate utility representatives and representatives from various City of Los Angeles departments including public works, fire, police, building and safety, transportation (LADOT), city administration, and the mayor's office. Also represented at the EOCs are the Los Angeles County Sheriff's Department, the MTA [Metropolitan Transportation Authority], the CHP [California Highway Patrol], and Caltrans. (U.S. DOT, 2002, p. 36)

This is a good example of the variety of organizational elements that will be represented in transportation-oriented emergency operation centers.

The EOC may be used throughout the recovery process as a coordination point for all aspects of recovery, reconstruction, and mitigation contracting. While the facility would be open around the clock during the emergency response phase, it may be open only during business hours once the recovery phase is reached.

Training and Exercises

For the EOP and EOC to function successfully, the staff members must be trained in ICS and NIMS, in their roles under the EOP, and regarding the functionality of the EOC. Emergency management staff training is an important part of the development and maintenance of emergency management systems. The Department of Homeland Security (DHS) provides guidance on the personnel who need ICS and NIMS training, as well as the content and frequency of the training (FEMA, n.d., b). FEMA offers many independent study training opportunities through its website (FEMA, 2011). Other classes are offered face to face in a classroom setting, which is especially useful for understanding complex systems like the higher levels of ICS training, notably ICS 300 and ICS 400.

Once emergency management staff members have received training, they need to practice their skills and test their equipment. Working in the EOC as part of an exercise will help staff members to become familiar with the facility and equipment and to understand what resources they will need to do their jobs in an emergency. Thinking through the checklist tasks presented in the EOP will enable staff members to determine what lists, directories, and contact information are essential for success during a disaster. For example, the Logistics staff will appreciate the importance of having vendor and contract information readily available in hard copy, while the Personnel Unit will understand the need for an updated list of callback information for the EOC staff members (Edwards & Goodrich, 2010a).

DHS has created a Homeland Security Exercise and Evaluation Program (HSEEP) with guidance on conducting a variety of types of exercises. While there is no transportation-specific information included in the materials, the general exercise types provide a progressive approach to learning. Starting with a seminar on the threats, moving through drills of specific skills, and including exercises of increasing complexity (DHS, 2007), the exercise system enables emergency management staff members to test their abilities to implement the emergency plan and manage the emergency management system under various circumstances (Edwards & Goodrich, 2010b).

Training and exercises are crucial to the success of emergency management in an event of any size. Staff members who are familiar with the EOP checklists and their EOC facility will experience less stress when working in these relatively unfamiliar surroundings. Synergies and relationships created during exercises will carry over into the actual events and make the coordination of activities and resources smoother.

Case Study

Northridge Earthquake Destroys I-10 Overcrossings

At 4:30 a.m. on January 17, 1994, the thrust fault under the Santa Susanna Mountains in northeast Los Angeles ruptured, causing a 6.8 magnitude earthquake that resulted in significant damage focused on the Northridge area of the city. However, damage was widespread throughout the metropolitan area, with significant disruption to transportation infrastructure. The I-10, also known as the Santa Monica Freeway, had four significant collapses, cutting a crucial multimodal transportation link for the Los Angeles area. Overcrossings at Venice, Washington, La Cienega, and Fairfax Avenues were destroyed (U.S. DOT, 2002, p. 10), representing a loss of 9.4 miles of freeway that linked two other major freeways, the San Diego and the Harbor (U.S. DOT. 2002, p. 21).

The U.S. Department of Transportation (DOT) considers the I-10 the busiest freeway in the world, running through eight states for 2,460 miles, from Florida to California (U.S. DOT, 2002, p. 5). The average daily trips in 1993 were calculated at 261,000 within Los Angeles east of I-405, making this an economically significant route. Post-earthquake studies estimated that the loss of the interstate links "was costing the community about $1 million per day" (U.S. DOT, 2002, p. 33). The I-10 is also important to the U.S. economy, as it carries freight from the Port of Los Angeles to the rest of the nation (U.S. DOT, 2002, p. 9).

By 2 p.m. on January 17 a Presidential Disaster Declaration was issued for Los Angeles County, and by 7:00 p.m. emergency work began on debris clearance and highway demolition (U.S. DOT, 2002, p. 9). The FHWA committed emergency relief funds for the rebuilding of the highway network, allowing the state to begin developing a contract for the repair work (U.S. DOT, 2002, p. 12). Using detour maps that Caltrans district 7 had designed for use in minor traffic incident response, Caltrans was able to manage the impact on the community's traffic circulation system effectively (U.S. DOT, 2002, p. 13). Caltrans' Intelligent Traffic System Traffic Management Center (TMC) served as the EOC for the immediate management of the event, using its backup generators to power the facility and land line telephones to coordinate the response (U.S. DOT, 2002, p. 14).

That same morning, the FHWA representative and Caltrans staff began developing the recovery plan for the freeway damage. Contracts with the various demolition companies were issued for labor, materials, equipment, and an agreed-upon profit, which allowed for a rapid start. By February 5 (Day 20), reconstruction of the I-10 corridor had begun with a contract that included incentives for early completion of the work. The work was completed on Day 85, 74 days ahead of schedule (U.S. DOT, 2002, p. 17). The contractor, C. C. Myers, was able to work around the clock and pay premium prices for the equipment and materials to complete the job because of the incentive funding of $200,000 per day, or a total of $14.8 million (U.S. DOT, 2002, p. 34).

This event shows the value of having an emergency plan in place that guided the response, including the ability to contract rapidly for the repairs. The response included rapid demolition and rerouting of traffic. The presence of the preplanned TMC with generator power enabled the coordination of work-arounds for damage across the freeway system. The recovery was facilitated by the FHWA financial support for the reconstruction of the roadways, notably I-10. The post-earthquake inspection of undamaged freeway bridges showed the value of the mitigation—bridge seismic upgrades and retrofitting—that had been done to 122 Los Angeles area Caltrans bridges in the wake of the Loma Prieta earthquake (U.S. DOT, 2002). "This costly disaster became a model of incident management" (U.S. DOT, 2002, p. 3).

Summary

Federal mandates for ICS/NIMS compliance, and security, emergency management, and COOP plans for transportation agencies, are intended to ensure that essential services will be delivered to communities, regardless of the emergency, disaster, or catastrophe that may occur. Pre-event planning, training, and exercising will ensure that emergency management staff members are prepared to respond to any community need.

While disasters and catastrophes stress the emergency management system and place a heightened demand on resources beyond the community, appropriate planning for emergencies should lead to the ability to save lives and facilitate community recovery, even under severe conditions. Transportation plays a role as both a responding agency and an important element of community economic recovery. Roads carry the response vehicles and the goods and personnel needed for repairs and restoration of community activity.

Transportation agencies are supported in their pre-event mitigation activities, planning and training efforts, emergency response, and ultimate recovery by a number of federal agencies. Transportation security is also enhanced by the work of federal partners. The roles of these agencies in ensuring the safety, security, and successful emergency management for transportation are the topics of Chapter 3.

Discussion Questions

1. What are the four phases of emergency management? How do they guide emergency planning for a transportation organization?

2. Describe the differences between an event, emergency, disaster, and catastrophe. Give one example of each in a transportation environment.

3. What would be the elements of a continuity of operations plan for a transportation agency?

4. What are the major recovery challenges for a transportation organization?

5. How would a mass transit agency develop an effective emergency plan? How would it integrate its stakeholders into the planning effort?

References

Bush, G. W. (2003a, February 28). Homeland Security Presidential Directive-5.

Bush, G. W. (2003b, December 17). Homeland Security Presidential Directive-8.

Botterell, A. (2002). A design language for EOC facilities. http://flghc.org/ppt/09-10/TS%20 EM7.pdf

California OES. (1995, March). *Northridge housing losses*. Sacramento, CA: Governor's Office of Emergency Services.

DHS (Department of Homeland Security). (2007). *Homeland security exercise and evaluation program, volume I. Overview and exercise program management.* Accessed April 3, 2010 at https://hseep.dhs.gov/support/VolumeI.pdf

Edwards, F. L. (2009). Effective disaster response in cross-border events. *Journal of Contingencies and Crisis Management, 17*(4), 255–265.

Edwards, F. L., & Afawubo, I. (2009). Show me the money: Financial recovery after disaster. *Public Manager, 37*(4), 85–90.

Edwards, F. L., & Goodrich, D. C. (2007). Organizing for emergency management. In W. L. Waugh & K. Tierney (Eds.), *Emergency management.* Washington, DC: ICMA Press.

Edwards, F. L., & Goodrich, D. C. (2009). *The role of transportation in campus emergency management* (Report 08-06). San Jose, CA: Mineta Transportation Institute.

Edwards, F. L., & Goodrich, D. C. (2010a). *Emergency management training and exercises for transportation agency operations* (Report 09-17). San Jose, CA: Mineta Transportation Institute.

Edwards, F. L., & Goodrich, D. C. (2010b). *Handbook of emergency management for state-level transportation agencies* (Report 09-10). San Jose, CA: Mineta Transportation Institute.

FEMA (Federal Emergency Management Agency). (n.d., a) *Continuity of Operations Plan (COOP) template instructions.* Washington, DC: FEMA.

FEMA (Federal Emergency Management Agency). (n.d., b). *NIMS training. Five year NIMS training plan.* http://www.fema.gov/emergency/nims/NIMSTrainingCourses.shtm

FEMA (Federal Emergency Management Agency). (2001, October). *Public assistance policy digest,* FEMA 321. http://www.fema.gov/pdf/government/grant/pa/pdigest.pdf

FEMA (Federal Emergency Management Agency). (2007, June). *Public assistance guide,* FEMA 322. http://www.fema.gov/government/grant/pa/pag07_t.shtm

FEMA (Federal Emergency Management Agency). (2008a, January). *Emergency support function annexes: Introduction.* http://www.fema.gov/pdf/emergency/nrf/nrf-esf-intro.pdf

FEMA (Federal Emergency Management Agency). (2008b, September 1) Missouri flood buyout saves lives, heartbreak and money. http://www.fema.gov/news/newsrelease.fema?id=45637

FEMA (Federal Emergency Management Agency). (2009a, March). *Community preparedness guide 101: Developing and maintaining state, territorial, tribal and local government emergency plans.* http://www.fema.gov/pdf/about/divisions/npd/cpg_101_layout.pdf

FEMA (Federal Emergency Management Agency). (2009b). Mitigation value to society. Fact sheet. http://www.fema.gov/txt/media/factsheets/2009/mit_value_society.txt

FEMA (Federal Emergency Management Agency). (2011). *FEMA independent study program.* http://www.fema.gov/txt/media/factsheets/2009/mit_value_society.txt

Howitt, A. M., & Leonard, H. B. (2009). *Managing crises: Responses to large-scale emergencies.* Washington, DC: CQ Press.

Integrated Waste Management Plan. (2010, April 30). *Mutual aid,* chapter 7. http://www.calrecycle.ca.gov/Disaster/DisasterPlan/chp7.htm

Perry, R. W., & Lindell, M. K. (2007). Disaster response. In W. L. Waugh & K. Tierney (Eds.), *Emergency management.* Washington, DC: ICMA Press.

Plenty Coups & Linderman, F. B. (2002). *Plenty-Coups, chief of the Crows.* Lincoln, NE: University of Nebraska Press.

Quarantelli, E. L. (2006, June 11). Catastrophes are different from disasters. In *Understanding Katrina: Perspectives from the social sciences.* SSRC.org. http://understandingkatrina.ssrc.org/Quarantelli/

Sylves, R. T. (2008). *Disaster policy and politics: Emergency management and homeland security.* Washington, DC: CQ Press.

U.S. DOT, FHWA. (2009, February). *A guide to the Federal-Aid Highway Emergency Relief Program.* http://fhwa.dot.gov/specialfunding/er/guide.cfm

U.S. DOT, ITS Joint Program Office. (2002, April 22). *Effect of catastrophic events on transportation system management and operations, Northridge earthquake, January 17, 1994.* Cambridge, MA: Volpe National Transportation Systems Center.

Water Emergency Transportation Authority (WETA). http://www.watertransit.org/

Waugh, W. L. (2000). *Living with hazards, dealing with disasters.* New York, NY: M. E. Sharpe, Inc.

Chapter **3**

Federal Agencies and Structures
Surface Transportation Security

Keywords: surface transportation, emergency management, homeland security, transportation infrastructure, Department of Homeland Security, Federal Emergency Management Agency, Transportation Security Administration, Coast Guard, Customs Service, Border Patrol, NAFTA, Department of Transportation, Federal Highway Administration, Federal Transit Administration, Transportation Research Board, Department of Energy

Learning Objectives

After reading this chapter you should be able to

- Identify the principal federal organizations with responsibility for emergency management and homeland security for the surface transportation sector
- Identify the sources of planning assistance and grants for emergency management and homeland security for the surface transportation sector

Disasters and the Surface Transportation System

"All disasters are local" is an often repeated quote from James Lee Witt, director of the Federal Emergency Management Agency (FEMA) in the Clinton administration. Every emergency, disaster or catastrophe starts in someone's local jurisdiction. Sylves (2008) notes that local capability to respond to these events varies widely, depending on the size of the community and the sophistication of its risk analysis. "In the United States, government management of major disasters is done through intergovernmental relations…[with] a tremendous degree of overlap" (p. 221).

The number of federal level organizations with responsibilities for emergency management and homeland security in the surface transportation sector may be surprising. Not only are there subunits within the Department of Homeland Security (DHS) that have unique responsibilities in all four phases of emergency management and elements of the U.S. Department of Transportation (DOT) that focus on emergency management, but even the Department of Energy (DOE) has emergency management responsibilities in the surface transportation sector, and the National Academy devotes one element to transportation, the Transportation Research Board.

Airports are an important part of the national transportation system overall and play a key role in emergency planning and response. However, because of the complexities of air transportation management for safety, security, and emergency management, air transportation will only be addressed in this chapter from the perspective of the Transportation Security Administration (TSA), which focuses on surface transportation as a critical infrastructure and multimodal system. Airport-specific Federal Aviation Administration (FAA) activities will be addressed in Chapter 9, again from the perspective of a multimodal interface.

Surface transportation systems in the United States are composed of privately owned enterprises, like trucking, intercity busses, freight rail and maritime transportation assets, and public enterprises, like urban mass transit, passenger rail, and ports, many of which are special districts. Prior to the terrorist attacks of 9/11, the focus of transportation security was crime: theft, vandalism, and human trafficking (Jenkins & Gerston, 2001). After the terror attacks of 9/11, which used commercial aircraft as missiles, there was a new emphasis on transportation security that looked at the possibilities for transportation assets becoming weapons, targets, or delivery systems for terror attacks.

Department of Homeland Security: Organization for Transportation Security

Following the 9/11 attacks, the federal government reorganized to create a more terrorist-resistant transportation system, aggregating organizations from various departments of the federal government into the DHS. In 2002 the Homeland Security Act was passed by Congress and signed by President George W. Bush to create the new cabinet-level department, merging 22 offices and organizations. Table 3.1 lists the agencies that became part of DHS in 2003.

The 22 organizations that were merged into the new DHS had their original responsibilities dispersed into the new department based on segmented administrative areas and five functional undersecretaries. Organizations that were formerly independent, with access to a Cabinet-level secretary, were now buried under several layers of reporting relationships (Figure 3.1).

The 2005 hurricane season included Hurricane Katrina, with its iconic views of a flooded city and drowned school busses, and Hurricane Rita, with its lasting images of cars full of stranded motorists who were out of gas sitting on the blazing hot interstate highway. Although FEMA had received positive evaluations of its support of Florida in the 2004 season of four hurricanes, the federal response to the 2005 events was generally evaluated as a "failure of initiative" (Select Bipartisan Committee, 2006). These disasters pointed out the need to reorganize the DHS to a streamlined reporting system—for example, to enable the FEMA director once again to have access to the president during disasters. While the original organization of DHS put many former Department of Justice staff members in charge of emergency management functions, because of the emphasis on preventing terrorist attacks, 2005's devastating disasters reinforced the importance of the all-hazards approach because most natural hazards are in fact not preventable, but can be mitigated against. Therefore, a "new FEMA" was created to take responsibility for a return to a more balanced view of the role of emergency management as an all-hazards effort. (DHS, 2008a) The 2010 DHS organization chart shows that the merged organizations that were formerly independent agencies, such as the Coast Guard and FEMA, now all have direct access to the secretary of DHS (Figure 3.2) (DHS, 2010c).

National Protection and Programs Directorate

The 2007 reorganization of DHS resulted in the dismantling of the Preparedness Directorate as FEMA was strengthened in its core mission of emergency management. However, there were elements of the directorate that

TABLE 3.1 Department of Homeland Security Components

Original Agency (Department)	Current Agency/Office
U.S. Customs Service (Treasury)	U.S. Customs and Border Protection—inspection, border and ports of entry responsibilities U.S. Immigration and Customs Enforcement—customs law enforcement responsibilities
Immigration and Naturalization Service (Justice)	U.S. Customs and Border Protection—inspection functions and the U.S. Border Patrol U.S. Immigration and Customs Enforcement—immigration law enforcement: detention and removal, intelligence, and investigations U.S. Citizenship and Immigration Services—adjudications and benefits programs
Federal Protective Service	U.S. Immigration and Customs Enforcement
Transportation Security Administration (Transportation)	Transportation Security Administration
Federal Law Enforcement Training Center (Treasury)	Federal Law Enforcement Training Center
Animal and Plant Health Inspection Service (part) (Agriculture)	U.S. Customs and Border Protection—agricultural imports and entry inspections
Office for Domestic Preparedness (Justice)	Responsibilities distributed within FEMA
Federal Emergency Management Agency (FEMA)	Federal Emergency Management Agency
Strategic National Stockpile and the National Disaster Medical System (HHS)	Returned to Health and Human Services, July 2004
Nuclear Incident Response Team (Energy)	Responsibilities distributed within FEMA
Domestic Emergency Support Teams (Justice)	Responsibilities distributed within FEMA
National Domestic Preparedness Office (FBI)	Responsibilities distributed within FEMA
CBRN Countermeasures Programs (Energy)	Science and Technology Directorate
Environmental Measurements Laboratory (Energy)	Science and Technology Directorate
National BW Defense Analysis Center (Defense)	Science and Technology Directorate
Plum Island Animal Disease Center (Agriculture)	Science and Technology Directorate

TABLE 3.1 (continued) Department of Homeland Security Components

Original Agency (Department)	Current Agency/Office
Federal Computer Incident Response Center (GSA)	US-CERT, Office of Cybersecurity and Communications in the National Programs and Preparedness Directorate
National Communications System (Defense)	Office of Cybersecurity and Communications in the National Programs and Preparedness Directorate
National Infrastructure Protection Center (FBI)	Dispersed throughout the department, including Office of Operations Coordination and Office of Infrastructure Protection
Energy Security and Assurance Program (Energy)	Integrated into the Office of Infrastructure Protection
U.S. Coast Guard	U.S. Coast Guard
U.S. Secret Service	U.S. Secret Service

Source: DHS. (2003). Components. http://www.dhs.gov/xabout/history/editorial_0133.shtm.

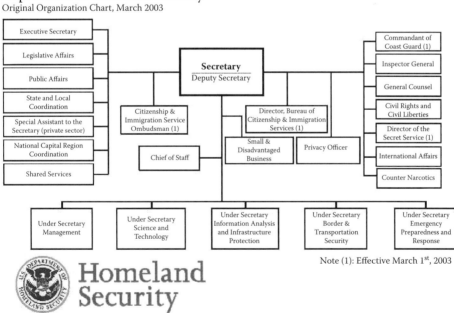

FIGURE 3.1   **Original organization chart, DHS, 2003. (DHS. 2003. Accessed 4/8/04 from http://www.dhs.gov/xlibrary/assets/dhs-org-chart-2003.pdf)**

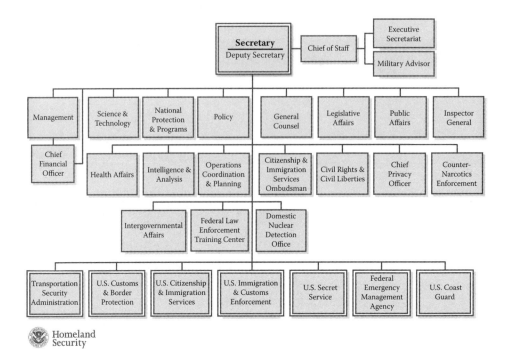

FIGURE 3.2   2012 DHS organization chart. (DHS. 2010c. Accessed 11/25/11 from http://www.dhs.gov/xlibrary/assets/dhs-orgchart.pdf)

fell outside FEMA's mandates, so a new National Protection and Programs Directorate was established. These programs included the Office of Cyber Security, US-Visit, Office of Risk Management and Analysis, Office of Intergovernmental Programs, and the one element that directly relates to transportation security: the Office of Infrastructure Protection (DHS, 2010a).

HSPD-7 established the national policy for the protection of critical infrastructure and key resources (CI/KR) from terrorist attacks. It defined how federal agencies work with state and local governments to identify and protect the systems and facilities essential to the nation's functioning. The nation's critical infrastructure is divided into 18 sectors, shown in Table 3.2.

TABLE 3.2 Critical Infrastructure Sectors

Agriculture and food	Banking and finance	Chemical
Commercial facilities	Communications	Critical manufacturing
Dams	Defense industrial base	Emergency services
Energy	Government facilities	Health care and public health
Information technology	National monuments and icons	Nuclear reactors, materials and waste
Postal and shipping	Transportation systems	Water

Source: DHS. (2010a). Critical infrastructure.
        *http://*www.dhs.gov/files/programs/gc_1189168948944.shtm

This directive made the DOT and DHS partners in the security of all forms of transportation systems and infrastructure (Bush, 2003b).

The transportation sector consists of six subsectors: aviation, highway, maritime transportation system, mass transit, pipeline, and rail (DHS, 2008c). The sectors cover vast areas and large amounts of resources, such as 95,000 miles of coastline, 360 ports, 450 commercial airports and many more civil air facilities, 4 million miles of highway, and 143,000 miles of railroad track (DHS, n.d.).

The National Infrastructure Protection Plan (NIPP) of 2009 details the activities required for securing all CI/KR, and ensuring its resiliency after any disaster (DHS, 2009). One important addition in this version of the plan was the acknowledgment by the secretary of DHS that natural hazards, as well as terrorist activity, pose a significant threat to the homeland (DHS, 2009). The NIPP also acknowledged specifically for the first time the threat of cascading events, when the failure of one CI/KR leads to the loss of another that was originally unaffected by the initial disaster. For example, damage to electrical transmission lines will lead to the loss of electrical power to a community or region. This in turn will lead to the shutdown of other CI/KR based on electrical power, such as water purification systems, sewage processing facilities, and electrified transportation systems like light rail. Even though such facilities generally have emergency backup power based on generators, additional fuel to run them for prolonged periods usually requires pumping from underground storage tanks that requires electricity. The goal of the NIPP is to have emergency planners evaluate the synergies and interfaces among all the CI/KR and plan for work-arounds, substitutions, or protections that will lessen or eliminate the damaging effects of a cascading event.

The 2009 version of the NIPP also notes the significant role of the private sector in developing resiliency for the nation's CI/KR. The 2002 National Strategy for Homeland Security acknowledged that 85% of all critical infrastructure is owned by the private sector (Office of Homeland Security, 2002, p. 8), so cooperation between the public and private sectors is necessary. In the transportation sector there are many privately owned elements that provide essential services: ambulances, ships, livery services, trucking lines, and many rail lines. The NIPP provides guidance for the coordination of risk analysis across regions, which integrates these private sector owners with public sector mass transit and highway administration.

The National Response Framework describes the coordinated response that will be led by the federal agencies when a disaster occurs (DHS, 2008b). It includes a Critical Infrastructure and Key Resource Support Annex that describes the coordination among various federal agencies and private sector owners of CI/KR to evaluate the risk to these assets and take steps to protect them from hazards (FEMA, 2008a). Many of the transportation sector-specific grants available through FEMA support the four phases of emergency management for CI/KR.

Many of the agencies merged into DHS have historic roles in the security of transportation, going back to colonial times. Although they are now components of the DHS, as shown in the next sections, many have their own histories and distinctive roles.

Customs Service and Border Patrol

The United States Customs Service dates back to colonial times, when it collected taxes at the ports and regulated the sources of trade goods coming into Britain's North American colonies. In 1789 the new government devoted its first legislative acts to establishing the Customs Service and setting tariffs on goods and the tonnage of ships to provide revenue for the new government. The 11 states that had signed the Constitution at that point had customs districts established under the Collector of Customs, part of the U.S. Treasury Department. Enforcement of customs regulations at sea was made possible by a fleet of revenue cutters, first launched in 1790 as the U.S. Revenue Marine (DHS, 2010b).

Border patrol did not emerge as a national concern until the twentieth century. Mounted guards began to operate out of El Paso, Texas, in 1904, focused on preventing illegal entries into the United States. Their major focus was the prevention of Chinese immigration into California (CBP.gov, 2010a). As immigration laws made legal entry into the United States more difficult, it became clear that restricting immigration and illegal importation of goods was impossible without a secure border. Then, in 1920, the start of Prohibition made patrolling the border more critical. In 1924 the Border Patrol was established to patrol the land borders, and in 1925 this was extended to the sea coasts. By 1932 districts were established in Detroit and El Paso to interdict illegal goods, especially liquor (CBP.gov, 2010a).

While early border patrol was based on horses, cars with radios were added before World War II, and during the war aircraft were added. The focus was on interdicting Axis saboteurs and running alien detention camps. After the war, the focus was on repatriation of illegal immigrants, mainly from Mexico, but the programs proved costly and were discontinued (CBP.gov, 2010a).

By 1970 air hijackings—notably efforts to go to Cuba—were a prevalent threat to trade and travel. The U.S. Department of Transportation signed an agreement with the Customs Service creating the Sky Marshals Program, which placed trained agents on flights considered likely to be hijacked. It was so successful at preventing hijackings that it ended in 1974 (DHS, 2010b).

Customs also developed automated data processing systems to track imports from "manifest declaration through liquidation" (DHS, 2010b). By the 1980s, antidrug operations were increased, using a fleet of air vehicles for surveillance and interdiction, including helium balloons and early warning aircraft (DHS, 2010b).

By 1993 when the North American Free Trade Agreement (NAFTA) had passed, Customs' role in transportation had become extensive. The new rules for importation of goods from Canada and Mexico led to changes in goods manifests and inspection protocols at the U.S. land borders. Electronic transmission of customs data became routine. The World Trade Center bombing in 1993 caused no direct damage to the New York Customs House, but it marked the beginning of a new era in border surveillance (DHS, 2010b), culminating in the apprehension of Ahmed Ressam, the "millennial bomber," at the Canadian border on December 14, 1999, as he drove his car full of explosives and circuit board timers, bound for Los Angeles International Airport (Bernton, Carter, Heath, & Neff, 2002).

In 2001 the automated commercial environment (ACE) replaced older customs systems for the processing of container cargo, marking a new commercial trade processing system to "facilitate legitimate trade" (CBP.gov, n.d., a). The program created a single point for shippers to register their transaction with all federal entities through one data entry session. In September the U.S. Customs House at 6 World Trade Center was destroyed in a terrorist attack, fortunately with no deaths in the Customs Service. Customs created the Terrorism Response Task Force to collect intelligence from its data to support the investigation of the 9/11 attacks and created an Office for Anti-Terrorism within Customs. The new Federal Air Marshals program was created by the FAA to prevent future use of airliners as terrorist tools. Initial staffing included 125 Customs officers (DHS, 2010b).

Recognizing the threat of terrorist use of chemical, biological, radiological, nuclear, and explosive/incendiary devices (CBRNE), Customs initiated a number of new programs to prevent the importation of weapons of mass destruction into the country in the normal supply chain. With thousands of containers arriving at the New York and Los Angeles port complexes, individual inspections would be prohibitively expensive and interfere with commerce. In 2002 the Container Security Initiative (CSI) was established to ensure that "all containers that pose a potential risk for terrorism are identified and inspected at foreign ports before they are placed on vessels destined for the United States" (CBP.gov, n.d., b). The program allows Customs officers to identify high-risk containers while they are in their country of origin and, in cooperation with the host nation, to inspect the containers using technologies like "large-scale x-ray and gamma ray machines and radiation detection devices" (CBP.gov, n.d., b). Details about this program are included in Chapter 8.

In 2003 the DHS was formed from existing government agencies. The Bureau of Customs and the Border Patrol were among the agencies incorporated into DHS, and on March 1, 2003, the Bureau of Customs and Border Patrol was created, merging the organization protecting the nation from contraband goods with the organization that prohibits the immigration of undocumented individuals. The largest law enforcement agency within DHS, it was placed in the Directorate for Border and Transportation Security (DHS, 2010b), emphasizing its role in global trade and transportation of goods. The mission is complex, ranging from preventing illegal entry into the United States to drug interdiction at ports of entry, from protection of intellectual property to collecting duties and enforcing U.S. trade laws (CBP.gov, 2010b).

In 2003 the Customs Trade Partnership against Terrorism (C-TPAT) was launched. Its goal is to bring the owners of all aspects of the global supply chain into partnership with the Customs agency to ensure that contraband is not imported into the United States. This initiative is different from CSI because it is a public–private partnership that offers the private sector a chance to expedite the movement of its materiel throughout the global supply chain. It also offers the opportunity for a business to develop a self-certification program that cuts down on delays in the movement of goods internationally (CBP.gov, 2007). Unlike CSI, C-TPAT covers all forms of goods transport, including trucks and rail cars. By 2008 more than 7,500 companies worldwide had developed a secure supply chain and operations within their facilities to "prevent terrorists and weapons of mass effect from infiltrating the supply chain" (Customs and Border Protection, 2008).

The Fast and Secure Trade (FAST) program is related to C-TPAT and designed to facilitate NAFTA trade. It allows drivers and shippers to register with Customs and Border Protection to use special clearance lanes at ports of entry between the United States and Mexico and Canada. By 2008 over 87,000 American, Mexican, and Canadian commercial drivers had completed background checks and been registered with FAST, which means that every link in the supply chain of the goods they carry has become part of C-TPAT. FAST provides dedicated lanes and front-of-the-line privileges when inspections are required (Customs and Border Protection, 2008).

In 2005 the threat of agroterrorism was recognized as having an international supply chain component. The Ag-Bio-Terror Countermeasures Program (ABTC) was started to keep out pathogens, supplies, and equipment needed to breed and disseminate biological materials. This represents an extension of Customs' historic mission of keeping agricultural pests and diseases out of the United States to protect the agricultural industry. In partnership with the Department of Agriculture, Customs has both enhanced staffing at U.S. border crossings and ports of entry and increased surveillance at and pre-clearance operations in Canada and Caribbean ports. Vulnerabilities are fresh produce introduced by returning tourists, insect larvae on maritime containers, and food service items loaded into aircraft galleys in foreign ports. In addition to canine inspectors, the ABTC uses technology, including handheld detectors for electronic chain-of-custody tracking (DHS, 2010b).

In 2007 the ACE was extended to truck manifests to facilitate clearance at 98 of the 99 land border entry points between the United States and Mexico and Canada (DHS, 2010b). Truckers can self-file the e-manifests to speed passage through the entry points, and duties are billed each month rather than having to be processed with each shipment (CBP.gov, 2011a). The e-manifest can be filed up to an hour before the truck arrives at the border portal, allowing processing to begin before the truck arrives. It includes information on the crew, the equipment, and the cargo for customs processing. Known shippers and designated freight can be cleared rapidly, while high-risk cargo can be referred to secondary inspection, with all paperwork available electronically to the inspector (CBP.gov, 2011c). By 2011 the ACE program had been expanded to include multimodal access for marine, rail, air, and truck cargo shippers. This common manifest makes the movement of goods through the global supply chain more efficient, while allowing Customs to monitor high-risk cargo (CBP.gov, 2011b).

Today the Bureau of Customs and Border Protection within DHS has a mandate to protect the United States from the importation of contraband like drugs and weapons and to prevent the immigration of terrorists, drug smugglers, and other undesirable persons. Transportation is protected through a variety of registration and inspection programs of the bureau, DHS's largest law enforcement agency.

Coast Guard

In 1915 the Coast Guard was created as a merger of the Revenue Marine—responsible for enforcing customs laws and revenue collections from seagoing vessels and the Life Saving Service—established in 1878 to aid mariners in peril. In time of war the Coast Guard is under the Navy, but in peacetime it was originally part of the Department of the Treasury. When the DOT was created in 1967, the Coast Guard was moved from Treasury to DOT, recognizing its significant role in maritime transportation safety, security, and emergency response. In 2003 it was transferred to the Department of Homeland Security because of its role in securing the nation's marine borders (Coast Guard, 2009a).

Today the Coast Guard has seven distinct missions. Four are related to maritime commercial and recreational activities and considered "nonhomeland security": search and rescue; marine environment protection;

aids to navigation; and polar, ice and Alaska operations. The three that are directly involved with transportation security are law enforcement, including enforcement of drug, immigration, and fisheries laws; marine safety, coastal and port security; and defense readiness, national security, and military preparedness (Coast Guard, 2011).

The Coast Guard's law enforcement mission began in Prohibition, but currently focuses on the economic issue of fisheries, drug interdiction, and migrant interdiction. Among its fisheries duties is the enforcement of the whaling convention and the 200-mile fishery zone. The Coast Guard has a law enforcement detachment (LEDET) program that operates jointly with the United States Navy for drug interdiction. After the Civil War, in response to perceived abuses by the Army of Occupation in the South during Reconstruction, Congress passed *Posse Comitatus* in 1878, forbidding active duty military personnel from acting as law enforcement agents within the United States (U.S. Statutes 1878). In 1986 Congress tasked the Coast Guard with performing drug enforcement duties at sea, using Navy ships as a platform to interdict ships suspected of drug trafficking. LEDET personnel monitor and board ships. LEDET operations are carried out from "ships of opportunity"—Navy ships operating in areas of known drug trafficking (Coast Guard, 2008). While many successful missions have been completed, the most notable was the dual captures of ships carrying 30,000 pounds of cocaine and 26,250 pounds of cocaine in 2004 (Coast Guard, n.d.).

Maritime security is overseen through the captain of the port program. The Coast Guard controls movement in and out of American ports, overseeing the security of piers and docks and establishing anchorages. Port security is the largest rating (job) in the Coast Guard today (Browning, 1993). Initially, the focus was on the movement and safe loading of explosives, but with the development of environmental protection laws, the responsibilities extended to management of all hazardous materials in the port and on navigable waterways. After the *Exxon Valdez* spill in Alaska, supervising oil-spill cleanups in coastal or marine environments and navigable waterways was also added to the Coast Guard role.

The attacks of 9/11 played a pivotal role in the structuring of the Coast Guard mission in the twenty-first century. On 9/11 the Coast Guard staff from the Marine Inspection Office in Battery Park just south of the World Trade Center acted as a coordinator and distributor of donated supplies, while continuing to provide maritime safety (Coast Guard Supervisor, 2001). Following this disaster, the role of the Coast Guard has focused on maritime security efforts, notably on crew identification, commercial vessels, and cargo moving through U.S. ports. Surveillance of vessels to prevent the transportation of improvised explosive devices has been enhanced, and port-scale nuclear detection projects have begun. The Coast Guard works with CBP to prevent the landing of terrorists and their weapons. They have developed a *small vessel security strategy* as part of the critical infrastructure protection program to protect ports from the disruptive effects of an attack. The combination of a risk-management approach to deploying resources and intelligence gathering to combat smuggling work together enhance security in U.S. ports (GAO, 2010).

In 2002 the Coast Guard established the antiterrorism maritime safety and security teams (MSSTs) with a defensive focus to provide a quick response capability to threats against harbors, ports, and internal waterways (Coast Guard, 2009b). The focus is on high-value naval assets and commercial high-interest vessels (Coast Guard, n.d.). There is also a counterterrorism organization called the maritime security response team (MSRT) that is offensive, and the first-responder organization when a terrorist act is in progress or terrorists have been discovered (Coast Guard, 2009b). Because of its unique position as both a military entity and a law enforcement entity, the Coast Guard has a role in all phases of homeland security work: "detection, prevention, protection and deterrence…response and consequence management" (Coast Guard, 2002, p. 9). This requires a coordinated response with other federal entities, such as Department of Defense assets including the Navy, Federal Bureau of Investigation (FBI), and FEMA.

As a means of enlarging its surveillance capabilities the Coast Guard created America's Waterway Watch (AWW). The program has a website and pages with information defining suspicious behavior that might be reported, and the collection of information for the report (America's Waterway Watch, 2011). This program encourages people who work around or spend time on the water to report suspicious activity to a central number. Information gained from the public is used to allocate professional resources for investigation and to create greater protection and deterrence for maritime critical infrastructure.

FEMA

The Federal Emergency Management Agency (FEMA) was created by President Jimmy Carter in 1979 in the aftermath of the Three Mile Island nuclear power plant accident. It represented a merger of existing offices and organizations from the White House, Department of Justice, Department of Commerce, and Department of Housing and Urban Development. It brought together organizations focused on preparedness like fire prevention and flood insurance, with post-disaster assistance and civil defense. The agency's focus was on all hazards preparedness, from natural disasters to war, and on all four phases of emergency management: mitigation, preparedness, response, and recovery. With the end of the Cold War, FEMA's civil defense programs were merged into the all-hazards framework of the agency (FEMA, 2010).

James Lee Witt was appointed by President Bill Clinton in 1993 as the first FEMA director with a background in emergency management. He reorganized the agency with a stronger focus on mitigation and preparedness as a means of cutting the misery, loss of life, and cost of disaster response. The FEMA director position was elevated to cabinet level and given direct access to the president during disasters. The Northridge earthquake, numerous floods, wildland fires, and seasonal hurricanes proved the benefits of the approach.

The September 11, 2001, attacks on the World Trade Center and Pentagon changed FEMA's mission focus from all hazards to a stronger focus on terrorism. President George W. Bush issued a number of homeland security presidential directives (HSPDs) that created a new environment for emergency management in the United States. As noted in Chapter 2, HDPS-5 led to the creation of the National Incident Command System (Bush, 2003a), and HSPD-8 set the national preparedness goals (Bush, 2003c), later revised by President Barack Obama in Presidential Policy Directive-8 to require that the goals be measurable (Obama, 2011).

When DHS was formed in 2003, FEMA was merged into the new department as one of the organizations under the complex five-level structure. As shown in Figure 3.1, the result was that the FEMA director had to report through an undersecretary for emergency preparedness and response, meaning that he no longer had access to the president during a disaster or even to the secretary of DHS, which proved disastrous in Hurricane Katrina. The emphasis was shifted away from natural hazards mitigation to terrorism prevention, and DHS's leadership was drawn from the Department of Justice with a strong law enforcement perspective. For 2 years FEMA underwent a number of reorganizations and lost many of its functions to other portions of the new DHS structure (FEMA, 2010). However, the post-Katrina Emergency Management Reform Act of 2006 created a new structure for FEMA and other elements of DHS in 2007 (DHS, 2008a).

Among the new initiatives was the use of a target capability list (TCL) to measure potential service delivery by first responders and emergency management organizations supported by FEMA terrorism grant funds (Table 3.3). Built around the homeland security rubric of "prevent, protect, respond, and recover," the TCL defines 37 core capabilities that jurisdictions should develop (FEMA, 2007). Grant funding required that achievement of target capabilities be the driver for spending plans, and an evaluation program based on exercises is used to measure the achievement of the organization in developing its capabilities (FEMA, n.d.).

In 2006 FEMA was reorganized with a new emphasis on preparedness. It also provided for immediate access to the president for the FEMA director during disasters. FEMA's new mission statement emphasized "a risk-based, comprehensive emergency management system of preparedness, protection, response, recovery, and mitigation" (FEMA, 2008c).

TABLE 3.3 Target Capability List, 2007

Common Capabilities	Respond Mission Capabilities
Planning	On-site incident management
Communications	Emergency operations center
Community preparedness and participation	Management
	Critical resource logistics and distribution
Risk management	Volunteer management and donations
Intelligence and information sharing and dissemination	Responder safety and health
	Emergency public safety and security
Prevent Mission Capabilities	Animal disease emergency support
	Environmental health
Information gathering and recognition of indicators and warning	Explosive device response operations
	Fire incident response support
Intelligence analysis and production	WMD and hazardous materials
Counterterror investigation and law enforcement	Response and decontamination
	Citizen evacuation and shelter-in-place
CBRNE detection	Isolation and quarantine
	Search and rescue (land based)
Protect Mission Capabilities	Emergency public information and warning
Critical infrastructure protection	Emergency triage and prehospital treatment
Food and agriculture safety and defense	Medical surge
Epidemiological surveillance and investigation	Medical supplies management and distribution
Laboratory Testing	Mass prophylaxis
	Mass care (sheltering, feeding, and related services)
	Fatality management
	Recover Mission Capabilities
	Structural damage assessment
	Restoration of lifelines
	Economic and community recovery

Source: FEMA (2007). Target capability list. http://www.fema.gov/pdf/government/training/tcl.pdf

FEMA's Grant Programs Directorate (GPD) manages several that focus specifically on transportation elements of a community. The Transit Security Grant Program (TSGP), Freight Rail Security Grant Program (FRSGP), Inter-City Passenger Rail and Security Grant Program (IPRSGP), Inter-City Bus Security Grant Program (IBSGP), and Port Security Grant Program (PSGP) funnel support to agencies that manage transportation assets (DHS, 2011). The grants focus on increasing the baseline of capability for all four phases of emergency management, but criticisms have been leveled at the lack of outcome data that makes measuring the change from baseline difficult (FEMA, 2009).

FIGURE 3.3 Amtrak security photo.

The TSGP is focused on the safety of the passengers and infrastructure of the nation's public transit systems. Experience in Europe and Israel suggests that improvised explosive devices (IEDs) and suicide bombers are likely causes of future damage, so grants focus on developing the target capabilities of critical infrastructure protection, communications, and intelligence. FRSGP is available to entities that ship "railroad security sensitive materials" and toxic inhalation chemicals (TICs), as well as owners of railroad bridges. IPRSGP is focused on Amtrak service areas and stations (Figure 3.3).

History shows that derailment is one attack option against heavy rail assets in the United States, while IEDs have been used against heavy rail assets in Europe. The focus for these grants' spending has also been on critical infrastructure protection and intelligence gathering, as well as planning. IBSGP is focused on charter and fixed-route intercity busses that serve any of the Urban Area Security Initiative (UASI) regions.[1] The grant focuses on the development of security plans, training, and exercises for employees, and public terrorism awareness campaigns. PSGP is aimed at the highest risk ports. Maritime commerce is critical to American economic stability, so protection of ports is essential. PSGP grants have focused on the same issues of critical infrastructure protection and intelligence gathering, but have also had a chemical, biological, radiological, nuclear, and explosives (CBRNE) focus (DHS, 2011). Transportation Worker Identification

Credential (TWIC) System installation at ports was a major subprogram within the grant (FEMA, 2009).

As the coordinator of the federal government's response to disasters, FEMA is responsible for the activation of the emergency support functions (ESFs), of which the first is transportation (ESF1). The emergency support functions list is part of the national response framework, which integrates federal agencies to provide support for 15 essential services to federal, state, and local governments and nonprofit organizations. The DOT is the coordinator for ESF1 and is supported by 10 other agencies, including DHS. During a disaster, the security of the national transportation system is the responsibility of ESF1 (FEMA, 2008b).

Transportation Security Administration

The Transportation Security Administration is the "youngest" of the entities to be merged into DHS in 2003. TSA was created in DOT in November 2001 as part of the Aviation and Transportation Security Act. Its mission is to screen baggage and passengers and to check travel documents at 450 commercial airports, as well as to provide security training and programs for all modes of transportation (TSA, n.d., b). Aviation security is its most well-known function, but it has a variety of other roles aimed at enhancing transportation security against the terrorist threat by using multiple layers of surveillance and many different programs. It collaborates with FEMA in administering the terrorism preparedness grant programs discussed earlier in this chapter, and it has law enforcement functions and security programs (TSA, n.d., c).

The use of commercial aviation as the weapon on 9/11 heightened congressional concern about the security of air transportation. The Pentagon was one of the targets of the aircraft attacks, but it was widely believed that another building was the original target. The hijacked plane that crashed in Pennsylvania was believed to have been headed for yet another Washington, DC, building. Because of the proximity of Reagan National Airport to many high-profile federal buildings, cancellation of all general aviation flights using that facility was considered, but the economic impact was evaluated to be too significant. TSA's law enforcement functions, therefore, now include providing armed security officers for general aviation flights serving Reagan International Airport, as well as air marshals for other flights deemed high risk because of their origin, destination, or fuel capacity. The air marshals also work closely with the FBI's Joint Terrorism Task Force and other law enforcement agencies to evaluate threats and prepare for potential disruptions on airplanes (TSA, n.d., c).

TSA also works with the air crews to enhance safety and terrorist attack resistance. The Crew Member Self-Defense Training Program equips aircraft crews to resist attempts to take over the planes, as well as deal effectively with disruptive passengers. Pilots, flight engineers, and navigators, known as federal flight deck officers, may be trained and authorized to carry a firearm in the cockpit to provide another layer of defense against attempts at air piracy. Under some circumstances, law enforcement officers may be authorized to fly armed, adding random antiterrorist assets to flights (TSA, n.d., c).

Canines are also part of TSA's law enforcement mission. The National Canine Explosives Detection Team operates in commercial airports, performing explosives identification missions that detect explosive materials, both to alert on a potential threat and rule out concerns about left luggage and forgotten packages. The dogs are trained to search airplanes, baggage, vehicles, and structures in the aviation environment (TSA, n.d., c).

TSA also has a variety of security programs working in the multimodal environment. Visible Intermodal Prevention and Response (VIPR) Teams were created after the attacks on commuter trains in Madrid. They are randomly deployed as a high-visibility security team at mass transit facilities, including ferries. These teams have been used since 2007 to deter terrorist interference with mass transit systems (TSA, n.d., c). The VIPR members wear readily identifiable clothing and actively seek out unusual behavior, like surveillance of facilities and operations. They have been successful in apprehending criminals during their deployments.

TSA has officers trained to detect behaviors that may indicate fear of exposure and may be indicative of terrorist activity. Because these behavioral observation officers are randomly deployed, they provide an important layer of uncertainty as terrorists evaluate security precautions. In the aviation environment, this training is used to target passengers for secondary screening based on behavioral cues. TSA also trains local law enforcement officers interacting with commercial vehicles to use behavioral screening techniques to identify suspicious behavior and false documents, like driver's licenses and vehicle registrations, and search trucks for potential terrorist weapons. This is called SPOT: screening passengers by observational techniques. Behavioral identification has caught a fleeing murderer in the Minneapolis–St. Paul Airport and helped stop a kidnapping at Newark Airport (TSA, n.d., c).

Surface transportation security is also a responsibility of TSA. Their Surface Transportation Security Inspection Program has placed 100 inspectors in the field to support mass transit and rail systems. The HAZMAT Endorsement Program ensures that drivers authorized to operate hazardous materials vehicles are screened before the endorsement is added to their commercial driver's licenses. The Intermodal Security Training and Exercise Program (I-STEP) serves public and private transportation operators in improving their knowledge of threats against their assets and methods for enhancing security for their facilities and vehicles. The program includes

FIGURE 3.4   Fire departments exercise with commuter railroads.

ports, mass transit, freight carriers, and highway personnel. Intermodal exercises also bring together various surface transportation organizations with first responders to enhance community preparedness across all transportation sectors (Figure 3.4) (TSA, n.d., c).

While passenger and baggage screening is accomplished in the funnel of an airport's boarding and luggage check system, similar screening for surface transportation has proven cumbersome. TSA is testing technologies and canine patrols that would permit rapid screening using mobile checkpoint equipment in train stations and mass transit stations. A pilot program in the metropolitan Washington area has been successful in screening hundreds of passengers expeditiously (TSA, n.d., c).

TSA's First Observer Program is designed to bring the eyes and ears of truckers, commercial bus drivers, and highway design and maintenance staff into the homeland security mission. Described as an "antiterrorism and security awareness program" (TSA, n.d., a), First Observer offers training on suspicious activity and provides a call center where concerns can be reported.

DHS has a number of programs and entities that focus on transportation security. From funding to training, DHS aims to bring its resources and the resources of the transportation community—public and private—into partnership to create a safe and secure transportation system. The lessons of 9/11 and Hurricane Katrina have sharpened the focus on preparing for inevitable natural disasters and working to prevent human-caused events. Other modal programs will be discussed in later chapters.

Department of Transportation and Transportation Security

The DOT was created in 1966 in recognition of the significant role of transportation within the economy, and the need for transportation policy to be developed in a logical and integrated fashion. It was created by taking the transportation activities out of the Department of Commerce and the mass transit oversight out of the Department of Housing and Urban Development. The goal was to create an intermodal system that would support commerce and economic growth (DOT, n.d., b).

The DOT played a significant role in management of the disasters of the 1980s and 1990s. Hurricane Hugo, the Loma Prieta earthquake, Hurricane Andrew, and the Northridge earthquake offered opportunities for DOT to lead response and recovery missions—even to supersede FEMA as the federal agency managing the Hurricane Hugo response. With the FAA and the Coast Guard as part of DOT, emergency response was a core mission. Right after 9/11 the department created the TSA (DOT, n.d., b).

Following the creation of DHS, DOT turned over the Coast Guard and TSA to the new department. Its other entities continued to play a significant role in transportation security and emergency management, including the Office of Intelligence and Security and Emergency Management, which is the lead office for ESF1 (Figure 3.5).

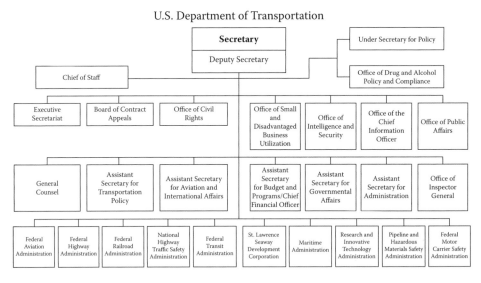

FIGURE 3.5 DOT organization chart. (US DOT. http://images.google.com/ imgres?q=US+DOT+organization+chart&hl=en&biw=1054&bih=484&tbm= isch&tbnid=dWgbvq3kNsj0-M:&imgrefurl=http://www.netage.com/economics/ gov/USTransport-chart-top.html&docid=iQEb8ZC8FxcUWM&imgurl=http:// www.netage.com/economics/gov/images-org/USTransport-orgchart.jpg&w= 750&h=432&ei=8HP-TsyUMsrTiAKsyl3MDg&zoom=1&iact=hc&vpx=72&vpy=158 &dur=4306&hovh=170&hovw=296&tx=145&ty=72&sig=111340061718528372088& page=1&tbnh=94&tbnw=164&start=0&ndsp=10&ved=1t:429,r:0,s:0)

The Federal Highway Administration (FHWA) has created the Natural Disaster Recovery Strategy to guide highway system managers to prepare for and recover from natural disasters. Quick release emergency relief funds are provided through FHWA to state and tribal highway system managers to cover the cost of emergency roadway and infrastructure repairs and reconstruction of roads and bridges damaged by disasters or catastrophes (DOT, n.d., a). Highway agencies are encouraged to consider resiliency in the rebuilding of damaged infrastructure, recognizing that transportation is a network that can have far reaching effects on the economy and quality of life beyond the immediate point of failure (DOT, n.d., a).

The Federal Transit Administration (FTA) focuses on the development and improvement of mass transit in the United States. Among its many programs is a safety and security focus. It offers guidance documents for transit agencies, including safety, security and emergency planning, employee training, and recommended protective measures. FTA is the sponsor for the nationwide Transit Watch Program, designed to bring employees and passengers into the surveillance of transit facilities. It has developed campaign materials in English and Spanish and has a program to incorporate transit watch training into the Citizen Corps Program of FEMA (FTA, n.d.).

DOT's most widely recognized program is the Pipeline and Hazardous Materials Safety Administration (PHMSA). This organization creates the *Emergency Response Guidebook,* which lists all the chemicals in transit in the United States, Canada, and Mexico, providing fire fighting, first aid, and emergency response information as well as chemical names and identification numbers (DOT, 2008). PHMSA also maintains a system of signage used to identify the materials carried in a truck or rail car so that first responders know what precautions to take in an accident or disaster. The signs are color coded for category and carry the chemical number that matches to the guidebook (Figure 3.6).

FIGURE 3.6 Sample DOT placards. (DOT. 2008. *Emergency response guidebook.* **Washington, DC: U.S. DOT.)**

DOT supports a number of university transportation research centers, as well as the Volpe Center, where guidance documents for safety, security, and emergency management activities are developed and maintained. For example, the Mineta Transportation Institute at San Jose State University has a collection of research reports on transportation security available as free pdf downloads at www.transweb.sjsu,edu. The Volpe Center materials include safety, security, and emergency management documents that can be accessed at http://transit-safety.volpe.dot.gov/publications/order/singledoc. asp?docid=21.

Department of Energy

The Department of Energy (DOE) was created in 1977 in response to the energy crisis that occurred due to OPEC members' decisions to withhold crude oil deliveries to the United States. DOE's purpose was to consider all forms of energy and develop a national energy policy for sustainability. Under its leadership the first solar power initiatives were tried. It brought together existing nuclear weapons and nuclear power programs with energy research initiatives (DOE, n.d.).

The Department of Energy oversees the management of nuclear fuel, including the shipment of fuel rods and spent fuel rods. Placards from the DOT PHMSA program are used to identify the vehicles to first responders. Through its Transportation Emergency Preparedness Program (TEPP), DOE ensures that local, state, and tribal first responders have the training they need to respond safely and effectively to any potential nuclear transportation-related accident. The Modular Emergency Response Radiological Transportation Training (MERRTT) Program trains first responders from fire, law, emergency medical, emergency services, and hazardous materials agencies in appropriate response to a potential transportation accident involving nonweapon nuclear materials, such as medical isotopes or spent fuel rods. Exercises are used at the end of the training to ensure that first responders can apply the principles of safe radiological materials management to actual events (DOE, 2009).

Transportation Research Board

The Transportation Research Board (TRB) is part of the National Research Council of the National Academy of Sciences, Engineering and Medicine. Its role is to support research and information exchange leading to innovation in transportation. U.S. DOT, state departments of transportation, and public and private organizations interested in the development of transportation jointly support the work of the TRB (TRB, n.d., a).

Transportation security is one focus of TRB. It funds research through its cooperative research programs and supports exploration of concepts through the IDEA program (TRB, n.d., b). The reports and studies are available through its website at www.TRB.org/SecurityPubs. Since 2001, the security work has focused on ways to protect transportation systems and thwart attacks using technology, science, and engineering. It has worked to develop security policies and programs for use by transit, air, maritime, freight, truck, and transportation agencies. Over 100 projects have been completed and more than two dozen are underway. The research is conducted in cooperation with the American Association of State Highway and Transportation Officials (AASHTO) and the American Public Transit Association (APTA).

Case Studies

Northridge Earthquake: Cascading Event

The Northridge earthquake occurred on a holiday weekend at 4:30 a.m. As a result, most people were at home. Once they examined their properties, many homeowners wanted to go to a store to buy needed supplies and repair materials. Because the area of Los Angeles that was damaged was limited to specific neighborhoods, there were shopping facilities in other areas of the city and in nearby towns that were open to meet their needs.

By noon on the day after the earthquake, people were complaining that they could not find gas for their cars or places to buy drinking water. The shift of demand from the damaged neighborhoods to the undamaged neighborhoods was causing a strain on gas stations and grocery stores. The problem was that there was no electricity in the damaged neighborhoods for the first week, with some areas not having power restored for more than 10 days. Gas stations simply closed because the gas pumps could not run without electricity. Grocery and convenience stores in the damaged area remained closed, even after they had cleaned up the spills and broken glass, because without electricity, they had no cash registers, no credit card readers, and no security systems. The imbalance in supplies could not be fixed because automated inventory information drove the delivery schedules of water and gas, rather than the actual demand. One store clerk said, "Each day I get a delivery of exactly what I sold on the day before 1 year ago. So next year I will have a glut of gasoline!"

AWW on the Bay

Many people believe that fall is the best time of year at the New Jersey seashore. The crowds are gone, the sun and water are warm, and the migratory birds fill the sky. Two friends decided to take a long weekend to enjoy fishing off their sailboat in the bay. By 10 a.m. on Friday morning they were floating along with the tidal current, hoping to catch some fish for their meals. They noticed two men in a rental boat from the marina who seemed to be having problems navigating into the channel. To these experienced boaters, it was a comical sight, so they remembered it. In fact, they remembered the code on the boat's side because it was the numerals of one fisherman's mother's upcoming October birthday: 1028.

As they fished and talked they kept catching glimpses of the same two guys in the rental boat floating around the shoreline of the power plant. One of them had a camera and kept taking photos of the shoreline—not a very picturesque area, covered with rip rap rock. Just before sunset, as the fishermen were cleaning their fish for dinner, they noticed the same guys trying to climb up on the rocks adjacent to the power plant's fence, an area clearly marked as off limits.

The fishermen were members of the Coast Guard Reserve Power Squadron and had received America's Waterway Watch training in June. The boat's owner got his clipboard, where he had put the guide sheet on information collection and reporting for AWW, wrote down the required details, and called the number on his cell phone to deliver his report. Within 30 minutes the two men in the rental boat were being towed to the marina by the Coast Guard.

At the end of their weekend, their ice chest full of filets and crabs, the fishermen stopped by the marina office to inquire about the guys in the rental boat. The clerk told them that they were copper thieves trying to figure out how to get the spools of wire that were stored at the back of the power plant property onto a boat. Their report probably stopped the men from drowning, as when the Coast Guard arrived their boat was stuck between some rocks, and neither of them could swim.

Coffee to Confuse the Dogs

The FAST lanes at California's San Ysidro port of entry provided a quick border crossing for the Mexican coffee roasting vendor who brought his supplies to San Diego restaurants each weekday. He had gone through the C-TPAT and FAST requirements to get documented to use the lanes after dutifully completing his e-manifest. The same Customs inspector saw him most mornings, and this morning the vendor looked different—nervous and upset. The inspector said a few words of greeting to the vendor and he only grunted, which was most unusual. Then the vendor noticed that the drug dogs were sniffing the truck's tires.

When the driver passed the clipboard back to the inspector with his signed paperwork, he included a shaky note that said, "Please don't stop me. The cartel has my wife. Meet me at McDonald's." The Customs agent realized that the vendor was probably importing contraband, most likely drugs, but he took a chance and smiled and waved him through, then went into the booth to call San Diego Sheriff's deputies for help. The plainclothes undercover officer met the driver in McDonald's and learned that members of a drug cartel had kidnapped his wife, filled his coffee cans with drugs, and topped them off with coffee to throw off the dogs. He was to meet his connection in a remote area of Chula Vista to make the delivery, at which time the receiver would call Mexico to get his wife set free, or so he had been told.

Quick cooperation between the San Diego Sheriff's Department, the Tijuana Police Department, and Customs led to the delivery being made just a few minutes late, and the driver was the undercover cop, not the vendor, who was in custody until the facts could be sorted out. The police were ready to trace the cell phone call in Tijuana and found the vendor's wife being led out of a warehouse blindfolded. The alert Customs guard and the preestablished relationships among law enforcement enabled one American drug dealer to be arrested and some cartel members to be detained in Tijuana. The vendor and his wife were taken into protective custody and later resettled in the United States after testifying in the trials of the drug dealer and cartel members.

Ships of Opportunity

American warships patrol the eastern Pacific as part of their precruise workups. On these short cruises, one oiler was always accompanied by a Coast Guard contingent with a helicopter and boarding party. Most days the helicopter went up for a look around while the ship slowly steamed south, testing its navigation and propulsion systems and holding man-overboard drills and fire drills.

One morning the helicopter was only gone a little while when it returned to pick up the boarding party. A fishing boat hung with nets was moving very quickly through waters teeming with fish, making no effort to catch any. The helicopter had gone low enough to take a look at the crew, and at least one crew member was armed. Concluding that they were carrying contraband, the Coast Guard officer mustered her crew to confer about a plan for interdiction. The decision was made to prepare a brig aboard the Navy ship and to test the engines at full speed to close the gap between the fishing boat and the oiler.

By early afternoon the helicopter went up again, this time with the boarding party. The fishing boat was too far out to sea to make port, and after a brief exchange of gun shots, the fishing boat surrendered. The Coast Guard was amazed to discover that the hold was filled with young girls. They had disrupted a human trafficking trip bound for the sweatshops of Los Angeles from El Salvador. The terrified girls explained that their families were told they would get jobs as nannies for rich movie stars, but once they were on the ship they were told that they would have to work for the gang in their garment industry factory until their passage was paid for. The smugglers were arrested and housed in the Navy ship's brig, and a Coast Guard ship repatriated the girls to El Salvador.

Summary

The federal government has a number of agencies and organizations that work together to enhance transportation safety in the United States. Some of these are within the Department of Homeland Security, while others are part of the Department of Transportation, the Department of Energy, and the National Academy of Sciences. Through research, training, and grant funding these organizations work with state and local governments, special districts and tribes to enhance the capability of transportation agencies to mitigate against, plan for, respond to, and recover from transportation security emergencies, regardless of their cause. In the following chapters some additional mode-specific terrorism and emergency preparedness programs will be described.

Discussion Questions

1. Name three sector-specific federal security agencies and describe the sector where they work and the services they provide.

2. What are the principal security concerns of the maritime sector, and how do the Navy and Coast Guard address these concerns?

3. How do the Customs Service and Border Patrol interact with the trucking industry? How does NAFTA affect the trucking industry?

4. What kinds of personnel regulations do federal agencies place on maritime, trucking, and rail sectors?

5. If you are the security director for the Port of Los Angeles, what modes of transportation do you have to integrate into your security plan? How does local government get integrated into your security plan?

Note

1. UASI is a terrorism preparedness program run by FEMA that provides funding for large metropolitan cities and their regions to support planning, organizing, equipping, training, and exercising of first responders and supporting agencies. A complete description of UASI is available in Reese (2009).

References

America's Water Watch. (2011, Aug. 17). Home page. Accessed 12/3/11 at http://aww. aww-sp.com/Americas_Waterway_Watch/Home.html

Bernton, H., Carter, M., Heath, D., & Neff, J. (2002, June 23). The terrorist within. *Seattle Times.*

Browning, R. M., Jr. (1993). *Captains of the port.* Coast Guard Historian's Office.

Bush, G. W. (2003a, February 28). *Homeland security presidential directive-5.*

Bush, G. W. (2003b, December 17). *Homeland security presidential directive-7.*

Bush, G. W. (2003c, December 17). *Homeland security presidential directive-8.*

CBP.gov. (2007, Dec. 13). C-TPAT overview. Accessed 12/3/11 from http://cbp.gov/xp/ cgov/trade/cargo_security/ctpat/what_ctpat/ctpat_overview.xml

CBP.gov. (2010a, Jan. 5). Border patrol history. Accessed 12/3/11 from http://cbp.gov/xp/ cgov/border_security/border_patrol/border_patrol_ohs/history.xml

CBP.gov. (2010b, Oct. 4). We are CBP! Accessed 12/3/11 from http://www.cbp.gov/xp/cgov/ careers/customs_careers/we_are_cbp.xml

CBP.gov (2011a, May 3). ACE at a glance fact sheet. Accessed 12/3/11 from http://www. cbp.gov/xp/cgov/newsroom/fact_sheets/trade/ace_factsheets/ace_glance_sheet.xml

CBP.gov. (2011b, May 4). ACE e-manifest: Rail and sea. Accessed 12/3/11 from http://www. cbp.gov/xp/cgov/newsroom/fact_sheets/trade/ace_factsheets/ace_rail_sheet.xml

CBP.gov. (2011c, May 15). ACE e-manifest truck fact sheet. Accessed 12/3/11 from http:// www.cbp.gov/xp/cgov/newsroom/fact_sheets/trade/ace_factsheets/emanifest_sheet. xml

CBP.gov. (n.d., a). ACE: Modernization information systems. Accessed 12/3/11 from http:// www.cbp.gov/xp/cgov/trade/automated/modernization/

CBP.gov. (n.d., b). CSI in brief. Accessed 12/3/11 from http://www.cbp.gov/xp/cgov/trade/ cargo_security/csi/csi_in_brief.xml

Coast Guard. (2002, December). *Maritime strategy for homeland security.* Washington, DC: U.S. Coast Guard Headquarters.

Coast Guard. (2008). Law enforcement detachments. Accessed 12/3/11 from http://www. uscg.mil/history/articles/LEDET_History.asp

Coast Guard. (2009a). Coast Guard history. Accessed 12/3/11 from http://www.uscg.mil/ history/faqs/when.asp

Coast Guard. (2009b, March 5). Office of Counterterrorism and Defense Operations. Accessed 12/3/11 from http://www.uscg.mil/hq/cg5/cg532/pwcs.asp

Coast Guard. (2011). Mission. Accessed 12/3/11 from http://www.uscg.mil/history/ MissionsIndex.asp

Coast Guard. (n.d.). Missions timeline. Accessed 12/3/11 from http://www.uscg.mil/ history/uscghist/USCGMissionsTimeline.pdf

Coast Guard Supervisor. (2001, Sept. 11). Personal communication, e-mail. Marine Inspection Office, Battery Park, New York City.

Customs and Border Protection. (2008). Free and secure trade (FAST). Accessed 12/3/11 from http://www.cbp.gov/linkhandler/cgov/trade/cargo_security/ctpat/fast/us_mexico/ fast_fact.ctt/fast_fact.pdf

DOE (Department of Energy). (2009). Transportation Emergency Preparedness Program (TEPP). Accessed 10/30/11 at http://www.em.doe.gov/Transportation/TEPP_Home.aspx

DOE (Department of Energy). (n.d.). History of the Department of Energy. Accessed 10/30/11 at http://www.lm.doe.gov/land/sites/oh/fernald_orig/AboutFernald/dhist.htm

DHS. (Department of Homeland Security). (2003). Components. http://www.dhs.gov/ xabout/history/editorial_0133.shtm

DHS (Department of Homeland Security). (2008a). Implementation of the post-Katrina Emergency Management Reform Act and other organizational changes. Accessed 11/25/11 from http://www.dhs.gov/xabout/structure/gc_1169243598416.shtm

DHS (Department of Homeland Security). (2008b). *National response framework.* Washington, DC: Office of the Secretary of Homeland Security.

DHS (Department of Homeland Security). (2008c). Transportation systems sector: Critical infrastructure and key resources. Accessed 11/25/11 from http://www.dhs.gov/files/programs/gc_1188404440159.shtm

DHS (Department of Homeland Security). (2009). *National infrastructure protection plan.* Washington, DC: Office of the Secretary of Homeland Security.

DHS (Department of Homeland Security). (2010a). Critical infrastructure. Accessed 11/25/11 from http://www.dhs.gov/files/programs/gc_1189168948944.shtm

DHS (Department of Homeland Security). (2010b). Customs and border protection timeline. Accessed 12/3/11 from http://nemo.customs.gov/opa/TimeLine_062409.swf.

DHS (Department of Homeland Security). (2010c, November). Organizational chart, November, 2010. Accessed 11/25/11 from http://www.dhs.gov/xlibrary/assets/dhs-orgchart.pdf

DHS (Department of Homeland Security). (2011). State contacts and grant award information. Accessed 11/25/11 from http://www.dhs.gov/xgovt/grants/

DHS (Department of Homeland Security). (n.d.). National infrastructure protection plan: Transportation systems sector. Accessed 11/25/11 from http://www.dhs.gov/xlibrary/assets/nipp_snapshot_transportation.pdf

DOT (Department of Transportation). (2008). *Emergency response guidebook.* Washington, DC: U.S. DOT.

DOT (Department of Transportation). (n.d., a). Natural Disaster Recovery Strategy. Accessed 10/30/11 at http://www.dot.gov/disaster_recovery/

DOT (Department of Transportation). (n.d., b). The United States Department of Transportation: A brief history. Accessed 10/30/11 from http://ntl.bts.gov/historian/history.htm

FEMA. (2007) Target capabilities list. Accessed 11/25/11 from http://www.fema.gov/pdf/government/training/tcl.pdf

FEMA. (2008a, January). Critical infrastructure and key resources support annex. Accessed 12/25/11 from http://www.fema.gov/pdf/emergency/nrf/nrf-support-cikr.pdf

FEMA. (2008b). Emergency support function #1—Transportation annex. Accessed 11/25/11 from http://www.fema.gov/pdf/emergency/nrf/nrf-esf-01.pdf

FEMA. (2008c). FEMA strategic plan, 2008–2013. Accessed 11/25/11 from http://www.fema.gov/txt/about/fy08_fema_sp.txt

FEMA. (2009, May). FEMA GPD grant program accomplishments report: Summary of initial findings 03-07. Accessed 11/25/11 from http://www.fema.gov/pdf/government/grant/GPD_grant_accomplish_report.pdf

FEMA. (2010). FEMA history. Accessed 11/25/11 from http://www.fema.gov/about/history.shtm

FEMA. (n.d.) Homeland security exercise evaluation program (HSEEP). Accessed 12/3/11 at https://hseep.dhs.gov/pages/1001_HSEEP7.aspx

FTA (Federal Transit Administration). (n.d.). Transit watch. Accessed 10/30/11 from http://www.fta.dot.gov/safetysecurity/12527_12547.html

GAO (Government Accountability Office). (2010, October 22). GAO responses to questions for the record. Accessed 12/3/11 from http://www.uscg.mil/history/docs/GAOd11140r.pdf

Jenkins, B. M., & Gerston, L. (2001). *Protecting public surface transportation against terrorism and serious crime: Continuing research on best security practices.* San Jose, CA: Mineta Transportation Institute.

Obama, B. (2011). *Presidential policy directive 8: National preparedness.*

Office of Homeland Security. (2002). *National strategy for homeland security.* Washington, DC: Office of the Secretary of Homeland Security.

Reese, S. (2009, Dec. 1) *Department of Homeland Security assistance to states and localities: A summary and issues for the 111th Congress.* Washington, DC: Congressional Research Service.

Select Bipartisan Committee to Investigate the Preparation for and Response to Hurricane Katrina. (2006). *Failure of initiative* (House Report 109-377). Washington, DC: Government Printing Office.

Sylves, R. (2008). *Disaster policy and politics: Emergency management and homeland security.* Washington, DC: CQ Press.

TRB (Transportation Research Board). (n.d., a). Mission and services. Accessed 10/30/11 from http://www.trb.org/AboutTRB/MissionandServices.aspx

TRB (Transportation Research Board). (n.d., b). Security and emergency publications. Accessed 10/30/11 at http://www.trb.org/securityemergencies/nasecurityproducts.aspx

TSA (Transportation Security Administration). (n.d., a). *First observer: Safeguarding America's transportation system against potential terrorist attacks.* Alexandria, VA: TSA/First Observer.

TSA (Transportation Security Administration). (n.d., b). Our history. Accessed 11/25/11 at http://www.tsa.gov/research/tribute/history.shtm

TSA (Transportation Security Administration). (n.d., c). Our programs. Accessed 11/25/11 at http://www.tsa.gov/lawenforcement/programs/index.shtm

U.S. Statutes. (1878). *Posse Comitatus* Act (Chapter 263, Section 15, U.S. Statutes, Vol. 20).

Chapter **4**

Layers of Security

Keywords: risk assessment, security technology, vulnerabilities, security plan, operational security, security clearance, need to know, physical security, policies and procedures, proprietary knowledge, surveillance, security strategies, acceptance, avoidance, diversification, transference, consolidation

Learning Objectives

After reading this chapter you should be able to

- Understand the security thought process
- Understand physical security terminology
- Employ a variety of strategies to enhance organizational security
- Understand the relationship between security and normal operations

Security Elements

In Chapter 1 the groundwork was laid to explore the application of security to transportation infrastructure and assets. As noted, security is often closely aligned with safety and emergency management within organizations, each of which has a slightly different approach to the challenge of providing a functional environment. Clear communication among the partners may be hindered because each discipline has its own understanding of the application of security principles. Risk, threat, and vulnerability are also related concepts that are part of the security evaluation process, but each discipline may see the challenge through a different lens.

Risk Assessment

The first step in creating a security program is the development of a risk assessment. Currently, most risk assessment is undertaken from the perspective of the security analyst. Hazards to the facility or community—natural, technological, and human caused—are identified, and an estimate is made of the damage that might result from each event. The security plan then considers the application of technology or engineering to maintain security when faced with such an event. The security expert tends to focus first on plans for defense of the facility, and then he or she evaluates the efficacy of such plans, asking how an adversary could overcome these protective measures.

Security Technologies

Most security technologies are centuries old in concept, meaning that they are well understood by adversaries. Modern locks, for example, are just more sophisticated versions of historical lock and key systems (Figure 4.1). Walls, fences, barbed wire, electrified barriers, and electronic detection systems evolved from protective ramparts. These well understood systems give the defenders little advantage over the attackers. More sophisticated systems like cameras (Figure 4.2) and biologically based identifiers are just

FIGURE 4.1   Antique locks.

FIGURE 4.2   Surveillance camera.

extensions of walls and locks. The plans for many systems are available from the manufacturer or on the Internet. YouTube has videos teaching key bumping and lock picking, and hackers successfully interdict even military computer security systems.

Technology itself is neutral. Its beneficial or destructive nature is determined by who is using it and when it is being used. A slim jim used by a tow truck driver in a parking lot at 2:00 p.m. is a tool to rescue a child trapped in an accidentally locked car. A slim jim in the hands of a 15-year-old in a parking lot at 2:00 a.m. is a burglar's tool.

The main security value inherent in these technologies is costing the perpetrator time, which in turn may allow the defenders to respond effectively and to summon additional assistance, such as from law enforcement, before a successful security breach. Locks are designed to slow down the entrance of unauthorized personnel by forcing them to stop and pick the lock. Walls require time for climbing. Cameras can cost time by forcing the adversaries into a longer path to their objective or stopping their forward motion to disable the cameras. In fact, if the adversaries are disguised or do not care that they are identified, the cameras may only be a deterrent in that they speed the protective response. If the perpetrator knows how many guards are on-site, the opposition force may simply overpower the defenders as they respond to the camera's notification of an attack.

Thinking Like a Perpetrator

One of the most effective ways to understand the nuances of security is to consider the vulnerabilities from the perspective of a criminal/terrorist seeking access to the facility, its personnel, and its secure contents and information. The most difficult part of developing this perspective is the requirement to suspend legal, moral, and ethical limitations on the evaluator's part, and to look at the security apparatus as an obstacle course instead of an unassailable barrier. Breaking down the physical security components and analyzing them will quickly reveal vulnerabilities to be exploited by adversaries. Observing the daily behavior of employees and security personnel over a period of time—a technique known as "hostile surveillance"—will expose many of the policies and procedures designed to protect the facility or infrastructure, some of which might not be properly employed.

Thinking like a perpetrator requires the security evaluator to take the role of a hostile observer who will seek all vulnerabilities in the chain of security measures and exploit them. All technologies can be overridden by denial of utility services; introduction of destructive elements, whether cyber viruses or explosive devices; or compromise of the human protector. A decision to take action against a secure facility will carry a cost, so the evaluator must determine the lengths to which an adversary would go, and then plan for protective measures against that level of potential attack. As will be discussed later in the chapter, a variety of means may be used that place barriers between the potential attacker and the protected facility to slow the attack and allow time for a successful interdiction. If the attacker does not want to get caught, this system may be effective as a deterrent before or during the attack. However, if the perpetrator is a suicide bomber with no need to escape capture, only a hardened physical protective barrier will deny him success.

The Human Element

While the structures' immobility is a benefit in developing physical security elements, the mobility of humans is a challenge to security. Once individuals have been identified by hostile surveillance operatives as associated with the target facility or infrastructure, further surveillance may be conducted off the facility, where detection is less likely to occur. Proprietary knowledge—information about the work of the organization; about the use of security systems like key codes or cards; and the names of key divisions, projects, or employees—might be gained by observing and talking with employees at local restaurants and coffee shops. When people go to lunch together, they may continue to "talk shop," oblivious to the eavesdropper at a nearby table.

A hostile observer may thereby be able to collect enough information to be accepted among a group of coworkers returning from lunch and pass through secure doors as part of the group, for example, because he or she is readily expressing an opinion about a project or a person by name. That inside—or proprietary—knowledge can be the key that bypasses all the physical security.

Some perpetrators have no regard for human life. Zealots in a political or religious cause might be willing to trade their lives and the lives of innocent bystanders for the success of the mission to destroy infrastructure or obtain critical intelligence. Such adversaries might be able to identify a specific employee, research the family through social media, and use threats to the family members to coerce key personnel to reveal information or provide assistance with access.

Testing the Threat Environment

All successful security plans require constant reevaluation and testing based on the evolving threat environment. Red teams/cells, tiger teams, and OPFOR (opposing force) are all terms for groups intended to test the security capability of an organization. They mimic the activities of potential threats to determine what vulnerabilities exist and assist in developing countermeasures. This approach is also used on an ongoing basis by security to do "what if" planning for potentially emerging threats. While the approach of thinking like a perpetrator may seem unscrupulous, it is necessary, as a dedicated adversary will readily use any mechanism available to him. Looking at the security plan from the other side and asking how it can be overcome is an effective way to reveal the weaknesses of a system while the opportunity exists to improve it.

Using the perpetrator's perspective is what differentiates security from safety and emergency management, where inanimate objects and unavoidable hazards may be the driving force of a reaction. Security focuses on the human actors. As technology changes, new ways of exploiting that technology are developed, which in turn creates the demand for newer technology. It is the race between offense and defense with the human element on both sides that makes security so dynamic and requires constant reassessment of the vulnerabilities and threats. This is also the reason why it is impossible to secure 100% of the assets all of the time. As motivational factors (like ideology, greed, and market value of recyclable materials) and skills (like bomb making, small-unit tactics, and computer hacking) change with different perpetrators, the risk analysis will constantly change.

Physical Security

The first challenge in adopting an integrated security program is developing a common vision of what a "secure environment" is, which has to begin by defining the concepts that will be used to evaluate the environment. There are three security *elements:* physical, policies and procedures, and proprietary knowledge. Although the individual elements can work alone, security is enhanced when all three elements are used in concert with one another.

The physical element of security establishes and maintains barriers to create a protective perimeter. It is designed to slow down an intruder, or make

FIGURE 4.3 Light rail station in San Jose, California.

the intrusion more obvious, to allow for a timely response and interdiction. Such barriers may include fences, lights, locks, doors, or windows. In some cases those barriers may not offer much physical deterrence, such as glass windows, but breaking or tampering with these barriers creates noise that triggers a defensive response. When facilities are designed and constructed, the security elements are often subordinated to the primary function of the building. For example, public transit stations are left open with multiple stairways to provide quick and easy access for passengers, but provide no deterrence to potential criminal or terrorist activity (Figure 4.3).

Physical security has at least to appear robust, even if there are unavoidable vulnerabilities. The key to successful physical deterrence is to create the image of consistent resistance to an adversary assessing the location. Invulnerability is theoretically possible if cost and convenience are unimportant. For example, Bio Level 4 labs require multiple layers of personal identification, a complete change of clothes, and passing through an air lock controlled from the outside by another person. Access to the passenger gate of an airport requires passing through a metal detector or back scatter x-ray and the screening of all carry-on items. In each case, a significant investment is required in equipment and in personnel time passing through the checkpoint. But for most transit and transportation applications, such measures are impractical.

Because perfect impenetrability is impossible for all transportation modes, the security analysis determines which elements must be strong and which elements can remain in a lower level of implementation. Access points with poor lighting and little activity are usually "hardened"—made more resistant to intrusion—by installing a solid-core door, steel door framing, and bullet-resistant glass. Well-lit open areas with high pedestrian traffic and personnel activity are left comparatively vulnerable with ordinary doors and glass because the presence of so many observers is an inherent deterrent to criminal activity.

Cameras, motion detectors, and other electronic alarm devices may serve as an adjunct system to either hardened areas or more open areas. Animals that are sensitive to intrusion, such as geese, may also enhance security. However, the operation of these systems determines whether they are actually a deterrent or just a means of catching the criminals after the fact. If a camera or detector is monitored in real time and tied to a rapid response to intrusion or tampering, such as by an on-site guard, the system's presence may deter criminal activity. This system depends on an astute observer watching the cameras either continuously or at least during the times when unlawful activity is most common. If the security staff member assigned to watch the camera is inattentive, the effectiveness of the surveillance is damaged.

Conversely, if a camera is merely recording the scene, or a detector triggers no response apparent to the observer, it is vulnerable to being disabled with impunity. The camera's recordings may be accessed to investigate criminal activity after the fact, as shown in the London subway bombings, but will not prevent the attack from occurring, unless the tapes are frequently reviewed. The camera assists law enforcement with the apprehension and prosecution of a perpetrator, but does not enhance the actual security of the site.

Cameras may also be used for countersurveillance. Recognizing that transit and transportation facilities have been popular targets for terrorist attacks—Madrid, 2004 (Johnson, 2005); London, 2005 (Rotella, 2006); Mombai, 2006 (Polgreen, 2009); and Moscow, 2010 (Nowak, 2010), for example—transit and transportation security staff members should be vigilant for people whose patterns of use of the facility are inconsistent with normal use. People who return frequently to the facility without actually boarding the vehicles may be studying the facility's security vulnerabilities in order to plan an attack on the system and its passengers. Camera systems with a human observer present will expose this unusual behavior—not only criminal behavior, but also people conducting their own surveillance of the facilities.

Even taped systems, if reviewed frequently enough, will reveal someone loitering or having an unusual pattern in using the transit or transportation facility. High-speed playback will cut the length of time a staff member has to watch the tape, but it will highlight loitering by some people as others move quickly through the frames. Computer programs have been developed that can monitor camera images for facial recognition and behavior recognition, such as leaving objects in the viewed area. This emerging technology depends for success on camera resolution, the processing power of the computer, and the sophistication of the programming behind the software.

At times public agencies with little funding may obtain placebo devices to heighten the impression of physical security in a public space. Dummy cameras, laser beams attached to no real alarm system, and locks that are easy to bypass are just a few examples of the items that can be purchased through any security catalog. Some agencies have used the less expensive dogs that are not trained to detect bombs to patrol platforms and carriages (Schaffer, 2006). Unfortunately, these placebos carry significant liability exposure, as the public is relying on security systems to protect them that actually have little functionality, except perhaps as a short-term deterrent to criminals.

If the placebos are used in connection with real security, they can maximize the use of real systems by forcing potential adversaries to take a different approach. An example would be using a dummy camera in a high-traffic area, thereby discouraging criminal activity from occurring there, but encouraging it in a nearby location that may be monitored by a hidden camera. Such tactics require considerable forethought and can pose significant risk if not properly managed.

While law enforcement agencies are security conscious, they have to let the crime progress to an articulable criminal activity before they can intervene, while security is focused on prevention. Success for law enforcement is prosecution and conviction, while success for security is preventing the crime from occurring. As an adjunct to human security guards, cameras and alarm systems can extend the reach of the patrol force, but cameras and alarm systems alone add little to security.

Policies and Procedures

Behind the physical security layers are the security policies and procedures of an organization. While physical security is transparent, the policies and procedures should be, and generally are, less apparent. They complement the physical security by ensuring that the physical security assets are being employed appropriately and that, when compromise of security occurs, it is met with an appropriate response. Ensuring that doors are locked and that a mobile patrol checks that those doors are locked is an example of a procedure. Not discussing an organization's security apparatus would be a policy, also known as "operational security" or OPSEC.

OPSEC is a military policy designed to deny information to the enemy in wartime and to potential adversaries in peacetime. The information involved might be related to troop movements, weapons capabilities, time schedules, mission objectives, or anything that might compromise the capability of the military to carry out its assignments. Because even scraps of information gathered through multiple sources can be compiled to obtain this information, OPSEC attempts to deny all information to those without a clear "need to know" in an attempt to create enough gaps in the available intelligence to make a clear operational picture unattainable. The slogans like "loose lips sink ships" and "the walls have ears" were created to convey the core concept of OPSEC and the responsibility of each individual in the organization to prevent sabotage and espionage.

In civilian terms, OPSEC is important because of the operational sensitivities that exist in every organization, particularly with security. Security plans are among the most sought-after intelligence by the opposition because access to the information enables the bypassing of those protective measures. This is why security plans are only known to a small, specific group whose members have a specific need to know.

Security clearances provide for another layer of security focused on personnel. This is a method of inspecting information about employees to ensure that they do not pose a future threat to the organization through criminal activity or disloyalty that would compromise sensitive information. Clearances can start with a simple "wants and warrants" check conducted through local law enforcement, to determine whether the employee has been involved in criminal activity in the past. A more complete background check may entail a review of confidential personal information such as bank records, personal history, family history, locations of prior residences, prior work history, political activity, and activity with foreign governments or questionable organizations. Personnel who must be bonded or who will routinely handle highly sensitive information may even have to take a lie detector test as part of the process.

There are two purposes for undertaking the time and expense of a thorough background check leading to a security clearance. The first is to prevent an individual who may be trying to infiltrate an organization from joining it. The second is to gauge the potential for the individual's loyalty to be subverted in the future through a threat to reveal embarrassing past events. These vulnerabilities include alcoholism, gambling, infidelity, sexual orientation, or anything that might be used by someone as leverage against the person to get him or her to comply with a perpetrator's demands. A security clearance, if formally structured, will identify what level of risk an individual may pose and whether that is acceptable from the organization's perspective. The higher the security clearance is, the lower the perceived risk must be.

The second component of security clearances, which is not generally discussed, is the access to critical and sensitive information that accompanies this level of trust. Those with clearances must have not only the appropriate level to gain access to plans and data, but also a need to know the facts. Only personnel who have a direct work-related involvement with the data will be made privy to them. This system of knowledge protection provides compartmentalization of information to minimize its potential compromise, as no one employee would know everything about a process or project.

Limiting those with access to sensitive information also narrows down the potential number of people who could be responsible for leaks.

Breaches of security policies and procedures are often unintentional but are very common, and they provide the weakest link in the security continuum as they rely on the compliance of personnel of the entire organization. The most advanced key card locking system can be easily defeated when a back door is propped open by a thoughtless employee during a smoke break. Employees who resist wearing their identification badges while inside the workplace make monitoring for intruders difficult. Friends who exchange door access codes to facilitate visits while on breaks create a breach, while polite people holding limited access doors open for "follow alongs" without badges open the facility to hostile intrusion.

Therefore, employee education is the key to successful implementation of security policies and procedures. Employees must understand that they are an essential part of the security apparatus and that their thoughtless or well-meant actions can lead to sabotage, criminal activity, or industrial espionage.

Information about the security operations is compartmentalized into several different subsections. Only the top personnel know how the various elements of the security apparatus interact. They are, in effect, the checks and balances within the system, ensuring that even if one portion has been compromised, another portion is likely to detect the compromise and be able to take protective action. Compartmentalization is reinforced by internal audits and surveillance detection.

Internal audits can be periodic or ongoing reviews of the effectiveness of a program using an evaluation by a separate source. The separate source will look at the efficacy of the security program and the responsibilities of the various elements of the program. The auditor will determine if there are violations of the security policies and procedures in the way the program is currently operating, and whether the circumstances require changes to or improvements in the interactions and relationships within the layers of security.

Surveillance detection is a separate program. The security staff members for a transit or transportation agency receive information from local, state, and federal law enforcement agencies about credible threats against critical infrastructure. They have a heightened awareness of the vulnerabilities within their systems that might assist an adversary in designing a successful attack. Knowing their own facilities, the internal security staff members "think like a perp" and determine which observation positions would be most advantageous for planning a successful breach of existing security. They then determine which vantage points would best enable the security staff to monitor others watching the points of interest and potential vulnerability. If hostile surveillance of the facility is begun, it will be detected through this system of countersurveillance. The observation of the critical

FIGURE 4.4   Reinforced security fence.

points can be accomplished by on-site security personnel or by video recording cameras as described before.

The countersurveillance operation is kept separate from the main security operations in order to avoid telltale activities by security staff in the areas of observation and potential vulnerability, which might alert the hostile observers. There is a danger that security personnel involved with the physical security components might act differently if they knew that they were being observed.

A countersurveillance response force is another security component, and it may be either a standing or composite unit. A standing response force is a dedicated entity whose sole responsibility is to respond to security breaches, as needed. Large metropolitan transit and transportation systems may have various full-time units, including a countersurveillance response force. A composite force would bring together already deployed roving security assets to form a response effort, resulting from specified activities (Figure 4.4).

Proprietary Knowledge

The third level of security is proprietary knowledge, which reflects the organization's language, behavior, and physical appearance, including badges, uniforms, or type of dress. Topics of conversation, vocabulary, and deportment allow one employee to identify another employee, even without a uniform or badge. Conversation in the workplace can be a key to security, as supposed employees are unable to supply commonly known business information. A person who cannot find the restroom or breakroom in the workplace should immediately be asked questions that reveal the reason for his or her presence. Information commonly known by employees but not known by outsiders makes a good test. For example, former Marines test each other by asking, "What was your MOS [military occupation specialty]?" A real Marine will respond with a four-digit number.

Each of these security elements has a function of its own, but when only one is used, the security level generated is weak. However, the three elements employed together create layers that result in a strong barrier to outside intrusion. A prime example of all three security elements working in concert is a bank. The primary asset being sought, money and valuable personal property, is located inside the vault. The physical security elements of the bank are the outside walls, the doors and windows, the alarm system, and the vault itself. The procedures include a roving guard patrol that checks the physical security systems at intervals that are shorter than the time it would take to defeat the physical barriers (penetrate the bank building and get into the vault).

Because the capital investment in the physical barriers has already been made, the greatest incremental cost is the guard force. Patrolling the building at intervals rather than continuously provides adequate deterrence because criminals would not have time to achieve their objective of robbing the vault in the period between visits by the guards. The guards, as part of their procedures, would have a manifest of who has permitted access to the bank after hours, such as the cleaning crew or senior bank officials. If unexpected individuals were discovered in the bank during a patrol, the procedure lists who should be called and what information would be reported to that person, normally a senior guard or a bank officer who would have been notified of an official deviation from access policy. That senior official could determine whether the unexpected individual had a need for after-hours access, which would be based on his proprietary knowledge.

Designing for Security

One reason that developing a rational security program for a facility is so difficult is that security is often an add-on rather than a principal component of a project or program. Security should always be among the first considerations in the development of a design for a new building or facility. For example, banks and prisons are designed with security as a principal consideration. When security measures are included in the design of the building, the costs are generally minimal. When retrofitting is required, it can be costly, unattractive, and dysfunctional, as observed at many airports, where management is still grappling with finding space for the security apparatus that is integrated into passenger and luggage flow. Stadiums were designed with security for the locker rooms, but security in the ticket-taking areas was added only after terrorism at sporting events became a concern.

The challenge is to develop a capability to respond continuously to developing technologies by allowing for space within access points, including conduit runs, for additional security assets to be added. Because cost is a significant factor in building design, security professionals find it challenging to get clients to build to standards that exceed mandated codes. While emergency management officials have had some success in promoting "value engineering" in earthquake country as a mitigation factor for seismic events, encouraging spending more money to create access for future unknown security threats is much more difficult (ABAG, 2003).

When remedial steps have to be taken to correct deficiencies in the initial design of a project, there is often conflict, as aesthetics and functionality compete with security. For example, older office buildings were not created with security systems like key-card-controlled elevators. If sensitive activities occur within the building, a security checkpoint may have to be established as a form of physical security, creating a choke point for employees arriving for work and clients arriving to do business. The new barrier creates unexpected congestion in the lobby, damaging the aesthetic designed by the architect and violating the fire code. The new security layer creates tension between the functionality of the building and the demand for security, leaving both the functional and security partners unsatisfied (Figure 4.5).

FIGURE 4.5 Water feature prevents trucks from accessing the plaza in front of San Jose City Hall.

Managing Security Assets

It is impossible to protect 100% of the assets 100% of the time. There are never enough resources to accomplish that goal. The cost in personnel and constant security upgrades would be detrimental to the long-term survivability of an organization. Even the military only accelerates to the maximum base security standards, for short periods of time under specific circumstances, because of the tremendous impact this has on normal operations. Condition Delta requires the reassignment of personnel and following invasive procedures that interfere with other aspects of readiness. Therefore, taking an approach to maximize the security resources available and exploit the potential threat's behavior is the best strategy to protect the most likely targeted assets.

One effective approach is to weaken the physical security visibly in a specific location to encourage the perpetrator to conduct more aggressive surveillance of that area. Security personnel would then determine where a potential attacker would set up an observation location and engage in countersurveillance in that area, looking for activity that does not match normal activity. Once this is done, a determination can be made that the area is being subjected to hostile surveillance. A variety of responses is employed, either to deter the individual through direct confrontation or to escalate to interventions, including eventual arrest. This may involve coordinating with law enforcement agencies to set the trap if the expected perpetrator is a civilian.

Other approaches to maximizing security include randomness, such as moving security assets around with no discernable schedule or pattern, thereby creating uncertainty for the perpetrator as to when and how many security assets may be employed at a specific location during a specific time frame. A good example of this is the VIPER program currently being used for surface transportation assets (TSA, 2007). Several federal and local law enforcement agencies will place personnel at a specific location for a period of time on a random basis. Their role is to increase the number of visible arrests on the transit system platforms and inside the vehicles to create an atmosphere that is unfriendly to all types of crime. The New York City Police Department also has its own internal program that follows the same deterrence concept for the city's subway system (Jenkins and Gerston, 2001).

Security Strategies

Beyond the security *elements* within the organization, there are also security *strategies* that follow the same approaches used for mitigation in emergency management. These are strategic managerial functions designed to lessen the impact of unwanted events on the transit or transportation system. These security mitigation strategies have a direct link to organizational operations. They are acceptance, avoidance, diversification, transference, and consolidation.

Acceptance

Economic circumstances may force a transit or transportation organization to accept that its assets cannot be effectively protected. Roads and rail lines cover so many miles that the systems' lengths preclude any effective system-wide security. Priorities are set for critical or irreplaceable assets, but most will not warrant protection because the incremental cost of widespread and effective security is greater than the replacement value of the asset.

Accepting that system security is not cost effective, asset users become the "eyes and ears" for system security. Road systems rely on the users to report disruptions, and rail systems have adopted a formal "see something, say something" program that will be discussed later.

This approach, however, inherently accepts the inevitability of attacks and losses, as most assets remain unguarded. Vandalism is common against railroad bridges, and theft from sidings spread along the rail line occurs frequently. The lack of protection invites attacks aimed at disruption, like train derailments. It also allows an adversary to attack different parts of the system sequentially, creating continuous disruptions to service along a route.

Avoidance

Another security strategy is moving assets out of geographical areas that are perceived to be too dangerous without significantly increasing the security. This approach may also include the reinforcement or overengineering of an asset to avoid future damage, in which case a cost benefit study will have to determine whether the extra costs are justified by the value of the asset. This approach is generally accepted only when human lives are at stake.

Reinforcement or "hardening the target" may actually be a strategy to deflect attention away from the asset that has been strengthened to a target that is easier to attack, especially if that target is also easier to secure.

Practically, the organization may not be able to move out of the area of concern because of its importance to the operation of the system. Transit has to continue to operate in high crime areas because the residents of such areas are often economically vulnerable and need the busses to commute to work. However, the bus yard can be located in a safer area, or the design can be more secure, reflecting the danger of the location.

Diversification

Assets may be intentionally dispersed over a broader area if compromise to a few of the assets will not adversely affect operations. Primary security for those dispersed assets is obscurity. In other words, the disbursed locations are also veiled—spread throughout a region without identification. This would make it difficult for an adversary to observe or track the organization's operations from a central point. The intent is to compartmentalize damage that may occur from an attack because of the increased vulnerability engendered by spreading out the assets, as noted in acceptance. One such approach is the increased use of rental or leased assets and equipment, which are stored and secured by their owners in many different locations.

This security strategy may hamper operations because the resources are dispersed over a large area, so gathering assets to meet a specific demand is more complex. There is also a tipping point that may occur if too many assets have been damaged or are unavailable in one region. Being able to marshal the remaining resources to deal with the organization's needs may be difficult if the needed resources are across a barrier or far away. For example, American Red Cross shelter supplies were moved out of the San Francisco Bay Area to Las Vegas as a precaution against earthquake damage. However, in the event of an earthquake in the Bay Area, bringing the shelter supplies back to the areas of need will be a challenge for the transportation system, as over 1,300 road segments are predicted to be damaged (ABAG, 2011), and air delivery service will have to wait until runways are inspected and repaired and air traffic control systems restored.

Transference

Buying insurance is one way of transferring the responsibility for security and replacement of assets following an attack. Entities may also contract out for services to other organizations, making the protection of expensive equipment their responsibility. The transit or transportation agencies may also have relationships with several vendors who provide similar services, to create redundancy in the event that one site or vendor is damaged or destroyed.

One problem with this strategy is the time required to acquire the replacement equipment when it is needed. Market fluctuations and activity in other sectors may have an impact on resource availability, including both materiel and contractors, who may have a contractual obligation to give priority to other customers. For example, a transportation organization may determine that a specified number of heavy equipment assets is adequate for day-to-day operations and that, if one is damaged in a disaster, it can be replaced through insurance reimbursement. However, all the available inventory of equipment in a region may already have been purchased or committed to other customers when the agency needs the replacement, leaving the organization with a delay in delivery that would significantly impact emergency response or recovery opportunity costs.

Consolidation

In consolidation, valuable assets are brought together to a highly secure site, where a large investment in the three security elements is made. This is the traditional approach encouraged by physical security professionals because it allows for maximization of security resources to monitor and protect assets. There is either one centralized point or as few regional centers as possible. Such consolidation allows for investment in sophisticated security systems and a concentration of personnel assets to protect the transit or transportation resources, while maintaining a low cost–benefit ratio. Bringing rolling stock into a few secure yards or centralizing all SCADA computer systems is an example of typical consolidations in transit and transportation.

This system, however, places all the organization's assets in one place. If there is a catastrophic failure of security at that location, the entire operation of the organization can be placed at significant risk. An attack on the single location could have dire consequences to the organization's ability to recover.

Strategies

Most organizations actually use all five of these strategies in different configurations as their overarching security strategy. It is the ratio of each one of the five types that varies among organizations. An organization may rely heavily on the consolidation strategy, yet have redundant assets secured through diversification to protect it in case the assets are compromised. Likewise, most organizations have some form of insurance for the replacement of critical assets. Most will try to avoid locating their resources in high-risk areas. Yet every organization has some elements of acceptance because it remains too costly to protect 100% of its assets 100% of the time.

See Something, Say Something

Riders have a vested interest in the continued operation of a transit system, whether it is for getting to work or just for their own personal safety. Therefore, a mutual dependence already exists. It is a matter of informing the system users of ways that they can become part of the organization's security solution. One method is to create a communication conduit into the security apparatus for passengers with knowledge about threats to the system to share. "See something, say something" started in New York City

FIGURE 4.6 "See something/say something" poster.

Transit following the 9/11 attacks, and similar campaigns have been adopted by transit agencies across the nation, Amtrak, and, most recently, by TSA for airports (Figure 4.6).

These programs drastically increase the size and scope of the security apparatus because of the number of "eyes and ears" helping the security system to identify and engage potential threats. The concept has been adopted from another environment where everyone's safety is mutually at risk: competitive shooting ranges. Anyone can call a cease fire on a shooting range. While there are only a few coaches and observers on the range, there are many shooters positioned across the space, who may be able to see a problem not visible to one of the officials. By encouraging those unofficial observers to notice and report unsafe situations, the size of the safety force has enlarged, and safety has been enhanced. This same approach is used in the campaigns to bring the riders into the security observer pool. By their numbers they increase the chance that something out of place will be noticed quickly or that unexpected or inappropriate behavior will be reported, thus increasing the security not only of their own site, but also of the system as a whole (Rohlich, Haas and Edwards, 2010).

There is also the need to reach out to organization staff members who do not have a direct security role. They need to be reminded that they are an integral part of the security apparatus as they follow the security procedures, as noted previously. Their actions or failures to act can have a significant impact on their organizations' security.

Case Studies

Security and Design for the New San Jose City Hall

The Problem

In the 1990s the city of San Jose, California, determined that consolidating city services into one city hall would decrease operational costs. The existing city hall, built in the 1950s, was not seismically resistant, had inadequate support for newer technologies in the work spaces, and could not be reconfigured to support more staff members. The city had negotiated leases for its growing staff during a period after the Loma Prieta earthquake when commercial space in the South Bay of the San Francisco Bay Area was readily available. When San Jose eclipsed San Francisco to become the third largest city in the state and the high-tech industry continued to flourish, the lease renewals on that office space were prohibitively expensive, so consolidation permitting the rents to be diverted to paying for the new facility's mortgage made sense.

Having city staff members scattered around the city's large downtown was also inefficient. People had to drive for several miles from some of the large downtown office buildings to the North First Street location of the city hall. Its parking lot was barely large enough to hold on-site senior staff members, so visiting staff had a challenge finding parking. One senior staff member calculated that, on an average workday, she spent more time in her car than she did in her office, as she drove back and forth between her office and city hall. She spent over 2 hours just looking for parking spaces as she went from meetings in the city hall to her office several times each day. Building a consolidated city hall would bring the senior staff members into one building, senior staff would have marked parking spaces, and people could "commute by elevator" for meetings with other departments, a time saver for busy executives.

The Best Laid Plans

The senior staff of the city began meeting with architects designing the interior spaces of the new city hall building. Early in the discussions, the chief of police and the director of the Office of Emergency Services (OES) requested that security measures be incorporated into the building's initial design. In 1993 New York's World Trade Center had been attacked using a truck bomb in an underground garage, and in 1995 the Murrah Federal Building in Oklahoma City, Oklahoma, had been attacked with a truck bomb by a disgruntled former soldier, pointing out the dangers posed by vehicle-borne explosive devices (VBIEDs). Taking steps in the design phase to protect the building and its occupants from VBIEDs and intrusions seemed like the appropriate strategy.

Elevator lobbies on each floor were designed to ensure that all visitors had to wait in a reception area to be escorted to the staff member they had come to visit. Department conference rooms, where meetings were held with members of the public, were located in the public area off the reception area, not in the employee work spaces. Each reception area's access door to the work spaces was locked. Each receptionist had a panic button. An internal automated dialer system permitted all receptionists and senior staff members to be notified by phone within 3 minutes if there were an intrusion or criminal activity in the building.

Street parking was controversial, with the police chief and the OES director insisting that vehicles should not be permitted to park on the four streets adjacent to the building. The north side was Santa Clara Street, a four-lane street with bus traffic. This side was designed as the formal entrance with a plaza and "water feature," providing a setback for the building, but the site plan called for a curved structure that stretched from 4th Street's to 6th Street's sidewalks. Fifth Street terminated at the back property line as a T-intersection, and public safety staff raised concerns that a truck could be driven down 5th Street, bumped over the curb, and parked directly beneath the walkway bridge that connects the administrative tower and the city council chamber.

Merchants with shops along 4th and 6th Streets protested that street parking was essential to their businesses, and a church and senior center on 5th Street demanded that parking for their use be retained, pointing out that they were already losing the spaces that had been located on the block of 5th Street that was to be closed and turned into the city hall footprint.

A larger security concern was the parking spaces beneath the city hall buildings and plaza. In the original design these spaces were to be reserved for city manager, senior and management staff, city council members, and their staffs. A card-reader-controlled gate was to limit access to the underground spaces, and a guard was to be posted to direct those without cards to other parking facilities. The new 4th Street garage just to the south was to open about the same time as the city hall.

A new employee parking garage was to be built on the north side of Santa Clara Street on 4th Street when the construction on city hall was completed, and one floor was originally to be designated for the public to use when they came to city hall for permits, council meetings, and development meetings. However, due to some challenges with assembling the land for the employee/public garage, its construction was delayed, initially for 2 years.

How It Actually Happened

Before the groundbreaking for the new city hall, a new mayor was elected. He immediately required that the city hall property be redesigned to include a rotunda. Because an internationally known architect had designed the city hall's structures, it was clear that the rotunda would have to be placed elsewhere on the property. The only possible location was the plaza. Rather than

FIGURE 4.7   San Jose City Hall rotunda.

being a substantial buffer between the building and the street, a portion of the area was filled with a glass rotunda building, adding the risk of flying glass to the existing concerns over possible attacks against the iconic building (Figure 4.7).

The original water feature had to be redesigned and downsized because of the added cost of the rotunda, which was not in the original budget. This left the curb as the only physical buffer to prevent a truck bomb from driving onto the plaza, clearly an inadequate solution. Late in the design process, the construction delay occasioned by the need to design the rotunda began to make a significant difference in the plans. The rock wall and water feature were changed to misters on tall poles, which no longer offered any protection from truck bombs. Faced with the conflicting concerns over budget shortfalls and security commitments, the architect's staff met with OES and police department representatives. An intern in OES, a former Marine well versed in the threat posed by VBIEDs, proposed the use of bollards—planters and boulders to create a visual rock garden that would actually serve as the needed barrier against trucks. Although this solution was adopted at the meeting, the cost of the boulders was too great.

After 2 years of dispute, the staff and community compromised on the street parking issue. There was no parking on either side of the four-lane Santa Clara Street from 4th to 6th Streets, but on the narrow two-lane numbered streets there would be street parking permitted on the opposite side of the street. A large city public parking lot was built on 4th Street immediately adjacent to the end of the city hall property, creating an exposure for vehicle-borne bombs on its north wall adjacent to the back wall of city hall.

In an excess of caution, the new city manager, appointed by the new mayor, determined that the employee elevator's key-card access system would be used to restrict the floors where staff members could exit, limiting the free flow of staff to the areas where they worked or that they visited frequently for work-related meetings. If a member got off at a floor where he did not have access, he would be locked in a small lobby area without access to the floor he was on and be forced to get back into the elevator. So the commuting-by-elevator dream ended.

It took 4 years to get the employee garage on the north side of Santa Clara Street built. The city council determined that it was not reasonable for the public to have to park in the new garage south of the city hall property, so they ordered that the underground parking be open to the public. The promised guard was cut in the first budget tightening after the move into the new city hall, and with the guards went the last important exterior security element of the new city hall.

Casing a Transit Station

A transit system in a major city decided to install surveillance cameras in the transit platform area with a view to deterring crime. The cameras were not staffed, but the recordings were reviewed at the end of each shift by the transit police officer on patrol. Over a period of several weeks the presence of the cameras did seem to deter graffiti and pick-pocketing: The equipment was cleaner and there were fewer passenger complaints about victimization. The chief of the transit police wanted to know at what point in the crime the perpetrators realized that their actions were being recorded, so he had all the recordings from the morning and afternoon commute periods downloaded for review by an intern.

The intern was instructed to look for people who seemed to be out of place among the usual commuters—too young, improperly dressed for a business day commute, or otherwise different from the heterogeneous daily passengers. The intern thereby became familiar with the faces that he saw on every tape, leaving in the morning and returning in the afternoon. Because of this intensive review, the intern realized that four young men arrived at the station by bus every morning at about 7:00 a.m. Two got off together but then separated, one going into the parking lot and the other going to the fence lines where he could watch the trains. Each had cameras. They stayed from 7:00 a.m. to 9:00 a.m. and then left on the 9:15 a.m. bus. At first he thought they were students of transportation systems or photography, but going to the same spots for 6 weeks, 5 days a week, for the same 2 hours seemed strange.

Another man got off the same bus every weekday for 6 weeks, walked up to the outbound train platform, and sat on one of the benches. He got out a notebook and wrote down things, never leaving the bench. A little after 9:00 a.m. each day he, too, boarded the bus and left the area.

A fourth man got off that same bus every day, walked up to the platform, and boarded the outbound 7 a.m. train, but was back on the same platform at 7:30 a.m. and boarded that train and then boarded trains again at 8:00 a.m. and 8:30 a.m.; at 9:00 a.m. he took the train but did not come back. When the intern, in curiosity, switched to the camera's recordings of the inbound track, he found that same man getting off the inbound train just minutes before he again boarded the outbound train.

The intern wrote up his findings, including the story of the four men, and gave them to the chief of police, noting this strange behavior. The astute chief immediately called the Federal Bureau of Investigation's counterterrorism office for that district and invited them to review the intern's notes and the tapes. Within 3 days all four men were in custody on suspicion of conspiracy to attack a train. A search warrant granted by a judge, based on the probable cause created by the strange behavior, revealed an elaborate plot to place IEDs on the train with the consistently largest number of passengers and to have the explosions synchronized to go off as the train passed close to an electrical substation.

Learning to "Think Like a Perp" Through YouTube

In *The Art of War*, Sun Tsu said, "If you know the enemy and you know yourself, you will be victorious every time." In the twenty-first century, a transportation security director is fighting a war against crime and terrorism every day. Attacks against public transit in Madrid (2004), London (2005), Mumbai (2006), and Moscow (2010) demonstrated the technological skill and tactical knowledge of the perpetrators. They have learned to "know the enemy" through surveillance of daily procedures and security measures in open public transit systems. The challenge is for the transit security professionals to become as knowledgeable about the methods used by criminals and terrorists so that they can now be "victorious" against disruptions to the public transit systems.

While there are many courses available through federal agencies that teach counterterrorism tactics, one of the most effective ways to become proficient in countering criminal and terrorist behavior is to go to school with them, and they get their skills training on the Internet! YouTube has revealed the secrets of crafts that have previously been obscure to the general public.

Locksmithing is one example of a skill that used to be revealed only to members of small societies known as craft guilds. During the Middle Ages people with the same skill banded together to share their knowledge and improve their practice within a closed group. Locks were built by skilled individuals, and it was the ingenuity of that locksmith and the training he had received that would result in a lock mechanism. They then marketed their products—in this case, locks—to consumers who had no understanding of how the product worked. They just knew how to employ the lock to their benefit, to protect valuables.

In the Middle Ages those who mixed elements together were called alchemists, and they also had a guild. The formulas for beneficial chemicals were closely guarded secrets within the guild. Customers were told how to use the product safely, but nothing about its components.

With the advent of the industrial revolution, locksmithing, chemistry, metallurgy, and other crafts were turned into commodities. Locks, chemicals, and metal alloys were mass produced by workers with little knowledge of the process overall, but who could perform parts of the work needed to create a finished product. Thus, the "secrets" of these crafts were taught piecemeal to many individuals working on an assembly line. Industrialization enabled the replication of a particular type of lock, chemical, or alloy at low cost for a mass market.

The wide distribution of products to consumers meant that more people had to have information about safety, use, and operation of these products. For example, this necessitated training locksmiths in how to overcome the lock if someone lost a key. It required training potential retailers and salesmen in how the lock worked so that they could promote the product to the consumer. Therefore, the internal mechanisms of these locks became public knowledge, but that knowledge was still limited to a relatively small number of people. Even today, most people have no idea how their front door lock works.

With the advent of the Internet, a significant amount of lock technology has been further disseminated. What started as promotions to potential retailers and training for salesmen by the manufacturers can now be found in various public locations, like YouTube. This information includes the manipulation and overcoming of those locks, otherwise known as lock picking.

Lock picking has also developed into "the sport of lock picking." A group of Michigan Institute of Technology (MIT) students developed *The MIT Guide to Lock Picking*, which was a catalyst for this sport. It particularly attracts computer programmers because of the challenge of solving problems in three dimensions required for successfully overcoming a lock.

Anyone with access to the Internet can access YouTube. Entering terms related to your area of interest will generate a list of related videos, in both the specific field and related fields. For example, if you want to know how to pick a lock, type in "lockpicking," "key bumping," "bump keys," "combination lock picking," "car door picking," and similar terms. These terms generate a list of videos that provide a clear understanding of what is involved in opening a lock without a key. Some personal practice will lead to the development of the capability to pick locks.

The same approach to learning can be used in acquiring knowledge about bomb designs, by typing in "cell phone detonator." YouTube videos made by experienced bomb makers detail how to create bombs from light bulbs, satchels, and other common items. There are also videos that teach how to make bomb materials, like ammonium nitrate and fuel oil (ANFO), and C-4 (a military explosive) at home. The fact that one bomb maker has lost several fingers should be cautionary!

Once a user has entered a search term, YouTube will generate a list of similar videos and related videos. This enhances the scope of knowledge related to crime and terrorism. Suggested videos for someone who typed in "cell phone detonator" might include marksmanship training and small unit tactics.

What once was proprietary information that required face-to-face training and hands-on experience is now being rapidly disseminated anonymously by video. By understanding these skill sets, a security professional can appreciate what knowledge a perpetrator might have acquired, which will in turn enable the development of countermeasures to deter, detect, delay, and deny criminal and terrorist activity.

Summary

Security is most effective when it is deployed in many layers and across all aspects of an organization. While physical barriers and monitoring systems may be the most visible aspects of the system, the human participation in observing actions and obeying procedures makes the greatest impact on security. From employee sensitivity to closing doors and identifying strangers in the workplace to the mass transit "see something, say something" campaign, human involvement is essential to ensure that all three layers of security—physical, policies and procedures, and proprietary knowledge protection—work effectively together.

The next chapter begins the second section of the book, with a specific mode as the focus for each chapter. The first mode to be considered is privately owned cars and trucks operating on the national highway system and state and local roads.

Discussion Questions

1. How would you conduct a threat analysis of a transportation agency? What hazards, vulnerabilities, and consequences would you evaluate?

2. How would you conduct a threat analysis of a mass transit agency? What hazards, vulnerabilities, and consequences would you evaluate?

3. What is the human element in security? What technologies can you use to minimize the human element threat?

4. What is physical security? What technologies enhance physical security? What are their limitations?

5. You are the security director for a rural bus company. What are the hazards to your agency? What technologies would you use to overcome or cope with those hazards?

References

ABAG (Association of Bay Area Governments). (2003). Riding out future quakes. Accessed June 26, 2010, from http://www.abag.ca.gov/bayarea/eqmaps/eqtrans/result.html

ABAG (Association of Bay Area Governments). (2011). Expected transportation losses in an earthquake. Earthquake and hazards program. Accessed June 26, 2010, from http://quake.abag.ca.gov/transportation/

Jenkins, B. M., and Gerston, L. (2001). *Protecting public surface transportation against terrorism and serious crime: continuing research on best security practices.* San Jose, CA: Mineta Transportation Institute.

Johnson, K. (2005, February 14). Terrorist threat shifts as groups mutate and merge; disparate radicals united to bomb Madrid trains, court documents reveal. *Wall Street Journal.* http://libaccess.sjlibrary.org/login?url=http://proquest.umi.com/pqdweb?did=792839451&Fmt=7&clientId=17867&RQT=309&VName=PQD

Nowak, D. (2010, March 29). Double suicide bombing kills 38 on Moscow subway. Associated Press. Yahoo News.

Polgreen, L., and Bajaj, V. (2009, November 25). India's guard is up after attacks, but weaknesses remain. *New York Times,* p. A.6.

Rohlich, N., Haas, P. J., and Edwards, F. L. (2010). Exploring the effectiveness of transit security awareness campaigns in the San Francisco Bay Area, California. *Transportation Research Record,* 4(2146), 92–99.

Rotella, S. (2006, March 6). Who guided London's attackers? *Los Angeles Times.*

Schaffer, A. (2006, January 17). Sorry, dogs don't do subways. Retrieved on Jan. 14, 2008 from http://www.slate.com/id/2134394/fr/rss/

TSA (Transportation Security Administration). (2007). VIPR teams enhance security at major local transportation facilities. http://www.tsa.gov/press/happenings/vipr_blockisland.shtm

Section II

Multimodal Surface
Transportation Security:
Threats and Strategies

Chapter 5

Road Transportation— Cars and Trucks

Keywords: bridges, tunnels, hazardous materials, state highway system, terrorism, VBIED, risk assessment, security, transportation

Learning Objectives

After reading this chapter you should be able to

- Identify potential vulnerabilities in road transportation
- Understand how construction methods generate vulnerabilities
- Understand the role of road system management in security
- Understand the interconnectedness of critical infrastructure within the road right of way

Components of the Road System

The road system in the United States has three components: paved surfaces on the ground, bridges, and tunnels. Each of these components has different characteristics that make it vulnerable to natural, technological, and human-caused damage, including being a potential target for terrorist attacks. The road system binds the American economy through drivers commuting to work and the movement of raw materials and goods. Loss of a road for even a short period of time can be costly. As noted earlier, the earthquake-induced loss of the I-10 corridor in Los Angeles in 1994 "cost the local economy $1 million per day" (U.S. DOT, 2002, p. 33), while the wider economy was impacted through the loss of access to the Port of Los Angeles (U.S. DOT, 2002.)

Road Surface

The paved surface of the road system is constructed of layers topped by asphalt or concrete. The roadway is engineered to specifications dictated by safety and efficiency factors. While "pervious concrete" is now available for use in some applications, thus allowing water to percolate through the paving into the ground, most road surfaces are impervious to water, meaning that drainage elements have to be included in the construction (Figure 5.1). Roads are generally "crowned," or higher in the middle, to facilitate water runoff because a sheen of water on the road can interfere with steering and braking and cause "hydroplaning," where a car's tires lose contact with the road surface and therefore the driver loses control of the car.

The sides of the road are designed to carry the water away through the use of curbs and gutters, ditches, or culverts, which are attached to a storm drainage system, sewer system, or natural water course. Piped connections to these systems may run under the roadway. Some sewer systems combine sanitary sewers and storm drainage, meaning that all the storm water runs through the water pollution control plant. When excess runoff occurs, it can cause the system to be overloaded, and sanitary sewage can be crowded out

FIGURE 5.1   Street draining system.

of the system by the storm water, causing untreated waste to enter the community at any access point to the system, including those along roadways. Because everything that is spilled on the road surface follows the drainage pattern created for storm water, spilled hazardous materials can also enter the drainage system and create a risk.

In many cases, the road becomes a conduit for other critical infrastructure. It is common to see telephone poles and electrical lines running along the road right-of-way. The road is usually constructed with a shoulder to accommodate vehicles that become inoperable due to lack of gas, tire problems, or mechanical problems. These shoulders are often used by utility companies as a location for their conduit or piping. It is common for conduit that will carry underground wires for telephone, electricity, and fiber optic cable to be laid during the construction of the roadway. Water pipes may be run through the same ditch or parallel to it. This co-location creates construction efficiencies, in that only one ditch has to be dug to accommodate all the utilities, but operational conflicts can occur as differing replacement or maintenance schedules cause the shoulder to be opened and inaccessible to motorists. Flooding may also compromise the utilities, as the shoulder is generally lower than the road surface, so if the conduit is cracked, the runoff may enter it and compromise the utility lines.

In urban settings, the road may have large pipe systems running beneath the driving surface. In cities like New York and Philadelphia, bricked sewer conduits beneath the streets carry sanitary sewage and storm runoff. As these brick structures age and the mortar dries out, the traffic-induced vibrations on the road surface disturb the bricks and cause them to fall apart. The street surface may then collapse into the sewer. Tunnels may use concrete pipe beneath the streets, and while it is not subject to mortar failure, its design strength may be exceeded by the traffic using the street above, and the pipe may deteriorate and ultimately fail. While it is desirable to create these piping lines in the gutter or shoulder of a roadway, congested older cities may not have adequate space for the dual location system.

Utility Tunnels

To avoid the risk of damage from failed pipes, some roads are constructed with utility tunnels. A tunnel may be a space dug through rock or an engineered structure designed to support the weight of the activity above it. The traditional piping relies on the pipe materials and surrounding earth to bear the weight of surface activity, but an engineered tunnel will provide a separate steel or wooden structure that bears the weight (National Terrorism Preparedness Institute, 2008, p. 6), while the pipes are simply artificial channels for drainage. In cut-and-cover construction, steel or concrete supports are augmented by backfilled dirt. The dirt surrounding the tunnel helps to stabilize its weight (National Terrorism Preparedness Institute, 2008, p. 6), but in some circumstances the dirt may contribute to its destabilization and redistribution of the weight burden, contributing to a surface failure.

Tunnels support the traffic load through engineered designs. Some tunnels have linings of circular cross sections designed as compression rings. Horseshoe-shaped tunnels carry the weight load around the perimeter of the tunnel openings (National Terrorism Preparedness Institute, 2008, p. 5). Modern materials, like shotcrete with lattice girders and bolted precast concrete sections, permit better constructed tunnels (National Terrorism Preparedness Institute, 2008, p. 7), but older infrastructure is still in daily use.

Some road tunnels are drilled through rock. These are common in mountainous areas, where tunnels allow the road to make a straight path rather than going up and down a mountain. The Pennsylvania Turnpike has several tunnels as it passes through the Appalachian Mountains. The Caldecott Tunnel in the San Francisco Bay Area is an example of an urban roadway that was tunneled through a hill to prevent a significant change of elevation for the road. Tunnels are also used to carry roads underneath busy waterways where bridges are impractical. The Holland and Lincoln Tunnels in New York City are good examples of tunnels that are drilled through bedrock underneath the Hudson River.

In tunnels drilled through bedrock, there is generally no access except at the ends, although there may be pedestrian emergency exits up stairways at the water's edge. Ventilation of these tunnels is also a challenge, as vents and fans have to be located in areas that are relatively near the surface. Tunnels going under water may have to limit air exchange systems to the ends and the water's edge, although they may use vent pipes that rise above the water surface out of the navigation spaces.

Surrounding geology is another consideration in the construction of transportation tunnels. Various types of rock have different load-bearing and motion characteristics. Earthquakes may disturb even bedrock. Landslides, subsidence, underlying substrata, and sinkholes are just a few of the geological aspects of the areas that must be considered when a site is selected for a tunnel. Core samples provide information, but underlying substrata may be different from the core sample material. Rock has different compressive strength: Chalk is soft and sandstone and limestone have medium strength, while dolomite and granite are hard. Tunnels have to be constructed to counteract weaknesses in the rock formations. Tunnels built in soil rely on the tunnel lining to maintain the opening (National Terrorism Preparedness Institute, 2008, pp. 9–10).

Some tunnels are actually boxes that are sunk into a subsurface trench below the surface of a body of water and then backfilled with soil to force out the surrounding water. Known as immersed tunnels, these tunnels rely on the integrity of the box structure and the strength of the compacted soil above it for structural integrity. The BART transbay tube is an example of this type of construction. Such tunnels require constant monitoring for leaks and cracks that could lead to water incursion (National Terrorism Preparedness Institute, 2008, p. 6).

Regardless of the type of tunnel construction, support systems are required. Ventilation systems remove contaminated air and help with fire fighting. Emergency access and egress stairways are required to remove users and allow access for emergency responders. Power is essential for lighting, for closed-circuit TV cameras to monitor traffic and safety concerns, and for signal systems and gas monitoring systems. Communications in subterranean areas require specially designed antennas to carry the radio signals to the surface. Rainwater and surface runoff from the ends must be pumped from the tunnel, and fire suppression systems with standpipes are required for safety (National Terrorism Preparedness Institute, 2008, p. 8). Tunnels must be designed to provide these support services essential to the safe management of the facility. While some access is provided through conduit within the tunnel, ventilation and access require breaches in the tunnel's structure.

Bridges

There are two major types of road bridges: overcrossings and bridges. Overcrossings are generally short spans that carry one street over a submerged portion of another street. They are a common interface between express highways and city streets and may also be used over other small depressed openings, like a rail line or creek. Overcrossings are a continuation of the street surface and because they are generally short spans, they usually require a simple deck girder construction.

Larger bridges span bodies of water, large ground depressions, and rail yards and may support elevated highways through urban areas. There are a variety of bridge designs selected by engineers based on the features of the site, the financial support available for construction, and aesthetic considerations. For example, a new bridge in Redding, California, was designed as a working sundial (Sundial Bridge, 2009), while the self-anchored suspension span cable's asymmetrical structure of the new Bay Bridge in Oakland, California, is designed as a visual asset to the skyline (Caltrans, 2011).

Bridges have two components: the approach and the main span. The span carries the road across the depressed space, while the approaches bring the traffic to bridge level, which is often elevated above road level. Approaches may start at ground level but be raised through various types of support: truss, arch, or beam spans.

The main span of a bridge may cover several miles, especially if it is supporting an elevated urban highway. The style of construction will be determined by the type of soil supporting the structure and whether it is

FIGURE 5.2   I-5 arch bridge in Dunsmuir, California.

in bedrock, some type of soil like bay mud, or even on man-made support under water. The length of the unsupported portions of the span will also determine which type of bridge is best, along with the expected weight that the bridge will have to carry.

Arch bridges are among the oldest style of bridge (Figure 5.2). Traffic may be carried above the arch or through the arch. The abutments support the arch and may be anchored in the ground on each side of the gorge or built of reinforced concrete. The deck may be supported on suspender cables or sit atop the arch. Roman aqueducts used the arch bridge to support the water run. The Ponte Vecchio in Florence, Italy, is a famous example of this style (Bridge Conference, 2006).

Deck spans use girders to construct the most common and basic bridges. Box girders are added for longer spans. Truss bridges may carry traffic above the truss system or through the truss system. Often a bridge will use deck truss construction for the approach and through-truss for the main span. Cantilevered truss bridges consist of a suspended span in the middle, with standard truss bridges on each end. The suspended span has hangers on each of the truss bridges and allows for the longest truss bridges, which are economical to build (Technical Support Working Group, 2006, p. 24).

Suspension bridges are more complex. Their iconic towers carry long cables that support the weight of the road surface. The cable anchorages at each end of the bridge are generally cast-in-place reinforced concrete (Technical Support Working Group, 2006, p. 38).

The cables are actually bundles of thousands of strands. The Hanshin-Awaji Bridge in Kobe, Japan (Figure 5.3), the Golden Gate Bridge in San

FIGURE 5.3   Cable anchorage for the Hanshin-Awaji Bridge in Japan.

Francisco, and the George Washington Bridge in New York City are good examples of suspension bridges.

New bridges are often of the cable-stayed design, especially for long-span structures. The cables are the main tension members, while the hollow towers and deck are in compression. Cable anchorages are at the deck and tower (Technical Support Working Group, 2006, p. 40). The Ravenel Bridge in Charleston, South Carolina, is an example of an American cable-stayed bridge (Figure 5.4) (Starmer, 2007). Cable-stayed bridges are also very popular in China, where the Sutong Bridge in Suzhou, the longest cable-stayed bridge in the world, carries traffic over the Changjiang River.

Movable bridges are required over navigation channels that serve ships of varying sizes. When large ship traffic is not frequent enough to justify the cost of a high bridge, a movable bridge will be constructed. Swing span bridges have a central pivot point that is often in the center of the navigation channel. The bridge swings parallel to the channel to allow taller ships to pass. Bascule spans allow one end of the bridge to lift up, providing a clear space for shipping. Vertical lift bridges have truss or girder structures that rise along towers to create adequate space for ships to pass under the deck. Movable bridges rely on power, often electricity, to operate (Technical Support Working Group, 2006, pp. 48–49).

Maintenance of the Highway System

All elements of the highway system require regular maintenance. The road surface is subject to deterioration from weather and use. Heat, ice, and rain

FIGURE 5.4   Ravenel Bridge, Charleston, South Carolina.

stress the surface materials and cause failures like potholes, cracks, and "alligatored" surfaces. Regular sealing of the surface will add years to the life of the road surface, but failure to perform routine maintenance may result in severe damage that requires reconstruction from the dirt level upward. America's major cities have been facing severe backlogs in road maintenance work due to budgetary constraints.

For example, the City of San Jose, California, America's 10th largest city, had an estimated road repair backlog of $298 million in March of 2012. While the city council voted to prioritize rebuilding and resurfacing for 400 miles of city streets at its March 27, 2012, council meeting, the $18 million per year budget for road maintenance means that the backlog grows each year. The importance of roadways to economic activity is demonstrated in the council's choice of priority street repair locations: six-lane roads, roads in two major shopping areas, VTA light rail and bus transit corridors, and streets serving major employers (Onaga, 2012).

Tunnels must be monitored not only for road surface condition, but also for cracks in the walls and damage to the supports. Traffic-induced vibrations can stress surface materials like tile or stucco, potentially leading to a lessening of structural integrity. Water intrusion is the greatest threat to tunnels (National Terrorism Preparedness Institute, 2008, p. 10). Small flows of water can erode structural components, while stronger flows could flood the tunnel.

Bridges are particularly vulnerable to weather conditions. Heat and ice can stress the metal elements, which must be kept painted to prevent rust and cleaned of bird droppings to prevent corrosion and weakening of bridge

FIGURE 5.5   Road repair crew and equipment.

connectors and components. Mechanical systems require regular service (Figure 5.5).

Failure to maintain road infrastructure is a national problem. The Sacramento, California, metropolitan region noted in a 2010 report that the annual spending by its six counties and 22 cities was $250 million for routine maintenance, but to keep the roads in a state of good repair, the spending would have to be $350 million. Road repair and road maintenance compete for the same funding streams: gas tax, sales tax, vehicle registration fees, and local government general funds. While the $0.18/gallon gas tax in California was designed to cover costs of road maintenance, today it covers only about 25% of the cost. In Sacramento, a typical community, 90% of the available funds are used for road repair, which means that deferred maintenance is backlogged, creating more damage to roads, which leads to more road repairs (Sacramento Area Council of Governments, 2010, p. 2). Deterioration of the roads makes them more vulnerable to all threats, enhancing the likelihood of loss of use.

Interconnectedness of Roads

Roads are useless as segments. They are part of a nationwide system that allows traffic to flow through cities, counties, and states across the nation. The Defense Highway System, commonly referred to as the Interstate Highway System, was designed to ensure the ability to move military supplies across the continent. Modeled on the German autobahn by President Dwight D. Eisenhower, this infrastructure investment is now maintained by each state with assistance from the Federal Highway Administration (FHWA). The federal allocations are determined by Congress as part of the transportation authorizations. In SAFETEA-LU the annual authorization was $100 million for each year from 2005 through 2010 for "resurfacing, restoration, rehabilitation and reconstruction (4R) work" on the interstate system. As costs for petroleum-based products like asphalt rose, costs for 4R work increased without a new source of funding, so fewer miles could be kept in good repair (FHWA, 2010).

States have gasoline taxes and sales taxes that can be used for maintenance and 4R work. While sales taxes increase with the cost of a gallon of gasoline, the gas tax per gallon stays the same. The gas tax is dedicated to road maintenance and repair, but sales taxes are divided among the state and local governments and may be used for other general government purposes.

Roads go from one city to the next, from one county to the next, and from one state to the next. Unequal maintenance means that drivers experience different driving conditions on the same road as they pass through different jurisdictions. Lack of maintenance leads to damage to tires and alignment, thus raising car maintenance costs for drivers, including commercial vehicles. People who use the roads or consume goods carried across the roads can pay either for road maintenance or for increased vehicle maintenance costs until an adequate source of road maintenance funding is established. As the nation waits for Congress to pass a new transportation bill, the solution is not in sight.

Risks to Road Transportation

Risks to road transportation fall into three categories: natural, technological, and human caused. As was discussed in Chapter 1, a threat analysis is the beginning of developing a security plan. The road system is spread out, which creates a benefit in redundancy and a detriment in its openness. Critical nodes, such as heavily traveled roads and congested areas, may not truly have an alternate route available that provides the same level of efficiency or access. Although New York City has surveillance cameras throughout Manhattan, most communities cannot afford to watch every mile of roadway. County roads and state highways may go through rural, forested, or remote areas where cameras may be inefficient or ineffective. Thus, security planners need to be able to evaluate the relative hazards, the vulnerability to those hazards, and the consequences of the occurrence to determine what investment in security strategies makes sense.

Natural Hazards

Different communities experience different levels of natural hazards that may lead to disasters. Dr. Kathleen Tierney, director of the Natural Hazards

Center in Boulder, Colorado, asserts that there are no "natural disasters"—only bad decisions by urban planners, builders, and buyers (Tierney, 2010). Today urban planners can make effective analyses of the inherent hazards of bad soil, seismic activity, and dangerous weather and direct development away from danger. However, land owners desire to maximize the value of their assets and buyers continue to be drawn to inherently dangerous areas like beach properties in hurricane country and hillside lots in earthquake country. The tension between safety and financial benefit generally causes elected officials to side with the landowner and voter and permit development in the community, even when it is not wise.

As discussed in Chapter 1, natural hazards include geological hazards like earthquakes, landslides, and sinkholes. Weather-related hazards include high heat, hurricanes, windstorms, tornadoes, ice storms, hail, avalanches, lightning, and floods. Generally, these events impact security only through their secondary effects, such as knocking out power, denying access, or damaging infrastructure.

Criminals and terrorists cannot manipulate the weather or geology, but they may plan in advance to take advantage of seasonal or cyclical events that, while unpredictable as to date, may be relatively predictable as to occurrence. So criminals plan bank robberies when a heat wave brings down the power grid, and terrorists could wait for an ice storm that slows police response to bomb a key infrastructure node.

Technological Hazards

Infrastructure failures induced by technology have occurred, and there is the potential for more events. The aging power grid failed catastrophically in California and Oregon in the mid-1990s because of an owl. The northeastern United States and parts of Canada experienced a cascading failure of the power grid in 2003, ultimately determined to have been caused by system operator failures (U.S.-Canada Power System, 2004). A heat-induced transformer fire in Mesa, Arizona, in July of 2011 left 100,000 homes and businesses without power as the temperature rose to 106° (Walsh, Randazzo, & D'Anna, 2011).

Design defects have led to the loss of critical infrastructure nodes, such as the I-35 bridge in Minneapolis that collapsed because the designer failed to provide strong enough gusset plates in the deck-truss design bridge. Increased loads due to construction work pushed the faulty design to fatigue and failure (*Roads and Bridges,* 2008).

Failure to design a structure with proper understanding of the surrounding conditions led to the failure of the Bay Bridge upper deck of I-80 and the Cypress Structure of I-880 during the Loma Prieta earthquake. Both structures were built on uncompacted bay mud and fill, which was unable to bear the seismic forces. Tests show that the seismic forces caused the hinges of the structure at the bottom of the upper deck and the top of the lower deck to fail (Bollo, Mahan, Moehle, Stephen, & Qi, 1990).

Similarly, the Tacoma Narrows Bridge was designed without adequate attention to the weight of the suspension bridge in relation to the windstorms in the area. The cables had already been replaced once but were still attached to the part of the bridge that was moving the most. The damper failed almost immediately, and the stiffening trusses were inadequate in length (only 2.4 meters), leading to significant swaying (Feldman, 2003).

Bridges are subject to cross traffic from vehicle traffic, if they are over other roads, rail equipment if they are over tracks, or marine traffic if they are over water. The supporting structure of the bridge may be rammed either accidentally or on purpose by land, rail, or marine vehicles, threatening the structural integrity of the bridge.

Bridges may also be overloaded because there are too many vehicles on the bridge, by the accumulation of ice and snow that, together with traffic, stresses them beyond their design limits, or by the introduction of heavy equipment on the bridge. This was determined to be the cause of the I-35 bridge failure in Minnesota. Rush hour traffic and multiple layers of asphalt from years of resurfacing had stretched the structure to near its weight limits. Construction equipment and material was staged on the bridge in preparation for post-rush-hour repairs. The cumulative weight together with weak gusset plates destroyed the structure (NTSB, 2008).

Hazardous materials accidents may also occur on roadways as a result of technological failures. Broken pipelines, faulty truck valves, and improperly installed or used safety devices have led to leaks and spills onto roads. One of the most spectacular hazardous materials spills was a tanker truck accident on the MacArthur Freeway in Oakland, California, in April 2007. The truck overturned and its load of gasoline spilled, caught fire, and burned down the deck of I-580 at the interchange with I-80. The tanker was theoretically designed to remain intact and retain its 8,600-gallon load, but failure of the tanker material or the operation of the valve resulted in loss of the load and $6 million in damage to the freeway system. The economic loss was estimated at $6 million per day for the 27 days that the interchange was closed (Cabanatuan, 2007).

Cyber Attacks

Computers control car and truck engines by monitoring the operations parameters and coordinating timing, fuel delivery, and synchronization with the transmission. More recently, systems like OnStar have included the ability to start and stop cars remotely. Some cars even have cell phone "apps" to permit remote operation of the ignition. Commercial trucks have GPS devices that monitor the location of the truck and can remotely shut it down. Sensors monitor tire pressure, fluid levels, and engine operation.

The road system itself uses computer-controlled traffic signals. Some controllers are tied to street sensors that trigger green lights for side streets only when a vehicle is present. Emergency vehicles can interface with the traffic light system through devices like Opticon that change the traffic light to green in the emergency vehicle's direction to prevent intersection accidents during Code-3 operations. Intelligent transportation systems (ITS) use sensors embedded in the road to monitor traffic performance, and this information is used to report road conditions to GPS units in cars and to handheld devices that inform commuters about the best route to the destination. It is also analyzed in the traffic management center to see if emergency response is needed for an accident.

Roadway lighting is also computer controlled in some cities. LED and induction lighting systems can be made brighter or dimmer depending on the needs of the driving public. Lights can come on gradually during twilight to augment natural light and maintain a minimum measure of lumens. Late at night, when traffic is light, the brightness can be reduced to save electricity costs (Hartnett, 2011).

Because of the ubiquitous presence of computer devices in the transportation system, a cyber attack could lead to chaos on the roads. Loss of traffic control devices could lead to accidents. Even the operation of cars and trucks could be compromised if the cyber attack were against the OnStar center or a tractor-trailer control center, which could become the conduit to randomly shut down vehicles on the road, leading to tie-ups and accidents. Attackers could also use these systems to eavesdrop on drivers trying to cope with the malfunction and redirect cars or trucks to desired locations for a hijacking or kidnapping.

Human Caused

Other forms of human-caused attacks could cause even more damage to the transportation system. Hijacking tractor trailers and tanker trucks for their loads has occurred at truck stops, rest stops, or along roadsides when well-meaning truckers stopped to help stranded motorists who were decoys. If the load is a hazardous material, the hijacker may be seeking to use the tanker or trailer as a destructive device. A tractor trailer filled with cans of evaporated milk was used by its own driver to ram the California capitol in 2001, causing a fire that evacuated the building during the legislative session and resulting in exploding cans of milk (Gledhill, Lucas, Martin, & Squatriglia, 2001). Although this truck was not hijacked, it demonstrates the damage that can be done by a seemingly innocent material.

Vehicle-borne explosive devices (VBIEDs) are a common weapon in Iraq. The Murrah Building in Oklahoma City was destroyed in 1995 by a truck bomb based on ammonium nitrate and fuel oil (ANFO) (Michael & Herbeck,

2001). The first attack against the World Trade Center in 1993 was a truck with a urea nitrate-hydrogen gas bomb parked in the underground parking garage. It killed six people instantly and created a 100-foot crater (FBI, 2008). Because detection is very difficult, VBIEDs make good terrorist weapons.

Security Strategies for Roads

Roads serve as both a surface for driving and a route for other infrastructure elements, which can lead to cascading events. Flooding of a roadway may lead to damage to the underlying conduit and piping from natural causes. A direct attack on the road's surface may inadvertently damage the underlying elements of the road, equally creating the loss of other infrastructure.

The conduits and pipes can also become the location for an attack, as these spaces can be packed with explosives, using manholes for access. Because sewage travels by gravity flow or pumping to the water pollution control plant, waterproof explosives can be introduced into the sewage system and floated downstream, timed to explode at a critical infrastructure node or in the plant itself.

Piped or tunneled areas underneath streets may also be attractive sites for attacks. The material around the utility tunnel entrance may be destabilized, causing rock or soil to block the entrance. Any area along a roadway that is prone to landslides or rock slides is also a potential target for induced slide activity. Additionally, attacking the slopes below the tunnel or road level may undermine the driving surface.

One solution to these threats is open communication among all the agencies responsible for the road surface and its underlying elements. First, a common risk assessment must be developed that looks not only at the individual risks, but also at the risks of cascading events. One difficulty of developing this complete threat analysis system is the challenge of getting all the participating agencies to share their most critical information. There may be a desire on the part of some participants to keep proprietary information confidential or activities secret to prevent unwanted attention.

Second, while the infrastructure may seem to be static, other systems tied to it outside the immediate area of risk assessment may be expanding rapidly, putting a greater load on the system or enhancing its criticality. For example, when the Owens Valley water system for the Los Angeles Basin was developed, only a few million people were being served. Today that system has been enlarged to serve almost 10 million people. Damage to the aqueduct running along a roadway would now have a much greater social and economic impact than the same damage when it was first activated.

Once the threats to the roads and their underlying systems are understood, a system must be developed and implemented for reporting planned activity on the roads or in the infrastructure systems, and unexpected activities that may indicate hostile interference with the systems. Even if the interference is only vandalism or "urban explorers," those who notice the event should generate an immediate request to the infrastructure owners for documentation of the damage or intrusion. There should be a response to evaluate the extent of the event and the precautions that could be taken to prevent future intrusions.

Law enforcement agencies must be included in the road and infrastructure reporting system. System service personnel need training in the rudimentary collection of evidence to support law enforcement investigations. These include photographing unusual markings, not handling foreign items found in the system, and being able to explain what the attraction would have been to a perpetrator in the area of the intrusion. This requires a holistic view not only of that particular entity's infrastructure, but also of the surrounding infrastructure that could be the actual target of the intrusion. For example, a road system culvert might be blown up to get access to the fiber optic cable in a nearby conduit.

Locks may be enhanced to deny access to underlying utilities. For example, after an AT&T fiber optic cable vault in southern San Jose was entered and the lines cut, the manhole covers were fitted with tamper-proof locking devices. As noted in Chapter 4, locks are intended to buy time for a response to an attempted intrusion, but they will also discourage less ambitious perpetrators. Alarm systems and monitored cameras on the access points can speed the response to an attempted intrusion.

Cell phone lines may be available for the communication channel for the alarm's or camera's signal, even in relatively remote locations, but costs for installing communications and reliable power supplies may preclude these installations. If there are no law enforcement personnel nearby, the response may be no better. Considering that the lock has to deter the perpetrator long enough for a response to occur, extreme distances may make an alarm system relatively ineffective as a deterrent, while the camera may provide recorded evidence for use in a prosecution. Antitamper devices can also be used to determine if the access point has been used by unauthorized personnel.

Access points for critical infrastructure, including the road's culverts and the underlying utilities in remote locations, should be masked and their locations disclosed only on a need-to-know basis for repair crews and first responders. In urban settings the opposite strategy is more effective. Placement of access points should be in highly visible locations and clearly marked, to bring the passing public into the surveillance, along with other public agencies working in the area. Activity around an access point that has not been announced on the common communication system should then generate a call to the owner and a response by security or law enforcement staff members.

Security Strategies for Tunnels

Tunnels are often high-profile routes of travel and even tourist attractions. The Lincoln and Holland Tunnels between New York City and New Jersey are an essential part of the commuting travel system for the region. North Carolina's Blue Ridge Parkway depends on a system of tunnels to carry travelers through the scenic Appalachian Mountains. Pennsylvania's Allegheny Mountain Tunnel goes under the Eastern Continental Divide. Tunnels are a potential choke point in the road system, offering a door from one region to the next. This makes them an attractive target for their economic value.

Additionally, tunnels may be an attractive site for a terrorist attack because they have limited access, creating a trapped group who become victims in the confined space. Tunnels often also carry communications lines, water lines, and other critical infrastructure, which can also be victimized in a tunnel attack. Because tunnels are underground or under water, they have limited surveillance points. Also, most tunnels change grade, making surveillance along the tunnel's route difficult.

Because underground tunnels have limited air exchange capacity, the introduction of fire or an inhalation hazard, including a chemical weapon, can quickly affect the occupants. Evacuating the victims is difficult, as most tunnels have limited shoulder capacity for breakdowns, and frightened or impacted drivers are more likely to have accidents that could block the lanes. It is equally difficult for first responders to get into the tunnel to conduct rescues because of the limited travel lanes. While car systems will filter some particulate matter from the air, they provide no protection against poisons or gasses, unless all vents are sealed with duct tape (American Red Cross, 2006).

The limited entry points to tunnels and the limited air exchange contribute to the difficulty of rescuing victims and mitigating damage in tunnel emergencies. While firefighters generally have air respirators that allow them to operate in confined spaces, few law enforcement officers have fully contained breathing apparatus. Most law enforcement agencies provide gas masks, which are effective in filtering particulate matter, but do not supply oxygen missing from the air and do not filter out all gasses.

The primary strategy for tunnel security is to deny access to potential perpetrators. For this reason some tunnels forbid the passage of hazardous materials, such as the Harbor Tunnel in Baltimore, Maryland. However, this may not be practical if an alternate route through the area is not available. Another strategy is to monitor the tunnel for any unusual behavior, such as a vehicle being abandoned in or near the tunnel. Such tactics are used by potential attackers to determine how long the response time will be for first responders in a real event.

Critical infrastructure owners may wish to monitor urban explorer websites to determine their marking styles so that they can observe if they have entered any potentially critical nodes or tunnel access points. For example, at each end, tunnels have air exchange facilities that may attract the curious as well as those planning to attack the tunnel.

Tunnels are often bored into rock. Grout and tie-backs are used to secure the surrounding loose rock. Tunnels can be blocked by damaging the tie-backs and destabilizing the loose natural material, causing it to slide down, blocking the entrance. Tunnels are also lined with tiles or suspended concrete panels, which can be destabilized in an explosion or by water intrusion, becoming missiles that can damage vehicles and their occupants. Poor workmanship or the use of improper adhesives can also lead to fatal tunnel ceiling failures, as in Boston's "Big Dig" Interstate 90 collapse of 2006 (Saltzman, 2009; NTSB, 2007).

When a tunnel is designed, using traditional construction methods will lead to a more robust finished product with more inherent resilience. However, old tunneling and finishing methods, like drilling through bedrock, are labor and time intensive and therefore costly. Even the old tunnels require sealing if below the water table. Currently, in order to keep to budget strictures, engineers often "push the envelope of design" to the minimum design standard, meaning that there is little excess capacity to absorb unexpected shocks. Tunnel construction may also make it more vulnerable to attack or accident.

Perpetrators need to evaluate the construction methods used to build the tunnel to understand how to create intentional damage that would close it long enough to generate economic harm. For example, the Big Dig tunnels in Boston were created in a channel that was dredged out of the bay bottom; precast sections of tunnel were placed in the channel and covered with natural material from the dredging. This means that the joints between tunnel sections present existing points of vulnerability to natural or human-caused disruption. For example, the joints are potentially vulnerable to leaks or to the effective placement of explosive charges. Even the older tunnel sealant methods may be susceptible to leaking in an explosives attack, but in bedrock, tunnels water intrusion at a joint failure is not a concern.

The design of an attack against a tunnel will be predicated on both the construction of the tunnel and on the access available to a perpetrator. A spot where someone can drill a hole and pack it with explosives unseen by security will enable a successful attack using few explosive materials. A timer may even permit the attacker to escape safely before the explosion. However, if robust surveillance prevents a prolonged attack procedure, a terrorist could place an adhesive charge against the tunnel wall as a car slows down briefly and, using a timed device, escape before the damaging explosion. The quantity of material needed for an external placement is much greater than for an internal placement, so the placement action itself and the presence of the device, appearing as an odd blob on the tunnel wall, might call attention to the action from other motorists or surveillance teams using cameras.

If there is no access to the tunnel wall, an even larger quantity of explosive material will be needed to be effective. For example, a VBIED would have to be parked in the travel lanes several feet away from the wall if there are barriers between travel lanes and shoulders and the wall itself. The Holland Tunnel is one such example, with a catwalk for the traffic officer in the tunnel creating a space with about 4 feet between the edge of the road surface and the tunnel wall. This approach to static security is known as creating a "standoff distance." A vehicle left in traffic will immediately draw attention from other motorists, roadway sensors, and cameras as the passage of surrounding traffic is impeded. This means that a rapid detonation would be required, probably needing a suicide perpetrator.

Tunnels also provide containment for large-scale explosives. The pressure wave from a blast would travel down the tunnel, covering a greater distance than in an uncontained environment, giving the tunnel a gun barrel effect. The overpressure wave traveling down the tunnel is lethal to humans, damaging the brain, ear drums, and internal organs. A good example of such an event is the blast wave contained in the London underground tunnel in the 2005 bombings.

Because tunnels are natural choke points, the approaches are restricted and easier to monitor than open roads. Fewer assets are required for surveillance of tunnel entrances, but the difficulty lies in being able to understand the contents of every vehicle going into the tunnel. VBIEDs seldom display external characteristics that differ from commercial freight carriers. Therefore, some tunnels that have been evaluated as especially vulnerable to terrorist attack have had portal monitors installed that detect radiation or chemical signatures. For example, New York City's tunnels have radiation detectors, license plate readers, and closed-circuit television cameras for surveillance of vehicles entering Manhattan. License plate numbers and photos of the drivers are matched by computer to a database of suspect vehicles and people as an early warning against VBIED and other attacks (Lanzano, 2008).

Surveillance inside the tunnels is an effective way of preventing any physical attack against the tunnel fabric. Because the lighting system is controlled and relatively constant throughout the 24-hour cycle, cameras can be managed effectively to monitor the passage of traffic and note unusual activity, such as stopped cars in the travel lanes or cars parked on the shoulder. If the cameras are monitored in real time and backed up with a rapid response team, traffic disruptions can be minimized and attacks interdicted. Similarly, road surface sensors can detect the regular passage of traffic at expected speeds, and slowing can then trigger a human observation of the cameras and the dispatch of an appropriate response, whether a tow truck or a response team.

Security Strategies for Bridges

Because bridges are over large, open areas, security for the structure poses several problems. Wear and tear on the structure create a constant demand for structure painting and road surface repairs and the need for regular bridge inspections. All of these activities take place within the bridge's most vulnerable areas. Vehicles pass over it and often under it, creating the threat of VBIED use, ramming, and vandalism, while making it difficult to limit access to the structure (Figure 5.6).

Prevention of accidental damage is best accomplished through safety devices. Bridge supports should have reflective paint in areas where vehicles travel close by, and shoulders should be maintained to increase the standoff distance between traffic and structure. In a marine environment, channel markers and buoys must be maintained in good repair. The Golden Gate Bridge in San Francisco also has fog horns to guide mariners.

As with tunnels, surveillance is the best method for protecting the bridge. Open spaces should be maintained free of weeds and debris that could hide explosive devices and provide a well-lighted, clear view for surveillance cameras. Access to bridge support structures should be limited through the use of reinforced fences and intrusion alarm systems, lighting, and cameras, if the threat level justifies the additional costs.

FIGURE 5.6 Hanshin-Awaji Bridge with commuter train.

Exclusion areas should be obvious in order to draw attention to any activities within them, making it more likely that bridge users will "see something and say something."

Inspection points for the bridge should be secured and accessible only to bridge maintenance personnel. All of the surveillance devices are only beneficial if they are backed up by a rapid response. This means that cameras and alarm systems must be staffed, including capability to summon a rapid law enforcement team.

Security Strategies for Cars and Trucks

Cars and trucks move over roads in no predictable patterns. Their freedom of movement makes providing security for the vehicle itself a challenge. It also means that interdicting attacks based on cars and trucks is very difficult.

Crime Prevention

Owners worry that their cars or trucks will be stolen. Manufacturers have created a series of systems to make the vehicle more difficult to steal, such as door locks and steering wheel locks. Manufacturers have to provide information on how to overcome these systems so that tow company operators, car repossessors, and individuals engaged in similar legal activities can do their jobs.

More recently, GM has installed OnStar in its cars to make it easy to trace them. Introduced as a consumer safety device to summon help in an emergency, OnStar also allows the car's engine to be remotely started or shut off and the car's location to be tracked. These systems can be viewed as providing added security to an owner in distress or as an added law enforcement tool for retrieving a stolen vehicle or a vehicle involved in a crime.

Roadside assistance phones have been provided along highways to allow stranded motorists to summon help. With the ubiquitous cell phone, these phones may be less important, except in rural and mountainous areas with spotty cell coverage. While many cellular phone systems have adopted technology that identifies their locations through GIS, not all law enforcement agencies can discern the location of the cell phone caller. Even with 9-1-1 systems, the call site may come back to the billing address. The roadside phones have cable technology to carry the signal regardless of the isolation of the location, and when the phone is used, its location is immediately identified to the operator answering the calls, which speeds emergency response.

Additional vehicle security features are routinely purchased by owners, with varying degrees of functionality and success. One popular steering wheel lock was "The Club." The problem was that the softest part of the automobile is the steering wheel. Tin snips or bolt cutters could be used to cut and bend the steering wheel so that the Club could be removed. Other devices are designed to interrupt the ignition system and are tied to an alarm, while some use proximity to sense the presence of an unauthorized person near the vehicle and set off an alarm. Generally, systems that are designed to produce noise are relying on someone in the immediate area to summon law enforcement. Unfortunately, car alarm malfunctions or alarms set off by loud exhaust systems have become so commonplace that bystanders seldom call for help. Systems that interrupt the ignition or fuel of the vehicle, thereby immobilizing it, are the most effective means of preventing unauthorized use.

Cars often have a variety of registration and access stickers on their exteriors. These may include parking and access permits for military bases and corporate facilities. These stickers can be the primary target for thieves and terrorists. Drivers should install as many of the stickers as possible inside the vehicle to enhance their security. For those that must be installed on the outside, like license plate renewal stickers, a razor blade should be used to score the sticker after it is installed so that it could only be removed in strips, making it useless to thieves.

Owners should also be careful that they do not provide access to personal information through the exposure of personal items in the car. For example, mail left in plain sight will provide the name and address of the vehicle's owner, and the thief can easily tie it to the car license plate and access stickers. This knowledge can be useful in obtaining additional information about the owner or in gaining unlawful access to locations covered by the stickers.

Drivers should also be situationally aware when approaching their vehicles, having their keys in hand, ready to open the door, and scanning the area for strangers or anyone paying unusual attention to their progress toward the car. Anyone finding himself or herself in a situation that feels threatening should return to the last building he or she occupied and contact local security or law enforcement for assistance.

Cars and Trucks as a Platform for Attack

Cars and trucks are ubiquitous in the United States. Obtaining a vehicle to be used as a platform for a VBIED is as simple as purchasing or renting the vehicle. Cars offer easy mobility, even on narrow streets, and are likely to draw less attention. Anyone with a driver's license can drive a car. Trucks, however, offer a more attractive platform for a bomb because of their ability to carry more weight. Because there are so many varieties of truck operating systems—transmissions, brakes, cargo space access systems—not everyone can drive one. Their size makes moving through crowded city streets harder, requiring some practice.

VBIEDs are not new. The first recognized incident of use of a VBIED occurred on Wall Street on September 16, 1920, in an incident known as "Buda's Wagon." An anarchist loaded his horse-drawn wagon with 100 pounds of dynamite and 500 pounds of scrap iron (Watson, 2007) and detonated it across the street from J. P. Morgan Bank at 23 Wall Street. Thirty-eight people were killed and a hundred more were injured, and there was $2 million in property damage ($23 million adjusted for inflation) (Davis, 2007).

While VBIED attacks have been used intermittently since the 1920 incident, it has become the weapon of choice for terrorist groups in recent years. The most famous American incident is the bombing of the Murrah Federal Building in Oklahoma City in 1995, but a VBIED was also used in the first World Trade Center bombing in 1993. The VBIED has become synonymous with the war in Iraq and has been used widely in the Chechen wars. The reason for its popularity is the availability of explosives, the understanding of the explosives train, and the widespread use of vehicles. The only limiting factors are the size of the vehicles, the amount of explosives, and the expertise of the individual putting the device together. For those lacking the necessary information, videos on YouTube clearly demonstrate how to make a variety of explosive devices, although the finger stumps of one bomb maker should be cautionary.

Triggering mechanisms can be timed via a burning fuse or an electrical device, like alarm clocks, cell phones, garage door openers, and remote control devices for toys. Run-down devices rely on a battery to hold the switch open and then detonate when the battery loses its power and the switch closes. The knowledge of the bomb designer is the only limitation to the switch design, as anyone with a rudimentary understanding of electrical circuitry would be able to grasp the concept of closing the switch to activate an electrical detonator.

Concealment of the explosive materials in the vehicles is limited only by the designer's imagination. Filling hollow door panels, seat cavities where stuffing and springs were removed, and the spare tire with explosives would all result in a car that would appear innocent in a visual inspection, but may contain several hundred pounds of explosives. Trucks are less consistent in design and therefore offer more potential hiding places for explosive materials. The only limitation on the amount of explosives used would be the ability of the suspension system to hold up under the increased weight of the explosive materials. Overload springs can be used to compensate in cars, allowing the vehicle to contain over 1,000 pounds of explosives. Trucks can be rated to carry tons of material, so weight limitations are fewer.

Terrorists want to increase the lethality of the VBIED. Upon detonation with a normal car or truck, the body panels and components of the vehicle will provide the fragmentation effect. This, however, is not the best use of the explosive resources. Additional shrapnel built into the car door panels in front of the explosives will create more of a Claymore mine effect, increasing the lethality of the vehicle. Nuts and bolts, BBs, and glass marbles have been favorites in Southwest Asia. Adding metal pieces would decrease the weight of explosives that could be carried in the car due to the weight of the metal, but increase the bomb's lethality several fold.

Because cars and trucks of all sizes are used every day, they are not perceived by most people as a potential threat. It is only after several bombings involving vehicles that people become suspicious. For example, after pictures of the Oklahoma City bombing showed a yellow Ryder rental truck parked near the building just before the explosion, the presence of Ryder rental trucks drew suspicion, causing them to change the color scheme of their rental vehicles from the yellow associated with the Murrah Building bombing to white.

Security Strategies for Trucks With Hazardous Cargo

Trucks carrying hazardous cargo provide yet another challenge for security. While their drivers are better trained and identified through the TSA's transportation worker identification credential and their routes are often dictated by law, hijacking and interdiction are still possible. Trucks with hazardous cargo in the long-haul trade are especially vulnerable during rest stops and sleep breaks. The driver may be asleep in the truck or in a motel room. The hijackers can tow the truck away, defeat the door locks and ignition locks, and drive the truck away, or force the driver to take the truck to their destination of choice.

Crime Prevention

Crime prevention systems for hazardous materials trucks are similar to those used in cars and commercial trucks. Door locks and steering wheel locks slow down a potential thief. Systems similar to OnStar enable the company to track the progress of the truck to its destination and to turn off the ignition if it goes significantly off course.

In 1998 the American Trucking Association developed a mutual aid surveillance system called Highway Watch, funded through the Department of Homeland Security (DHS), which started in 2002. In 2008 it was renamed

First Observers and moved into DHS's Trucking Security Program (TSP) (firstobservertrainthetrainer.com, 2010). The training is designed to enhance the awareness of toll takers, road repair crews, bus drivers, and truck drivers regarding the potential for safety, security, and terrorist threats using the highways (Poovey, 2009).

Truckers call 1-888-217-5902 to report suspicious, dangerous, or unusual activity to the central call center in Alexandria, Virginia. Appropriate law enforcement or other support is sent to the site. The information is loaded into a database for additional investigation by the Information Sharing and Analysis Center (ISAC) (First Observer Call Center, 2008).

Terrorism Prevention

Trucks moving hazardous cargo have long been placarded for the safety of first responders, making the materials being carried obvious. The U.S. Department of Transportation publishes the *Emergency Response Guidebook,* which decodes the placards and provides detailed information about the characteristics of the hazardous materials, including their explosive and incendiary aspects (Figure 5.7). The 2008 edition is available online (U.S. DOT, 2008). After 9/11 there was concern that this information would attract terrorists seeking bomb-making components to steal or hijack trucks.

FIGURE 5.7 Trucks carrying hazardous materials move along the I-5 corridor over the Lake Shasta Bridge.

In 2003 amendments to the Department of Transportation's (DOT) hazardous materials rules required that organizations moving hazardous materials that could be precursors to the production of explosive materials or otherwise attractive to terrorists had to create a security plan and provide security awareness training to all their employees (Deitz, 2011). DOT also created a risk assessment tool for companies to use in the development of their security plans (http://hazmat.dot.gov/rmsef.htm).

As mentioned before, placarding allows criminals to easily identify bomb making precursors in transit, which may make them attractive targets for hijacking or theft. Placarded tankers might contain diesel fuel, peroxide, acetone, chlorine, or other common chemicals that can be used to create explosives. The FBI and the Department of Homeland Security's Office for Bombing Prevention have developed the Bomb-Making Materials Awareness Program (BMAP) to educate wholesale, retail, and transportation companies about the importance of security for products that are bomb material precursors (DHS, 2010).

Researchers have reviewed other safety systems available to truckers. One idea was to install panic alarms that would transmit a distress signal to a central location. While useful in concept, the question arises as to who would respond to the distress signal. Research from the Mineta Transportation Institute considered a variety of issues, including the involvement of first responders and the assumption of the costs created by the response. Consequences of a false alarm were also reviewed (Jenkins, Butterworth, & Edwards, 2010).

The Department of Defense has long tracked its shipments of arms and ammunition, and commercial truck operators are benefiting from the efficiencies gained through the use of GPS technologies to create more efficient routes and better use of personnel. These systems also enhance the security of the materials being transported by making estimates of expected routes and arrival times so that shipments that have gone off the plan can be quickly identified and tracked.

With the availability of satellite communications technology, onboard security systems for trucks have become more sophisticated. One example is the Astrata Box, which allows the industry to provide protection for drivers and their loads through integrating GPS tracking, wireless communication, and a Linux-based computer system. The box can be programmed to require the driver to pass a breathalyzer test and provide a thumbprint before starting the truck. Cameras watch inside the cab. If the truck is speeding or veers off course, it can be remotely slowed to 5 mph or stopped completely. The device will lock the doors to prevent a thief from fleeing and can sound the horn and flash the lights to warn other drivers of a truck in distress (Russo, 2007).

Platforms for Attack

Hazardous materials trucks have many of the same characteristics as standard load trucks. Their size and complex safety systems make it even more difficult for an untrained operator to drive the vehicle. However, their loads of hazardous materials potentially make them extremely attractive for use in either developing explosives or serving as a weapon. As early as September 2002, the FBI was warning law enforcement agencies that tanker trucks of hazardous materials and petroleum fuel depots were potential targets for terrorist thefts (policeone.com, 2002).

A tanker truck loaded with a hazardous material can be used as a rolling bomb. The tanker can be stolen and parked on a railroad track to cause a fiery derailment or driven into a hazardous materials storage facility to create a deadly witches' brew of an unknown chemical mixture. In Tunisia in 2002, a truck loaded with propane was detonated next to a synagogue. In 2004 a fuel truck was used to burn down a section of Baghdad during Defense Secretary Donald Rumsfeld's visit (Clayton, 2006).

Unfortunately, the theft of tanker trucks is not unusual and is not always associated with terrorism. For example, in September 2011 when the price of gasoline was high, a tanker truck with 3,000 gallons of gasoline worth $12,000 was stolen in Maryland and taken to Philadelphia. While investigation suggested that this was a commodity theft for profit, the tanker truck was considered a possible terrorist asset while it was missing. One unique feature of the case was the success of a cell phone application in alerting the police officer to the theft just at the time when he was in the vicinity of the stolen vehicle, which led to its recovery (ABC News, 2011).

Just a few days earlier, on September 9, 2011, an empty tanker truck was stolen in rural Kern County, California, and then used to steal 2,400 gallons of diesel from a storage tank on a ranch (taftmidwaydriller.com). Because diesel fuel is a component of the explosive ANFO (ammonium nitrate and fuel oil), its theft so close to the 10th anniversary of the 9/11 attacks caused concern.

Case Studies

Obtaining Explosives for VBIEDs

Over 5 billion pounds of explosives are used in the United States annually (Davis, 2003) for mining, construction, and similar industrial applications. That is 2.5 million tons. The remote locations of many of these industrial production and mining sites means that the owners perceive that the general public and would-be thieves have no knowledge of the availability of explosive materials. Therefore, the security for stored explosives is often primarily through obscurity—meaning that they are not readily visible from public areas. Frequently, only some fencing and a padlock prevent access to the material.

For example, the County of San Mateo's Sheriff's Department had an explosives storage bunker in a remote hillside area, whose security relied primarily on its obscurity. The materials were confiscated explosives, training materials, or explosives used to destroy dangerous chemicals, pipe bombs, and similar threats. The bunker contained county property, materials belonging to the city of San Francisco, and also explosive materials belonging to the FBI (Lee, 2005). In addition to locks and fences, there was an alarm system, and a sheriff's patrol beat was supposed to include the site, but budget cutbacks had led to fewer patrols to the remote location and poor maintenance of the alarm, leading to a failure of the system.

In 2004 on the Fourth of July weekend the explosives locker was broken into, resulting in the theft of 200 pounds not only of county materials, but also of those of a federal agency. The thief defeated the heavy-duty fencing and locks with an acetylene torch as his "key" (Kim, 2004). The obscure location and loss of regular sheriff's patrols provided adequate time for the crime. While these explosives were later recovered, many tons go missing each year.

Timothy McVeigh, the Oklahoma City bomber, used stolen explosives to build his VBIED. The ANFO charge, which is generally the main explosive described in Oklahoma City bombing articles, required significant booster explosives to initiate its detonation. McVeigh and accomplice Terry Nichols stole 18 crates of Tovex, 18 spools of shock tube, and 500 electric blasting caps that were used in the Ryder truck bomb from a quarry in Kansas (Michael & Herbeck, 2001).

Explosives are difficult to track because of the open environment in which they are used. Stolen and missing explosives are often not reported because the owners fear loss of their licenses for violations of the strict federal requirements for storage, security, and record keeping (Stolz, 2007). Some are reported by employees as being used in production but are actually misappropriated and sold on the black market for a profit. A taggant is added to plastic explosives to help track them through airports and other sensitive portals. However, due to cost and safety issues, taggants are not added generally to commercial explosives.

The Institute of Makers of Explosives notes that both Oklahoma City and the 1993 World Trade Center bombing were perpetrated with homemade, not commercial, explosives (IME, 2006), referring to the ammonium nitrate fertilizer and nitro methane that were the majority of the bomb materials in Oklahoma City, although prepared ANFO was also used (Michael & Herbeck, 2001). A few years later, a major theft of ANFO from a mining site in northwest Arizona drew the attention of the Bureau of Alcohol Tobacco and

Fire Arms (Stolz, 2007). In June 2011 ABC News noted that in 2010 there were 31,000 pounds of ANFO stolen in the United States (Thomas, 2011).

Water Pipes Destroy the San Jose Transit Mall

In 1992 the city of San Jose had a new light rail system that included a transit mall in the downtown area. On Columbus Day weekend an emergency call was made to Fire Dispatch reporting that the transit mall was collapsing. Light rail operations were suspended and emergency response personnel went to the scene to try to determine the cause of the failure. As-built designs showed no void under the transit mall.

Upon arrival, the fire personnel saw rainbows floating on the surface of water that was gushing down the gutters and into a storm drain that flowed to Coyote Creek and the San Francisco Bay. Recognizing this as a sign of the presence of petroleum products, they sandbagged the storm drain and tried to find the source of the water. Calls to utilities using the transit mall for their pipes and conduit revealed that the private water company that served the area had been pressure testing the system and apparently had a significant leak. Soon 9-1-1 was getting calls that phone service in the area was disrupted.

A door-to-door search of the area led to the discovery that one building on the transit mall had a basement that contained an old fuel oil tank unused for years after conversion to natural gas heat. The broken water pipe had flooded the basement, permitting water to enter the fuel storage tank and rehydrate the old oil residue, which flowed out with the water and into the street, creating the petroleum rainbows. It was also discovered that conduit in the street carried the telephone lines, which had been laid while the mall was under construction. The phone company had backfilled its trench with sand to provide a flexible support for the phone line conduit in an earthquake and to support the street's surface weight. The rushing water carried away the sand, exposing the telephone conduit and leaving the street without support, permitting the collapse under the weight of the light rail tracks.

Summary

Roads are the backbone of the American economy, carrying workers in their cars and commodities in trucks throughout the continental nation. Roads run through open rural areas and congested urban environments, each of which creates its own security challenges. Cameras and road sensors extend the reach of surveillance over long distances, provided that they are staffed by attentive monitors and backed up by a rapid law enforcement response.

Tanker trucks of hazardous materials pose a special risk of theft because of their value to terrorist bomb makers. Onboard security systems may deter or prevent theft, but protecting the driver from hijacking is more complex.

Transportation security is enhanced by the involvement of all the users of the roads. The First Observer program brings toll takers, road repair crews, and bus and truck drivers into a mutual aid surveillance network. The BMAP program incorporated storage and wholesale and retail outlets into the prevention program through a heightened awareness of the value of commodities to terrorists.

Fee-for-service carriers of passengers face different challenges in using the road system. The management of vehicle and passenger security is the subject of the next chapter.

Discussion Questions

1. Describe the security vulnerabilities of road transportation systems. What technologies can be used to overcome these vulnerabilities?

2. How can construction methods, security methods, and technologies be integrated to enhance the security of roads, bridges, and tunnels?

3. How does the road system integrate other critical infrastructure of the community? What are those critical infrastructure elements? How do they relate to a road security plan?

4. You are the security director for a large retailer that gets most of its goods from overseas. Your EOC regularly monitors highway conditions for weather-related emergencies. What kinds of security issues would you have to include in a security plan for your organization?

5. You are the security director for a state highway system. You are about to build a new bridge over a ship channel. What security concerns would you have for the new bridge, and what strategies and technologies would you use to address them?

References

ABC News. (2011, September 14). Officer uses 6ABC app to identify stolen tanker truck. http://abclocal.go.com/wpvi/story?section = news/crime&id = 8353871

American Red Cross. (2006). Shelter-in-place during a chemical or radiation emergency. Accessed November 11, 2011, from http://www.redcross.org/preparedness/cdc_english/Sheltering.asp#vehicle

Bollo, M. E., Mahan, S. A., Moehle, J. P., Stephen, R. M., & Qi, X. (1990). Observations and implications of tests on the Cypress Street viaduct test structure. Earthquake Engineering Research Center, University of California at Berkeley, UCB/EERC-90/21.

Bridge Conference. (2006). Bridge construction Europe. Ponte Vecchio. http://www.bridgeconference2006.com/?q = node/76

Cabanatuan, M. (2007, May 24) I-580 reopens. *San Francisco Chronicle.* http://www.sfgate.com/cgi-bin/article.cgi?f =/c/a/2007/05/24/BAG2GQ1BD111.DTL

Caltrans. (2011). Self-anchored suspension span. San Francisco-Oakland Bay Bridge seismic safety projects. http://baybridgeinfo.org/projects/sas

Clayton, M. (2006, July 7). Hazardous materials trucks: Terror threat? *Christian Science Monitor.*

Davis, M. (2007). *Buda's wagon.* London, England: Verso.

Davis, W. C. (2003). Introduction to explosives. In J. A. Zukas & W. Walters (Eds.), *Explosive effects and applications.* New York, NY: Springer Verlag.

Deitz, H. (2011). *Special report: U.S. DOT hazardous materials security plan rules, September 2003.* https://www.nrca.net/rp/safety/specrpt/0903_hazmat.aspx

DHS (Department of Homeland Security). (2010). Bomb-making materials awareness program. http://www.dhs.gov/files/programs/gc_1259938444548.shtm

FBI. (2008). First strike: Global terror in America. http://www.fbi.gov/news/stories/2008/february/tradebom_022608

FHWA (Federal Highway Administration. (2010, May). Interstate maintenance discretionary program information. http://www.fhwa.dot.gov/discretionary/imdinfo.cfm

Feldman, B. J. (2003, February). What to say about the Tacoma Narrows Bridge to your introductory physics class. *Physics Teacher, 41,* 92–96.

First Observer Call Center, Transportation Security Administration. (2008). http://firstobserver.com/callcenter.php

Firstobservertrainthetrainer.com. (2010). First observer train the trainer.

Gledhill, L., Lucas, G., Martin, M., & Squatriglia, C. (2001, January 17). Truck rams capitol/legislators' narrow escape. *San Francisco Chronicle,* p. A1.

Hartnett, B. (2011). New induction and plasma lighting technologies proven superior to LED for street lighting and high lumen applications. Deco Lighting. http://getdeco.com/products/plasma

IME (Institute of Makers of Explosives). (2006). Taggants in explosives. http://www.ime.org/files/Issue%20Briefs/Taggants%20In%20Explosives.pdf

Jenkins, B. M., Butterworth, B., & Edwards, F. L. (2010). *Implementation and development of vehicle tracking and immobilization technologies.* San Jose, CA: Mineta Transportation Institute. http://transweb.sjsu.edu/mtiportal/research/publications/summary/MTI-0904.html

Kim, R. (2004, July 9). Budget cuts left cops' weapons storage depot accessible. *San Francisco Chronicle.* http://articles.sfgate.com/2004-07-09/bay-area/17435050_1_explosives-depot-surveillance-cameras

Lanzano, L. (2008, September 9). NYPD transformed since Sept. 11. *USA Today.* http://www.usatoday.com/news/nation/2008-09-09-nypd-changes_N.htm?csp=34

Lee, H. K. (2005, February 2). 37-Month sentence in explosives case. *San Francisco Chronicle.* http://articles.sfgate.com/2005-02-05/bay-area/17359844_1_explosives-san-mateo-county-possessing

Michael, L., & Herbeck, D. (2001). *American terrorist.* New York, NY: Harper.

National Terrorism Preparedness Institute. (2008, May). *Tunnel vulnerability assessment: Best practices guide.* St. Petersburg, FL: St. Petersburg College.

NTSB. (2007). Ceiling collapse in the Interstate 90 connector tunnel, Boston, Massachusetts, July 10, 2006. http://www.ntsb.gov/doclib/reports/2007/har0702.pdf.

NTSB. (2008). *Collapse of I-35W highway bridge, Minneapolis, Minnesota, August 1, 2007: Accident report* (NTSB/HAR 08/03, PB 2008 916203). http://www.dot.state.mn.us/i35wbridge/ntsb/finalreport.pdf

Onaga, K. (2012, March 28). SJ city council paves way for road repairs. *San Jose Mercury News,* B-1.

Policeone.com. (2002). FBI warns law enforcement to be on the lookout for stolen fuel tanker trucks. http://www.policeone.com/terrorism/articles/52570-FBI-Warns-Law-Enforcement-to-Be-on-the-Lookout-for-Stolen-Fuel-Tanker-Trucks/

Poovey, B. (2009, February 6). Government enlists truck drivers in DHS anti-terror program. www.securityinfowatch.com

Roads and bridges. (2008, December). NTSB releases report on I-35W bridge collapse.

Roadtraffic-technology.com. (2011) Sutong Bridge, Jiangsu Province. http://www.roadtraffic-technology.com/projects/sutong/

Russo, F. (2007). The hijack-proof truck. *CNN Money.* http://money.cnn.com/2007/10/03/technology/hijack_proof_truck.biz2/index.htm

Sacramento Area Council of Governments. (2010). MTP2035 issue papers: Road maintenance. http://www.sacog.org/mtp/pdf/MTP2035/Issue%20Papers/Road%20Maintenance.pdf

Saltzman, J. (2009, May 8) Big Dig contractor Modern Continental pleads guilty. *Boston Globe.*

Starmer, C. F. (2007). Changing the face of Charleston: Building of the Arthur Ravenel, Jr. Bridge. http://ravenelbridge.net/

Stolz, M. (2007, March 10). Explosives are missing from mine in Arizona. *New York Times.* http://query.nytimes.com/gst/fullpage.html?res=9E07E2DB1331F933A25750C0A9619C8B63

Sundial Bridge. (2009). http://www.turtlebay.org/sundialbridge

Taftmidwaydriller.com. (2011, September 9). Stolen truck used to steal diesel fuel. http://www.taftmidwaydriller.com/news/x219212363/Stolen-truck-used-to-steal-diesel-fuel

Technical Support Working Group. (2006, June). *Best practices for identifying potential threats to bridges.* Arlington, VA: Technical Support Working Group.

Thomas, P. (2011, June 19). Tons of explosives routinely disappear. *ABC News.* http://abcnews.go.com/WNT/story?id=130286&page=1

Tierney, K. (2010). Closing speech delivered at the Natural Hazards Conference, July 13, 2010, Broomfield, CO.

U.S.-Canada Power System Outage Task Force. (2004). *Final report on the August 14, 2003 blackout in the United States and Canada: Causes and recommendations.* https://reports.energy.gov/BlackoutFinal-Web.pdf

U.S. DOT. ITS Joint Program Office. (2002, April 22). *Effect of catastrophic events on transportation system management and operations, Northridge earthquake, January 17, 1994.* Cambridge, MA: Volpe National Transportation Systems Center.

U.S. DOT. (2008). *Emergency response guidebook.* http://www.phmsa.dot.gov/staticfiles/PHMSA/DownloadableFiles/Files/erg2008_eng.pdf

Walsh, J., Randazzo, R., & D'Anna, J. (2011, July 1). SRP fire affects 100,000 homes and businesses. *Arizona Republic,* p. 1.

Watson, B. (2007). *Sacco and Vanzetti: The men, the murders, and the judgment of mankind.* New York, NY: Viking Press.

Chapter **6**

Road-Based Busses, Livery, Paratransit, Ambulances, and Delivery Vehicles

Keywords: busses, limousines, taxis, paratransit, ambulances, delivery services, terrorism, IED, VBIED, suspicious packages, suicide bombers, risk assessment, security, transportation, smuggling, illicit goods, human trafficking

Learning Objectives

After reading this chapter you should be able to

- Identify potential vulnerabilities in scheduled road-based transit
- Understand how road system use generates vulnerabilities
- Understand the role of vehicle storage systems in security
- Understand the importance of security planning, training, and exercising
- Understand the strategies used by terrorists and criminals to disrupt transit

Components of Road-Based Transit and Delivery Systems

In the last chapter, the components of the highway system were described. The same roads, bridges, and tunnels may serve mass transit and delivery companies, as well as individual cars and trucks. While cars and trucks, intercity busses, and delivery vehicles may operate on roads in rural areas with open spaces between populated communities, mass transit systems are most often operating in urban and suburban settings marked by congestion and anonymity induced by high concentrations of population.

Chapter 5 addressed the road system and its components and the individually operated cars and trucks that use the road system. These vehicles were characterized by driver-based decisions as to route and exact timing of trips. This chapter deals with another set of vehicles that use the roads but have predetermined routes, or timed and tracked routes, often using global positioning systems (GPS) to determine routes and automatic vehicle locator systems (AVLSs) to track a vehicle's location. The use and location of the for-hire, mass transit, ambulance, and delivery vehicles contribute to both their vulnerability to attack and their potential for use as vehicle-borne explosive devices (VBIEDs) because they are ubiquitous and therefore invisible in urban settings.

Busses form the backbone of urban mass transit, operating in large and small communities and providing access to rural areas unavailable by other mass transit. In 2008 there were 845,308 busses of all types serving transportation needs (U.S. DOT, 2011, p. 12). By 2008 mass transit, commercial, federal, and school busses drove 7,114,000 miles (U.S. DOT, 2011, p. 15), operating 150,827,000 passenger miles (U.S. DOT, 2011, p. 16). In 2009 over two million passengers crossed from Mexico into the United States by bus, and another two million passengers crossed from Canada (U.S. DOT, 2011, pp. 19–20).

Threats to Busses, Livery, Ambulances, Paratransit, and Delivery Systems

In November of 2011, on the eve of its 10th anniversary, the Transit Security Administration (TSA) issued a bulletin in preparation for the holiday season, Terrorist Concerns Regarding Mass Transit Bus Systems. It warned that "[b]uses remain an attractive terrorist target due to their open architecture and accessibility for use by millions of travelers" (McCarter, 2011). The timing was based on the knowledge that millions more people travel by bus than air during the holiday season. TSA Administrator John Pistole noted that Al Qaeda in the Arabian Peninsula had plotted to attack American mass transit. Through its magazine *Inspire,* it urged followers to hijack busses to use as weapons against crowds, buildings, and infrastructure (McCarter, 2011).

Mass Transit Busses

Mass transit includes two types of busses: intracity and intercity busses. Busses are attractive targets because they operate in open areas where security is difficult and they carry a number of people in a confined space (TRB, 2008). Internationally, busses have been targeted by terrorist groups in countries where bus travel is the primary means of transportation. While attacks against busses in Israel are probably the best known in the United States, India, Russia, Turkey, Sri Lanka, Pakistan, and the Philippines have also experienced terrorist attacks against busses, perpetrated by both religious and secular terror groups (Jenkins, Butterworth, & Schrum, 2010).

Intercity busses are also operated by private companies that provide sightseeing services and transportation services to tourists. They are also contracted by large companies in metropolitan areas to provide their employees with easy access to work each day. For example, Apple in Cupertino, California, contracts for daily commuter service for its employees from several locations in San Francisco, Alameda County, and Santa Cruz County. Genentech, located in San Mateo County, provides daily commuter services for its employees from Santa Cruz County, Santa Clara County, and Alameda County. Whether the busses contain tourists or scientists and engineers, an attack leading to the disruption of the service and injury to passengers would have a significant economic effect on the area. Loss of workers could hinder product development and production. Loss of tourists could cause financial losses for hotels and sites of interest.

Internationally, 41.55% of all attacks against surface transportation are against busses (Jenkins et al., 2010, p. 19). Data collected by Jenkins et al. show that, since 2009, there have been 684 attacks against busses worldwide, of which 439 used explosive materials. They note, moreover, that busses provide desirable terrorist targets because terrorists can "with high confidence, achieve a death toll of 25 to 50" (p. 13). While no U.S. busses have been terrorist targets, Jenkins et al. note that international attacks have provided the terrorists with "an extensive playbook of [successful] attacks against public surface transportation" (p. 13), so such attacks in the United States are possible.

Intracity busses are generally operated by mass transit agencies and serve specific communities on specified routes with operating schedules. Passengers pay their fares with cash or tokens or sometimes with monthly or annual passes purchased in machines, making the passenger untraceable. The busses are generally crowded during rush hour, meaning that individual passengers may not be noticed, and packages are less noticeable when carried onto the vehicle and left behind (Figure 6.1). Therefore, bombs in packages can be left behind with a timer or carried aboard by a suicide bomber, as in London on July 7, 2005, when a double-decker bus was attacked. While routes with regular passengers might offer the chance that a stranger would

FIGURE 6.1 Backpack left behind in a transit vehicle.

be noticed boarding the bus, it is unlikely that anyone would notice a stranger on an intracity bus because random riders are also common.

Intercity busses generally operate on a prepaid fare system and cost more per trip than intracity busses. Passengers buy their tickets in a terminal or a shop that acts as a bus stop and are more likely to use credit cards to buy them, which could make those passengers traceable. However, those using cash are generally not required to show identification and can give any name for the checked luggage tag. Because the stops are less frequent, passengers are likely to wait in the bus stop area and may be photographed on a routine commercial surveillance camera. However, terminals and bus stops may be crowded, and experienced criminals are likely to avoid identification by wearing sunglasses and a hat or consciously keeping their faces turned away from the camera.

Passengers are able to take more luggage on the intercity bus, and some of it is stored in the hold below the passenger seating area. Because baggage is not routinely scanned for weapons or explosives, an improvised explosive device (IED) could be included in luggage. Passengers can also exit at any stop and leave their luggage behind, meaning that a timed IED can be placed in luggage in the hold and abandoned, detonating by a timer or cell phone after the bomber has left the vehicle (Figure 6.2).

While a bus bombing is not likely to kill many people, it has tremendous disruptive effect in an urban setting. The Israeli experience suggests that in addition to killing several dozen people on the bus, a bus bomb releases shrapnel and flying glass that will kill or injure people on the sidewalk and even in buildings along the street. It can set fire to adjacent structures as the flaming gasoline or diesel fuel runs down the street and can cause secondary explosions by entering storm drains and sewer systems and igniting gasses trapped there.

FIGURE 6.2   Tool box bomb on a transit vehicle.

Busses are also used for the movement of contraband items, including human trafficking. Void spaces in the vehicle may be used, such as the inside of door panels, quarter panels, underneath the vehicle, and areas like spare tire wells and gas tanks that can yield additional space. These techniques date back to the Greeks and the Trojan horse. The only limitations are the physical restrictions of the vehicles, the physical characteristics of the items being smuggled, and the imagination of the person designing the hiding space. This presupposes that the smuggler who is designing the hiding space has unlimited time to develop the concealment. In many instances, limited access and limited time are available, which may make the design and execution of the concealment more difficult.

Livery and Medical Vehicles

Taxis are used by anonymous passengers. Especially in urban settings, cabs are hailed on the street; the passenger rides a short distance and then alights, paying the fare in cash. Likewise, limousines may be used by an anonymous individual using a false name who summons a limo to an apartment building or office building with many occupants. Passengers may carry parcels, briefcases, and other small luggage in the seating area. Larger bags may be placed in the trunk. Either offers the opportunity for a suicide bomber to transport an IED that can cause havoc in a congested urban setting.

Limousines are often used by people going to airports or train stations, justifying a large amount of luggage. Such trips may include travel through tunnels, over bridges, and on crowded roadways. A taxi or limousine carrying an IED that was detonated in a tunnel could create further death and disruption because it is in an enclosed space and surrounded by tanks full of gasoline. If the explosive wave ruptured gas tanks or set off a fire, the results could be catastrophic, as noted in the discussion of tunnels in Chapter 5. Detonation on a busy highway could have immediate destructive consequences for the other vehicles and the road surface, and it could possibly impact urban circulation patterns for hours to days. Detonation on a bridge might damage the road surface and close a bridge for extended periods for repair.

Ambulances and paratransit vehicles are used by people with limited mobility who have casts, wheelchairs, and cylinders of medical gasses— all of which offer opportunities for concealment of IEDs. These rides must be scheduled in advance, and the origin and destination are known, but they have access to parking spaces adjacent to sensitive areas of hospitals and medical care facilities, making them attractive for terrorist bombers. Vehicles in legitimate use could be scheduled by suicide bombers for supposed relatives with functional and access limitations for a trip to the hospital or medical center to ensure close-proximity delivery of an IED. Oxygen cylinders could be placed in the vehicle without question and become part of a large bomb. Other bomb components could be hidden in casts, wheelchairs, satchels, and personal support equipment.

Ambulance and paratransit vehicles are also attractive vehicles to steal for the delivery of explosive devices because of their access to facilities not open to the general public. For example, an ambulance might receive less careful inspection than a pickup truck when entering a parking structure and might not be denied access to security areas like loading docks or executive entrances (Figure 6.3). Pre-event surveillance or elicitation that generated

FIGURE 6.3   Ambulance in Portugal.

the name of an important person in one of these facilities could result in security personnel letting down their guard to take an action they thought would accommodate an important member of the organization.

British Intelligence reports that terrorists in the Middle East have been using ambulances to perpetrate terror attacks. In February 2008, in Iraq, an explosives-laden ambulance drove into a police station, exploding when it was fired on at a checkpoint. The Israeli Defense Force has reported that Palestinians in the West Bank have used ambulances for the covert transportation of terrorists and explosives since at least 2002 (Edwards, 2008). One of the most spectacular uses of an ambulance bomb was October 27, 2003, when an ambulance laden with explosives crashed through the security gate at the International Committee of the Red Cross headquarters in Baghdad, killing at least 15 people. The blast left a crater 6 feet deep, damaged buildings on both sides of the street, and shattered windows a mile away (*Chronicle* staff, 2003).

Delivery Vehicles

Delivery vehicles such as those used by UPS, FedEx, and even the postal service pose multiple threats. In a hazardous materials awareness class for community members, the instructor stated that the most dangerous truck in their neighborhood was the UPS delivery truck because it carries numerous types of hazardous materials in consumer packaging, and therefore it does not have to be placarded on the exterior. People place online orders for pool chemicals, gardening supplies, pet care products, and hobby supplies like model rocket fuel and photographic chemicals that are delivered by UPS and FedEx.

The unmarked packages are stored on the truck's shelves based only on delivery address, meaning that dangerous combinations like ammonia and chlorine, or acids and bases, can be adjacent to each other in transit. A shipped package bomb with a timer could wreak havoc in a neighborhood as the bomb detonated and set fire to the other materials in shipment. It could be constructed to create an airborne hazardous materials release that would shut down a neighborhood and tie up first responders for hours. Such an action might be used as a diversion to enable criminals to carry out a large robbery or terrorists to attack a sensitive target.

Hijacking would permit a terrorist to obtain a properly registered delivery truck or bus for use in an attack. Delivery trucks or busses make good VBIEDs (Figure 6.4). Their cargo capacity would enable a terrorist to pack a truck with explosives like ammonium nitrate and fuel oil (ANFO) and drive it to a government building or critical infrastructure component. Single-axle trucks are rated with a 10,000 pound capacity, meaning that large chemical, biological, radiological, nuclear, and explosive (CBRNE) incendiary devices

FIGURE 6.4 Beverage delivery truck on a downtown street.

could be transported in them. Multiaxle vehicles have a capacity of up to 60,000 pounds and can pose an even greater threat (TSA, 2010).

Vehicles do not have to be stolen. In the United Kingdom, National Health Service ambulances and police cars, often still marked, have been sold on eBay (Edwards, 2008). In the United States, surplus vehicles are sold at auctions. Most agencies remove all identifying markings before selling the vehicles, and sometimes they are repainted. However, they can easily be repainted appropriately and have new decals applied to mimic the correct markings. TSA security training warns against these "cloned vehicles"—those painted to look like "legitimate businesses, law enforcement or first responder vehicles, or other federal or private entities" (TSA, 2010, p. 9) as they can obtain the same access as legitimate vehicles of the same type.

In addition, ambulances, limousines, and delivery trucks often loiter in areas without raising a question. Ambulances can be parked anywhere without attracting attention because it is assumed that they are picking up a patient. Taxis and delivery trucks are parked in loading zones and even red zones so often that they seldom draw attention. This means that they make an excellent platform for surveillance of sensitive sites and desirable getaway vehicles for criminals, as well as attack vehicles.

Types of Attacks Against Street-Level Mass Transit Vehicles

There are two primary types of attacks against street-level mass transit and transportation vehicles: explosives and small arms. The two types of explosive devices—military ordnance and improvised explosive devices—use commercial, homemade, or military explosives.

Improvised Explosive Devices

An IED consists of any trigger, any container, and any explosive material. The combinations are endless, based only on the ingenuity of the bomb maker (Figure 6.5). Containers can be as small as a letter or greeting card, as long as they can hold the trigger mechanism and the explosive material. When a vehicle is packed with explosives and used as the bomb, as in the 1993 attacks on the World Trade Center in New York, it is called a vehicle-borne IED (VBIED). They can be as large as a semitruck.

The explosive materials may be purchased, stolen, or made by the bomber. Dynamite is used in mining and for removing tree stumps from farm fields and orchards. In some states it may be purchased by individuals, but the buyer has to provide identification and an explanation of the purpose of the purchase. Ammonium nitrate is a common fertilizer that can be purchased in home-improvement stores and farm stores. Fuel oil includes #2 diesel fuel, available at gas stations. Gasoline and nondetergent motor oil and other fuel types can be substituted for the diesel to make an explosive mixture called ANFO. ANFO can also be purchased as a binary mix for use in stump removal, as well as for digging irrigation ditches. Five thousand pounds of ANFO was used in the Murrah Building VBIED bombing in 1995 (Whitlock, 2007).

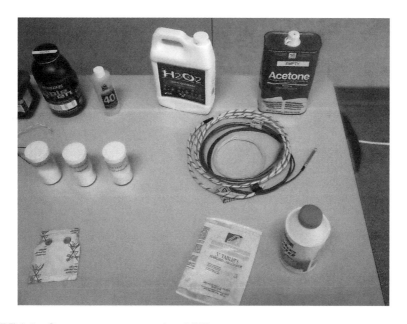

FIGURE 6.5   Common components of IEDs.

Al Qaeda manuals have advised terrorists to use available chemicals to make their own explosives mixes. On a laptop found in an Al Qaeda safe house in Pakistan, there was an instruction book for would-be bombers. "[T]he manual advised a shopping trip to a hardware store or pharmacy, where all the necessary ingredients for a terrorist attack are stocked on the shelves." (Whitlock, 2007). In 1993 the VBIED used at the World Trade Center bombing was composed of 1,500 pounds of urea nitrate—a fertilizer-based explosive—and hydrogen-gas cylinders (Whitlock, 2007). The London bombings of 2005 used tri-acetone tri-peroxide (TATP). The ingredients—nail polish remover and hair bleach—were purchased in a beauty supply store. "TATP wields about 85 percent of the explosive power of TNT and can be made in a kitchen or bathroom. A dime-size amount of the explosive can ignite a fireball the size of a basketball" (Whitlock, 2007).

Because so many commercially available chemicals can become components of an IED's explosive material, the Federal Bureau of Investigation and the Department of Homeland Security have created an outreach program called Bomb-Making Materials Awareness Program (BMAP) that aims to educate local law enforcement and fire department personnel, as well as store managers and staff, about the use of common household and industrial products by terrorists. There are two messages in the program. The first is that salespeople seeing unusual transactions should collect as much information about the purchaser as possible and then notify local law enforcement. The second is that bomb-making activities can look like drug labs, so law enforcement and fire personnel should carefully evaluate the scene before collecting evidence, which may be sensitive to touch or friction and explode on contact (DHS, 2011).

In the United States commercial activities consume five billion pounds of explosive mixtures and materials every year (Figure 6.6). As was noted in Chapter 5, theft of explosives in the United States is not unusual. Detasheet, det cord, and other high explosives and initiators are stolen from legitimate users and retailers. For example, in 2010, 31,000 pounds of ANFO were stolen from mining and construction sites (Thomas, 2011). In 1990, President Vaclav Havel of the Czech Republic said, "There is enough uncontrolled Semtex in the world to support terrorism for 150 years" (DHS, 2011, p. 27).

Information on the creation of the explosive mixes or the assembly of an IED is readily available at any library and on the Internet. However, many of the instruction manuals leave out crucial safety steps or fail to emphasize appropriate precautions when handling the unstable mixes or sensitive devices. Table 6.1 lists some examples of IED containers and the amount of explosive materials that they can hold.

Triggers or switches can be made from any combination of items that creates a circuit for an electronic detonation or produces adequate friction for

FIGURE 6.6 **Common explosive materials.**

TABLE 6.1 Improvised Explosive Devices (IEDs) and Vehicle-Borne Explosive Devices (VBIEDs)

	Description	Explosive Capacity (pounds)
IEDs	Small package or letter	1
	Pipe bomb	5
	Express-mail box 10	
	Vest bomb	20
	Container bomb: briefcase, backpack, small suitcase, large purse, shopping bag	20
	Parcel/shipping box 50	
VBIEDs	Compact car	500
	Full-size car/minivan	1,000
	Full-size van/SUV/pickup truck	4,000
	Single-axle truck	10,000
	Tandem-axle truck	30,000
	Semitruck	60,000

Source: AFT bomb card, 2002.

a mechanical detonation. A mousetrap, light switch, clothespin, or salvaged parts from old electronics could be used. The motion sensor in an outdoor light, the remote control from a child's toy or garage door opener, an alarm clock, or the alarm function of a cell phone have all been used in IEDs. The remote control for a child's toy car was a favorite of roadside bomb makers in Iraq until an alert Marine Corps captain placed his own remote control on the dashboard of his Humvee with the levers taped down to detonate any IEDs up to 100 yards ahead of him (Simmons, 2007).

Islamist terrorists have increased the lethality of their IEDs by adding shrapnel. Containers are packed with nails and screws, nuts and bolts, and washers and other small metal parts to ensure that when the bomb explodes small missiles fly with the blast wave to kill victims. Recently, bomb builders have begun using glass marbles because they cannot be detected by x-ray scanners and metal detectors, yet their density makes them lethal.

There are two primary methods of using these devices. One is to deliver the explosive into the bus itself. This can be done by a passenger placing the device and leaving it behind or staying on the bus and becoming a suicide. Devices can be thrown through an open window or door. In both cases, the device would have to weigh less than 50 pounds for a person to be able to carry or throw it. Such devices would include military devices, like grenades or satchel charges, and IEDs. The other option is to blow up an explosive device in close proximity to the vehicle. Roadside bombs, land mines, or VBIEDs near the bus could be used.

An attack from the outside would require the vehicles to be stopped, as throwing an object into the window of a moving vehicle is difficult. Attacking from the outside requires an ambush methodology, monitoring the vehicle's route and timing, as well as speed, but may still require bringing the vehicle to a halt in close proximity to the device to ensure success.

Small Arms

Small arms attacks include assaults using pistols, shotguns, submachine guns, rifles, and machine guns. Attacks may be made by passengers on the bus; this type of attack favors close-proximity weapons, like pistols, shotguns, and submachine guns because of the high volumes of fire and compactness for working in restricted spaces. Rifles and machine guns are more likely to be used for an external ambush that would require not only high volumes of fire, but also penetration through the outside shell of the bus in order to ensure maximum damage.

While the possibility of a rolling ambush—that is, a vehicle with several heavily armed individuals pulling alongside the bus and opening fire while it is moving—exists, it is also more complex to execute. The stationary ambush using the bus's known route and schedule would ensure a higher degree of success.

There are also combinations of attacks using both explosives and small arms. The explosives are used as the initiator of the attack, and then small arms are used to ensure maximum lethality. Explosives are also used to prompt the attackers to begin their assignment. Although most such attacks have been perpetrated against armored cars in the United States, the techniques could be used against any high-value vehicle.

Hijacking

Hijacking is the forceful acquisition of a vehicle or theft of a specific vehicle, usually to gain the vehicle for use in a criminal enterprise. This could be for smuggling people or illicit goods or for the creation of a VBIED. In either case, the use of that specific vehicle will be for a short duration because the police will quickly place "be on the look out" (BOLO) alerts for its apprehension. Longer term smuggling operations are more likely to use a cloned vehicle that is less likely to draw law enforcement attention.

Vehicle hijackings have two phases. First, the perpetrator has to stop or immobilize the vehicle. This can be done by either tricking the driver into stopping or physically blocking the vehicle's passage. One method is to have a stranded motorist flag down a truck on a lonely road. However, there is no guarantee that anyone will stop, and it is not useful if a specific target vehicle is needed. A more successful ploy is to bump the target vehicle with another vehicle from the rear, inducing the driver to stop to inspect for damage and exchange insurance information.

Another technique is used most successfully at remote traffic lights or late at night when there is little traffic. Two vehicles work in concert with an individual on the street to block the vehicle at the stoplight and force the driver from the vehicle. Blocking the vehicle requires two vehicles to block the forward and rear avenues of escape. One hijacking used a baby carriage pushed in front of the car to stop it, allowing two other vehicles to box it in (Deatherage, 2006).

Cloned Vehicles

Criminal enterprises and terrorists may be more successful in acquiring a vehicle legally and turning it into the vehicle that they need for the crime. Cloned vehicles with very accurate markings have been used along the United States/Mexico border for smuggling drugs. Only subtle cues have given away the cloning, such as high-end radios, older model vehicles, and extensive use of "vehicle wrap" (vinyl-coating advertisements that would be excessive for standard commercial vehicles). Misspelling of signage has also been noted, along with misuse of departmental serial numbering (Florida Department of Law Enforcement, 2008).

Security Strategies for Busses, Livery, Paratransit, Ambulances, and Delivery Vehicles

Human Factors

The safe and secure operation of vehicles starts with the capability and competence of the driver. Federal rules limit the number of hours that professional drivers can work. Lack of sleep, injuries, and emotional stress are among the factors that lead to distraction and decreased reaction time. In a crisis, the driver has first to recognize that there is a problem, determine how to react to the problem, and then carry out the appropriate action, often within just a few seconds. If the driver has had training that leads to situational awareness, is well rested, and is in a relaxed but alert state, the speed of decision-making ability should be increased.

Pre-event actions can enhance driver focus. For example, the windshields and mirrors of the vehicle should be cleaned and properly adjusted for maximum vision. The brake system should be working appropriately. The vehicle's power train should be functioning properly. Knowledge that the vehicle is in proper operating condition makes the driver more confident in managing unexpected situations.

Many times, attempted attacks against professionally driven vehicles can be disrupted by the driver's speed of reaction. The attackers rely on the driver to be surprised and remain immobilized for a few seconds. During that period, an opportunity is presented for the attack. If the operator is able to recognize the threat and immediately take an appropriate course of action, there is a possibility of disrupting the attack, thereby protecting the vehicle and its occupants. Jenkins and Gerston (2001) have noted that fleet security officials are more concerned with the day-to-day threats from criminal and gang-related activities than terrorism, and these strategies provide equal attack deterrence in either situation.

The second factor in preventing attacks is security at the storage and repair facilities that denies access to the vehicles. Hydraulic lifts, overhead cranes, and spare parts may be attractive to criminals and terrorists as a means of damaging vehicles and disrupting service. For example, damaged parts could take a vehicle out of service, which could allow terrorists to substitute a cloned vehicle on a regular delivery route. In addition, repairs done with parts that have been damaged, such as damaged brake lines, may enhance the chances for hijacking a vehicle when it breaks down after it has left the yard.

An adequately protected facility would include a roving patrol and a secured fenced area to prevent casual access. In addition, critical assets like fuel lines and utility connections should be identified and managed through security procedures, and information about their locations and operation should be controlled based on security concerns. Adequate lighting for the roving patrol is required, as well as a reaction capability, either with additional guards or local law enforcement. Cameras can be used to supplement the visual range of the roving patrol, but an attentive guard will be required to monitor the cameras and act on what is being broadcast.

Even with these precautions, controlled access to the vehicles cannot be guaranteed. The intent is to reduce the window of time for the perpetrator to the minimum amount, thereby disrupting the ability to introduce explosive devices or damage vehicle operating systems. For example, a bomb with magnets can be introduced onto a vehicle's exterior in a few seconds, but it may also fall off as soon as the vehicle moves. With 30 seconds, the IED might be secured with zip ties, enhancing the likelihood that the bomb will stay with the vehicle until detonation. Lessening the time that a perpetrator would have to tamper with the vehicle means that the tampering is less likely to be extensive or effective.

Roving patrols are also important for disrupting surveillance. Perpetrators may be observing the facility to ascertain operational schedules, or vehicle appearance for cloning. The patrol should observe people outside the storage area who are taking photographs or notes, or who are behaving in an unusual manner, such as loitering in an industrial area. Vehicles that appear inappropriate to the area, especially abandoned or damaged vehicles, should be reported to the patrol's control point, and removal should be coordinated with the local law enforcement agency, as they may provide cover for covert surveillance or recording of storage area activities (Figure 6.7). Security patrols should be coordinated with neighboring facilities to ensure that neighbors' properties are not being used to conceal surveillance of transportation facilities.

Surveillance is just one indicator that a facility may be being studied to plan for a criminal event or terrorist attack. Perpetrators have to acquire materials, devise a plan, and test aspects of the plan. Table 6.2 lists some indicators that an attack or crime is being planned.

Randomization of operations is an important feature of effective patrol, as perpetrators will be unsure when they can safely enter a secure area. Transportation agencies and companies should vary their patrol schedules as much as possible to make it difficult for perpetrators to undertake surveillance or intrusion unobserved. Activity schedules should be randomized

FIGURE 6.7 **A mobile home parked in an industrial area near a secure transportation facility should raise questions.**

as much as possible to defeat surveillance and interference with operations. However, for most commercial activities, a routine has been developed to enhance efficiency and meet customer needs, so there are limited activities that can vary.

The third element in human factors is the selection of drivers, security, custodial, and repair personnel. Companies already routinely check driver's license levels and accident records, and for drivers and security personnel they may coordinate with local law enforcement to do a "wants and warrants" check to ensure that these personnel are not known criminals. More detailed background checks, which become expensive, are usually only conducted for personnel who will be routinely driving hazardous materials, high-value shipments, or sensitive cargo. For example, as mentioned in Chapter 3, drivers routinely entering ports unescorted will be required to have a transportation worker identification card (TWIC), which requires a full criminal history and terrorist watch list check. TWIC credentials are good for 5 years and require payment of a fee (TSA, 2010).

Custodial and repair personnel are generally not given a background check beyond possibly a "wants and warrants" check, and not all positions require credentials. Contractors and temporary personnel are seldom given any background checks. All personnel have access to the facility and could engage in surveillance, information collection, or tampering to further the cause of a terrorist or criminal organization.

An important element of employee and contractor security is the personnel identification system. Employee identification cards should have the employee's photo and, ideally, a thumbprint, and they should be coded

TABLE 6.2 Pre-incident Indicators

Indicator	Description	Activities
Surveillance	Potential target	Level of protection; existing security measures; security/law enforcement response patterns and times
	Suspicious surveillance activity	Recording; drawing diagrams or monitoring activities; watching the facility through binoculars; trying to acquire site plans; looking for access points
Elicitation	Acquisition of information about the facility and security from personnel	Gain employment at the facility; contact by mail, phone, or e-mail
Test security	Procedures and response times	Leave unattended items and monitor response times; trespass and monitor response times
Funding	Crimes for funding terrorism	Trafficking drugs and people; burglary; sales of illicit merchandise; moving money from charities to businesses
	Indicators	Large transaction paid for with cash or gift cards; donations to unknown charities
Acquiring supplies	Legal purchases and theft	Weapons, vehicles, communications equipment
	Report activities	Vehicles out of place or in restricted areas; one-time use cell phones; purchase of large amounts of products at odd times or by inappropriate people; false identification documents; theft of uniforms
Impersonation	Law enforcement, mail carriers, utility workers, delivery company workers	People who do not belong or look out of place; suspicious actions; suspicious conversations; suspicious uniforms
Rehearsal	Criminals and terrorists may attempt a dry run of an attack	Strangers in odd places; suspicious people monitoring police and fire radio channels; monitoring police and fire response times
Deployment	Attack	Place assets, take action

Source: TSA. (2010). *Motorcoach counterterrorism guide.* Montreal, Canada: QuickSeries Publishing.

to make clear the areas of access for each member of the workforce. For example, custodians would have to access the interior of parked busses, but should never operate a vehicle. Therefore, they should not have access to ignition keys, which should be kept in a supervised area and issued only to properly identified drivers or kept in a locked cabinet for which only the drivers have combinations or keys. For vehicles with push-button starters, access keys should be checked in and checked out. Drivers have no need to be in parts cages, and security guards have no need to access spare parts or cleaning supplies. Compartmentalization of employee access will provide another layer of vehicle security.

Employees of many companies wear distinctive uniforms as another layer of security. Clothing items, including hats and badges or embroidered insignia, should be safeguarded and not distributed as souvenirs at public events or during tours. Employees should be careful to wear appropriate uniform items for the season and to note anyone wearing a partial, obsolete, or unserviceable uniform. Employees being terminated or retiring should have the last paycheck withheld until all uniform items and identification cards and badges are collected. Companies that use temporary or seasonal workers should be especially vigilant about collecting clothing and badges when employees have finished their work periods. Criminals have gained entry to facilities dressed as firefighters and emergency medical technicians, for example.

The fourth element of human factors-related security considerations is vehicle inspection. Before the beginning of each shift, the vehicle operator should start with a perimeter search of the area immediately surrounding the vehicle. Any indications of leaking fluids, loose parts, or other abnormalities should immediately be reported to the chief mechanic, and a new vehicle should be obtained for an on-time start. The inspection should include fluid levels, tire pressure, and operation of the vehicle's lights and doors. The driver should check along windowsills, the front of the vehicle, the sides and wheel wells, and the back of the vehicle including the exhaust pipe. Signs of tampering include broken plastic trim pieces, rubber trim bent at an angle, and access points left ajar or pried open. The driver should check under the vehicle for leaks and hanging parts, as well as signs of material having brushed against the underside, which might indicate that someone has accessed the underside to place a foreign object. Table 6.3 provides details of areas that should be checked for tampering or vandalism.

The inside of the vehicle should also be searched. Every vehicle operator should have a daily checklist with a comprehensive guide to vehicle searches for the specific vehicle. Starting with the driver's area, all operating parts should be checked including radios, pedals, gear shifts, and mirrors. The driver's seat should be checked for unusual thickness or torn upholstery and for anything under the seat that does not belong. The interior should be checked for abnormalities in door surfaces and floors, including torn or replaced materials. Unexpected left-behind items should be noted and removed. Vehicles with passenger spaces should be checked for abnormalities in the seat cushions, walls, doors, overhead bins or compartments, and floors.

TABLE 6.3 Security Inspection Checklist

Critical Areas

Exterior: bumpers, tires, walls, under carriage, roof
Compartments: engine, baggage
Interior: ceiling, seats, floor, luggage racks

Routine Checks

Lumps in seats
Missing screws or rivets on walls (inside and outside)
Inconsistent sounds when tapping walls
Unusually thick space—ceiling, roof, walls
Unusually heavy doors
Torn or repaired flooring
Uneven or thick floor
Damaged upholstery
Items left in baggage racks or storage areas

Source: TSA. (2010). *Motorcoach counterterrorism guide.* Montreal, Canada: QuickSeries Publishing.

The fifth element of human factors-related security is planning, training, and exercises. A comprehensive security plan based on evaluated risks should be developed for the entire facility and all rolling stock assets. Vehicle checklists should be developed in concert with drivers and local law enforcement. Staff members should be viewed as stakeholders in security plans and be involved in the creation of checklists and inspection protocols.

All staff members should receive training on appropriate parts of the security plan, such as the requirement to wear identification at all times, how to report security breaches or unusual activity, and definitions of unusual activity. Specific portions of the security plan should be delivered only to those employees working in the area of concern. For example, hazardous materials storage precautions training would be delivered to repair and custodial crews, while bus inspection information would be given to drivers and security personnel.

Exercises should include scenarios based on the local facility and its resources, as well as exercises that integrate local law enforcement and other responder agencies. These exercises should be conducted by the transportation agency so that the focus remains on transportation assets. Participation in other agencies' exercises should also be encouraged, recognizing that transportation will then be used as a resource to the organizing entity.

Busses

Busses operate in an open environment without any special security mechanisms. In Israel bus drivers are trained to recognize potential indicators of terrorist activity and are authorized to deny entry to the bus or remove someone from the bus if such indicators are observed. However, in the United States only specific actions and threats by individuals can generate action by the driver, not just suspicions and indicators. Every transit agency has its standards for acceptable passenger deportment and standard operating procedures for drivers to follow when faced with unacceptable and disruptive passenger behavior. Drivers must put their personal safety first followed by the safety of their passengers.

Technology inside the bus can assist drivers. Drivers should have a "panic button" or silent messaging capability to summon law enforcement assistance when faced with threats or disruptions on the bus. Each bus should have an automated vehicle locator system (AVLS) connected to the dispatch center. Drivers should have a mobile data terminal to exchange information with the dispatch center. The bus number should be clearly visible on the body of the bus and also on the roof (TCRP, 2009).

Basic safety precautions should be observed to prevent the bus from being hijacked or taken over. Drivers should never leave an unattended bus unlocked. The driver should note the bus number and license plate for the assigned vehicle at the beginning of each shift and keep that information with him or her during breaks. Drivers should never deviate from the route unless directed by law enforcement personnel, and then the rerouting should be reported to dispatch immediately by radio or cell phone.

Some bus companies use commercial driver monitoring systems to solicit input from the public on the operation of a bus or other professionally driven vehicle. For example, Driver Check offers a toll-free number that the public can use to report unsafe driving. Placards are placed on the back of the vehicle with the toll free number and vehicle identification number to facilitate reporting of unsafe driving practices. Such placards can also enable drivers of other vehicles to alert the company of erratic driving that may be a signal of a driver in distress or to report a vehicle that has been left in a suspicious or unusual location for a period of time that exceeds normal driver breaks. Jenkins et al. (2010) note:

> It would be prudent to learn from the attacks elsewhere and to develop a program of bus operator security-awareness training and corresponding procedures and equipment that mitigate the risk of terrorist attacks and also assist bus operators in dealing with the much more likely dangers they face from common crime and deranged individuals. (p. 16)

Bus Stops

Busses have to stop at specific locations on a specific schedule to meet the needs of passengers. Steps can be taken to lessen the security concerns associated with these stops. For example, landscaping at bus stops should be kept trimmed to avoid providing concealment for criminals. Lighting should be adequate for the driver to observe passengers before they enter the bus. The bus stop shelter should be designed to allow waiting passengers a quick escape in an emergency. Emergency call boxes should be available to allow waiting passengers to notify law enforcement or the bus company of problems.

Bus shelters should also be designed with natural hazards in mind. The shelter structure should be designed to resist seismic forces or wind in hazard-prone areas. Furniture and light fixtures should be properly secured to prevent them from moving around. Shelters should not have wraparound advertisements that provide a hiding place (TCRP, 2009).

Professionally Driven Vehicles

Drivers with commercial licenses have received training in the appropriate operation of the vehicle. They may not have received adequate security training at that time. Operators of commercial fleets should ensure that their drivers have appropriate training for the secure operation of the vehicle as well. A security orientation should include reminders about precautions such as never leaving a vehicle unlocked when unattended, and to stop the vehicle as seldom as possible during the journey.

At the start of a shift, the driver should follow the vehicle inspection procedures noted before, write down the vehicle number and license plate, keep this in his possession, and review the complete route to the destination. Many delivery companies rely on prearranged routes programmed into a GPS system, but drivers should also have a printed route map or at least a printed map of the area in case the GPS fails.

Professional drivers should be reminded that their responsibility is for the safe and secure delivery of their passengers or cargo on time. Therefore, they should never pick up hitchhikers or stop to assist stranded motorists, both of which expose the company to liability and the vehicle to hijacking. Drivers can notify their dispatch centers of motorists needing assistance or unusual behavior along the route and leave the resolution to local law enforcement agencies.

Case Studies

Commercial Chemical Purchase

Two young men went to a beauty supply shop outside London. They bought a large quantity of nail polish remover and hair bleach. The young female clerk thought the size and content of their order was odd and asked them what they were going to do with these products. They seemed surprised and confused, and then said it was for their sisters. They paid for the large purchase with cash. The young woman thought about the purchase but did not mention it to anyone at the time.

On July 10, 2005, the woman called her local police station and said that she had something that might be of interest to them. When she was interviewed at the shop, she showed the officers the two items that the men had bought. She had read in the paper that the London subway and bus bombs had used TATP, and that got her thinking about the two men who had bought so much nail polish remover and hair bleach, which are dilute acetone and peroxide. The police thanked her for her assistance. They had now found the source of the bomb materials.

Attacks on Tourist Busses in Egypt

In 1992 and 1993, a terrorist group called Gamma'A launched a campaign against tourists in Egypt. Tourism is Egypt's main source of foreign income, estimated at $3 billion per year at that time, so disruption of tourism would have an effect across many sectors of the economy. The stated goal of the Islamist militants was to replace the secular government with a religious ruling power.

In one attack in the southern Nile Valley, a boy acted as the lookout and alerted gunmen when the bus was coming; they then fired on the bus from both sides, killing one woman and injuring two men. Over the next few months, busses carrying German and Japanese tourists were also fired on. Later a bomb was thrown at a bus, shattering its back window but causing no injuries to the riders. The campaign of terror against tour busses continued, even with police escorts. One attack was thwarted by a vigilant bus driver. In another attack, the gunmen hijacked a taxi in an attempt to escape responding police. By the end of 1993, an attack on a bus with bombs and guns injured eight Austrian tourists and eight Egyptians. One bomb was thrown into the bus, causing the injuries. The three attackers also fired small arms at the bus (Stubblefield & Monday, 1994).

In 1995 Gamma'A joined forces with Egyptian Islamic Jihad to assassinate President Mubarak. The plot failed and Mubarak instigated strong measures to eliminate Gamma'A. In 1997 they formally renounced violence as a means of regime change in Egypt. But in 1997 rogue elements of Gamma'A with ties to Islamic Jihad killed 58 tourists and four Egyptians in a tomb in Luxor, devastating the tourist industry and ending much of the popular support for the group (Wright, 2006).

Limousine Attack

Alfred Herrhausen was the chairman of Germany's Deutsche Bank. He had a security detail that accompanied him on his daily commute. Unfortunately, he kept to the same schedule and route every day, and terrorists' surveillance successfully revealed his routine. The first car in the convoy passed the roadside bomb, hidden in a bicycle, without incident, but as Herrhausen's armored limousine passed, the bomb was detonated. The 2½-ton vehicle was thrown 83 feet. Herrhausen was the only fatality, bleeding to death from the shrapnel injuries (Deatherage, 2006).

The bomb was made of 22 pounds of TNT, a shaped charge at the right level to impact someone sitting in a limousine, and it propelled the shrapnel through the limousine's rear door. It was set off using a cable that had been laid and covered earlier. The remote control detonation was timed for the specific car that the target was using (Stubblefield & Monday, 1994).

Driving Through the Ambush

In 1990 a busload of U.S. Air Force personnel was returning to their base from a recreational tour. Three gunmen attacked the bus with automatic weapons fire. Eight soldiers were wounded, two seriously. The driver kept driving through the area, thereby saving the lives of the passengers (Stubblefield & Monday, 1994). The attackers were from the Morazanista Liberation Front that was opposed to the U.S. military presence in Honduras. American troops were supporting the right-wing Contras in opposition to the Sandinista government in neighboring Nicaragua (START, 2010).

Bus Driver Awareness

A transit bus was moving through town when one of the passengers in the back of the bus began fighting with another passenger. It appeared that he was mentally unstable, and he seemed determined to create problems for the other passengers. Not wanting to provoke him to further violence, the driver pushed her panic button but said nothing. When the dispatcher did not get a verbal response from the driver, she noted the bus's location from the AVLS, and through the driver's earpiece she said that a law enforcement unit would meet the bus at its next regularly scheduled stop.

The quick thinking driver realized that the officer would need more time to get to the stop than she would, so she pulled the bus to the curb. The unruly passenger protested, and she said that she was ahead of schedule and had to wait a few minutes to stay on time. This quieted him and allowed her to meet the officer at the appointed time and place, where the unruly passenger was removed by police.

Summary

Vehicles driven by professional drivers on known routes have specific vulnerabilities that need to be addressed by the vehicles' owners. Situational awareness of the drivers and security personnel is critical. The operators of the vehicles are aware of safety issues and observe unusual occurrences that might point to criminal or terrorist activity. They drive many miles using large vehicles that require attention and skill to operate safely. Transit and transportation agency leadership needs to be responsible for the development of safety and security plans and operating procedures to ensure that appropriate precautions are taken by all personnel every day.

Mass transit vehicles that operate on fixed guideways and rails have additional security challenges. In the next chapter, the strategies for the protection of light rail, subways, and monorails will be discussed.

Discussion Questions

1. Describe the security vulnerabilities of mass transit busses in urban areas and compare the American experience with the international experience of security concerns.

2. What are an IED and a VBIED? When and where should a state transportation system security manager be concerned about VBIEDs?

3. What is the role of passengers in security for mass transit? What programs and systems are used to enhance their security?

4. A hazardous materials class instructor once said that the most dangerous truck on the road was UPS. Why? As the director of security for a local UPS district, how can you enhance the security of your vehicles, personnel, and cargo?

5. You are the security director for an urban mass transit system based on busses. How do you rate your concerns for terrorism, crime, and vandalism, and how do you leverage available counterterrorism funding to best address crime and vandalism?

References

Chronicle staff. (2003, Oct. 27). Bomber kills 15 at Red Cross in Baghdad. *SF Gate.* Accessed 10/25/11 from http://articles.sfgate.com/2003-10-27/news/17514309_1_red-cross-suicide-attack-rocket-attack

Deatherage, Jr., R. H. (2006). *Survival driving: Staying alive on the world's most dangerous roads.* Boulder, CO: Paladin Press.

DHS. (2011). Bomb-making materials awareness program. Delivered at Chico, CA, December 9, 2011.

Edwards, R. (2008, June 29) Al-Qa'eda style terrorists planning UK attacks with ambulances bought on eBay. *The Telegraph*. Accessed 10/25/11/from http://www.telegraph.co.uk/news/uknews/2217076/Al-Qaeda-style-terrorists-planning-UK-attacks-with-ambulances-bought-on-eBay.html

Florida Department of Law Enforcement. (2008). The roadmap to cloned vehicles. www.patc.com/special/cloned-vehicles.pdf

Jenkins, B. M., Butterworth, B. R., & Schrum, K. S. (2010). *Terrorist attacks on public bus transportation: A preliminary empirical analysis*. MTI Report WP 09-01. San Jose, CA: Mineta Transportation Institute.

Jenkins, B. M., & Gerston, L. (2001). *Protecting public surface transportation against terrorism and serious crime: Continuing research on best security practices* (MTI Report 01-07). San Jose, CA: Mineta Transportation Institute.

McCarter, M. (2011, November 14). TSA warns of terrorist interest in attacking buses during busy holiday season. HSToday.com. http://www.hstoday.us/industry-news/general/single-article/tsa-warns-of-terrorist-interest-in-attacking-buses-during-busy-holiday-season/2a198ccb0399cab8d0e250a5a3e1db24.html?goback=%2Egde_106846_member_81331340

Simmons, D. (2007). June/July 2007 message from Dan. Retrieved on Jan. 14, 2008, from http://www.dansimmons.com/news/message_jun07_2.htm

START. (2010). Morazanist Patriotic Front. http://www.start.umd.edu/start/data_collections/tops/terrorist_organization_profile.asp?id=4132

Stubblefield, G., & Monday, M. (1994). *Killing zone: A professional's guide to preparing or preventing ambushes*. Boulder, CO: Paladin Press.

TCRP. (2009). *Synthesis 80—Transit security update*. Washington, DC: TRB/National Academies.

Thomas, P. (2011, June 19). Tons of explosives routinely disappear. http://abcnews.go.com/WNT/story?id = 130286&page = 1

TRB. (2008). *Transit Cooperative Research Program synthesis 80: Transit security update*. Washington, DC: National Academies.

TSA. (2010). *Motorcoach counterterrorism guide*. Montreal, Canada: QuickSeries Publishing.

U.S. DOT. (2011). *Pocket guide to transportation 2011*. RITA, Bureau of Transportation Statistics. Washington, DC: RITA.

Whitlock, C. (2007, July 5). Homemade, cheap and dangerous: Terror cells favor simple ingredients in building bombs. *Washington Post*. http://www.washingtonpost.com/wp-dyn/content/article/2007/07/04/AR2007070401814_pf.html

Wright, L. (2006). *The looming tower: Al Qaeda and the road to 9/11*. New York, NY: Borzoi Books.

Chapter 7

Mass Transit on Fixed Rails and Guideways

Keywords: light rail, subways, monorails, cable car, commuter rail, street cars, trolleys, fixed guideways, tunnels, stations, electricity, diesel power, risk assessment, security, surveillance, closed circuit TV, suicide bombers, sarin, arson, cyber security

Learning Objectives

After reading this chapter you should be able to

- Identify potential vulnerabilities in systems using vehicles that run on tracks
- Understand how fixed operations generate vulnerabilities
- Understand the role of technology in security
- Understand the strategies used by terrorists to disrupt rail-based mass transit

Components of Rail and Guideway-Based Mass Transportation Systems

A visitor to San Jose, California, can ride a horse-drawn trolley in History Park and a modern light rail system in the same day. The nation's 10th largest city has reclaimed its transit history with a short restored trolley route past the historic homes in the park, but the city's planners have also seen the use of rail-based transit as an important part of the city's future. The light rail system began in the downtown and now extends to the high-tech hubs for Yahoo! and Google in Sunnyvale and Mountain View, the Great Mall in Milpitas, and the commuter suburb of Campbell. Extensions of the light rail system have been constructed in areas designed for transit-oriented development, denser housing, and commercial sites that are intended to give people an alternative to car-dominated living, as congestion reaches disruptive levels.

This chapter will discuss the security challenges and strategies for self-powered mass transit vehicles that run on rails or tracks. Some run as trolley or light rail systems, while others are subway/surface cars, subways, elevated systems, cable-driven, monorail, or heavy short-haul passenger rail. They share the common characteristics of having an absolutely fixed route, because they cannot leave the rails, and of depending on fixed locations for discharging and receiving passengers safely. Further, except for some diesel heavy rail, these systems depend on electricity to operate.

While electric power makes these forms of urban mass transit more environmentally friendly than livery vehicles or busses, consuming little or no petroleum products and generating no exhaust at the vehicle's location, those that operate co-located in street rights-of-way can cause traffic congestion as they take on and discharge passengers into driving lanes. Those that operate at grade, even in dedicated lanes, pose a roadblock to cars turning left across their paths.

For these reasons, transportation planners encouraged the removal of rails from city streets in America' largest cities after World War II. Individual car ownership increased after the war, lowering demand for urban mass transportation except in the largest and most densely populated cities. Even there, busses offered more flexibility for operating in congested city streets, and the removal of the trolley tracks added a driving lane for cars.

The "gas crisis" of the 1970s brought into focus the need for an urban mass transit system not dependent on gasoline or diesel fuel.[1] Cities began adding commuter trains to existing heavy rail lines and creating new subway lines in cities like New York and San Francisco. Light rail systems were added to urban mass transit options in many newer and growing cities, like Los Angeles, San Diego, Houston, Phoenix, Portland, and San Jose. Seattle added a monorail to its downtown in preparation for the World's Fair.

By 2011 the U.S. Department of Transportation (DOT) reported that trolleys were operating on exclusive rights-of-way, controlled rights-of-way, and mixed traffic systems, with 456 directional route miles in service. Light rail systems had 1,477 directional route miles, while commuter rail had 7,561 directional route miles. Over 13,000 vehicles were in service providing urban mass transit service on rails, with another 6,494 commuter rail cars and locomotives (U.S. DOT, 2011, pp. 12–13). Transit rail vehicles traveled 762 million miles in 2008, and commuter rail systems traveled 337 million miles (U.S. DOT, 2011, p. 15). Mass transit rail systems accounted for 18,931 million passenger miles in 2008, while commuter rail accounted for another 11,032 million passenger miles (U.S. DOT, 2011, p. 16). By 2002 more than six thousand agencies operated bus, rail, ferry, and other transit systems (Guerrero, 2002).

Locations

Rail-based transit may operate at grade level, on elevated tracks, or in subways. Some systems, like Philadelphia's subway system and San Francisco's BART, may operate on all three levels. Tunnels are often used to traverse waterways, travel through mountains, or pass through buildings. Systems operating at grade level generally have a curb or fence separating the tracks from the streets (Figure 7.1).

Elevated tracks offer few access and egress points, often through second floor spaces in existing commercial buildings or through dedicated stations. Subways are spaces beneath urban development, often in tunnels or tubes, with limited access from the street level—usually only through stations and specific emergency exit systems. Tunnels through mountains or under waterways may have access only at the portals. The systems' rights-of-way extend not only to the "pathway on which a train travels" but also to "any

FIGURE 7.1   San Jose light rail station at grade level.

piece of equipment or person within twenty-five feet of the track" (Schulz & Gilbert, 2011, p. 5).

Unlike busses that can be redirected onto any street, rail-based transit vehicles can only go forward or backward on the rail. Some tunnels or tubes have only one set of one-way tracks, with the other direction in a separate tube or bore. Because the subways, tunnels, and elevated tracks have limited space and track-only access, repair, recovery, or rescue vehicles generally have to arrive using the same tracks.

Trolleys

Trolleys, also called streetcars or trams, were developed in the nineteenth century to meet the demand for longer trips in urban settings. Originally, urban mass transit was provided by horse-drawn wagons, but vehicles on rails could move faster, and the rails meant that a horse or mule could pull more weight, meaning more passengers per vehicle. Steam engines and cable car systems were used to power the cars initially, but electricity proved to be the best source of power. The term "trolley" comes from the overhead pole and electrical connection that powered most systems. Trolleys still operate today in San Francisco, Philadelphia, and New Orleans, among other cities, although the sleeker modern light rail cars have often replaced the traditional vehicles.

Trolley systems use single cars that travel along a fixed set of tracks. The schedule is generally based on intervals between cars rather than set times. Trolleys run on tracks that may be set in the street with cars running on the same roadway. This is called "mixed traffic" and provides challenges for both the car drivers and trolley motormen. Rails are slippery when wet, adding a hazard for drivers. Drivers wanting to turn left have to cross the path of the trolley. Passengers have to cross car traffic to get to and from the sidewalk, creating a passenger safety challenge.

Light Rail

Light rail systems are common in growing cities, often using existing street rights-of-way to create rapid transit (Figure 7.2). Cars are electrically driven and operated as single cars or in sets for rush hour. Because they have their own operating space, they are faster than busses. While an average free-way can carry about 2,000 cars per hour, an average light rail car can carry 20,000 riders per hour (Parkinson & Fisher, 1996).

Modern light rail systems often create a light-rail-only channel in the center of the street that is marked off by a curb, keeping cars and light rail vehicles separated. Intersections where drivers have to cross light rail tracks to make a turn are generally protected with traffic signals for both the light

FIGURE 7.2   Light rail in Istanbul, Turkey.

rail and the drivers. Passenger access and egress is from a central platform, with marked and often signal-protected access from the central platform to the sidewalk. In some cases, raised platforms are provided for easier access for passengers with mobility challenges, making the car floor flush with the platform (Figure 7.3).

FIGURE 7.3   Raised light rail platform in downtown San Jose, California.

Subways

Subways are underground commuter systems using rail cars powered by electricity. They are a key element in mass transit in many large cities worldwide. These rapid transit systems are also called "metro," "underground," or "tube" in recognition of their service area, location, or construction method. London's "underground" was opened in 1863, the world's first such system, and New York City's subway opened in 1904 (Figure 7.4) (APTA, 2004). Philadelphia's system of subway, elevated, and subway/surface cars opened in 1907 (Philadelphia, 2007).

Subway systems, which are dependent on electricity, require extensive infrastructure to operate, consisting of tunnels, usually beneath city streets, electric wires and transformers, ventilation systems, and stations. Within the system, there are large operating rooms where signals, lighting, ventilation, and power are coordinated. Openings are usually at street level, with stations at the basement level of surrounding buildings offering ticket purchasing options and information kiosks. Stations may have a single entry to a single line, with a crossover to the opposite direction track, or multiple corridors leading to several systems in both directions.

Subways pose special challenges for safe operation and passenger use. The long corridors require constant lighting and ventilation, making them susceptible to disruption during any power outage and policing manpower intensive. Limited passenger access points make evacuation difficult during rush hour and medical response a challenge at any time. Access to the

FIGURE 7.4 Entrance to New York City subway system.

underground areas is generally by stairs, although since the passage of the Americans With Disabilities Act in 1990 (Mayerson, 1992), all stations have to provide accessible methods for reaching boarding areas. Stairs pose a disaster response challenge for first responders carrying medical equipment or wearing self-contained breathing apparatus. Newer systems like the Metro in Washington, DC, serve most stations with escalators, but operation is disrupted at times because of ice and snow or extreme heat at the top exposed area, loss of power, or mechanical problems.

Subway tunnels share construction characteristics with the road tunnels described in Chapter 5. Some run underwater or through rock, as well as under city streets. The depth of the subway tunnel depends on surrounding geology and infrastructure. For example, London's King's Cross subway station is built on five levels to accommodate the operation and connection for the five lines converging there: Metropolitan, Circle, Piccadilly, Victoria, and Northern Lines. Because of the depth of the various platforms, most passengers rely on the six escalators that were built in 1939, although staircases are also available (Parsons, Brinkerhoff, Quade, & Douglas; Science Applications International Corporation; & Interactive Elements Incorporated, 2006).

Access to the tunnels is limited. Ventilation shafts and emergency evacuation points have been included in newer systems, and older systems with multiple tracks may offer crossover options to other tunnels carrying trains in the other direction or on another line. However, most tunnels have access only at the station portals.

Tunnels are ventilated using fans and forced air, as well as through the pneumatic action of the trains themselves. Natural ventilation intakes are often located on the sidewalks of the streets above the subway system, with obvious gratings in city systems like Philadelphia and New York. Tunnels are lighted with electric bulbs, and in many systems they are triggered to light only by the passage of the train, to save energy—meaning that empty tunnels may be dark except for emergency exit signs.

Elevated Systems

The Chicago El is probably the most famous elevated rapid mass transit system in the United States, although other systems include elevated portions, like Philadelphia's Market Street Line. Elevated systems share characteristics with subways, being based on rail cars operated by electricity.

While subways are underground, elevated lines are aboveground on limited-access tracks built above traffic at about the second floor level of buildings. Like subways, the principal access is through stations that are accessible by stairways, and sometimes by escalators, with mandated ADA accommodations. Unlike subways, the ventilation is provided by open air, and the tracks are usually not enclosed beyond safety fencing, so emergency access from the ground can be achieved by ladders, although ladder evacuation is a slow and inherently dangerous process. Catwalks are also present along most lines for routine service needs and can be used for evacuations.

Cable Cars

Cable cars power the vehicles by a continuously moving cable that runs under the street. Most often used today for pulling vehicles up steep inclines, they provide centralized power for transit vehicles. San Francisco's cable cars—called the traction railway—remain in service in the hilly downtown area and are a major tourist attraction. The operator disengages the car from the cable to stop for passenger access and egress and uses a handbrake to hold the car steady on inclines.

Monorails

Monorails were a futuristic mass transit concept designed to use urban air space and leave the ground for cars. Disneyland in Anaheim, California, and Disney World in Orlando, Florida, have monorails that connect their branded hotels to the parks and Downtown Disney. Seattle created its monorail for the World's Fair in 1962 (Seattle Center Monorail, 2011), and the Tokyo monorail was created to support the Tokyo Olympics in 1964, moving people from Haneda Airport to downtown (Monorail Society, n.d.).

Heavy Passenger Rail

Heavy rail commuter trains generally share tracks with freight railroad companies and carry passengers in a variety of cars (Figure 7.5). Some use traditional railway carriages, while others have double-decker cars offering amenities like WiFi, tables, restrooms, and bicycle storage. Commuter trains are generally self-propelled using electricity or diesel engines. On some lines, the trains may be on a push–pull system using a locomotive, which may be electric or diesel. Commuter rail usually travels longer distances at higher speeds and at a higher cost than light rail systems. While light rail stations may be a mile or less apart to support a walking environment, commuter rail stations are usually 10 or more miles apart, supported by bus line connections or car parks.

Commuter rail systems usually operate at grade, but they will use bridges and tunnels in urban environments. Rights-of-way may be open or protected by fencing. Grade crossings are common in less populated portions of the route, but over- and undercrossings are more common in densely populated

FIGURE 7.5   Altamont Commuter Express (ACE) connects the Central Valley to the Bay Area in California.

areas. Access is generally at designated stations, which may be at grade, underground, or elevated. Stations are frequently multimodal exchange points that include bus stops, taxi stands, parking lots for commuters' cars, "kiss and ride" lots with short-term parking for picking up commuters, and access to other mass transit systems like subways or light rail.

Cyber System Controls

Modern rail-based mass transit systems rely on computer controls to manage train schedules and announcements, signals, switches, ventilation, heating and air conditioning, ticketing, and access to stations. Some systems even operate the cars by computer without human drivers. Modern security systems like closed circuit television, fire alarms, smoke detection systems, and intrusion detection alarms all have computer tie-ins to the system's operations center. Known collectively as SCADA (supervisory control and data acquisition) systems, they are dependent on computer functionality (SCADA, n.d.) and are crucial to the safety and security of passengers and employees.

Mass transit rail-based systems almost all operate on electricity from the public grid. Electric power transmission and distribution is dependent on SCADA systems. Many of mass transit's computer-based systems transmit information over telephone or wireless systems to the computers, and communications systems are also dependent on SCADA infrastructure. Thus, collectively, the ability of rail-based mass transit systems to operate effectively is based on systems dependent on computer functionality.

Threats to Rail-Based Transit Systems

In the mid-1980s the threats to rail-based transit systems were homeless people living in the stations, unruly youths annoying and threatening other passengers, and graffiti defacing cars and station walls. The most common violent criminal acts were robbery, drug dealing, and shooting. In this same period in other nations, terrorists had targeted rail-based mass transit, but the goal had generally been to hurt the economy or the government's credibility, not to injure passengers. For example, the Irish Republican Army (IRA) waged a war of terror against British interests for over 80 years, frequently targeting the London subway system and commuter rail throughout the country. Generally, the IRA would contact law enforcement in advance of an attack, with enough warning time to remove people but not to protect the system (Jenkins, 1997). British tube riders accepted the inconvenience and cooperated with evacuations.

Targeted enforcement campaigns like New York City Transit's have largely eliminated the worst criminal violence from rail-based urban mass transit systems (Gladwell, 2002), yet international terrorism has increased its focus on rail-based transit as a target. While liberation groups like the Chechen rebels and Tamil Tigers continued to perpetrate attacks against mass transit during the 1990s and into the twenty-first century, the rise of Islamist terrorists has resulted in the spread of violence against all types of transportation.

Jenkins's chronology of attacks against passenger rail lists 639 instances of attacks or threats of attacks against commuter systems or their component parts, like stations, tunnels, and bridges, between 1920 and 1997 (Jenkins, 1997). The updated 2009 chronology, which covers all attacks against transportation since 1970, and train derailments since 1920, included 522 attacks against rail-based mass transit alone, of which 434, or 83%, used explosives or incendiary devices (Jenkins & Butterworth, 2010). From numerous bus bombings in Israel to the spectacular attacks of 9/11, transportation has become a more common site, victim, and weapon for terrorists.

Most of the attacks and threats against rail-based urban mass transit have occurred outside the United States. Notable successful attacks have included the bombing of subways in Moscow and London and commuter trains in Madrid and Mumbai. While plots against the New York City subway, its stations, and the PATH train tubes have been thwarted by law enforcement agencies before they came to fruition, the future may hold a successful attack in America.

As Secretary of DHS Janet Napolitano recently told Congress, "Home-based terrorism is here….And like violent extremism abroad, it is now part of the threat picture that we must confront." Since public transportation is in the terrorist playbook and has yielded many successes, possible attacks against the public transportation system in the United States must be considered. (Jenkins & Butterworth, 2010, p. 18)

Urban mass transit in the United States is an open system, making the provision of safety and security challenging. Terrorism expert Brian Jenkins has noted several factors that make public transit systems an especially attractive target to contemporary terrorist organizations:

> For those determined to kill in quantity and willing to kill indiscriminately, public transportation offers an ideal target. Precisely because it is public, and used by millions of people daily, there is necessarily little security with no obvious checkpoints, like those at airports, to inspect passengers and parcels. The passengers are strangers, promising attackers anonymity and easy escape. Concentrations of people in contained environments are especially vulnerable to conventional explosives and unconventional weapons. Specifically, attacks on public transportation, the circulatory systems of urban environments, cause great disruption and alarm, which are the traditional goals of terrorism. (Jenkins, 1997, p. 1)

Beyond the loss of human life caused by real and potential terrorist attacks against mass transit and the attendant psychological damage to commuters and communities, urban mass transit system attacks cause significant economic harm. Densely populated urban areas depend on rail-based mass transit for the efficient movement of passengers above or below the street-level congestion. Because of the high cost of parking and the length of time it takes to drive on congested roads, many commuters choose rail-based mass transit for their daily trips to work. Those living in the city may not even own a car. Thus, a significant portion of the economy depends on rail-based transit for getting its workers to work (Figure 7.6).

A shutdown of the system would cause financial losses to businesses and workers. Having no alternative, workers might drive their cars to work, worsening street-level congestion, which would then delay goods deliveries by trucks operating on the same streets and deter shoppers from going to the city, enhancing the economic damage.

For example, in December 2005 the Transit Workers Union Local 100 called a strike against New York's Metropolitan Transportation Authority, which was observed by New York City Transit workers, effectively ending bus and subway service in New York City. The strike occurred during the week before Christmas, from December 20 through December 22, one of the busiest shopping periods of the year. The financial impact resulting from lost workdays and retail sales was estimated to be $400 million on the first day and $300 million each succeeding day. The city's controller said that

FIGURE 7.6 **New York City's rebuilt PATH station at the World Trade Center.**

losses to the city overall would be $1.6 billion if the strike lasted a week (NY1.com, 2005).

In this case, commuter heavy rail services and ferries substituted for the transit system for some commuters. However, not every city has an alternative mass transit system if its primary system is closed, whether through labor action or terrorist action. Some commuters arranged carpools, while others living nearer to their jobs took taxis or walked, but most workers and even students suffered economic disruption.

As noted before, cyber systems are part of the critical infrastructure of mass transit, creating another vulnerability to attack. Homeland Security Presidential Directive 7 (HSPD-7) directed the Department of Homeland Security (DHS) to protect the nation's critical infrastructure, including its cyber systems (Bush, 2003). The National Cyber Security Division of DHS is responsible for the protection of critical cyber systems from attack and for the development of a response capability, including the National Cyber Alert System (DHS, 2010).

Cyber systems are recognized as potential targets for criminals, terrorists, and cyber warfare (SCADA, n.d.). Cyber security professionals warn that while computer hacking is one way to disrupt a system, physical intrusion is also possible. "[P]hysical access to network switches and jacks related to SCADA provides the capacity to bypass the security on control software and control SCADA networks" (SCADA, n.d.). Therefore, protection of SCADA systems and their components through firewalls and virtual private networks (VPNs) is needed, as well as well-documented and exercised redundancies and work-arounds to keep the critical infrastructure working to support mass transit and civil society.

Types of Attacks Against Rail-Based Mass Transit Vehicles and Systems

In the United States, mass transit systems are open and accessible. Scholars like Dornan and Maier (2005) have suggested that these factors make prevention of terrorist attacks against mass transit impossible. Features of the rail-based mass transit infrastructure heighten its attractiveness to terrorists. People cannot flee easily, as they are constrained by tracks, fences, elevation, or tunnels. Their light and air depend on power from the outside, although generator backup systems may be provided, and electric vehicles require electricity from the community grid to move.

As noted by Jenkins (1997) before, mass transit gathers large groups of people in a contained space for specified periods of time (the travel time between stations at a minimum when egress is not possible), making these vehicles attractive targets for disruption and attack. The attack mechanisms against rail-based vehicles are the same as for busses—small arms or explosive devices—although the limited air exchanges in subway systems have added biological and chemical attacks to the arsenal of weapons tried or planned by terrorists. The mechanisms of delivery include placement or tossing into the vehicle or station, similarly to busses.

One difference is that stations and service corridors offer many more areas to hide destructive or disruptive devices in advance of an attack. Such weapons can be set off by remote control or timed devices long after the criminal who placed the device is gone. This complicates both prevention and pre-event recognition, as well as apprehension after the event.

Criminals and the mentally ill pose the greatest threat of attack or disruption to mass transit, but terrorists' intentional attacks are designed for the maximum death, destruction, and psychological impact. Weapons used against rapid transit systems have included small arms, chemical, fire, and explosives. Disrupted plots have included biological weapons, and accidental disruptions through cyber malfunctions point the way to potential terrorist activities.

Jenkins's chronologies investigate attacks on mass transit back to 1920. He notes that attacks on surface transportation have increased over the past 25 years, with Israel suffering the most attacks while India and Pakistan have had the most fatalities related to attacks (Jenkins, 1997, p. 103). Of the more than 600 attacks against surface transportation between 1920 and 1997, attacks on rail-based mass transit have focused on commuter rail and light rail, with 27% of the attacks against vehicles and 13% of the attacks against stations. The IRA in the United Kingdom and the Algerian extremists in France have targeted railed-based urban mass transit. The chemical attack in Japan was on subway lines in Tokyo, and, starting in 1993, Islamic extremists began plotting attacks on the New York City subway systems (Jenkins, 1997, p. 107).

Long Island Railroad Murders

The worst commuter rail crime in America occurred in December 1993 on the Long Island Railroad Line just outside the Merillon Avenue station in Garden City, Long Island, a commuter suburb of New York City. Colin Ferguson murdered six people and 19 others were injured as he walked through the rail car shooting people, apparently randomly. Ferguson was an unemployed man in a battle with the state over a worker's compensation claim at the time of the shooting. His mental health problems included paranoia, and his defense was "black rage," a sense that he was being ill treated because of his race (Rabinovitz, 1993). The perpetrator was stopped and detained by three passengers and arrested by an off-duty officer who was waiting at the station to pick up his wife, a passenger on another part of the train (Schemo, 1993).

In addition to physical injuries, many passengers suffered severe psychological injuries from being trapped with the dead and dying while a response was organized. Congressmember Carolyn McCarthy lost her husband in this event, and her adult son was permanently disabled by his injuries. She ran for a seat in Congress on the basis of fighting for gun control as a result of her traumatic loss (CQ Staff, 1997). In a 2007 television interview after the Virginia Tech shootings, she stated that she still could not ride a train.

Aum Shinrikyo Attacks Tokyo Subway

Sarin was the weapon of choice in the religious cult's attack on the Tokyo subway in 1995. Cult members, many of whom were scientists, brewed a homemade version of the military nerve agent sarin. The Chiyoda Line, Marunouchi Line, and Hibiya Line, which all converge at the Kasumigaseki Station, were attacked by teams of cult members with small plastic bags of sarin that they punctured with sharpened umbrella tips. The bags were left behind in train cars and the movement of the train helped to further disperse the gas. The Kasumigaseki Station served the Tokyo Metropolitan Police Headquarters, and one strategy was to kill as many police officers as possible. The Aum Shinrikyo cult's goal was to discredit and bring down the government as part of an apocalyptic vision, but they in fact killed 12 people, injured several hundred, and exposed or contaminated thousands (Parsons et al., Science Applications International Corporation, & Interactive Elements Incorporated, 2006, p. 34).

Emergency response was complicated by the slow recognition of the attack and the movement of the contaminated trains through the system for some time after the attacks. Cleaning up the cars and ventilating the affected stations required the movement of workers and equipment below grade. Escape, for the exposed passengers, was complicated by the need to climb stairs as the nerve agent took its toll. Long-term effects included permanent disability, memory loss, and posttraumatic stress disorder (Parsons et al., Science Applications International Corporation, & Interactive Elements Incorporated, 2006).

Arson on Korean Subway

In February 2003 at the Jungangno subway station in Daegu, Korea, a subway car was set afire by a mentally unstable man. In an apparent attempt to commit suicide, he threw flammable liquid inside a subway car carrying 600 people. He lit the fluid as the car entered a station four levels below the surface. Apparently changing his mind at the last minute, the arsonist escaped. The contents of the car contributed to both the fire and the toxicity of the flames, and the flames destroyed electric circuits, locking the doors. By August, confirmed deaths had reached 198, with 147 injured and more than 50 people missing (Parsons, Brinkerhoff, et al., 2006).

The response to the fire was complicated by central control's management of the other trains and the train crew's actions that locked passengers in. Although trapped passengers called for help immediately, official communications took 10 minutes. The electrical failure spread to the station, shutting off emergency lighting and the ventilation system. The only access to the platform was by three levels of stairs from the street, hampering the arrival of first responders and emergency equipment. There was no standard evacuation procedure for the station. Seventy people were incinerated in the train car, while 50 died on the stairs trying to escape (Parsons et al., Science Applications International Corporation, & Interactive Elements Incorporated, 2006).

European IED Attacks

The most famous attacks on rail-based transit were on the Moscow and London subways and the Madrid commuter rail lines and station. All of these attacks used explosive devices that were placed on the trains. The Moscow attack was a suicide attack by Chechen terrorists that killed 39 and injured over 100 (Parsons et al., Science Applications International Corporation, & Interactive Elements Incorporated, 2006), while the London suicide attack on four lines was by Al Qaeda sympathizers, killing 54 and injuring dozens more (*Times of London,* 2005). The Madrid attackers left their backpacks of explosives behind with cell phone-based detonators. In each case, the goal was mass carnage to draw attention to a political cause.

These examples show that a variety of attacks have been perpetrated against rail-based mass transit vehicles and their passengers. Therefore, security strategies have to be developed to address the challenges.

Security Strategies for Rail-Based Mass Transit Vehicles and Systems

In Chapter 1 the philosophy and theory of security were described, encompassing physical, policy and procedure, and proprietary elements. It was noted that perfect security is not possible in the open environment of transportation systems. Cars and trucks, busses and livery, and scheduled fixed-route vehicles all operate in a completely open environment where security has to be built into the vehicle or provided through driver training.

In this chapter the focus is on vehicles that run on rails. Not only do they have fixed routes and schedules, but they also cannot deviate from their routes because they are bound to the rails. Within these restrictions, they have to use specified stations, tunnels, and bridges. In one way, this enhances their vulnerability to crime and terrorism because of the predictability of their locations. However, the limited range of their operation and the fixed nature of some of their assets permit the development of a security system that includes more coverage by technology like cameras, detectors, and alarms. Dornan and Maier (2005) note that even though prevention is extremely difficult, response and recovery can be planned for and implemented successfully through strategies like redundancy and dual purpose plans.

The Security Cycle

Because the rail-based assets are also in an open environment, many sources of information about the safety, security, and operations of the systems have to be accessed to understand the threats to the system and to create policies and procedures that lead to the desired outcome of enhanced safety and security in operations—to deter, detect, interdict, and mitigate security breaches of all kinds, including crime and terrorism.

Many groups observe the daily operations and conditions of the rail-based mass transit system. Graffiti, tampering with fences and barriers, and damaged system components like lights may first be noticed by system users and casual observers. The organization must have a routine and simple way for all concerns to be reported. Currently, many agencies have a counterterrorism program modeled on "see something, say something" that should be enlarged to accept comments about all types of inconsistencies and damage, not just packages that have been left behind and suspicious people.

Staff members of other organizations have the opportunity to observe mass transit facilities while doing their own work. Street repair crews, utility repair personnel, and grounds maintenance crews for other agencies may be working adjacent to mass transit property and observe changes in the condition of the property or its components, or unusual behavior by strangers to the area. Partnerships should be developed for the rapid exchange of information when anything unusual or out of place is observed, whether it is a damaged fence or a person photographing critical nodes of the rail system.

The employees of the organization are its "eyes and ears" every day. Train operators, ticket sellers, and station cleaning crews interact with the passengers and the system every day. They will be conscious of changes in passenger behavior, breakdowns of equipment, and operational problems with facilities. Vendors working in stations, like newspaper sellers and food vendors, should receive the same security vigilance training as mass transit staff, and all these station and system employees should have a central point of contact who receives all reports of damage, vandalism, and unusual behavior.

Mass transit systems have law enforcement personnel, whether on contract or as an internal department. Law enforcement personnel will be aware of increases in petty crime, passenger complaints, and staff concerns. They will also have connections with other law enforcement agencies in the area serving the community at large or other transit agencies. Through these connections, they can collect information on crime trends and security concerns, including developing gang activity and terrorism threats. Their reports must be included in the internal analysis of system operations and threats.

Finally, there are staff members whose job is to monitor and service the technology that provides security enhancements. These systems include intrusion detection, fire and smoke alarms, and closed circuit television cameras. The information collected from these systems should be analyzed by the operator and reported to the analysis section on a regular shift basis, with items of special concern reported immediately to analysis and law enforcement, as appropriate. The cameras are only a deterrent to crime if there is a quick response to inappropriate action. As noted in the previous chapter, cameras must be accompanied by the capability for a rapid response in the field through law enforcement or security staff.

All this information generated at the operational level must be passed through an accessible and easily understood system to the analysis group that develops proprietary intelligence from the various threads of information collected from the field-level staff members. Using information from DHS, National Critical Infrastructure Protection programs, regional intelligence fusion centers, and the Federal Transit Administration's weekly bulletins, these analysts will track trends in threats against transit and local crime and gang activity, as well as damage to the system and the presence of unexpected persons and property, to develop an evolving understanding of the threats to the system in their immediate area and within the region (Figure 7.7).

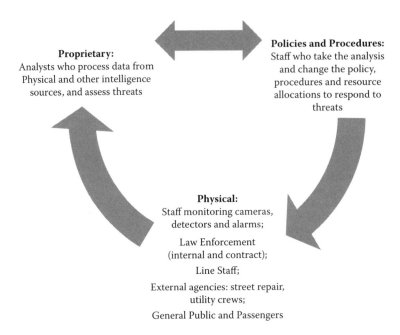

FIGURE 7.7 Security cycle.

The intelligence only becomes beneficial to the organization when it is applied to the current policies and procedures to determine what changes need to be made to enhance safety and security. Knowing crime trends and modes of damage will lead to enhanced attention to specific elements of the system, either through more physical presence in the vulnerable areas or the installation or redirection of lighting and cameras. For example, when the theft of copper became lucrative, the areas where spare wire was stored had to be kept locked at all times, not just at night, and the lighting around access points to electrical systems had to be enhanced to deter theft.

Once new strategies for thwarting attacks against the system are developed, training on the changes has to be delivered to the staff members of the system. Brief bulletins may be adequate for simple adjustments to lighting or changes of contact information for reporting inappropriate behavior or crime. Changes to policies regarding access to areas of the property or enhancements in security systems may require shift-change briefings for some or all staff members. New policies and procedures will not be used unless all affected staff members have been trained effectively in the new strategies.

Security Technologies

Many technology-based systems are available to enhance safety and security in the rail-based mass transit environment. Lighting, ventilation redundancy, roving patrols, and fire protection systems have dual use for day-to-day system operation and emergency service. Other strategies, like bomb-sniffing dogs and CBRNE detectors, may have increased cost and limited day-to-day benefits. A cost benefit analysis is an important part of every purchasing decision, as some systems will show immediate benefits, while others would only be worthwhile in a heightened threat-specific environment, and only for short durations. For example, the bomb-sniffing dogs are only effective for brief work intervals of 15 to 20 minutes each (Schaffer, 2006) over a 3- to 5-hour workday (Parsons et al., Science Applications International Corporation, & Interactive Elements Incorporated, 2006). Explosive detectors are not useful if the threat is a chemical attack. Conversely, enhanced lighting in the parking lot may deter car burglaries and also prevent pedestrian accidents.

There are many technologies and strategies that can be applied to counter crime and terrorist activities, but not all are equally effective, and some are very expensive. Table 7.1 provides an evaluated list of possible strategies and technologies that could be used on rail-based vehicles, rights-of-way, parking facilities, and stations, including an analysis of whether they would deter, detect, interdict, or mitigate against terrorist activities and crime. Technical specifications for the installation and implementation require situation-specific engineering.

Human Element in Security Systems

Some technologies that counter terrorism and crime work without human interface once they have been designed and installed. A ventilation system operates as designed as long as the required power is provided. Lighting requires only replacement of burned-out bulbs to perform as designed. Some systems, however, require continuous human involvement to be useful.

The best example of such a system is the camera. Cameras can be placed in strategic locations to create an archive of events that will only be accessed after a defined event. These camera recordings may be kept for hours, days, weeks, or longer. In 2005 the London Underground had a camera system that provided extensive coverage of the system and its components but was only making recordings that could be accessed as needed. After the bombings in July 2005, the cameras were useful in identifying the perpetrators, but they were not managed to aid in the recognition of the disaster or the rescue of the victims.

Many American mass transit entities have cameras installed in the passenger areas, in the driver's area, and on the front and back of the vehicle. These cameras are used to recognize and generate a response to traffic accidents, to determine who was on the vehicle for liability purposes, and to determine if the driver was distracted or in some other way at fault. Many

TABLE 7.1 Security Strategies for Rail-Based Mass Transit

Functions	Relative Effectiveness	Costs	Physical or Operational?	Strategy	Benefits/ Dual Use
Minimum Strategies					
Lighting	High	Medium	Physical	Deter	Antitheft, safety
Ventilatilon enhancements	High	Very high	Physical and operational	Mitigate	Safety
Fire detection system	Medium	Low	Physical	Detection	Safety
Fire protection system	High	High	Physical and operational	Mitigate	Safety
Cameras	High	Medium	Physical and operational	Deter, interdict	Traffic surveillance, facility design efficiency
Security awareness training: employees and passengers	High	Low	Operational	Deter, mitigate	Safety, security
Roving patrols	Medium	Low	Operational	Deter, detect, interdict	Safety, security
Employee background checks	Low	Low	Operational	Deter, detect	Identify unqualified employees
Full-scale emergency response exercises	High	Low	Operational	Deter, interdict, mitigate	Meet first responders and adjacent agency personnel
Seismic/wind reinforcement of structural members	High	Medium	Physical	Mitigate	Damage from explosions, earthquakes, hurricanes, windstorms, and tornadoes
Cyber security: firewalls, antivirus software, data backup, computer room security system	High	Low	Physical and operational	Deter, detect, interdict, mitigate	Damage from power surges, loss of power, natural hazards, system failures

TABLE 7.1 (continued) Security Strategies for Rail-Based Mass Transit

Functions	Relative Effectiveness	Costs	Physical or Operational?	Strategy	Benefits/ Dual Use
Additional Strategies for Elevated Threats					
Guards at station entrances	High	Low	Operational	Deter, detect, interdict	Public assurance
Inspections— baggage, carry-ons	High	Low	Operational	Deter, detect, interdict	Public assurance
Bomb-sniffing dogs	Medium	Low	Operational	Deter, detect	Public assurance
Explosive detectors—fixed	High	Medium	Physical	Detect	
Explosive detectors—mobile	High	Low	Physical	Detect	
Redundant systems	High	High	Physical	Mitigate	Increase usable life of systems
Robots: rescue	High	Medium	Physical and operational	Detect, interdict	Bombs, search and rescue, sensors

Sources: Adapted from Parsons, Brinkerhoff, Quade, & Douglas, Inc.; Science Applications International Corporation; and Interactive Elements Incorporated. (2006). TCRP Report 86/NCHRP Report 525. Washington, DC: Transportation Research Board, and Rose, D. M. (2003). TCRP Report 86. Washington, DC: Transportation Research Board.

agencies also have cameras focused on parking areas and station platforms and passageways. These camera images are often both recorded and monitored, meaning that they not only serve the archival function for investigation and litigation purposes, but also serve as a means of rapidly generating a response to an event, especially if the driver or passenger is incapacitated and unable to summon help. The mere presence of a camera may have a deterrent effect on crime. For example, cameras in parking lots have been shown to lower the incidence of vandalism and car burglary.

Cameras that are monitored offer the opportunity to interdict crime and terrorist activities, as well as identify passengers with medical emergencies. They can be broadcast to first responder command posts to provide a better operating picture as the incident commander creates the incident action plan. But all these benefits are only realized if the camera monitor is properly trained and alert. The camera is only as good for emergency response as the employee who is watching it.

Roving Patrols

Security or law enforcement personnel who are regularly patrolling a facility or a vehicle route will enhance the passengers' sense of safety. Careful surveillance, however, will allow criminals and terrorists to become familiar with the deployment schedules and to create their plans for criminal activity in the intervals between patrol presences. However, randomness forces the potential perpetrator to conduct surveillance for a longer time, trying to discern the pattern in law enforcement presence. This slows down the tempo of their operation and may lead them to seek a softer, less prepared target. Therefore, roving patrols must also be random to be effective.

Changing the number of personnel and the direction of their patrol routes is part of a random pattern. In addition, plainclothes officers and officers from other agencies can be introduced into the environment to increase the unpredictability of law enforcement presence. After the Long Island Railroad shootings, the agency offered free rides to law enforcement officers going to and from work, whether uniformed or in plain clothes, as long as they were armed. This was widely publicized and proved effective in lowering petty crime on the railroad (Rabinowitz, 1993).

Random patrols can include random visual inspections of passenger baggage or explosive trace wipes. Although airport-style baggage checks would lead to unacceptable delays in the open system of American mass transit, the random checks seem to be acceptable to passengers. The Massachusetts Bay Transportation Authority (MBTA) in greater Boston, Metropolitan Transit Authority (MTA) in New York City and vicinity, Washington Metropolitan Area Transportation Authority (WMATA) in the nation's capital, and New Jersey Transit have institutionalized random inspections effectively (Nakanishi, 2011).

The roving patrol by local resources can be enhanced by outside agency personnel to add another layer of randomness to transit. DHS has created visible intermodal prevention and response (VIPR) teams to enhance law enforcement capabilities of passenger rail and mass transit agencies, noting that randomness is a key to their operational posture: "[U]npredictable security measures...deter potential terrorist activity."

DHS promotional materials for transit agencies emphasize that VIPR teams "can be assembled on short notice in an emergency," and routine visits can be scheduled as little as 2 weeks in advance (TSA, n.d.). Teams are intended to be highly visible, interdicting petty crime, providing perimeter control, and conducting passenger baggage checks on trains, as well as patrolling stations and platforms. One high-profile detail was on WMATA during the 2009 presidential inauguration (TSA, n.d.).

Explosives Detection

Jenkins's research has demonstrated that the greatest threat to mass transit is explosive devices, which are usually easily concealed in carry-on items or clothing. Backpacks were used in London and Madrid. Shoes, vests, and even underwear have been used to conceal explosive devices in vehicles. Because explosive devices are not usually easily seen, other clues must be used to lead to detection or interdiction.

Behavioral assessment is one way to detect people who may be about to commit a crime, including using an explosive device. DHS has a variety of research projects focused on behavioral assessment as an actionable indicator of terrorist intent. The Science and Technology Directorate is supporting research into unintentional behaviors that reveal the intent to commit a crime. One such project, the Hostile Intent Detection—Validation of Observable Indicators of Suspicious Behavior Project, is validating behavioral components currently used by TSA and Border Patrol agents to screen for smugglers as indicators of other types of criminal behavior. Insider threats and violent intent modeling are related projects (DHS, 2011c).

Random searches are lawful provided there is no discrimination in the selection of those to be searched. Constitutional freedoms and civil liberties protect people from being targeted for unlawful searches and seizure of their property. The law requires that law enforcement officers detaining a person or searching his property must have articulable probable cause for their actions. DHS has developed a civil rights/civil liberties impact assessment program to determine which types of searches would be lawful. Screening passengers by observation techniques (SPOT) is a confidential process currently used at the border to assess truckers. "This program is designed to be a nonintrusive means of identifying potentially high-risk individuals who exhibit behavior indicative of high levels of stress, fear, or deception" (DHS, 2011a). It is lawful because border searches have been deemed routine by the courts (DHS, 2011b).

A related program is future attribute screening technology (FAST), still in the research phase, that would use "noncontact sensors to measure physiological and behavioral indicators of 'malintent'—defined as the mental state and intention of an individual planning or intending to cause harm to the United States or the general public" (DHS, 2011b). The DHS legal advisers have determined that FAST would require cause or consent in general application, but might be a permissible action in lawful random transit screening and would be considered reasonable (DHS, 2011b).

The behavioral clues being developed by DHS human factors projects can be used to explain why one person is targeted in a nonrandom search.

They can also be used to determine who should be screened for explosives. DHS has developed guidance documents like handbooks, guides, and cards for use by law enforcement and security teams. For example, "Suicide Bomber Recognition and Response" guides observers in recognizing suspicious behaviors in people and appearance in baggage. VIPR teams and local law enforcement may conduct random sweeps for explosives using dogs that move through crowds, mass transit vehicles, and baggage storage spaces.

Portable explosives detection units can be used for rapid evaluation of left-behind packages or suspicious objects; however, to swab an item in someone's possession, probable cause has to be established. Behavioral cues can be a valuable tool in selecting people and objects to be screened from a crowded mass transit facility. In high-value target facilities, permanent explosive detection devices could be installed at entrances to the station, but for most mass transit facilities, a portable detection machine for use during sensitive events or during heightened threat levels would be more cost effective.

Training and Exercises

Effective security depends on employees. They work in the environment every day and are most likely to notice when something is out of place or some person does not belong. Harnessing this knowledge requires two elements of training: what to report and how to report it. Security awareness training is available through independent study courses online, through video-based training, and through in-person instruction. Initial training like the AWR-160 WMD Terrorism Awareness course can be taken online or in person. Transportation-specific courses like System Security Awareness for Transit Employees are available through the Federal Transit Agency.

Employees must also be trained on emergency and security plans of the agency. This can be done initially through new employee training and briefing training, fliers, or formal courses. This training would include agency protocols for emergency response and security events, including medical emergencies, fire-related events, and crimes in the vehicles or facilities. The training should be repeated regularly to reinforce the information and to provide updates of any changes to policies and procedures.

Passengers should also be reminded that they can contribute to their own safety and security by notifying the transit agency of unusual items, items left behind, and people behaving strangely. Ubiquitous cell phones make sending messages easier, and video of emergency events is often taken by the public, which could be used to augment surveillance camera recordings.

For example, video sent from cell phones of passengers in the 2005 London attacks assisted investigators in their understanding of the events.

FIGURE 7.8 **Multiagency emergency response training is sponsored by the ACE Train Urban Area Security Initiative.**

Many transit agencies have sponsored "see something, say something" campaigns to solicit the help and cooperation of the public. An MTI study by Rohlich, Haas, and Edwards (2009) suggests that existing campaigns in San Francisco Bay Area transit agencies have attracted the attention of passengers and have contributed to heightened awareness of left-behind items and suspicious behaviors.

Training should be reinforced by exercises. This may be as simple as a brief discussion of the proper management of a theoretical event during briefing or as complex as agency participation in a full-scale exercise involving other agencies, first responders, and even community members. For example, California sponsors an annual "Great Shakeout" in which the entire community is encouraged to take protective measures against earthquake shaking at the same time. Transit agencies could join such events to involve employees and passengers in safety and security practice. Exercises must be designed to reinforce training and be conducted in concert with the emergency plans (Figure 7.8).

Cyber Security

Cyber security is another focus of mass transit security cycles. As noted previously, many aspects of mass transit rely on SCADA and other computer-based systems. Failures may be caused directly by intentional hacking or the introduction of viruses into the system. Criminals could gain physical access to server rooms or other system components to damage, shut down, or change the security system protocols. Remote or automated control of mechanical, electrical, and communication systems also offers a potential access point for intrusion.

Security mechanisms to overcome many of these threats are routinely available. Firewalls, antivirus software and redundant manual controls of mechanical, electrical, and communications systems are available. Again, the human element is the key to security success. Employees must be taught to maintain tight security standards at all times. System computers should not be used to access the Internet. Personal USB drives and similar media that might contain viruses should not be introduced into the system. Passwords must be safeguarded. Physical locks on computer system facilities must be kept locked, and doors must not be propped open for smoke breaks or to help out a colleague who is arriving late or forgot the key. Codes on access points and passwords for systems should be changed regularly. Hot sites and cold sites should be established to ensure continued operations in the event of local disruption to power, Internet access, or other support systems or access to the physical space used by the computers.

Case Studies

PATH Train Evacuation Success on 9/11

The 9/11 attacks on the World Trade Center towers were not designed as an attack against mass transit, yet multiple transit systems were victims of the terrorists. The twin towers were built on a plaza above a large underground complex of five stories. The first two floors were a shopping mall, while the third through fifth floors were the parking garage. Running through the parking garage on the fourth level down was the tube that carried the PATH train from New Jersey. The PATH station was under the World Trade Center (WTC) complex. Also within the footprint of the plaza were connections and tunnels for New York City Transit subway lines 1 and 9 (Jenkins & Edwards-Winslow, 2002).

When the towers collapsed, the transit infrastructure under it was destroyed, yet no lives were lost in the stations or on the systems because of the quick reaction of well trained employees who followed the emergency plan that they had exercised. When word of the plane crash into the first tower was received by PATH employees, the first reports were of an explosion or fire in Tower One. A PATH deputy director working in the tower ordered the train master to begin emergency operations, having trains bypass the WTC station. A train that arrived and discharged passengers immediately had them reboard and returned them to safety in New Jersey. Remaining passengers were evacuated from the station by Port Authority police officers and operations personnel. Another train arriving from New Jersey passed through the station without stopping and returned to New Jersey. A third train left its passengers in Hoboken, the last stop on the New Jersey side of the river, and went to the WTC station to take on remaining passengers and staff, ensuring that no one was left in the WTC station (Parsons et al., Science Applications International Corporation, & Interactive Elements Incorporated, 2006).

Effective communication following a well-documented plan led to the safe evacuation of the transit spaces under the WTC footprint. When the towers collapsed, the infrastructure was destroyed and was only replaced in 2003, but rolling stock and passengers were all safely in New Jersey that day.

WMATA Cyber Failures as a Paradigm of Possible Terrorist Attack

Modern mass transit systems are dependent on radios and computers for running the systems. Train signals along the tracks and track switches are operated by remote control devices that are automated using radio signals. The equipment that sends the audio radio signal is out in the open on the track. On Monday June 22, 2009, about 5:00 p.m., one WMATA metro train struck another from behind, killing nine people and injuring another 52. The accident was blamed on the malfunction of the audio signal that should have warned that the track was in use. Five days before the accident, a part for the track circuit where the accident occurred was replaced, but the signal strength for the automatic train protection (ATP) system was not adjusted after the new part was installed. The National Transportation Safety Board's letter to WMATA's general manager suggested that this missing step caused the accident because the second train did not receive a signal that the first train was on the same track (Hersman, 2009).

While this event was an accident, it demonstrates the vulnerability of radio- and computer-based communications systems that operate many aspects of the rail-based mass transit systems in the United States. Some monorail and light rail systems routinely operate without human drivers. Other systems rely on cyber and radio linkages for safety systems like track signals, as in this case. Terrorists or criminals could exploit these system designs and use false cyber information to cause accidents that generate loss of life and economic damage.

Summary

In the open environment of rail-based mass transit, perfect security is not possible. Steps can be taken to encourage public participation in the security of the system. Employees can become partners in observation and reporting suspicious objects and people. Mitigation measures can be taken to lessen the likelihood of damage and the amount of damage from crime or attack. Deterrence, detection, and interdiction systems can be applied. Rapid response will limit damage and losses, and a recovery plan will limit economic impacts.

In the next chapter, the topic of freight rail will be considered, with operations in a similar rail-based environment, but with fewer human observers available to the system.

Discussion Questions

1. Why is mass transit operating on rails an attractive target for terrorists? What other security concerns would a mass transit security plan have to address?

2. What special vulnerabilities come from operating in subways and tunnels? What strategies and technologies can enhance security in these environments?

3. What are the security concerns for light rail and trolley systems? What strategies and technologies can enhance security in these environments?

4. How does cyber security impact rail-based transit security? What are the specific vulnerabilities that cyber systems induce in rail-based transit, and how can they be addressed through security strategies and technology?

5. While the rail-based transit systems are predictable as to their time and place of operations, they also have the potential for a more robust security structure for these same reasons. Describe the layers of security that can be applied to a light rail surface system and to a subway system.

Note

1. America's long-standing alliance with Israel and the provision of military supplies during the Yom Kippur War led to the Organization of Petroleum-Exporting Countries (OPEC) placing an embargo on oil exports to the United States in 1973. In 1979 the Iranian Revolution led to another oil embargo. Each time, diminished supplies of gasoline led to long lines at gas stations, rationing, limited days of access to gas, and a significant increase in the cost of gas after years of relatively steady and inexpensive prices.

References

APTA (American Public Transportation Association). (2004). New York celebrates centennial of subway opening. Accessed July 23, 2011 at http://www.apta.com/passengertransport/Documents/archive_1077.htm

Bush, G. W. (2003). *Homeland Security Presidential Directive 7: Critical infrastructure identification, prioritization and protection.* Washington, DC: The White House.

CQ staff. (1997, Jan. 4). Carolyn McCarthy, D-NY (4). *CQ Weekly,* 75.

DHS. (2010). National Cyber Security Division. Accessed July 23, 2011, at http://www.dhs.gov/xabout/structure/editorial_0839.shtm

DHS. (2011a). Civil rights/civil liberties impact assessments. Accessed Dec. 23, 2011, at http://www.dhs.gov/xabout/structure/gc_1273849042853.shtm

DHS. (2011b). Future attribute screening technology. Accessed December 23, 2011, at http://www.dhs.gov/xlibrary/assets/crcl/crcl-assessment-fast.pdf.

DHS. (2011c). Human factors/behavioral sciences projects. Accessed July 23, 2011, at http://www.dhs.gov/files/programs/gc_1218480185439.shtm#8

Dornan, D. L., & Maier, M. P. (2005). *Incorporating security into the transportation planning process* (NCHRP Report 525). Washington, DC: Transportation Research Board.

Gladwell, M. (2002). *The tipping point.* New York, NY: Back Bay Books.

Guerrero, P. (2002, Sept. 18). Statement in testimony before the Subcommittee on Banking, Housing and Urban Affairs, U.S. Senate. GAO 02-1075T.

Hersman, D. A. P. (2009, Sept. 22). Letter to Catoe, J. B., Jr., general manager, WMATA. Washington, DC: National Transportation Safety Board.

Jenkins, B. M. (1997). *Protecting surface transportation systems and patrons from terrorist activities* (IISTPS Report 97-04). San Jose, CA: Mineta Transportation Institute.

Jenkins, B. M., & Butterworth, B. (2010). *Explosives and incendiaries used in terrorist attacks on public surface transportation: A preliminary empirical analysis* (MTI Report WP 09-02). San Jose, CA: Mineta Transportation Institute.

Jenkins, B. M., & Edwards-Winslow, F. L. (2002). *Saving city lifelines: Lessons learned in the 9-11 attacks* (MTI Report 02-06). San Jose, CA: Mineta Transportation Institute.

Mayerson, A. (1992). The history of the ADA: A movement perspective. Accessed July 23, 2011, at http://www.dredf.org/publications/ada_history.shtml

Monorail Society. (n.d.). Monorails of Japan: Tokyo-Haneda. Accessed July 23, 2011, at http://www.monorails.org/tMspages/TokyoH.html

Nakanishi, Y. (2011, July-August). Addressing vulnerabilities in transit security. *TR News,* 20–28.

NY1.com. (2005). TWU leaders refuse to back down despite threat of jail time. Accessed July 23, 2011, at http://www.ny1.com/content/top_stories/55772/twu-leaders-refuse-to-back-down-despite-threat-of-jail-time

Parkinson, T., & Fisher, I. (1996). *Rail transit capacity.* TCRP Report 13. Washington, DC: Transportation Research Board.

Parsons, Brinkerhoff, Quade, & Douglas, Inc.; Science Applications International Corporation; and Interactive Elements Incorporated. (2006). *Making transportation tunnels safe and secure* (TCRP Report 86/NCHRP Report 525). Washington, DC: Transportation Research Board.

Philadelphia. (2007). Accessed July 23, 2011, at http://urbanrail.net/am/phil/philadelphia.htm

Rabinovitz, J. (1993, December 10). Death on the LIRR: Police look for the spark that led to the shootings. *New York Times,* p. 9.

Rohlich, N., Haas, P., & Edwards, F. (2009). *Exploring the effectiveness of transit security awareness campaigns in the San Francisco Bay Area* (MTI Report 09-19). San Jose, CA: Mineta Transportation Institute.

Rose, D. M. (2003). *Robotic devices: A guide for the transit environment* (TCRP Report 86). Washington, DC: Transportation Research Board.

SCADA. (n.d.). SCADA systems. Accessed July 23, 2011, at http://www.scadasystems.net/

Schaffer, A. (2006, January 17). Sorry, dogs don't do subways: Canine sniffers won't make mass transit safer. Slate.com. Accessed January 19, 2006; retrieved January 14, 2008, from http://www.slate.com/id/2134394/fr/rss/

Schemo, D. J. (1993, December 9). Death on the LIRR: The confrontation; 3 credited in capture of gunman. *New York Times,* p. B 9.

Schulz, D. M., & Gilbert, S. (2011). *Video surveillance uses by rail transit agencies.* TCRP Synthesis 90. Washington, DC: Transportation Research Board.

SeattleCenter Monorail. (2011). A brief Seattle monorail history. Accessed July 23, 2011, at http://www.seattlemonorail.com/history.php

Times of London. (2005, July 14). Four suicide bombers caused London blasts, police say. Accessed July 15, 2005, DHS listserve

TSA. (n.d.) *Visible intermodal prevention and response (VIPR) teams: Working with security partners for a safe and secure transportation network.* Brochure and FAQ sheets packet. Washington, DC: TSA.

U.S. DOT. (2011). *Pocket guide to transportation.* Washington, DC: RITA.

Chapter 8

Freight and Long-Distance Passenger Heavy Rail

Keywords: heavy rail, freight trains, passenger trains, tunnels, stations, bridges, electricity, diesel power, risk assessment, surveillance, weapons of mass disruption, safety, security, trespassing, vandalism, derailments, rails, locomotives, class I railroad, regional railroad, short line railroad, hazardous materials, acutely hazardous materials, toxic inhalation hazards, TIH, high threat urban areas, HTUA

Learning Objectives

After reading this chapter you should be able to

- Identify potential security vulnerabilities in heavy rail systems
- Understand how rail-based, long-distance operations generate vulnerabilities
- Identify hazardous materials and toxic inhalation hazards (TIHs) in shipments
- Understand the role of technology in long-distance operations security
- Understand the strategies used by terrorists to disrupt freight and long-distance passenger rail systems

Components of the Freight and Long-Distance Passenger Heavy Rail System

Americans' fascination with trains is clearly demonstrated in the culture of its toys and pastimes. Thomas the Tank Engine toys, books, and videos for toddlers give way to HO scale layouts for the elementary school child's "Christmas platform" and the adult hobby of "train watching." The railroads are among the most desirable properties on the Monopoly board in recognition of their tremendous economic importance. There is something about the romance of the train whistle and the trip into the unknown that catches the imagination. "The Chiefs, the Limiteds, the Zephyrs. They were more than passenger trains. They surrounded us with impeccable comfort and tantalized our palates with elegant dining fare as they whisked into a world of romance and mystique" (Amtrak Historical Society, n.d.).

American History and the Railroad

The railroad made the America that we know today. The industrial North had hundreds more miles of privately operated track than the agrarian South when the Civil War, or War Between the States, began. Historians credit the North's success to this greater industrial mobility, allowing raw materials for the war machine to move rapidly to the manufacturing centers, and people and equipment to move from battlefield to battlefield by rail. Starting with McClellan's Peninsula Campaign in 1862, the "railroad gun" was an important artillery piece up to World War II. The Leopold, a famous German 280 mm rail gun used at the battle of Anzio, used railroad tunnels for concealment by day and fired its 550 pound shells at night (McCall, 2008). It is currently stored at Fort Lee, Virginia.

Railroads created the United States' continental identity. The transcontinental railroad tied the westernmost state of California to the ports of the Mississippi River, Philadelphia, Baltimore, and New York in 1869. The construction of the transcontinental railroad was accomplished with financial assistance from the federal government, including land grants, creating a tie that lasts through the twenty-first century. The trains changed the economic balance among the nation's regions, allowing people to move freely and in relative comfort between the coasts, allowing the agricultural and mineral products of the West to reach eastern markets easily and finished industrial products to reach formerly isolated farmers on the Great Plains and consumers on the Pacific coast.

America's railroads are the busiest in the world, moving more freight than any other system. They earn $42 billion annually in revenue transporting 12.7% of the nation's goods by volume. Most of the income derives from moving coal, chemicals, nonmetal minerals, food, and automobiles

(TSA, n.d.). Many of the chemicals are hazardous materials, and the toxic inhalation hazard (TIH) chemicals pose a special concern for security and accident prevention.

Categories of Rail

The rail system in the United States is divided into four categories of service. First is long-distance passenger rail, which was consolidated under the National Railroad Passenger Corporation in 1970 and called Amtrak. After struggling to compete with the convenience of passenger cars for short trips and the speed of airlines for longer trips, many of the nation's passenger lines were no longer able to operate as profit-making private enterprises, leading to the publicly funded consolidation. Road congestion and post-9/11 airport searches have once again made rail travel attractive to more people. The 9/11 attacks resulted in the closure of American air space for 48 hours, making long-distance passenger rail transportation a critical element in the ability of stranded travelers to get home (Jenkins & Edwards-Winslow, 2002).

Amtrak travels 272 million vehicle-miles a year, or 6,179 million passenger miles (U.S. DOT, 2011, p. 16). Amtrak operates 21,178 miles of rail for passenger use, with 278 locomotives and 1,177 cars for long-distance passenger trips (U.S. DOT, 2011, pp. 11–13).

Freight rail companies in the mid-twentieth century struggled to support aging infrastructure and deficit-generating commuter passenger services. Federal regulations made it difficult for freight rail to compete with trucks in freight delivery. When the six railroads that served the Northeast corridor and the Midwest all filed for bankruptcy, Congress formed Conrail in April 1976 and provided subsidies to repair aging infrastructure and replace rolling stock, recognizing the economic importance of the rail system. By 1980 Congress turned over the operation of commuter railroads to the states, and Conrail was operating without federal funding. In March 1987 Conrail was sold for a $1.9 billion initial public offering (IPO) of stock, the largest in history, becoming a for-profit private company. In 1997 CSX and Norfolk Southern acquired Conrail through a joint stock purchase, and Conrail operates as a switching and terminal railroad within the corporations (Conrail, 2003).

There are over 550 freight railroads operating in the United States (Figure 8.1). Freight railroads are in three categories: Class I or long haul, Class II or regional, and Class III or short line. Their characteristics are listed in Table 8.1.

Class I railroads have 94,082 miles of freight lines, Class II have 16,690 miles of regional freight lines, and Class III have 28,554 miles of local freight lines. Class 1 railroads have 24,003 locomotives and 450,297 freight cars, with additional rail vehicles in daily service that are owned by the shippers or

FIGURE 8.1   Freight railroad engine.

TABLE 8.1 Classes of Freight Railroads

Freight Railroad Class	Description
Class I	Operates over large areas, in multiple states, and concentrates on the long-haul, high-density, intercity traffic lines with annual revenues over $250 million
Class II (regional)	Operates on at least 350 miles of active lines and has annual revenues between $20 and $250 million
Class III (short line)	Operates on less than 350 miles of line and generates less than $20 million in annual revenues

Source: TSA. (2011).Freight rail overview. Accessed July 20, 2011, at https://www.tsa.gov/what_we_do/tsnm/freight_rail/index.shtm

non-Class 1 railroad companies (U.S. DOT, 2011, pp. 11–13). There are seven Class I railroads (two of which are Canadian): Burlington Northern Santa Fe, CSX, Union Pacific, Kansas City Southern, Norfolk Southern, Canadian Pacific, and Canadian National (TSA, n.d.). Class 1 railroad freight travels 37,226 million vehicle-miles per year, about 25% of the distance traveled by freight trucks (U.S. DOT, 2011, p. 16). Freight rail statistics are shown in Table 8.2.

Single track operation is common throughout the United States. Dual tracks and sidings are provided in limited areas to permit trains going in opposite directions to pass, and faster passenger trains to pass slower freight trains. The coordination of the timing of the two trains' passage is critical, and switches control the location of trains on tracks, spurs, and sidings.[1] Track is owned by individual railroads but shared across the system. Freight

TABLE 8.2 Freight Rail Statistics

Class I	93% of freight revenues
89% of railroad workers	
Miles of railroad operated	140,000+
Freight cars in service	642,405
Locomotives in service	22,548

Source: TSA. (n.d.). Freight rail modal annex, p. 3. Accessed July 20, 2011, at http://www.tsa.gov/assets/pdf/modal_annex_freight_rail.pdf

is transferred between companies while en route at rail yards and sidings, where new consists[2] are created for the trains (TSA, n.d.). In addition, Amtrak and even commuter rail services operate on track owned by the freight railroads. According to the GAO (Guerrero & Rabkin, 2004), 95% of Amtrak's 22,000 mile network operates on freight railroad-owned tracks. Conversely, Amtrak owns most of the Northeast corridor between Boston and Washington on which commuter and freight trains also operate.

In some places, especially in the West, railroad track runs straight across open plains. In the East and mountain West, trains depend on tunnels and bridges. Their characteristics are the same as those discussed in Chapter 5. While they speed trains to their destination, they also provide potential choke points when they are damaged. Many rail bridges are maintained in a nonusable position until the train reaches a sensor, at which point the bridge is lowered, aligned with the track, or closed to permit passage across newly joined rails. These operations depend on power and working sensors.

Freight Rail Operations

The freight rail system consists of trains made up of locomotives, which weigh about 200 tons each, and rail cars in a number of configurations: boxcars, hoppers, gondolas, flatbed, tankers, automobile racks, refrigerated vehicles, well cars for containers, and other specialized vehicles. Most freight locomotives are diesel powered, but much of passenger rail operates on electrified networks. Multiple locomotives may power one train, and most locomotives can pull or push a train. Each train averages 100 cars and weighs about 6,000 tons. Trains travel an average of 55 mph and require a mile to stop in emergency mode (Illinois State University Police, 2012).

The freight rail system is operated to move large quantities of heavy goods across the country or through a region. However, the Class I trains seldom go from origin to destination without stops. Cars are added and removed from trains at sidings and rail yards along the train's route, and they are then picked up by another long haul, regional, or short line railroad to get to the final destination. The cars to be removed at the first station are placed directly behind the locomotive, and each station order block is loaded into the consist from there.

A train car goes through three processes on its journey from origin to destination. It is assembled as part of the "local pickup and set out of cars." The cars are then classified for DOT regulation purposes and the consist is finalized. Finally, the car moves down the track in "line haul" (Thompson, Zamejc, & Ahlbeck, 1992, p. 139).

Train consists are created in station order blocks based on the stations where the train will go and the cars will be removed. Movement of train cars within rail yards requires the presence of the train's crew as well as yard staff, meaning that time in the yard moving cars around adds to the cost of the shipment to the rail company. At the origin, the conductor receives the consist showing the cars in station blocks, and he determines where the train cars have to be removed and added at each exchange point. It is estimated that each movement requires 15 to 20 minutes, so being able to remove and add cars in blocks significantly cuts down on the time for dropping off and picking up cars (Thompson et al., 1992, p. 131).

Nonrail Components

The American rail system has numerous components in addition to the rails. Switches and signals that control rail traffic are operated from remote locations by radio signals, often controlled by computers. Cyber-based elements include computer scheduling of trains and rail car movements, tracking of rail cars in transit, and management of grade crossing signals and other safety warning devices. These systems depend on the provision of electrical power from the community grid. As mentioned earlier, while most freight is moved by diesel locomotive, many passenger lines are electrified.

Stations allow for the exchange of passengers and freight, often having auxiliary activities like intermodal transfer to trucks or maritime, and parking lots for passenger and employee cars. Rail yards store cars that are waiting to be transferred to different trains and those that are out of service, some of which may contain hazardous materials including TIHs. Rail yards are also the repair facilities for the railroad. The roundhouse services and repairs locomotives and their component parts, such as boilers and electric motors. The train cars are repaired in railroad shops within the yards (USMC, 1942).

Repair of rail lines requires a fleet of specialized vehicles. Large self-propelled machines lay and repair track. Small pickup trucks with rubber tires and steel wheels at rail gauge manage small maintenance projects. Rescue cranes, towing vehicles, electrical systems repair vehicles, and snow removal equipment all operate on the same rails as the trains. Because the rails run through so many otherwise inaccessible areas, all emergency equipment has to run on rails to get it to the point of accidents in remote areas, so tracks that have been destroyed can slow emergency response.

Rail and Commerce

Today, heavy freight rail has become the "land bridge" between the industrial production in East Asia and consumers on the American East Coast and in Europe (TSA, n.d., p. 3). There are more than 1.2 million intermodal containers on the equipment registry of the American Association of Railroads (AAR), and many more containers owned by maritime and trucking companies (Blaszak, 2006) that carry trade goods. Within the U.S. domestic transportation system, $436 billion of commodities travel by rail alone, while combined truck and rail shipments account for $187 billion, and combined rail and water shipments account for $14 billion. In the international trade, rail accounts for the transportation of $35,263 million in exports and $60, 361 million in imports (U.S. DOT, 2011, pp. 32–33).

While trucks carry a higher dollar value of merchandise, trains account for the heavy bulk commodities that cannot pass over roads and much of the toxic hazardous materials transport within the country. Forty percent of all intercity goods travel by train. Grain, petroleum products, and ethanol account for a large proportion of goods traveling by rail. Of the coal used for creating electricity, 67% travels by rail. Hazardous materials travel 72 trillion ton-miles on rail every year. They include chlorine that is used to process safe drinking water and chemicals used in refining gasoline, fuels for vehicles and home heating, "farming, medical applications, manufacturing and mining" (TSA, n.d., p. 3). Table 8.3 lists the freight rail hazardous materials/TIH data.

Railroads remain a key to military support and supply. The Department of Defense Strategic Rail Corridor Network (STRACNET) includes 30,000 miles of rail to support military bases throughout the nation (AAR, 2011). Because military equipment is heavy, it is usually moved by rail rather than

TABLE 8.3 Freight Rail Hazardous Materials/TIH Data

Category/Type Annually, 2003	Number
HAZMAT originations in the United States and Canada	1.6 million
Tank car originations	1.2 million
Liquefied petroleum gas (LPG) tank car shipments	85,198
Chlorine tank car shipments	30,254
Anhydrous ammonia tank car shipments	30,687

Source: TSA. (n.d.). Freight rail modal annex, p. 3. Accessed July 20, 2011, at http://www.tsa.gov/assets/pdf/modal_annex_freight_rail.pdf

road. Although the National Defense Highway System—the "interstate"—was created specifically to accommodate the movement of war materiel, including airplanes, from coast to coast, the railroads routinely carry most of the military's weapons, ammunition, and vehicles.

Thus, the rail system is a key element in national critical infrastructure protection planning. The Freight Rail Modal Annex to the National Infrastructure Protection Plan provides a list of security goals and the existing gaps that need to be filled (TSA, n.d.). "The fundamental challenge to securing the freight rail network is to protect against a constantly changing, unpredictable threat environment without impeding the continuous movement and free flow of commerce that is required in today's 'just-in-time' supply chain" (TSA, 2011).

Threats to the Freight and Long-Distance Passenger Heavy Rail System

On May 1, 2011, Navy Seal Team Six apprehended and killed Osama Bin Laden, head of Al Qaeda, the group responsible for the 9/11 attacks on the World Trade Center and Pentagon. In his papers they found plans for attacks on American rail systems. Although freight trains have not been the target of many terrorist attacks in the past, the notes in Bin Laden's journal raised concerns in the rail industry that countermeasures needed to be enhanced (Cloherty & Thomas, 2011). DHS reported finding plans to derail trains "to send a train off a bridge" on the 10th anniversary of 9/11. Passenger and freight trains share the same tracks. Attacking any train could close the rail line, impacting the whole supply chain and potentially having significant economic impact. Attacking a freight train with toxic materials could create damage in adjacent communities as well (Boyd, 2011).

Open System

Amtrak's system is concentrated in the Northeast corridor, but extends across the continent. After the review of Bin Laden's papers, Amtrak security was reevaluated. Amtrak's chief of police noted that the high speed passenger trains on its system provide the potential for significant loss of life in a derailment. The security profile is concentrated on detection and deterrence of IEDs in a station or train, as well as active shooters.

> Historically, Amtrak has used a range of security strategies, such as high security fencing, bollards, blast curtains, access control and technologically driven initiatives to protect stations, bridges and tunnels. Amtrak is exploring the expanded use of these strategies for right of way protection. (Cloherty & Thomas, 2011)

FIGURE 8.2   Rail cars awaiting pickup.

"The size of the freight system and the diversity of freight hauled" create unique challenges in managing security for freight rail systems (Guerrero & Rabkin, 2004, p. 7). With over 100,000 miles of freight rail that extend into Canada and Mexico, "the extensiveness of the infrastructure creates an infinite number of targets for terrorists" (Guerrero & Rabkin, 2004, p. 8). The size of the system also makes protection of all of it impossible.

Its very size is also one of its protective mechanisms. While train cars are tracked and train consists are well documented, the length of time and the distances traveled by freight create tremendous uncertainties regarding where any specific car or type of car will be at any given time. Although regional rail yards are located only in large junction areas, sidings along tracks to allow for changing consists en route are scattered throughout the system, with rail cars left unguarded but protected to some degree by their isolation (Figure 8.2).

Human trespassing onto the thousands of miles of rail poses one of the greatest challenges to rail system security. "Railroad security has been traditionally defined as a problem of trespass and liability for deaths, injuries, and property damage sustained or caused by trespassers" (Plant, 2004, p. 293). For example, in 2009 there were 428 fatalities among railroad trespassers, and 66 people were hit by trains at grade crossings (TSA, 2011, p. 3). Urban facilities are usually fenced, locked, and covered by roving patrols and surveillance cameras—the same techniques, as noted in Chapter 7, used by rail-based mass transit.

Although rail systems are traditional targets for wartime operations (USMC, 1942), no American facilities were damaged during World War II. In 1942 a German submarine landed commandoes in plainclothes on the coast of Long Island. Their mission was to damage rail infrastructure, including a major Ohio bridge. The apprehension of the spies led to the development of a railroad security focus based on denial of access to rail facilities. "Before 9/11, the issue of rail security was tied heavily to concerns about protection from vandalism and liability for the numerous injuries and fatalities incurred by unauthorized persons on rail facilities" (Plant, 2004, p. 297). The Federal Railroad Safety Authorization Act of 1994 (49 U.S.C. § 20151) encouraged states to pass stricter punishments for trespass and vandalism.

The attack on the Tokyo subway in 1995 and the ongoing IRA campaign in Great Britain raised the security concerns of railroad owners and operators. Competition from trucking forced freight rail to focus on efficiency in a new era of just-in-time shipments and global supply chains. The elimination of cargo choke points and NAFTA-related changes to border inspections, as well as the introduction of cyber systems for information sharing, enhanced the attractiveness of railroads as targets (Plant, 2004).

Intermodal System

The evolution of freight transportation to a multimodal system further enhanced the security threat against rail freight. There are 9.2 million intermodal rail shipments every year—the fastest growing segment of rail freight services (TSA, n.d.). Quicker transitions through port security (which will be discussed in more detail in Chapter 9) and shorter transit times into the main freight system mean that there is less time buffer between foreign shippers and the entrance of cargo containers into the U.S. freight stream, as many of the shipments travel unopened to the East Coast or even Europe.

Global supply chain port services enhancements have further cut the time from port to shelf. From ship to crane to waiting flatbed rail car, the system has to be designed to minimize costs to the customers. Eric Soderberg of the Port of Oakland, California, America's 20th largest dollar value port, said, "The whole system has to work. Between the yard and the cranes, your slowest link is what's going to slow you down" (Hull, 2008). The Port Authority in Charleston, South Carolina, recently purchased four new cranes that accelerate the movement of containers from ship to dockside transport, going from 30 moves per hour to 40 moves per hour (Hull, 2008). The Alameda Corridor Transportation Authority serves the Port of Los Angeles and the Port of Long Beach. The $2.4 billion express rail line connects the port to the transcontinental rail yard in Los Angeles in 30 minutes, rather than the 4-hour route previously required. This corridor handles 20% of the nation's Asian imports and is the busiest international trade gateway in the nation (White, 2010), with over $250 billion in combined imports and exports each year (U.S. DOT 2011, p. 36).

The loss of border controls through land crossing programs (as noted in the discussion of trucks in Chapter 5) and maritime interfaces (as discussed in Chapter 9) may lead to the introduction of contraband or weapons into the supply chain. The current problems with drug and human trafficking demonstrate that border security is imperfect. For example, according to the Department of Health and Human Services, more than 20,000 people are trafficked into the United States each year (Clawson, Dutch, Solomon, & Grace, 2009).

With the loss of restrictive cargo searching protocols, there is a concern that illegal or dangerous materials may be introduced into the U.S. supply chain through the freight rail system. For example, a weapon of mass destruction introduced into the country initially through a marine cargo container could be transferred to rail freight, leading to the bomb being delivered to a populated area, and detonated using a timer or remote control. While the challenge of tracking a single container among millions is high, GPS units placed in the container may make it easier. The GAO noted in testimony to the Senate that although

> ...the original security breach occurred in the port, the rail or trucking industry would be affected as well. Thus, even if operators within one mode established high levels of security, they could be affected by the security efforts, or lack thereof, in the other modes. (Guerrero & Rabkin, 2004)

Trusted shipper programs like C-TPAT (discussed in Chapter 3) and offshore inspection programs like the Container Security Initiative are designed to deter, detect, and interdict such shipments before they leave the country of origin, but only a small percentage of the containers are actually inspected once the trusted shipper program is in place (Edwards & Goodrich, 2010).

This global interconnectedness creates another threat to rail freight security. A disruption in the supply chain may directly impact other seemingly unrelated elements. In 2002 the West Coast ports had a strike, which caused a decline in rail freight of almost 30% in the first week (GAO, 2003). The immediate impacts were notable in the Bay Area's high-tech and auto industries. Within a few days of the beginning of the port strike, the NUMI auto plant in Fremont, California, stopped production on pickup trucks and passenger cars because of a lack of parts that should have arrived "just in time" from Asia. They usually received 40 containers a day. On the export side there was also a stoppage. Jim Cuneen, executive director of the Silicon Valley Chamber of Commerce, stated that the majority of Silicon Valley companies operate on an international customer basis, so they were producing American products that could not be shipped to Asian and South American customers. Thus, the economic impact of the port strike in three American states created a global supply chain crisis.

Plant (2004) has called these disruptions and exposures "viruses":

> Little insulation is possible from a host of viruses that can disrupt rail operations, ranging from containers brought in by sea to breakdowns of information systems that provide safety of operations to traditional sabotage of bridges, rails, and signaling devices to the unknowing employment of terrorist operatives. As a middleman in an evolving seamless intermodal transportation system, railroads can be infected by these viruses originating elsewhere, or be the agent of moving them to other points in the logistics chain.

Hazardous Materials and TIH

The U.S. Environmental Protection Agency has designated classes of chemicals as "hazardous materials." Broadly defined, these are chemicals that pose a health risk to humans who are exposed to them through inhalation, ingestion, contact, or exposure (FEMA, 1996). The risk is different for different chemicals, based on the concentration of the material in the air and the length of time the person is exposed. One class of chemicals causes fatalities almost instantly, and these have been categorized as "acutely hazardous materials," while other chemicals are only damaging at very high concentrations or with prolonged or chronic exposure.

Toxic inhalation hazards are "poisonous by inhalation" (TSA, 2006b) and may pose a risk to adjacent communities during transport if there is an accidental release. The Belfer Center at Harvard's Kennedy School of Government has identified the most dangerous of the TIH chemicals that are regularly in the transportation stream. "Chlorine gas and anhydrous ammonia are the most common TIH chemicals; others include sulfur dioxide, ethylene oxide, and hydrogen fluoride, and a variety of other products that are important manufacturing inputs" (Branscomb, Fagan, Auerswald, Ellis, & Barcham, 2010, p. 3).

The U.S. DOT *Emergency Response Guidebook* (ERG; U.S. DOT, 2008), which was introduced in Chapter 3, offers a comprehensive list of chemicals transported on U.S. highways, railroads, and waterways. The guide was created to inform first responders of the characteristics of the materials that might be present at the scene of an emergency, such as a fire or transportation accident. Federal regulations require that every chemical shipment have a material safety data sheet (MSDS; Figure 8.3) in the possession of the driver or operator that lists the hazardous materials in transit, the quantity, state (solid, liquid, or gas), origin, and destination, including a 24-hour contact number and any special considerations in managing the material (e.g., it must be kept refrigerated or it cannot be mixed with water). The U.S. DOT ERG divides hazardous materials into nine classes, as shown in Table 8.4.

FIGURE 8.3   Material safety data sheet.

In 1907 the American Railway Association, predecessor of the AAR, created regulations for the rail transport of explosive materials through its Bureau of Explosives. It prescribed standards and practices for the safe shipment of explosives, including the placarding of rail cars carrying explosives. The rules developed then form the basis for all hazardous materials shipment regulations today, including 49 CFR (Bureau of Explosives, 2012).

A series of diamond-shaped placards has been created to identify the contents of a hazardous materials transport vehicle clearly from a distance, so that first responders can stay safely upwind and uphill of the material while its characteristics are being evaluated. The placards are color coded and have symbols and four-digit numbers to provide the most information with the largest lettering possible in the space available. The four-digit number may also be displayed on a separate orange panel below the placard. For example, a red class 3, 1203 placard indicates that the vehicle is carrying gasoline. Chlorine is 1017, a class 2 inhalation hazard. Examples of the placards are shown in Figure 8.4.

Over 83 million tons of hazardous materials were shipped by rail in 2001 (Guerrero & Rabkin, 2004). They are usually on freight trains with mixed shipments, with the chemical tankers placed among empty and full rail cars of all types, according to the requirements of 49 CFR Part 174 Subpart D. Between 1982 and 1985, there were 435 accidents involving trains carrying hazardous materials cars, of which 10 were significant derailments. Fifty-three of the accidents that involved tankers carrying hazardous materials included a release of the hazardous materials (Thompson et al., 1992, p. 135). One accident resulted in the jackknifing and "piling" of a cluster of 32 cars in close proximity (Thompson et al., 1992, p. 134). Consequences of the

TABLE 8.4 U.S. DOT Hazardous Materials Placards

Class Number	Class Name	Categories
1	Explosives	Division 1.1 explosives with a mass explosion hazard
		Division 1.2 explosives with a projection hazard
		Division 1.3 explosives with predominantly a fire hazard
		Division 1.4 explosives with no significant blast hazard
		Division 1.5 very insensitive explosives with a mass explosion hazard
		Division 1.6 extremely insensitive articles
2	Gases	Division 2.1 flammable gases
		Division 2.2 nonflammable, nontoxic[a] gases
		Division 2.3 toxic[a] gases
3	Flammable liquids	Flammable liquids
		Combustible liquids
4	Flammable solids; spontaneously combustible materials; materials that are dangerous when wet/ water-reactive substances	Division 4.1 flammable solids
		Division 4.2 spontaneously combustible materials
		Division 4.3 water-reactive substances/materials that are dangerous when wet
5	Oxidizers	Division 5.1 oxidizing substances
		Division 5.2 organic peroxides
6	Toxics	Division 6.1 toxic[a] substances
		Division 6.2 infectious substances
7	Radioactive	
8	Corrosive	
9	Hazardous	Miscellaneous hazardous materials/ products, substances, or organisms

Source: U.S. DOT. (2008). *Emergency Response Guidebook.* Washington, DC: US DOT.
[a] "Poison" or "poisonous" is synonymous with toxic.

FIGURE 8.4 Examples of hazardous materials placards.

releases included fires that spread to other cars, explosions, and the evacuation of surrounding communities (Thompson et al., 1992, p. 135).

By the 1990s the Federal Railroad Administration (FRA) had recognized that transportation of hazardous materials in freight trains created the potential for unwanted contact between incompatible chemicals. Battelle Laboratory scientists researched "the top 101 chemicals (by volume movement) and fuming nitric acid...for chemical incompatibility, a total of 5,151 binary combinations" (Thompson et al., 1992).

Their research generated a list of 1,210 incompatible substances that would have adverse consequences if mixed in the course of a train derailment. They observed that a 30-car separation would be preferred to ensure that there would be no contact, but a 15-car separation would be acceptable. Based on a review of the actual train derailments from 1982 to 1985, in which there was no actual mixing of hazardous materials cited, they determined that the safest place for chemical tankers in a derailment is the rear quarter of the train, "but the longer the train, or the higher the speed, the more cars derailed on the average" (Thompson et al., 1992).

The goal of Battelle Lab's research was to recommend "the placement of hazardous material cars in a train consist in order to reduce the potential for being involved in a derailment, and, if the cars are in an accident, to reduce the potential for mixtures of incompatible materials" (Thompson et al., 1992, p. 133). They noted that the standard for creating train consists is first to evaluate efficient operation of the train related to the delivery and acquisition of cars along the route: "The basic goal is to minimize the number and/or complexity of switching movements within terminals and yards, as well as those associated with the transport, set-out, and pick-up of cars while en route" (Thompson et al., 1992, p. 138).

The second consideration is compliance with the federal rules for the placement of hazardous materials cars within the consist. The third is directed toward avoiding building trains having "inherent dynamic operating characteristics which could promote, or contribute to, derailments" (Thompson et al., 1992, p. 138). Battelle Lab recommended adding an additional consideration of keeping incompatible cars adequately separated and preferably located at the rear of the train. However, cost-benefit analysis demonstrates that by changing the traditional station order block consist development, the company is trading ongoing costs of extra rail car movements for greater safety in a derailment involving hazardous materials tankers (Thompson et al., 1992, p. 142).

When the AAR undertook its security plan development, it identified several streams of hazardous materials traveling by rail that were essential to the American economy and defense. For example, as mentioned previously, the railroads carry weapons and munitions that are in the hazardous materials category of explosives for the military. They carry hazardous chemicals that are essential for water purification, industrial processes, and agricultural activities.

Some of these chemicals are explosive, while others create clouds of hazardous vapor, and an accident in transit can generate a community impact. For example, in Graniteville, South Carolina, in 2005, four people, including the engineer, died when a train carrying hazardous materials derailed, spilling two-thirds of a 90-ton tanker of chlorine. Two hundred people were injured and 5,400 were evacuated for 2 days. A train with three locomotives and 42 cars struck a locomotive with two parked cars. Because the accident occurred at night when it was cold and damp, the chlorine vapor crawled along the ground and remained for hours (Edgar, 2005).

Although the FRA has strict rules regarding the construction of rail tankers that carry chlorine, the power of a moving train can sometimes overcome the strength of the double-walled tankers. In this case, the coupling of one of the derailed cars was pushed into the side of the ninth car—the tanker—during "piling" of 14 cars caused by the derailment, and the gash allowed the chlorine to be released as a vapor. It took 12 days to unload the ruptured car, including several efforts to patch the hole and preclude the release of more chlorine (NTSB, 2005).

This accident demonstrates how terrorists could use tanker cars as weapons. A tanker containing a hazardous material could be fitted with an explosive that would rupture its wall and cause a catastrophic release of its contents. Acutely hazardous materials, including chlorine and anhydrous ammonia, regularly travel on trains, as shown in Table 8.3. The intentional derailment of a train carrying hazardous materials tankers might also generate a similar outcome, although derailments are difficult to create and unreliable as to time and place.

Freight cars have also been considered as potential transport devices for weapons of mass destruction or weapons of mass disruption. Various researchers have suggested that a shipping container with a nuclear device could be sent from a foreign port to the United States and then detonated. The realistic difficulty of actually obtaining the device, shipping it through the nuclear detection-protected ports, and getting it onto a rail car is relatively simple compared with the challenge of setting off a nuclear bomb by remote control. While perhaps possible, it is not plausible.

A more reasonable concern, however, is the shipment of an explosive material like ammonium nitrate in a rail car, with the intent of detonating the car as it passes through a critical node or densely populated urban area or is adjacent to critical infrastructure. Because the main rail lines of the United States were built to serve its large population centers, many rail cars daily pass through the largest cities of the East Coast, as well as Chicago, Denver, and Los Angeles, among other major cities. Because GPS locators can be placed in cars and monitored, a remote control device could be placed in the car and detonated at the desired location. However, this strategy requires considerable planning, access to the rail consist, the ability to introduce a booster charge, and proximity to the car to be detonated, unless a cell phone is being used as the remote detonator.

Types of Attacks Against Freight and Long-Distance Passenger Heavy Rail

Earlier in this chapter, the size of the U.S. freight rail system was described. Much of the track is in wide-open spaces and limited access mountains, where physical protection is neither cost effective nor possible. In the early days of the transcontinental railroad, the trains were targets for attack by robbers using firearms. Later, frontiersmen and Indians who wanted to discourage further incursion into their lands took random shots at train cars. In 1907 train placards were designed by the Bureau of Explosives to identify the cars carrying explosive materials as a way of deterring shooting that would lead to an explosion.

Traditional Attacks on Rail Systems

Modern freight rail systems operate with two train crew: the engineer and the conductor. Therefore, attacking freight trains would only lead to numerous fatalities if the attack occurred in a congested area and the population along the tracks was the real target. The purpose of attacking freight trains, then, is a denial of service: delay train traffic and reduce the number of locomotives and rolling stock available to meet community needs. Because of the military value of rail in moving personnel and equipment, rail attack strategies are part of military tactics for use against enemy infrastructure (Figure 8.5).

Jenkins (1997) notes that derailment caused by sabotage is the greatest threat to long-distance rail systems. Jenkins and Butterworth (2010) note that there have been 181 attempts to derail trains with bombs or mechanical sabotage between 1920 and 2010. There were 15 attacks between 1920 and 1970, with 11 derailments. During the period of their data collection, there were only 45 attacks on freight trains, or less than 3% of all attacks. Forty of these attacks used bombs, representing just over 3% of all bomb attacks.

> Derailments can be the consequence of several factors which may act alone or in combination to cause an accident. The primary factors are track-related conditions (e.g., a broken rail, "sun kinks" due to high longitudinal compressive stress, poor track geometry), equipment failure (e.g., a broken wheel, an overheated journal), poor train makeup (e.g., unfavorable relative placement of empty and loaded cars), and poor train handling practices (e.g., improper use of throttle and/or brake, or excessive speed). (Thompson et al., 1992, p. 133)

FIGURE 8.5 Railroad tracks at Dunsmuir Station in California.

FIGURE 8.6 Fish plate and bolts on railroad track.

"Derailment can be accomplished in two ways: creating a gap in the rails or through an obstruction that will cause the flange of the train's wheels to ride up and off of the rail" (Rigden, 2004). The gap may be created by prying up a series of stakes, undoing the fish plates, and then forcing the rail in and wedging the fish plate between the two rail sections (Figure 8.6). In this way, an approaching train would come off the rail because the flange sections would be diverted to the outside of the track (Von Dach, 1965). Straight sections of track permit a much larger gap to be created without derailing the train.

Most modern rail lines, however, have the track sections welded together. This means that the gap has to be created by cutting the rail line with an oxyacetylene torch, or similar cutting instrument, explosives, or thermite.

Studies conducted by the Office of Special Services (OSS, precursor to the Central Intelligence Agency) during World War II discovered that the tampering would have to be on curved track, and the gap created would have to be longer than 36 inches (YouTube, 2011). Mudslides or large amounts of sand burying the tracks can also cause the train to derail through the wheels riding up onto the piled-up sand instead of the track, going over the track, and derailing. Also, derailing equipment used by the rail industry can be purchased or stolen and carried by one person, but it is primarily designed for low-speed operations.

Military tactics recommend going to an inaccessible spot where the train affords the only access. These include tunnels and long cuttings, steep embankments, or entrances to bridges (Rigden, 2004). Because these are narrow areas, it is difficult to bring in the repair equipment, and there is limited space to work to put the train back on the track.

While bridges and tunnels appear to be attractive targets for damaging track sections and causing a derailment, the tunnel portals and bridge abutments are the strongest portions of the structures. Tamped charges could be used, but the depth of placement required to be effective would demand a large number of people working for several hours, thereby enhancing the likelihood of detection before the sabotage was complete. Also, each type of bridge design would require a different type of demolition design for success, meaning that the attackers would need to have significant knowledge of civil engineering (U.S. Army, 1987).

Another means for interfering with the operation of the rail system is to tamper with or destroy the switches that are used to move trains from one track to another. The reason for targeting switches is that they are more difficult to repair than a normal section of track. The damage can be created by the use of explosives (Schmitt, 2005) or a sledgehammer to destroy the switching mechanism or bend the connecting rod (Von Dach, 1965). The damage to the switch also has the potential to cause a derailment.

Repair facilities are primary targets for attack in a traditional warfare model (nation versus nation), but should also be considered as a possible terrorist strategy for inducing delays in rail service. Of specific interest would be the overhead crane assemblies, train turntables, oversized lathes, furnaces, and any proprietary equipment that does not have a commercial equivalent, such as cranes rated for 200 tons (USMC, 1942).

Ancillary equipment that is crucial to rail operation provides another target for sabotage or destruction. For example, electrical lines, radio repeaters, and phone lines run parallel to the tracks and are used to control signals and switching points on the rail and to monitor train activities. Loss of these will force train operations to switch to alternate means that are not as efficient, such as manually turning and monitoring the switches or using signal flags. Often, attacks on rail will target not only a derailing of the train or damage to the switch, but also damage to these auxiliary systems that increase the time to diagnose the problem and begin appropriate repairs.

Attackers against the freight system will increase their effectiveness by engaging in repetitive attacks, requiring continuous repairs and rail operation interruptions. For example, if a section of rail is destroyed and the train is derailed but does not fall over, it will take 12 hours to repair the damaged rail segment and restore operations. During those 12 hours, the problem is identified, resources are mobilized and dispatched to the scene, repairs to the track are made, and the train is placed back on the tracks. Other trains that were to use that section of track have to be diverted or placed in a holding status, creating a backlog in operations.

If an attack team were then to hit another section of the track after the repair crew had returned to its base and restored normal operations, it would take another 12 hours to repair the second section of track with the same damage, creating a cumulative loss of use of 24 hours. If the attackers blew up two sections of rail at the same time, simultaneous repairs could be undertaken, requiring only slightly longer than repairing one section of damage (Von Dach, 1965). Similarly, attacks against the ancillary equipment could generate serial outages that would cause extended disruptions of freight movement.

Cyber Attacks on Freight Rail Operations

Much like mass transit rail systems, freight rail is dependent on cyber systems for a variety of operational elements. First, computers control most signals today. In addition to indicating whether the track is available or in active use by another train, signals also inform engineers whether bridges are closed to receive the train or still open. Many rail bridges over navigable waterways are closed only during the passage of the train to minimize the disruption to maritime traffic. Train bridges may be drawbridges that split in the middle and rise upward on hinge systems at each bank, parallel bridges that are turned parallel to shipping channels until train operations require them to turn 90° to align with the banks, or raised bridges that are pulled up intact above the shipping lanes until train operations require the whole bridge to be lowered into place to join the track sections on each bank.

These movable bridges are vulnerable to two types of attack. The bridge mechanism may be damaged to prevent its operation, thereby blocking the track for use until the bridge operation is restored. Modern bridges are generally operated by computer controlled systems triggered by sensors on the rails several miles away from the bridge. The sensor triggers the movement of the bridge so that it is aligned with the tracks when the train arrives.

Hacking into the cyber control system could permit attackers to induce a false signal from the sensors that would trigger bridge activation. Thus, when the train arrived, the bridge would be in its open position. Because a freight train needs at least 1 mile to stop, it is possible that the train would crash through the guardrails and move into the empty space, creating a derailment that might include the train running down the embankment or even into the water.

Other strategies could include reprogramming remote control equipment to interfere with the remote signals that operate some railway equipment. For example, in Poland a teenager in Lotz used a modified TV remote control to interfere with the operation of commuter rail, causing property damage and injuries to riders. "Transport command and control systems are commonly designed by engineers with little exposure or knowledge about security using commodity electronics and a little native wit" (Leyden, 2008).

Cyber attacks can also take the form of a penetration test of the SCADA systems. The Boston "T" was subject to hacking by some MIT students whose short-term goal was to make a presentation to DEFCON 17 in 2008 on the security vulnerabilities of the Boston T, using the creation of counterfeit fare cards as proof of success. Their well-documented digital exploration demonstrates how to conduct a penetration test that would lead to access to a SCADA system. Even more important, they demonstrated the failures of many layers of traditional security, like failure to monitor the surveillance system, leaving critical equipment unlocked, and leaving keys in the locks. They were also able to purchase Boston T identification items on eBay that could have facilitated physical penetration of the security systems (Ryan, Anderson, & Chiesa, n.d.).

Once the SCADA system has been penetrated, attackers could go into the management of the freight rail system, creating numerous disruptions to service. For example, manipulation of the station blocks for tankers on the consist could result in hazardous materials falling into the hands of attackers, for future use. Containerized goods could be intentionally sent to the wrong receiver, tying up staff time to reroute and deliver the goods, and even causing destruction of food and other perishable items. Manufacturing could be disrupted by the misdirection of just-in-time materials to the wrong source. As demonstrated by the West Coast port strike, losses can run into the millions of dollars for each day of delivery failure.

Train routes are managed through SCADA systems. Hackers could change switches, causing whole trains to travel to the wrong locations. Derailment could also be caused by changing the switch while the train is traveling over the switch. Hackers could mask a train's GPS signal by removing the train from inventory, raising the specter of collision. The full potential for the abuse of computers is only now being realized, so additional results of hacking are likely. As a result, the human train crews must be more vigilant than ever before as they travel the networks.

Hazardous Materials as Attack Modes

TSA has conducted extensive investigations into the potential for the inter-action between terrorists and hazardous materials. While hazardous materials are a valuable commodity that may be stolen, TSA's principal security focus is the use of hazardous materials as weapons against populated areas. As noted before, hazardous materials travel on rail lines that pass through the heart of America's largest cities, with high concentrations of population well within the evacuation distances for hazardous materials releases. A rail tanker car can become a rolling bomb that could emit toxic fumes that could kill, require widespread evacuations, and contaminate and damage property and the environment, resulting in expensive cleanups, as well as tying up freight and passenger movement on the rail lines serving that area.

Actual events like the Graniteville, South Carolina, accidental derailment discussed earlier in the chapter demonstrate the impact that can be created by one punctured rail car. In 1994 the Department of Transportation con-tracted with the Transportation Research Board to review DOT 112, which regulates the design of hazardous materials tanker cars used on the rail-road (TRB, 1994). Post-1980 accidents resulted in fewer releases of materi-als as a result of strengthened manufacturing design requirements for tank cars. The introduction of double-shelf couplers was credited with lessen-ing the number of tank car punctures. The double-shelf couplers are better able to withstand the stresses of passing through switches, changes in train makeup, and accidents, so the coupler does not ride up and puncture the car's wall. The tank walls for TIH transport vehicles have a double wall with insulation between the layers, and the layers, which are 1/8 inch thicker than those of other tank cars, must withstand 300 psi.

Most accidental releases studied by TRB resulted from damaged fittings and valves (TRB, 1994). However, during a derailment when over a dozen cars pile up, even the extra thick walls and insulation of a TIH tanker can-not withstand the weight and pressure of the colliding cars.

A concerted attack using a TIH car could be accomplished with less than 5 pounds of explosives properly placed on the outside of a TIH car. Using a remote control device like a cell phone and a GPS tracking device, a terror-ist could detonate the car as it passed through a selected critical node or in a built-up area. Properly placed, the explosives could cause a large hole that would lead to a catastrophic release of a TIH.

Likewise, a shipment of explosives in a boxcar or intermodal container, hopper, or flatbed car could be used to create damage to buildings, critical infrastructure, and population centers along the tracks. The truck bomb set off in Oklahoma City at the Murrah Building was reputed to carry 5,000 pounds of ANFO, and it not only demolished one building, but also dam-aged buildings in a 48 square-block area, and blew out windows a mile away

(Oklahoma Department of Civil Emergency Management, 1995). The average train car carries about 50,000 pounds of freight, while a well car with intermodal containers has a load limit of 176,000 pounds (AmericanRail.com, 2011).

TSA and AAR have recognized the threat to America's population centers posed by the transportation of dangerous goods on railroads and also the attraction of railroads for terrorists. They have partnered to create security standards and programs to make this essential economic linkage safer and more secure.

Security Strategies for Freight and Long-Distance Passenger Heavy Rail

As noted earlier in this chapter, the interconnecting railroads of the United States and Canada are open systems covering 140,000 miles of track, making the security of all assets impossible. Vandalism is the most frequent crime against freight rail, with 12, 280 incidents in 1994.[3] Three thousand of these events were vandalism against signals, while 154 events resulted in derailment (Jenkins, 1997). In recent years the FBI has noted a shift to theft of specific cargo and copper wire, while as shown in Table 8.5, the overall crime rate has dropped in most categories, probably because of heightened vigilance after 9/11.

Ordinary Crime

Trespassing on railroad property, which is a codified crime in most states, is a gateway crime that leads to other problems, such as vandalism of the property or death of the trespasser. The FRA notes that most trespassing is just a shortcut to other destinations, but trespassers also loiter, hunt, bicycle, fish, snowmobile, and ride ATVs, some of which activities damage railroad

TABLE 8.5 Property Crimes Committed on Heavy Rail, 2001 and 2010

Type	Number (2001)	Number (2010)
Theft	7,807	2,504
Vehicle theft	1,143	140
Burglary	119	266
Vandalism	984[a]	101[a]
Trespassing	1,228[a]	633[a]
Fare evasion	24,852[a]	24,684[a]

Source: Bureau of Transportation Statistics, 2011.
[a] Number of persons arrested.

FIGURE 8.7 Hazardous materials car with graffiti.

embankments and other property (FRA, 2010). These activities put people in harm's way, either inadvertently or as a suicide strategy (Sturgeon, 2008).

But trespassing is the first step in vandalism, theft, and tampering with railroad security. A spokesman for Norfolk Southern Railroad said, "If you don't have people trespassing you don't have thefts, you don't have vandalism, you don't have tampered switches, debris placed on rails, because they're not out there." Graffiti creates an illegal moving exhibit for artists, some of whom even advertise on websites, but it is vandalism and an expense to the railroad (Figure 8.7) (Sturgeon, 2008). The FRA encourages the use of security by design strategies like vegetation management and lighting, and technology applications like motion sensors, video cameras, and infrared lighting to discourage and apprehend trespassers (FRA, 2010).

Copper theft has become a focus of railroad security as the price has risen 500% since 2000. The FBI has reported that many elements of American's critical infrastructure have been a target for copper thieves, including the railroads, resulting in disruption of operations (FBI, 2008). For example, in 2010 three men from Utah were convicted in federal court of stealing 750 pounds of copper wire from the railroad tracks in eastern Nevada, causing $50,000 in damage. The loss of the wire "completely disabled the Union Pacific's detection system, and broken rails or landslides within a 40 mile section of track would have been undetected by control operators, thus presenting a serious hazard." It caused two Amtrak trains and one freight train traveling on the line to slow to 20 mph and stop at every control point. It also damaged the system controlling grade crossings, posing a threat to motorists (U.S. Attorney, District of Nevada, 2010).

In November of 2011 the FBI began to collect cargo theft statistics for the Uniform Crime Report for the first time. Norfolk Southern Police battled street gangs in Chicago that targeted idling trains. One group entered the cars to search for cargo that they could easily move and sell, and others outside hid the stolen merchandise for later pickup. In New Jersey the "Conrail Boys" (named for the consolidated freight system) rented tractors to use to steal trailers from rail staging areas (Sturgeon, 2008). Theft from all modes has reached $30 billion annually, and this includes theft of cargo from railroad rolling stock and fixed facilities (FBI, 2010). Selected crime statistics for heavy rail are shown in Table 8.5.

Security Enhancements

While trespassing, tampering, and theft are the primary security concerns during the movement of ordinary freight shipments, TIH shipments add the concern that terrorists might use the tank cars, hoppers, and boxcars as weapons of mass disruption, harming communities adjacent to the rail line and closing down rail operations to create an economic impact.

Traditionally, safety on the railroad has focused on accident avoidance and preventing trespassing. The new post-9/11 focus on security has created a second layer of regulation focused especially on TIH. Branscomb et al. (2010) have noted:

> Accidents and deliberate attacks may result in similar consequences. Therefore many safety regulations and policies will also mitigate, to some degree, the consequences of a security breach. The domains of safety and security overlap with respect both to mitigation and to consequence.

Security on freight and long-distance passenger rail systems has benefited from the same technology enhancements as those for mass transit rail, which were discussed in Chapter 7. Lighting, cameras, sensors, VIPR teams, bomb dogs, random patrols, and access control have all become an integral part of the rail security system for stations, rail yards, and repair facilities. However, the 140,000 miles of rail spread across the continent defy the provision of security, except to the degree that their very remoteness protects them.

After the 9/11 attacks, the AAR conducted a vulnerability assessment of its constituent organizations and determined that security changes and improvements were required in four areas: hazardous materials operations, infrastructure, information technology and communications, and military movements (AAR, 2011). The new security plan began with an assessment identifying and prioritizing over 1,300 critical assets, examining their vulnerabilities and threats, and calculating the risks. Then a set of

TABLE 8.6 AAR Security Threat Levels

Level	Description
1	New normal day-to-day operations
2	Heightened security awareness
3	A credible threat of an attack on the United States or the railroad industry
4	A confirmed threat of attack against the railroad industry or actual attack in the United States (implemented up to 72 hours and reevaluated)

Source: AAR. (2011). Security Plan. Accessed on July 23, 2011, at http://www.aar.org/Safety/Rail-Security.aspx

countermeasures was developed to address the identified risks. A four-tier threat level was established for managing countermeasures, and an AAR operations center and a railroad alert network were created. The four tiers are shown in Table 8.6.

Significant countermeasures began with employee involvement. Security awareness training was delivered to over 200,000 railroad employees, making them the "eyes and ears" of the security system. This training is reinforced in daily briefings, with video examples of suspicious activities, reminders about reporting procedures, and rewards for employee suggestions for security improvements. Posters and fliers, e-mails, and brochures are distributed periodically. Background checks have been conducted on key personnel and random identification checks have been instituted.

As noted earlier, railroads in the United States and Canada carry 1.6 million hazardous materials shipments each year. The safe operation of the railroads depends on the proper management of hazardous materials. Employees receive hazardous materials training on awareness, safe and secure management of hazardous materials shipments, and identification of potential problems.

Also, the cyber security threat was addressed by enhancing security systems to safeguard radio systems, signals and switches operated remotely, and computer-based operational infrastructure, including encryption technology for the most critical processes. More robust tracking of hazardous materials shipments and munitions movements was begun. Random patrols were added, and the physical security of assets and infrastructure was increased, including the use of technologies like intrusion detection, explosive detectors, and various sensors in key locations.

A major development was the creation of the ARR 24/7 operations center to coordinate information on rail security issues. The center establishes a permanent link with a number of federal agencies, including the Department of Defense, FBI, DHS, and DOT. They also network with state and local law enforcement agencies. The freight system and Amtrak share the information generated in the Surface Transportation Information Sharing and Analysis Center.

Hazardous Materials Security

In 2004, S. Mark Lindsey of the Department of Transportation testified before the Rail Security Senate Committee on the Judiciary to request stricter laws for the punishment of terrorist activity against railroad property. At that time he noted:

> Freight trains haul nearly a million rail tank cars and 238,000 intermodal loads of hazardous materials annually. Rail is the predominant method of transportation for certain classes of hazardous materials that pose an especially high risk, including explosives, radioactive materials, and flammable solids. (Lindsey, 2004)

In requesting stronger federal punishments for wrecking trains and using dangerous weapons on the property of a railroad, Lindsey was highlighting the need to safeguard TIHs in transit better.

TSA emphasizes three aspects of security for hazardous materials in transit: system security, access control, and en route security (TSA, 2006b). Of these three, only the last is controversial. While heavy rail transportation networks have improved their system security and access control as discussed earlier, they contend that the existing freight routes through population centers pose no special risk, while TSA supports rerouting as a security strategy. In its first guidance, issued in June 23, 2006, TSA (2006b) states, "Movement of large quantities of TIH materials by rail in proximity to population centers warrants special consideration and attention. These materials have the potential of causing significant numbers of fatalities and injuries if intentionally released in an urban environment." The first 19 recommendations in the TSA freight rail security TIH guidance are largely encompassed in the AAR's actions since 9/11.

The TSA June 2006 TIH guidance for en route security states, "Consider alternative routes when they are economically practicable and result in reduced overall safety and security risks. Work with the DHS and DOT in developing better software tools to analyze routes" (TSA, 2006b). This was followed by a supplement in November that emphasized the special concerns about high threat urban areas (HTUAs) and TIH. The security plans for railroads operating in HTUAs had to be updated to include additional provisions for the secure storage of TIH cars in HTUAs and the minimization of the time during which full TIH cars remain unattended in HTUAs. This poses a challenge for management of TIH in rail yards and on sidings. In addition, special consideration was to be given to allowing TIH to sit in storage yards or sidings in proximity to sensitive receptors such as "hospitals, high-occupancy buildings, schools, and public venues" (TSA, 2006a).

In January 2007 an additional supplement was issued with guidance for safeguarding TIH shipments. This one focused on contractor employee background checks for all those with unmonitored access to railroad critical infrastructure. Procedures included criminal history checks, social security number checks, and verification of immigration status (TSA, 2007).

Plant (2004) had considered a similar blend of security approaches, calling them "policing, cordoning and risk assessment" (p. 8). He noted that the Northeast corridor passes through Baltimore and Washington, carrying hazardous freight daily. He suggested that the conflict between DHS's risk assessment-based approach to TIH safety and the railroad's efficiency approach would have to be resolved for security to be enhanced. The networked approach that he proposed appears to be embodied in the AAR's operations center and information sharing, but the physical movement of hazardous materials on the rail network continues to pose a problem.

Kaplan (2007) wrote that Congress had considered a law making it mandatory to reroute trains carrying TIHs around major cities (noting that this represents about 1% of all the freight in transit) because FRA and TSA issued only guidance and requested voluntary compliance. However, terrorism expert Stephen Flynn, a former Coast Guard captain, stated that many of the hazardous chemicals are in fact bound for activities within the HTUAs, such as drinking water processing with chlorine (Kaplan, 2007). Another strategy might be to lessen the need for such TIHs to be taken to HTUAs by changing processes instead, creating inherently safer technologies (ISTs). For example, cities could use bleach instead of chlorine for water processing, and refineries could use sulfuric acid in place of hydrofluoric acid for petroleum refining.

AAR notes that mandatory rerouting "doesn't end the risk and could cause unintended consequences to our health and economy" (AAR, 2011). It points out that rerouting just changes the communities that are exposed to the passage of the TIH cars, and that rerouting would almost inevitably mean that the TIH cars are in transit longer because the current routes are the most efficient.

Case Studies

Dunsmuir, California, Derailment

In the evening on July 14, 1991, a 6,000-foot train carrying metam sodium was traveling through the 10.5-mile Cantara Loop, a descent in the train's route through the mountains along the Sacramento River that is the steepest in California's rail system. It was the single track main line in the north–south route through California and carries 7,600 trains per year (Alves, 2003). The train had 97 cars, of which 86 were empty when the derailment occurred. The cause of the accident was a combination of an improper consist, with gondolas of heavy scrap metal at the end of the train, and too much speed (Schneider, 1991). The NTSB also determined that the rails had been greased to assist the train with negotiating the curve and the grease was excessive.

The cars slid off the isolated track into the river, but the one carrying metam sodium, identified on the manifest only as weed killer, did not appear to be damaged. The engineer detached from the derailed cars, including the metam sodium car that was in the river, and proceeded into Dunsmuir to clear the track so that the rescue equipment could retrieve the derailed cars; 19,000 gallons of metam sodium emptied into the river (Schneider, 1991).

Metam sodium was used as a soil fumigant and usually diluted before application. Up to that time, there had been no indication that it was in fact a hazardous material. However, when the sun came up, the damage was plain to see. Everything in the river was dead, and the water was traveling at 1 mph toward Lake Shasta, 40 miles away—a major reservoir supplying drinking water throughout the state. When mixed with water, the metam sodium creates methyl isothicyanate, methylamine, and hydrogen sulfide (Cantara Trustee Council, 2007).

The gasses released in the chemical reaction were respiratory irritants that began affecting the people living along the river and in the town of Dunsmuir. Dunsmuir was protected by a volunteer fire department with no hazardous materials response capability. The Southern Pacific dispatcher notified the state of the derailment, but had no indication that hazardous materials were involved. The dispatcher did not call 9-1-1 because the derailment was on railroad property, so local first responders did not know about the derailment until morning. The people in Dunsmuir and along the river were exposed for 8 hours before the evacuation began. In the first month, 705 people were identified with exposure to the chemical. Another 483 people were evacuated from the area (Koehler & Van Ness, 1993).

The pristine river area had long been a trout fishing center. The economy depended on the railroad and the tourist industry. The chemical spill destroyed wildlife along the banks as well as every living thing in the river, all the way down to Lake Shasta, where the state and federal EPAs had arranged for barges to aerate the water to hasten the decomposition of the chemical. It took 2 weeks for the lake water's chemical balance to be restored (Cantara Trustee Council, 2007).

Southern Pacific Railroad settled with the California Department of Fish and Game for $38 million; $13 million reimbursed the agencies for their emergency response and $14 million created a restoration account (Report to congressional requesters, Superfund, 1996). The railroad also installed concrete rail ties, heavier rails and inline rails to help prevent derailments, and a better guard rail on the curve. The U.S. DOT strengthened shipping requirements for chemicals with environmental and public health effects, including chemicals banned from disposal in landfills (TRB, 1994).

Baltimore Tunnel Fire

On July 18, 2001, a CSX train of 60 cars, including several hazardous materials tankers, derailed in the Howard Street Tunnel in Baltimore, Maryland. The brick-lined tunnel was built in 1896. It is 3 feet below ground level at Camden Yards and 46 feet below Martin Luther King Boulevard. Four of the tankers ignited, and the fire was fueled by paper and wood in adjacent cars. At least 2,500 gallons of hydrochloric acid were released (Styron, 2001). The engineer was able to uncouple the engine and move it to safety. The derailed cars were left to burn themselves out.

The emergency response was complicated by the limited access to the tunnel, the toxic smoke, and the presence of the hazardous materials tankers. Firefighters tried to access the tunnel through a manhole on Howard Street but were driven back by the venting smoke. The 40-inch water main in Howard Street ruptured from the heat of the underground fire below it, fortuitously pouring water into the tunnel. Eventually, the firefighters were able to pour water through the manhole to speed the end of the fire (Styron, 2001).

There was a concern that there could be a boiling liquid explosion (BLEVE) in the tankers that could have damaged the tunnel's structure. Due to concerns about safety, the Camden Yards ballpark was evacuated and remained closed for 4 days at the height of the baseball season, and the Inner Harbor was closed. Businesses in a 1.3 mile radius around the tunnel were closed for at least 5 days.

Secondary impacts of the fire were numerous. The fire resulted in the closure of the major highways into the area, including I-395, I-83, and I-40. Freight service along the whole east coast and mass transit in Baltimore were disrupted by the fire. The communication infrastructure was affected when a fiber-optic line routed through the tunnel itself was burned, affecting voice communications and data transmissions as far as Lusaka, Zambia, in Africa (U.S. DOT ITS, 2002).

It took 5 days for the fire to be extinguished and 55 days before all services were restored (U.S. DOT ITS, 2002). The break in a city water main on Howard Street above the derailment complicated the investigation of the cause of the accident, as most of the evidence had either been burned up or washed away by the time the NTSB investigators could access the tunnel.

Cleanup costs were $1.3 million; the Baltimore Orioles baseball team estimated its losses at $4.5 million. All freight traffic had to be rerouted hundreds of miles out of the way when the main north–south rail line was severed by the fire (U.S. DOT ITS, 2002).

Sunset Limited Derailed in Arizona

In 1995 the Amtrak Sunset Limited was traveling from New Orleans to Los Angeles. It had two locomotives and 12 cars with 248 passengers and

20 Amtrak employees. In the desert west of Phoenix, Arizona, the train derailed, killing one employee and injuring 65 passengers. The derailment occurred 18 miles from a paved road, 18 hours after the last train had passed safely. An unknown terrorist group called Sons of the Gestapo claimed credit for the derailment that was perpetrated in retribution for Ruby Ridge and Waco, Texas, gun battles between dissident groups and federal agents (Jenkins, 1997).

The sabotage to the track on a 30-foot high trestle was extensive. The damage was done on a curve leading to the bridge to hide the damage from the engineer's view until it was too late to stop the 55 mph train. Twenty-nine spikes were removed from the rails, nuts and bolts were removed from the rail joints, and the joint bars holding the rails together were removed. The signal system was tampered with to keep the signal green, meaning to travel at maximum speed. The track was then bent inward and respiked to hold it in place as the train passed over it (Jenkins, 1997).

The locomotive remained upright, and the damage to the passenger cars was limited. There was no fire or hazardous materials involvement. The safety features built into the cars and locomotive to protect the passengers and crew in case of an accident all performed as intended. The damage was limited to $2,979,000, and passengers were able to self-evacuate through emergency windows. Emergency response personnel evacuated 70 people from the area by helicopter. Evacuation of the injured passengers was completed within 4 hours. The Red Cross established a shelter for the rest of the passengers in Phoenix (Jenkins, 1997).

Ethanol Trains

Long trains of tanker cars are a staple of East and West Coast main railroad lines as petroleum products go from coastal refinery to inland consumer. Midwestern trains hauled corn and corn oil, wheat and meat from fields and stockyards. Ethanol, a corn-based fuel, has changed the consist of Midwestern trains to include more tankers of flammable liquids.

Someone in Menlo, Iowa, wanted to derail the 130-car ethanol train in June of 2011. The lock was cut off the switch box, and the track was "gapped open" about 2 inches. A black bag was placed over the switch to mask the tampering. A slow moving Union Pacific train passed safely over the disrupted switch, but noted the black bag and reported the trouble, causing the line to be shut down (Cloherty & Thomas, 2011). The section of rail that was tampered with is owned by the Iowa Interstate Railroad Limited (IAIS), a Class II regional railroad that connects with all of the Class I railroads—BNSF, UP, CN, CP, KCS, CSXT, and NS—at various points between Council Bluffs and Chicago and carries 1 billion gallons of ethanol per year (IAIS, n.d.).

The IAIS chief operations officer estimated that a train traveling at 40 mph or more would have been derailed by the vandalism. Unlike gasoline fumes that will explode, ethanol will only burn, but if numerous cars were set ablaze, the fire could have been disastrous (Cloherty & Thomas, 2011). While no one took responsibility for the June 2011 damage, it provided a paradigm for one kind of derailment scenario and demonstrates the vulnerability of the far-flung rail infrastructure.

On October 7, 2011, 26 cars of a 131-car train did derail, including ethanol tankers containing 30,000 gallons each. Nine of the tankers derailed and seven caught fire (Walberg, Nickeas, & Wang, 2011). The residents of the nearby town of Tiskilwa, Illinois, were evacuated in the early morning hours as a precaution, and no one was hurt. However, the quantity of spilled ethanol raised environmental concerns, and the Illinois EPA has sued the railroad, as the "spiller," for the costs of instituting environmental monitoring and cleanup for several private wells and two creeks. The cause remains unknown, and it may take up to 18 months for the NTSB to determine what happened (Barker, 2011).

Summary

Freight rail is invisible to the average consumer who shares the roads with trucks, yet its loss can quickly cripple the economy. While the rail system carries less freight than trucks, it carries the heavy and hazardous, keeping them off highways. The freight rail and long-distance passenger systems are open and operate in many remote areas, but they have a unique capability to restore their operations through internally provided repair services. The AAR's rail and government partners have created a networked approach to the provision of safety and security that incorporated the employees of the railroad and its contractors into the security force. The challenge of moving TIHs through the system, especially through HTUAs, continues to seek a solution. Cyber enhancements to operational efficiency may open a new vulnerability for safe and secure operations.

Freight in the global supply chain joins the rail stream through maritime deliveries. Their relationship and synergies are the topic of the next chapter.

Discussion Questions

1. What are the hazards and vulnerabilities of heavy rail systems? What security concerns would a plan have to address?

2. Heavy rail systems operate in remote and desolate areas and over long distances. How do these factors make heavy rail more vulnerable to security breaches? How do these same factors contribute to system security?

3. What aspects of heavy rail operational infrastructure enhance its vulnerability to attack?

4. Describe the Sunset Limited derailment. What security enhancements might have been useful in preventing the attack or speeding the response to the derailment?

5. Thinking of freight rail as a multimodal system, what features of the equipment enhance its vulnerability? What security strategies and technologies have been applied to lessen vulnerability? Evaluate their effectiveness.

Notes

1. Spurs are short lines that serve a customer's facility, such as a factory or warehouse. Sidings are track sections owned by the railroad where cars wait to join a new train.
2. A consist is the list or order in which the engines and cars on a train are lined up. It notes which cars are empty, which full, and any special handling instructions.
3. The Federal Railroad Administration and the Association of American Railroads no longer collect vandalism incidence statistics.

References

Alves, R. (2003). Dunsmuir train derailment spurs public safety forum. The Fish Sniffer Online, 8/11/2003. Retrieved February 8, 2009, from http://www.fishsniffer.com/steelhead/030811trainwreck.html

AAR (American Association of Railroads). (2011). Security plan. Accessed on July 23, 2011, at http://www.aar.org/Safety/Rail-Security.aspx

AmericanRail.com. (2011). Well cars, hauling today's intermodal needs. Accessed July 20, 2011, at http://www.american-rails.com/well-cars.html

Amtrak Historical Society. (n.d.). Experience the spirit…the history…. Accessed July 23, 2011, at http://www.amtrakhistoricalsociety.org/bah.htm

Barker, D. (2011, October 31). Tiskilwa derailment: Investigation continues. *Bureau County Republican*. Accessed January 20, 2012.

Blaszak, M. (2006, May 1). Intermodal equipment: flat cars, well cars; containers and trailers. *Trains: The Magazine of Railroading* (http://trn.trains.com/en/Railroad%20Reference/ABCs%20of%20Railroading/2006/05/Intermodal%20equipment.aspx)

Boyd, J. D. (2011, May 6). DHS warns of Al Qaeda rail plot. *Journal of Commerce On-Line*. Accessed July 20, 2011, at http://www.joc.com/security/dhs-warns-al-qaida-rail-plot?page = 2

Branscomb, L. M., Fagan, M., Auerswald, P., Ellis, R. N., & Barcham, R. (2010). *Rail transportation of toxic inhalation hazards: Policy responses to the safety and security externality.* Discussion paper 2010-01, Belfer Center for Science and International Affairs, Harvard Kennedy School. Accessed July 20, 2011, at http://belfercenter.ksg.harvard.edu/publication/19929/rail_transportation_of_toxic_inhalation_hazards.html

Bureau of Explosives. (2012). History of the Bureau of Explosives. Accessed January 20, 2012, at http://www.boepublications.com/about_us.html

Bureau of Transportation Statistics. (2011). Table 2-38: Reports of violent crime, property crime, and arrests by transit mode. http://www.bts.gov/publications/national_transportation_statistics/html/table_02_38.html

Cantara Trustee Council. (2007). Final report on the recovery of the Upper Sacramento River—Subsequent to the 1991 Cantara Spill. Retrieved February 14, 2009, from http://www.dfg.ca.gov/ospr/spill/nrda/cantra_loop-final_report2007.pdf

Clawson, H. J., Dutch, N., Solomon, A., & Grace, L. G. (2009). Human trafficking into and within the United States. Accessed July 20, 2011, at http://aspe.hhs.gov/hsp/07/HumanTrafficking/LitRev/index.shtml#Trafficking

Cloherty, J., & Thomas, P. (2011, June 14). FBI investigates train carrying flammable ethanol—Rules out terrorism. Accessed July 20, 2011, at http://abcnews.go.com/Politics/train-disaster/story?id=13840108

Conrail. (2003). A brief history of Conrail. Accessed July 20, 2011, at http://www.conrail.com/history.htm

Edgar, A. G. (2005, January 6). South Carolina train crash leaves four dead, 200 injured. *Firehouse Magazine,* http://www.firehouse.com/news/10512869/south-carolina-train-crash-leaves-four-dead-200-injured

Edwards, F. L., & Goodrich, D. C. (2010). Supply chain security and the need for continuous assessment. In A. R. Thomas (Ed.), *Supply chain security.* Santa Barbara, CA: Praeger.

FBI. (2008). Precious metal: Copper theft threatens U.S. infrastructure. Accessed July 20, 2011, at http://www.fbi.gov/news/stories/2008/december/copper_120308

FBI. (2010). Inside cargo theft: A growing multi-billion dollar problem. Accessed July 20, 2011, at http://www.fbi.gov/news/stories/2010/november/cargo_111210/cargo_111210

FEMA. (1996). *Guide for all-hazard emergency operations planning. Attachment C, hazardous materials.* Washington, DC: FEMA.

FRA. (2010). Railroad trespassing, vandalism, and highway-rail grade crossing warning device violation prevention strategies. Washington, DC: US DOT, Office of Railroad Safety.

Guerrero, P. F., & Rabkin, N. J. (2004, March 23). *Rail security: Some actions taken to enhance passenger and freight rail security, but significant challenges remain* (GAO 04-598T). A report to the Senate Committee on Commerce, Science and Transportation.

Hull, P. (2008, March 10). Port relies on high tech cranes to speed flow of cargo. *Post and Courier.* Accessed July 20, 2011, at http://www.postandcourier.com/news/2008/mar/10/cranes33078/

Illinois State University Police. (2012). Railroad general safety tips. http://policeillinoisstate.edu/crime_prevention_safety_tips/railroad_safety/index.shtml

Iowa Interstate Railroad Limited. (n.d.). About us. Accessed July 20, 2011, at http://www.iaisrr.com/

Jenkins, B. M. (1997). *Protecting surface transportation systems and patrons from terrorist activities* (IISTPS Report 97-04). San Jose, CA: Mineta Transportation Institute.

Jenkins, B. M., & Butterworth, B. (2010). *Explosives and incendiaries used in terrorist attacks on public surface transportation: A preliminary empirical analysis* (MTI Report WP 09-02). San Jose, CA: Mineta Transportation Institute.

Jenkins, B. M., & Edwards-Winslow, F. L. (2002). *Saving city lifelines* (MTI Report 02-06). San Jose, CA: Mineta Transportation Institute.

Kaplan, E. (2007). Rail Security and Terrorist Threat Council on Foreign Relations. http://www.cfr.org/United-States/rail-security-terrorist-threat/p/28000

Koehler, G. A., & Van Ness, C. (1993). The emergency medical response to the Cantara hazardous materials incident. *Prehospital and Disaster Medicine, 8*(4), 359–365. Retrieved February 14, 2009, from PubMed database.

Leyden, J. (2008). Polish teen derails tram after hacking train network. *Enterprise Security.* Accessed January 20, 2012, from www.theregister.co.uk/2008/01/11/tram_hack/

Lindsey, S. M. (2004, April 8). Testimony of S. Mark Lindsey before the Rail Security Senate Committee on the Judiciary. Accessed July 23, 2011, at www.fra.dot.gov/Pages/1650.shtml

McCall, J. H., Jr. (2008). When railroad guns ruled. Accessed July 23, 2011, at http://www.historynet.com/when-railroad-guns-ruled.htm

NTSB. (2005). *Collision of Norfolk Southern freight train 192 with standing Norfolk Southern local train P22 with subsequent hazardous materials release at Graniteville, South Carolina, January 6, 2005: Railroad accident report* (NTSB/RAR-05/04). Washington, DC: National Transportation Safety Board.

Oklahoma Department of Civil Emergency Management. (1995). *After action report, Alfred P. Murrah Building Bombing, 19 April 1995.*

Plant, J. F. (2004). Terrorism and the railroads: Redefining security in the wake of 9/11. *Review of Policy Research, 21*(3), 293–305.

Report to congressional requesters, Superfund. (1996). Outlook for and experience with natural resource damage settlements, appendix I—Restoration status for five largest settlements. United States General Accounting Office, 24-26. Retrieved February 8, 2009, from http://www.tpub.com/content/cg1996/rc96071/index.htm

Rigden, D. (2004). *How to be a spy: The World War II SOE training manual.* Toronto, Canada: The Dundurn Group.

Ryan, R., Anderson, Z., & Chiesa, A. (n.d.). Anatomy of a subway hack. Accessed January 20, 2012, at http://tech.mit.edu/V128/N30/subway/Defcon_Presentation.pdf

Schmitt, P. J. (2005). *The partisan's companion: Deadly techniques of Soviet freedom fighters during World War II.* Boulder, CO: Paladin Press.

Schneider, K. (1991, July 27). California spill exposes gaps in rail safety rules. *New York Times.* Retrieved February 17, 2009, from LexisNexis database.

Sturgeon, J. (2008, March 13). On the track of crime. *Roanoke News.*

Styron, H. C. (2001). CSX tunnel fire, Baltimore, MD. FEMA. http://www.usfa.fema.gov/downloads/pdf/publications/tr-140.pdf

Thompson, R. E., Zamejc, E. R., & Ahlbeck, D. R. (1992). *Hazardous materials placement in a train consist—Volume I (review and analysis).* U.S. DOT, Federal Railroad Administration. Washington, DC: Office of Research and Development.

TRB. (1994). *Ensuring railroad tank car safety* (Special Report 243). Washington, DC: National Academies.

TSA. (2006a). *Recommended security action items for the rail transportation of toxic inhalation hazard materials.* Supplement No. 1, issued November 21, 2006. Accessed July 20, 2011, at http://www.tsa.gov/assets/pdf/Supplement_No%201_TIH-SAI.pdf

TSA. (2006b). Toxic inhalation hazards. Accessed July 20, 2011, at http://www.tsa.gov/what_we_do/tsnm/freight_rail/tih_materials.shtm

TSA. (2007). Recommended security action items for the rail transportation of toxic inhalation hazard materials. Supplement No. 2, issued February 12, 2007. Accessed July 20, 2011, at http://www.tsa.gov/assets/pdf/sai_for_tih_supplement2.pdf

TSA. (2011). Freight rail overview. Accessed July 20, 2011, at https://www.tsa.gov/what_we_do/tsnm/freight_rail/index.shtm

TSA. (n.d.). Freight rail modal annex. Accessed July 20, 2011, at http://www.tsa.gov/assets/pdf/modal_annex_freight_rail.pdf

U.S. Army. (1987). *Engineer field data: FM5-34*. Ft. Belvoir, VA: U.S. Army Engineering School.

U.S. Attorney, District of Nevada. (2010). Defendants' sentences for stealing copper wire from the railroad tracks in northern Nevada. Accessed January 20, 2012, at http://www.fbi.gov/lasvegas/press-releases/2010/lv082510.htm

U.S. DOT. (2008). *Emergency response guidebook*. Washington, DC: US DOT.

U.S. DOT. (2011). *Pocket guide to transportation*. Washington, DC: RITA.

U.S. DOT ITS Joint Office Program. (2002). *Effects of catastrophic events on the transportation system management and operations: Baltimore, MD—Howard Street Tunnel Fire—July 18, 2001*. Washington, DC.

USMC. FMF. (1942). *Destruction by demolition, incendiaries and sabotage*. Field training manual.

Von Dach, H. (1965). *Total resistance: Swiss Army guide to guerrilla warfare and underground operations*. Boulder, CO: Paladin Press.

Walberg, M., Nickeas, P., & Wang, A. L. (2011, October 7). Small town lit up by explosive early morning train derailment. *Chicago Tribune*. Accessed January 10, 2011, at http://articles.chicagotribune.com/2011-10-07/news/chi-authorities-evacuating-central-illinois-town-following-train-derailment-20111007_1_train-derailment-train-cars-131-car-train

White, R. D. (2010, December 25). Moody's cuts Alameda corridor's bond rating despite strong year. *LA Times*, p. B1.

YouTube. (2011). Experiments to derail trains, 1944. Accessed on July 23, 2011, at http://www.youtube.com/watch?v=D-8gV4DJZUw

Chapter 9

Maritime Transportation

Keywords: Boat, ship, ferry, tug, port, navigable waterway, flotation, propulsion, steering, GPS, AIS, pilot, harbor, buoys, channel markers, lighthouses, beacons, MDA, MTSA, C-TPAT, cargo container, container ship, tanker, freighter, crew, dock, pier, intermodal, surveillance, sabotage, weapons of mass disruption, safety, security, trespassing, vandalism, piracy, hazardous materials, TIH, NFPA placards, LNG

Learning Objectives

After reading this chapter you should be able to

- Identify potential security vulnerabilities in maritime transportation
- Understand how maritime operations generate vulnerabilities
- Identify hazardous materials and toxic inhalation hazards (TIHs) in stationary storage and transit
- Understand the role of technology in maritime operations security
- Understand the strategies used by terrorists to disrupt maritime transportation systems

Components of the Maritime Transportation System

Chicago, Duluth, San Francisco, and Boston celebrate their sailing heritage by hosting tall-ships events. The grace and beauty of a ship under sail draws spectators to a parade of brigantines, sloops, schooners, and square riggers—part of America's maritime past. In Chicago, Olympic match racing is conducted in the shadow of the historic vessels, while in San Francisco the Navy's Blue Angels fly over the parade of tall ships. Coast Guard cutters float among the visiting ships as the law enforcement agency for America's maritime territory. In the background, the working ports are filled with huge cranes that serve the tankers, freighters, ore carriers, and container ships that reflect the continuing importance of maritime vessels to America's security and economy.

American History and the Sea

America is inextricably tied to the sea. Archeologists believe that America's earliest inhabitants crossed the Bering Sea from Asia. Viking remains demonstrate the seafaring visits to the western coasts of the Atlantic Ocean. The first European settlers arrived by sea and stayed to dominate two continents. American's Revolutionary War pivoted on the sea power of the British, French, and nascent United States. The Constitution reflects the critical importance of maritime security by giving Congress the explicit power to "provide and maintain a Navy" (Constitution, Article 1, Section 8). While the army is only raised for 2 years at a time and can be abolished, the navy is a responsibility of the government.

The ocean was long America's first line of defense. Territorial waters were defined by the distance that could be protected by land-based defenses. In 1982 the United Nations created a Convention of the Law of the Sea that established the width of the territorial waters of coastal nations at 12 miles (UN, 1982, Part II, Section 2, Article 3) and a 200-mile limit over which the adjacent nation has economic control (UN, 1982, Part V, Article 57). Although the United States never ratified the treaty, it and most nations recognize these internationally agreed upon territorial limits.

The Atlantic Ocean was America's initial economic engine, with many Americans drawing their livelihoods from fishing and shipping. Agricultural products like cotton, indigo, and tobacco were sent in ships to Europe to obtain hard currency for the new republic. The American Navy and Marine Corps demonstrated the new nation's maritime strength by defeating the Barbary pirates on "the shores of Tripoli," in the words of the Marine Corps Hymn. The War of 1812 was won on Lake Erie and the Mississippi River, in the Caribbean, and in the Atlantic. By the end of the Civil War, American

FIGURE 9.1   Container ship in the Port of Seattle.

trade goods included food, manufactured goods, and raw materials for European industry, like cotton and iron ore.

Ships brought the first Europeans to settle North America, with the *Mayflower* giving its name to the first written law of the colonies, the Mayflower Compact. The ports of Philadelphia, Baltimore, New York, Boston, and Charleston welcomed new immigrants, and with the boom in immigration Ellis Island in New York became the center of immigration in the 1800s, while Philadelphia remained the world's largest freshwater port until the 1960s. The shipyards of America produced the myriad types of military vessels needed to blockade Southern commerce in the Civil War and later to protect the economy of the growing nation. Teddy Roosevelt's Great White Fleet showed the flag around the world in the early twentieth century. Military ships won World War II, and the American nuclear navy projected U.S. sea and air power around the world during the Cold War. The evolution of intermodal shipping to support the growing globalization of trade led to the development of new port facilities with high-speed cranes and new maritime vessels whose containers mated directly with trains and trucks (Figure 9.1).

Categories of Maritime Vessels

Maritime vessels are vehicles that are designed to float, that are self-propelled, and that can be steered. The maritime domain in the United States is divided into four categories: pleasure craft, fishing and extraction craft, military craft, and commercial craft. Commercial craft are divided between passenger vessels and cargo vessels.

Pleasure craft include vehicles as small as jet skis and as large as seago-ing yachts. In 2009 there were 12,721,541 recreational boats "numbered in accordance with Chapter 123 of Title 46 U.S.C." (RITA, 2011), meaning they were smaller than 5 tons and 30 feet and not used in commerce or fishing. These boats are registered with the state of the owner's residence rather than with the Coast Guard. They are regulated by the U.S. Coast Guard regarding safety features, navigation aids, and respect for the maritime rules of the road.

Unfortunately, these craft have also been involved in smuggling operations, starting during Prohibition, which led to the nickname of "rum runner" for small, fast boats. Currently, illegal operations using these "go fast" or "cigarette" (an allusion to their shape) boats include gun running, drug importation, and human trafficking, drawing the attention of law enforcement to their operation, configuration and berthing. Pleasure craft may have sails or engines or a combination, and cigarette racing boats can travel at speeds close to 90 mph, while sail boats can run before the wind in races at speeds over 50 mph (Yachtpals, 2008); at slower speeds, they travel almost silently.

Fishing and extraction craft include oil rigs in tow, fishing vessels, and undersea mining vessels. They are regulated by a combination of commerce-driven requirements, hazardous materials management laws, Department of Agriculture food production requirements, and international treaties, as well as standard Coast Guard requirements. Furthermore, activities of the paid crew may come under the jurisdiction of union contracts, Occupational Health and Safety Administration (OSHA) regulations, and industry-specific laws and regulations. Under the Bureau of Labor Statistics, they are categorized as "fishers" (BLS, 2009). In 2012, the Coast Guard estimated the value of U.S. fisheries at $30 billion annually (Coast Guard, 2012).

Military vessels operate under the Department of Defense, subject to the Uniform Code of Military Justice and the oversight of military commands.

These three categories of vessels are not part of the American economy's global supply chain, although they may contribute protection or support, raw materials, goods, and fuel to it.

Passenger Vessels: Cruise Ships

The focus of this chapter is the commercial transportation sector. Passenger vessels include ferries and cruise ships (Figure 9.2). A cruise ship is regulated by the country in which it is registered, and that is the flag that it flies. There are a very limited number of American flag cruise ships. The newest, *Pride of America,* part of Norwegian Cruise Lines, was christened in 2005 for the Hawaiian inter-island itinerary denied to foreign flag ships, which are forbidden to stop at consecutive American ports (Smith, 2005). In 2010, 2.7 million passengers went on 1,083 cruises on 101 different ships that had at least one stop in an American port. Most cruise ships have about 2.6 passengers for each crew member (U.S. DOT MARAD, 2010).

The construction, safety features, and operation of American cruise ships are regulated by the Coast Guard, and the crew is generally subject to union

FIGURE 9.2   Cruise ship in the Port of Seattle.

rules and contracts (doubling wages as compared with foreign flag vessels) (Smith, 2005), OSHA rules, and public health regulations related to food handling and cleanliness. Some passenger ships are designed mainly for transportation from one continent to another; however, most passenger ships today are operated as floating resorts, with onboard entertainment and gourmet cuisine, whose ports of call are generally single-day visits for sightseeing activities.

Passenger Vessels: Ferries

Ferries are part of the nation's mass transit system, comprising 697 directional route miles (U.S. DOT, 2011, p. 12). Ferries operate in place of or in addition to bridges over bodies of water that divide urban areas or disrupt road layouts (Figure 9.3). For example, the Staten Island Ferry is owned and operated by the New York City Department of Transportation, which also maintains the city's roads and bridges.

Some ferries are operated by intermodal mass transit companies. For example, the Massachusetts Bay Transportation Authority that operates Boston's "The T" subway system also operates commuter boats and ferries in Boston Harbor, even offering a transit pass that includes bus, subway, ferry, and commuter boat trips (MBTA, 2011). Ferries owned by the Washington State Department of Transportation, called Seattle's best tourist attraction, carry commuters and their cars around the harbor (Washington State DOT, 2011), while the Water Emergency Transportation Authority in San Francisco operates both daily commuter ferries across San Francisco Bay and an emergency transportation system (WETA, 2009).

FIGURE 9.3   Car ferry in the Seattle harbor.

The Coast Guard regulates the operations of ferries, including their safety equipment and loading requirements. Following a number of ferry accidents overseas that were attributed to overcrowding, the Coast Guard has raised the estimated weight per average American passenger to 185 pounds from 160 pounds, thereby lowering the number of passengers allowed per ferry, to increase operational stability (*ABC News,* 2011). Ferry operators from Seattle to Galveston protested the change in their income generated by the reduction in passenger loading, but as noted in Chapter 3, the Coast Guard makes the final determination on all maritime safety regulations of U.S. flagged vessels. It also issues all merchant marine operator licenses, and amended those regulations with stricter medical clearance requirements (Yanchunas, 2008) after the fatal accident on the Staten Island Ferry in 2003, which was caused by the pilot being on pain killers at the time of the crash. The accident killed 11 people and injured dozens of others (Associated Press, 2008).

Crew Members: Merchant Marine

The merchant marine is made up of the professional crew members of waterborne vessels, with more than 81,000 jobs (BLS, 2009). Unlike a modern railroad that runs trains with a crew of two on-duty personnel—the engineer and the conductor—the modern ship has a variety of specialized positions. The crew of large and oceangoing ships requires training and licensing, called a merchant mariner's credential (MMC), as specified by the Coast Guard. Ancillary unlicensed crew may include a cook, electrician, and machinery mechanics. Some ships offer apprentice positions for

TABLE 9.1 Typical Licensed Crew Titles

Title	Role	Special Information
Pilot	Guides ship through confined areas, like straits, harbors, and rivers; supervises the ship's operation during these maneuvers	Harbor pilots are independent contractors; pilots on river boats are crew members.
Master/captain	Overall command, supervise the crew; responsible for safety, for loading and unloading of passengers and goods and compliance with all regulations; maintain logs of all ship movements; oversee course and speed of vessel and navigation	
Deck officer or "mate"	Supervise and coordinate the activities of the crew; alternate standing watch with the captain	Can have second, third, and fourth mates on large oceangoing vessels. Chief mate assumes command if captain is incapacitated.
Ship's engineer	Operate, maintain, and repair all elements of the propulsion system	Seagoing vessels have four engineering officers: chief, first assistant, second assistant, and third assistant. Assistants alternate watch standing.
Marine oilers	Assist engineers with maintenance of ship's propulsion system components	Qualified members of the engine department (QMED) work with oilers.
Sailors or deckhands	Operate the vessel and maintain the nonengineering aspects of the ship; stand watch for navigation obstructions and navigation aids; steer the ship; take depth soundings; handle the lines at the dock	On liquid cargo ships some are called pumpmen and operate the hoses, pumps, and tanks. Oceangoing ships call them able seamen, and the boatswain is the head seaman.
Communications officer	Operates and maintains radios and other communications equipment on the ship	Does not need an MMC but is licensed by the FCC.

Source: BLS. (2009). *Occupational Outlook Handbook,* 2010–2011 ed. Accessed April 20, 2011, at http://www.bls.gov/oco/ocos247.htm.

unlicensed personnel studying to become licensed. Table 9.1 lists the typical professional crew positions licensed by the Coast Guard. As shown in Table 9.2, the makeup of the crew depends on the type of ship.

Commercial Vessels: Tugboats

Commercial vessels come in a variety of configurations. Tugs move larger vessels in ports, through narrow transit points, and in other areas where the

TABLE 9.2 Typical Crew Configurations

Ship Type	Titles	Total Crew
Oceangoing	Captain or master Deck officers or mates (3) Chief engineer and three assistant engineers Seamen (6+): able seamen, oilers, QMEDs Cook	15 or more
Large coastal	Captain Mate Engineer Seamen (7 or 8)	11 or more
Small vessels: Harbor and rivers	Captain Deckhand	2

Source: BLS. (2009). Occupational Outlook Handbook, 2010–2011 ed. Accessed April 20, 2011, at http://www.bls.gov/oco/ocos247.htm.

ship's internal propulsion and steering are not adequate. Tugs, which are essentially floating engines, also provide emergency support to ships that have had engine problems or run aground, for example. Service and supply vessels support offshore drilling platforms or ships anchored offshore—moving parts, supplies, and personnel from the shore. Typical supplies include food, spare parts, and replacement equipment, and crews at shift change.

Commercial Vessels: Barges

Among the vessels moved by tugs are barges, barge carriers, and lighters, which do not have their own engines. These watercraft have flat bottoms and generally operate in inland waterways such as rivers and canals. According to the U.S. DOT, in 2008 there were over 25,000 miles of canals in service (U.S. DOT, 2011, p. 12), and over 9,000 barges were in operation in the United States in 2009 (RITA, 2011). Barges carry cargo on deck and can operate singly or in "trains." Barge carriers can carry barges or cargo containers. Lighters are smaller craft that move cargo between ships anchored in the channel and the shore, often in areas where the port facilities cannot accommodate the ship's draft. Barges generally carry foodstuffs, bulk materials like rock and sand, liquid food products like wine and corn oil, and some chemicals.

Barges have also been used as floating land. In Mississippi before Hurricane Katrina, gambling was only permitted on floating barges. However, after one ended up in the main street of a town, marooned by the hurricane, the state changed the law to permit gambling also on dry land. One of the most unique uses for a barge is the New York City prison barge, Vernon C. Bain, that holds 870 prisoners in medium- and maximum-security sections (Rocchio, 2010).

Commercial Vessels: Cargo Ships

Cargo ships move the economy. In 2009 there were only 196 U.S. flagged oceangoing ships (RITA, 2011), but international cargo vessels regularly call at U.S. ports. More than 7,000 commercial ships per year transit between Asia and the U.S. West Coast (Gordon & Parker, 2007).

Cargo ships come in several configurations, as shown in Table 9.3. They operate at 12 to 25 knots, depending on the type of ship and whether the company is trying to save money by "slow steaming" or to meet a deadline (*Copenhagen Post,* 2011). Slow steaming allows ships to save fuel, which is crucial to staying in business during the economic downturn. For example, at the typical steaming speed of 21 knots, a cargo ship needs 125 metric tons of fuel to go 500 miles, while at 15 knots it only needs 80 tons. At the 2010 cost of bunker fuel, that change represents a $250,000 savings on a voyage from Hong Kong to Long Beach. Although some customers complain about the longer delivery time, environmentalists applaud the decrease in greenhouse gas emissions—approximately 30% reduction through slow steaming (White, 2010).

TABLE 9.3 Types of Cargo Vessels

Type	Description	Typical Cargo
General cargo	Roll on/roll off	Vehicles, wheeled heavy equipment, large crates, palletized material
	Refrigerated ships	Food, bulk frozen food
	Livestock carrier	Animals
	Breakbulk	Bundled, bagged, drummed cargo; heavy equipment
Dry bulk cargo	Cargo hold with hatches or removable deck plates	Solid food, bulk materials, scrap and recyclable materials
Liquid bulk cargo	Oil tankers with multiple tanks	Crude oil, refined petroleum products
	Chemical tankers with multiple tanks	Bulk liquid industrial chemicals, both inorganic and organic, including items for human consumption like wine and corn syrup
	Gas carriers with multiple pressurized tanks	Liquefied gas, hazardous TIH
Container ships	Stowage spaces above and below deck divided into cells, with intermodal containers placed on slots or guides and stacked in tiers	Intermodal containers include any type of trade goods, often in consumer packaging; some containers may be refrigerated

Source: Department of Defense. (2006). *Merchant Vessel Inspection Guide,* vessel and cargo types, 55–71.

FIGURE 9.4 Container ship in Istanbul.

Commercial Vessels: Container Ships

Container ships are the principal method for moving the global supply chain, from raw materials to finished high-tech equipment (Figure 9.4). Globalization of the economy results in component parts for a consumer product being made in several countries and assembled in yet another, which necessitates the movement of components across oceans, creating demand for shipping services.

Unlike other types of cargo ships, the freight in container ships is packed at the point of origin and not unpacked until it reaches a warehouse or customer destination. Containers are designed to fit into cells aboard the ship. A fully loaded ship has the containers packed so tightly that a person cannot move between them and needs climbing gear to get from the deck to the top of the stack.

There are international containers and domestic containers. International containers are 20, 40, or 45 feet long. The shorter boxes are used for heavy goods like machinery and metal parts due to the weight limits of cranes and load limits on highways, because many containers go onto trucks. The bigger boxes are for lightweight articles like clothing and small electronics in consumer packaging. Domestic containers are sized for use on standard U.S. truck trailers: 28, 40, 45, or 53 feet (Blaszak, 2006).

For maximum stability at sea, the heaviest loads need to go on the bottom of the stack, which makes developing the loading plan a challenge, as stack configuration has to take into account the length and weight of each container. Fully packed containers are more stable than partial loads, which may be necessitated by the shape and weight of the item being shipped. At the end of the sea voyage, the containers are stacked onto specially designed railroad "well cars" (as described in Chapter 8) or onto specially designed truck trailers.

Nonvessel Components of the Maritime Transportation Environment

Waterside components of the maritime transportation environment are the oceans, bays, rivers, deltas, and harbors—natural features—and piers, ports, and canals that are the result of human intervention. These words designate the different parts of the Blue Planet's surface, the 70% that is covered by water (deBlij, 2005). The watery portions of Earth defy protection because of their size. Water is three dimensional, ever moving, and essential to human life. This means that, unlike other surface modes that operate on a two-dimensional plane, ships contend with operating in a medium that moves up and down as well as forward and backward.

Most of the Earth's water is currently navigable, providing a highway for maritime trade. The U.S. Coast Guard has law enforcement authority, including oil spill enforcement power, over all navigable waterways in the United States. The oceans border the east and west coasts of the United States, with bays left behind by Ice Age sea level rise (Long Beach Island Foundation, 2008; KQED, 2012). The southern coast is the Gulf of Mexico, a larger coastal indentation divided from the Atlantic Ocean by a string of islands.

Rivers have their origins in the mountains of the inland areas and flow across the continent, emptying into larger bodies of water—sometimes lakes but often the oceans. Where the river joins the ocean, it may form a delta where the water slows down and fans out, creating a challenge to navigation and often resulting in the creation of channels to support the movement of ships between the river and the ocean. Natural harbors are sheltered portions of oceans or bays where wind and waves are calm, and ships can ride out a storm or anchor safely and transport people and goods to shore using lighters, ferries, or other small vessels.

Canals are water highways built to supplement rivers as access to inland areas. Most American canals were created in the early days of the Industrial Revolution to move raw materials to factories and finished goods to consumers. Barges typically operate on canals and may be towed by tugs or be internally powered. There are few canals in operation in the United States today, as the flexibility of railroad track made digging canals less economically desirable. However, they are attractive for short connections, and road congestion adjacent to container ports has resulted in reconsideration of the benefits of waterway transportation inland.

America's Marine Highway Program, developed through the U.S. DOT Marine Administration, is studying the creation of more robust waterborne movement of goods in areas of high congestion or undesirable levels of greenhouse gas emissions. Secretary of Transportation Ray LaHood announced the proposal for 18 marine corridors, eight projects, and six initiatives on August 11, 2011 (U.S. DOT, 2012).

For example, in California there is congestion around the Port of Oakland, the 20th busiest port in the nation and the 6th busiest container port. Its major export is agricultural products from the Central Valley going to Asian customers. The products currently are delivered by truck on the I-580, one of the most congested highways in the nation. A marine highway connecting the ports of Oakland, Stockton, and West Sacramento could "eliminate 180,000 truck trips from I-580, I-80, and I-205 annually, saving approximately 7 million gallons of fuel and reducing air emissions in the process" (U.S. DOT, n.d.). Other proposed routes include the development of the East Coast Intercoastal Waterway, Gulf Coast, Mississippi River, Ohio River, and Great Lakes (U.S. DOT, 2012).

Humans create harbors through dredging, and erecting sea walls and jetties to provide calm waters. Harbors may become ports, a place where goods are imported and exported. Ports have piers, extensions of the land constructed to allow ships to tie up to them for the transfer of cargo and personnel. Piers can be built on pilings or support structures that extend far enough into the waterway to permit safe berthing during change of tides. Areas with little tidal change will have shorter piers. Ports also have docks for the loading, unloading, and storage of goods. Today, container ports, like Charleston, South Carolina, have large, high-speed cranes that move 40 containers per hour (Hull, 2008), requiring partner land transportation companies to speed their forward movement of goods into the supply chain (Figure 9.5) (Carmel, 2011).

While other methods of surface transportation operate on limited routes dictated by paving or rails, ships have vast expanses of water as their area to transit. Coastlines, islands, reefs and shoals, underwater formations, and floating debris restrict access to some areas of the ocean. Ships' officers have to plot the most efficient and safest route from port of origin to destination. In recent years, global positioning systems (GPSs) have become integral to the operation of commercial vessels. GPS has led to the creation of electronic chart display and information systems to replace paper charts with more accurately plotted courses. The Integrated Bridge System combines the GPS data and radar information to create accurate navigation charts based on route and time data for journeys, to minimize cost (GPS.gov, 2011).

While ships do not run on restricted routes in the open sea, coastal areas pose different problems. Therefore, coastal nations have created a series of navigation aids, including maps and charts. Lighthouses were used for thousands of years to warn sailors away from rocky coasts. Originally just

FIGURE 9.5   High-speed crane.

large fires on towers or headlands and then mirrors and candles or kerosene lamps, modern lighthouses are generally automated with flashing LED beacons. Lightships were used in areas where a lighthouse could not be built, but all American lightships have been decommissioned.

In addition to buoys and channel markers, positioned with the help of GPS (GPS.gov, 2011), and lights, the Coast Guard maintains electronic systems to guide safe passage along coasts and into harbors (Coast Guard, 2012). The Automated Identification System (AIS) and Vehicle Tracking Service (VTS) help to locate ships in distress as well as chart the locations of ships to help avoid underway accidents. Radar, VHS-FM radio, and GPS all provide data for safe navigation in harbors, coastal areas, and other restricted navigation areas (Coast Guard, 2010).

Maritime Cargo Operations

Maritime cargo operations are part of a complex network that includes shippers, customers, warehousing, maritime transportation, intermodal transfers, land use management, GPS, and cyber systems (Carmel, 2011). Ship movements are monitored by long-range identification tracking (LRIT), which was originally intended to provide assistance for ships in distress, but can also be used for commerce management. AIS, which was originally intended to allow vessels to exchange information and avoid collisions when they were within 20–30 miles of each other, now allows the Coast Guard, using new technologies, to communicate with ships farther out at sea (GAO, 2009). These systems allow for scheduling of pilots and berths based on actual passage rather than just estimated arrival times, which can be affected by storms, tides, and winds.

TABLE 9.4 Top U.S.-International Trade Freight Gateways

Rank	City	Exports (Billions)	Imports (Billions)	Total (Billions)	Container Ranking	No. of Full Containers (Thousands)
1	Los Angeles	$28.0	$167.7	$195.6	1	5,521
2	New York/ New Jersey	$38.3	$104.5	$142.8	3	4,103
4	Houston, TX	$48.4	$57.7	$106.1	8	1,371
8	Long Beach, CA	$24.2	$44.4	$68.5	2	4,843
12	Savannah, GA	$18.9	$27.7	$46.6	4	2.086
14	Norfolk, VA	$18.9	$24.0	$43.0	5	1,645
20	Oakland, CA	$12.7	$21.1	$33.8	6	1,548
N/A	Tacoma, WA	N/A	N/A	N/A	7	1,458

Source: U.S. DOT. (2011). *Pocket Guide to Transportation.* Washington, DC: RITA, p. 36.

Once the ships' cargoes are unloaded onto the dock, the goods have to be moved into the supply chain. Currently, cargo moves on and off the docks by truck or rail. In 2007, 146 million tons of domestic freight moved by water and truck, while 55 million tons moved by water and rail (U.S. DOT, 2011, p. 32). As noted in Chapter 5 and Chapter 8, trucks and railroads carry the maritime goods into the U.S. supply chain and consumer outlets.

Maritime Commerce

The GAO (2009) estimates that U.S. ports handle more than $800 billion annually in goods. Water transportation accounts for 44.5% of all U.S. trade by value, with $368 billion in exports and $795 billion in imports in 2009 (U.S. DOT, 2011, p. 33). Water carries 78% of total trade by weight (U.S. DOT, 2011, p. 34). The top-dollar-value international trade freight gateway in the United States is the port of Los Angeles, with $195 billion in 2009, followed by New York/New Jersey with $142.8 billion. Of the top 20 international freight gateways by value of trade goods, seven are water (U.S. DOT, 2011, p. 36). Table 9.4 lists some top U.S.–international trade freight gateways.

Threats to the Maritime Commerce System

Open System

The marine environment has some similarities to the rail system environment. It operates on a vast open system of navigable waterways. The Government Accountability Office (GAO) has evaluated the maritime domain threat as including large merchant vessels carrying WMDs, smaller boats with explosives on suicide missions, and vessels smuggling "people, drugs, weapons and other contraband" (GAO, 2009, p. 12).

While modern tracking systems (discussed earlier and in a later section on security) provide some methods for monitoring the progress of ships at sea, guarding every vessel individually is difficult and cost prohibitive. The openness and size of the system's area is a type of protection from specific vessel targeting, although sea lanes in some areas are limited, such as the Singapore Strait or the Straits of Malacca, making it possible to find random vessels.

Intermodal Goods Transfer

Maritime commerce is intermodal, which also creates a vulnerability to theft, sabotage, vandalism, and damage. As noted in the previous chapters on trucking and railroads, complete security over the supply chain is not possible. Movement of goods from ships to docks to warehouses to forward transport carries inherent opportunities for financial and economic losses. Employees in warehouses and trucking have opportunities for diversion of goods in transit. Experts estimate that cargo theft is about $30 billion per year worldwide, and about $10 billion of that is in the United States. Additional losses accrue through the cost of investigations and insurance company losses (Cisco-Eagle, 2010).

As noted in Chapter 8, the customer in a just-in-time business may lose manufacturing or assembly time when parts do not arrive, adding to the financial losses associated with theft. "A successful attack on a major seaport could potentially result in a dramatic slowdown in the international supply chain with impacts in the billions of dollars" (GAO, 2008).

Smuggling

Sequestration of unwanted contraband materials in legitimate container shipments is another threat to the global supply chain (U.S. DOT BTS, 2011). Human trafficking and drug running can lead to damage to adjacent cargo or injury to the crew, while gun running can lead to destruction of property to facilitate theft. Post-9/11 concerns about shipments of nuclear materials or dirty bombs have led to the development of inspection protocols that will be covered in a later section of this chapter. Maritime security experts question the value of the extra security inspections, but note that a port security war game, postulating the delivery and detonation of a dirty bomb in a U.S. port, projected a 10-day shutdown and $58 billion in economic damage (Weinberg, 2003).

Piracy

Piracy is theft at sea. Long considered a major criminal offense in international and national law, it has been a continuing scourge to small fishing boats and pleasure craft, historically in the South China Sea. With the rise in the American and Asian importation of oil from the Middle East by tanker ship, piracy in the Straits of Malacca and the Singapore Strait required the presence of the U.S. Navy's Seventh Fleet to keep the sea lanes open. The Sixth Fleet was active in the Mediterranean Sea to protect shipping transiting from the Atlantic to the Suez Canal. The Gulf of Aden, Gulf of Oman, Arabian Sea, and Red Sea have also been areas of pirate activity against tankers.

More recently the failed state of Somalia has generated an apparently endless supply of out-of-work young men in speedboats who attack slowly moving boats off their coast, tow them into Somalia, and hold the crew or owners for ransom. Most of the larger ships have been able to outrun the pirates. However, in 2009, an American flag ship was attacked by pirates for the first time in 200 years, and the captain was held for ransom in a lifeboat (Mazzetti & Otterman, 2009). At the time the *MV Alabama* was attacked, there were 16 ships and 200 crew members being held for ransom by pirates (Edwards & Goodrich, 2010, p. 1).

Maritime piracy has been a subject of public concern since the kidnapping of the *MV Alabama*'s captain in 2009 brought this scourge to the attention of the general public. While the risk to human life is an ongoing concern, the remedy may be more in route and speed selection than in guards and technologies. Less than 2% of U.S. commerce is carried on U.S. flag ships, and this is mostly food aid or Department of Defense cargo. The head of Maersk, one of the world's largest marine cargo companies, notes that the cost of piracy to the global supply chain is in "distracting attention and resources away from more immediate and consequential threats" (Carmel, 2011, p. 50).

Hazardous Materials

Hazardous materials are an important part of the United States' import and export chain. Table 9.5 shows some of the major exports that fall into the hazardous materials or dangerous goods category, and Table 9.6 shows some of the imports.

All shipments must be labeled according to the U.S. DOT *Emergency Response Guidebook* standards. Movement of hazardous materials and dangerous goods in international maritime commerce is controlled also by the International Maritime Dangerous Goods Code (IMDGC), which requires placards like the U.S. placards on all hazardous cargo in transit. The 1965

TABLE 9.5 U.S. Hazardous Materials Exports, 2010

Code and Name	Value in Thousands
(11020) Coal and fuels, other	$2,207,801
(11100) Crude oil	$1,327,571
(11110) Fuel oil	$32,625,202
(11120) Petroleum products, other	$33,077,550
(11130) Natural gas liquids	$3,733,241
(11200) Gas, natural	$4,488,194
(11300) Nuclear fuel materials	$1,896,261
(12510) Chemicals, fertilizers	$7,873,606
(12530) Chemicals, inorganic	$7,486,464
(12540) Chemicals, organic	$34,074,610
(12550) Chemicals, other	$25,580,546
(50050) Tanks, artillery, missiles, rockets, guns, and ammunition	$3,608,421

Source: U.S. Census Bureau. (2011a). Foreign trade: U.S. exports. Accessed January 20, 2012, at http://www.census.gov/foreign-trade/statistics/product/enduse/exports/c0000.html.

TABLE 9.6 U.S. Hazardous Materials Imports, 2010

Code and Name	Value in Thousands
(10010) Fuel oil	$33,708,227
(10020) Other petroleum products	$37,934,367
(10030) Liquefied petroleum gasses	$12,157,987
(10100) Coal and related fuels	$2,136,052
(10110) Gas, natural	$16,086,289
(10300) Nuclear fuel materials and fuels	$5,640,679
(12530) Industrial inorganic chemicals	$6,345,266
(12540) Industrial organic chemicals	$20,512,237
(12550) Other chemicals (photo chems, print inks, paint)	$9,347,354
(16040) Sulfur and nonmetallic minerals	$1,100,719

Source: U.S. Census Bureau. 2011b. Foreign trade: U.S. imports. Accessed January 20, 2012, at http://www.census.gov/foreign-trade/statistics/product/enduse/imports/c0000.html.

IMDGC covers not only placarding of hazardous materials, but also packing and stowage of the materials. Some liquid hazardous materials, such as crude oil, are carried in dedicated tankers, while others are in the mixed liquid supply chain, in solid form on cargo ships, and even in containers. The IMDGC covers the segregation of hazardous materials from each other based on hazard class, which is similar to mandated rail car order in train consists.

At times bulk hazardous materials are also stored in warehouses and holding facilities at ports and marine terminals. If the hazardous materials will remain in the building for more than 30 days and the quantity of bulk material exceeds the reportable quantity, the building must be marked with National Fire Protection Association placards to warn first responders of the dangerous goods within the building. The reportable quantities are 55 gallons of a liquid, 250 pounds of a solid, or 500 cubic feet of a gas. This is critical in case of fire, as the products of combustion may be toxic, the material may accelerate a fire or contribute to a medical emergency, or the material may explode when heated. Some chemicals, like lithium and magnesium, react with water to accelerate the fire or create an exothermic reaction that might ignite a fire. Figure 9.6 shows the placard and its codes.

Bulk storage for flammable liquids is not unusual in ports and harbors. The materials are delivered there and stored for use in that urban area. A good example is the Port of Boston, where tankers of liquefied natural gas (LNG) sail past the urban area on their way to the terminal in Everett. The LNG is used to power the electricity plant that produces 40% of New England's electricity and to provide heating and cooking fuel for half of the homes in Massachusetts. The concern is that the tankers are coming from places where terrorism is a threat, like Yemen, and terrorist sabotage of the tanker or a terrorist stowaway sabotaging the terminal is why Boston spends $25,000 in police patrols of the harbor area during each delivery from the

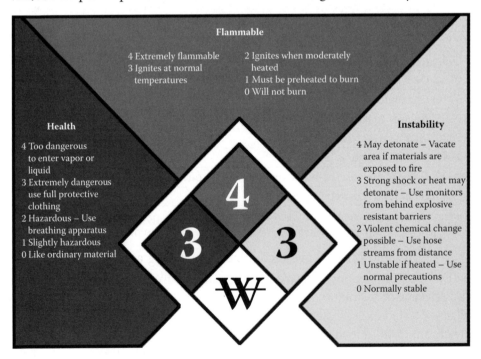

FIGURE 9.6   NFPA placard. (Source: Oklahoma State University, 2003.)

Middle East. A 1977 study by the Federal Energy Commission estimated that 3,000 people would die if the Everett facility had a catastrophic event (Schwartz, 2010).

Boston's concerns were heightened when the security of an LNG facility in Lynn, Massachusetts, was breached by vandals cutting through chain-link fence. The vandals accessed the top of the LNG tank, where the gas forms the vapor that will ignite and explode. In this event, the intruders left behind only graffiti. Although the event had been recorded when it occurred on Wednesday, August 16, it was not reported until the following Monday (WCVB, 2006), demonstrating the importance of regular monitoring of surveillance camera tapes if they are to have any security value.

Crime, Accidents, and Attacks on Maritime Vessels

The openness of the maritime environment has led to crime, accidents, and attacks against shipped goods, including some by terrorists. Scholars are concerned that some of the ordinary accidents and crime might become a paradigm for terrorist attacks in the future. For example, the ease with which people introduce counterfeit merchandise into the supply chain might suggest avenues for introducing an IED or WMD into the United States. Attacks in other nations might be viewed as "dress rehearsals" for attacks inside the United States.

Ordinary Crime in the Maritime Environment

Every year the maritime supply chain is interfered with for criminal purposes. As noted before, cargo "shrinkage" through theft during shipping amounts to over $30 billion, of which $10 billion in losses occurs within the United States. As Ritter, Barrett, and Wilson (2007) note, "Savings from reduced product losses (shrinkage) can compensate in part for the cost of implementing various security measures.…[T]he ability to account for and track goods, at the item level" could result in significant reductions in thefts (p. 71). Groups as diverse as whiskey distillers and Target have battled organized crime's impact on their operations (p. 72).

The GAO and others have recognized smuggling as an ongoing threat. The Interagency Commission on Crime and Security at U.S. Seaports Report in 2000 noted that internal conspiracies led to pilferage of goods in transit (Stodder, 2011). While DHS has focused on the introduction of WMDs, the Business Alliance for Secure Commerce has noted the potential for other contraband to be part of the global supply chain. Goods containing banned chemicals like CFCs, counterfeit merchandise, and other contraband like drugs and weapons enter the supply chain and through it the U.S. economy (Stodder, 2011).

A "nuke in a box" could be placed in a container and delivered to a target seaport city where it would be detonated before the container was unpacked (Stodder, 2011). As noted in Chapter 8, many containers use the United States as a land bridge from Asia to Europe and are never unpacked within the country, traveling from a port in Asia to ports on the U.S. East Coast by water and then rail or truck. The rail and interstate road systems provide routes into and through major cities that could create a location for a significant detonation of a WMD or an IED.

Hijacking and Piracy: *Achille Lauro*

On October 7, 1985, four men from the Palestine Liberation Front (PLF) hijacked a cruise ship in the Mediterranean Sea off Egypt. Two of the operatives had previously taken two cruises on the ship for reconnaissance:

> These scouting trips were meant, among other things, to assess security measures, meal times, normal activities of passengers and crew, relative competence and aggressiveness of specific crew members, likely response of ship's captain and crew, and the layout of the ship. (Anderson & Spagnolo, n.d.)

They had weapons in their cabins and were wearing bomb vests. The weapons included "four Soviet-made Kalashnikov automatic rifles, eight hand grenades, and nine detonators" that they smuggled aboard ship in their luggage (Anderson & Spagnolo, n.d.).

The ship, the *Achille Lauro,* was owned by the Italian government and had 748 passengers. The original plan was for the terrorists to attack port operations during a planned stop in Israel, but a cabin steward discovered the hijackers cleaning their weapons, and that precipitated the ship hijacking (Anderson & Spagnolo, n.d.). They entered the dining room at noon and fired their weapons over the heads of the diners, consolidated the passengers and kitchen staff in the dining room, and ultimately took over the ship and threatened the 97 passengers who had remained onboard rather than take an overland tour. They were demanding the release of 50 Palestinian prisoners from Israeli prisons (Lieberman, 2012).

After determining which passengers were Jewish, they shot Leon Klinghoffer, a disabled retired Jewish businessman, in the head and chest and then made two crew members throw his body and wheelchair overboard (Lieberman, 2012). Klinghoffer had suffered a stroke and had slurred speech and hand tremors, which seemed to upset the hijackers (Anderson & Spagnolo, n.d.).

The ship returned to Port Said in Egypt, and after 48 hours of negotiations, the terrorists agreed to abandon the cruise ship for safe conduct to Tunisia, location of the PLF headquarters. The plane, which was denied permission to land in Tunis, was intercepted by U.S. Navy fighters and forced to land in Sicily on a NATO base. The Italians took custody of the terrorists and let the senior terrorist, Muhammad Abu Abbas, go to Belgrade, Yugoslavia, causing a diplomatic rift between the United States and Italy. Italy tried him in absentia and sentenced him to five life terms (*BBC News*, 2003). Abu Abbas, leader of the Palestinian Liberation Front and a prime planner of the ship hijacking, was later captured in Iraq in 2003 during the U.S. invasion (Ensor, 2003) and died in U.S. custody in 2004 (Anderson & Spagnolo, n.d.).

Piracy involves not just theft of merchandise but also taking of the vessel itself. It involves violence against the crew and passengers and even, as in this case, murder. The terrorists were making a political statement against the state of Israel, and their demand for the safe return of the hostages was a release of fellow terrorists.

Explosives: Super Ferry 14

Abu Sayyaf, a Philippine Muslim separatist group, claimed credit for the bombing and sinking of Super Ferry 14 on February 26, 2004. A terrorist packed 8 pounds of TNT into a television set, placed the set in a box, and carried it aboard the ferry. Posing as a passenger he went to his seat in the crowded cheap area, left the box on his seat, and left the ferry just before it left port for the overnight trip from Manila. There were 1,747 passengers on board. A timing device detonated the bomb at midnight (Elegant, 2004), setting a fire that killed at least 115 people (Lipton, 2005). Because the ferry was half sunk in the bay, an investigation was difficult, but the terrorist confessed to the bombing when he was captured 4 weeks later (Elegant, 2004).

Abu Sayyaf is a radical Muslim group seeking an independent Muslim nation in the southern Philippines. They are allied with Al Qaeda and have developed a relationship with the Moro Islamic Liberation Front, a longstanding separatist group (Elegant, 2004).

Cyber Dependencies of Maritime Transportation

Global positioning systems are critical to the safe passage and accurate navigation of ships on the open sea. The integrated bridge system relies on GPS transmissions to create navigation charts. Navigation beacons, LRIT, and AIS all depend on cyber interfaces. Security systems such as

CSI and C-TPAT use cyber systems to communicate information about the contents of scanned containers. The scheduling of shipping, including acquiring pilots and berthing or anchorages, relies on computers, while operational controls for container ships and tankers rely on SCADA systems similar to those described in Chapter 8. Carmel notes that there is "the potential for an attacker to tap into ship controls via the satellite communication system."

Carmel (2011) has noted that GPS jammers are available for $30 (p. 47) and SCADA system attacks would lead to significant economic losses, as well as potential property losses. "A Stuxnet type of attack on critical controls" is possible. "The Stuxnet worm demonstrated that physical proximity is not necessary to achieve physical damage" (p. 47).

Hazardous Materials as Attack Modes

As noted earlier, security analysts have posited that hazardous materials in transit could be used as weapons against the cities through which they travel. Ships travel into ports of the Atlantic and Pacific Oceans and the Gulf of Mexico, as well as along the St. Lawrence Seaway into the Great Lakes. Most of the nation's largest cities are adjacent to large port complexes, and in some cases the ships travel through city harbor areas along busy waterfronts and through heavily populated areas.

Tankers carrying flammable materials or toxic inhalation hazards could become floating bombs. Explosive materials and munitions could be used against targets in a port. The port itself as a critical infrastructure and economic engine for a region could be damaged. Explosion, fire, and release of toxic chemicals are all possible with the materials routinely carried in international commerce.

Security Strategies for Maritime Transportation

In the preceding sections the threats to maritime commerce and actual attacks and accidents have been examined. Security strategies have been developed as part of the "lessons learned" from these events. Some security strategies provide multiple benefits, such as preventing theft, discouraging vandalism, and removing an easy transportation method from terrorists.

Ordinary Crime in the Maritime Environment

Security against "shrinkage" and tampering with the global supply chain begins with simple precautions similar to those used in other modes of transportation. Goods need to be tracked from the shipper to the customer in a reliable way. Manifests and bills of lading have long been used to identify what is being moved and where it is going. GPS systems enable the tracking of containers, and recently radio frequency identification (RFID) devices have been added to the cargo itself, as well as to the containers, to allow them to be tracked throughout the journey (Ritter et al., 2007). This has helped to lessen the number of containers that get lost in transit and assists the loading and unloading of cargo in the port, where thousands of containers are stacked awaiting shipment.

Good locks are another method used to prevent theft, tampering, and pilferage. Tamper-proof electronic seals are affixed at the beginning of shipment. The seal shows that the inspection of the cargo has been completed and that the contents match the manifest. "Smart containers" go a step further by "collecting data on the time, date and location of an intrusion into a container. Manifest information (provides)…data about container ID, contents and chain of custody" (Ritter et al., 2007, p. 138). A sealed container with intact seals facilitates the passage through customs at the receiving port and movement into the intermodal system.

GPS, RFID, electronic seals, and "smart" containers are all systems designed to make theft of containers and their contents more difficult. They also make it harder for criminals to add contraband to legitimate shipments, as once the customs inspection is complete, the seals are applied and intrusions after that will be identified, causing the container to be subjected to extensive inspection at the receiving port and likely identification of added items. The technologies designed to defeat thieves and smugglers of drugs and guns can also help to protect against introduction of IEDs and WMDs by terrorists.

Terrorism

U.S. ports are critical infrastructure for America's global economy. As shown previously, globalization of the economy has resulted in increased vulnerability to loss of seagoing supply chains, potentially through the destruction of vessels, ports, and adjacent intermodal transfer points.

In 2010 DHS provided $288 million in grants through the Port Security Grant Program. The focus was on preventing the importation of "improvised explosive devices and other non-conventional weapons" (DHS, OPS, 2010). Another $150 million in funding was provided under the recovery act. Ports could use the funding for training, exercises, and implementation of the transit worker identification card (TWIC) program.

TWIC

Transit worker identification cards (TWICs) provide another layer of security to ports and shipments. This is a joint program of the U.S. Coast Guard and the Transit Security Administration (TSA). The TWIC program is focused on ensuring that all maritime workers with unaccompanied access to the docks, cargo, and transportation vehicles have received background checks (U.S. DOT BTS, 2011). The initial focus was on ensuring that transportation workers were not on the terrorist watch list, but it has been expanded to a full commercial background check (Edwards & Goodrich, 2010).

Maritime workers include the port employees as well as the transportation mode workers, such as truck drivers and train crews. TSA enrolls the workers through a Lockheed Martin-created system that assigns a biometric identification card (Edwards & Goodrich, 2010). The Coast Guard enforces the TWIC requirement in the ports. By December 2010, 1.7 million workers had been enrolled, with 1.6 million identification cards activated (DHS, TSA, 2010).

MDA

Maritime domain awareness (MDA) is a Coast Guard approach to securing maritime transportation activities through ongoing risk assessment and threat identification. This global view of the maritime environment includes (1) collection of information, (2) fusion of information from different sources, (3) analysis through the evaluation and interpretation of information, and (4) dissemination of information to decision makers (GAO, 2009). The key to the system is the collection of vessel movement information to look for anomalies that might indicate criminal or terrorist activity.

MTSA

The Maritime Transportation Security Act (MTSA) and its amendments in 2004 and 2006 required the application of technology to the information-collection function. The GPS-based LRIT and AIS systems (discussed earlier under cargo operations) are used as part of the vessel monitoring activity. The AIS, required for all vessels over 65 feet long and tankers regardless of length, broadcasts the vessel's name, location, course, and speed while it is in U.S. waters (GAO, 2009). This information is received with adequate time available for the Coast Guard to react to unexpected or inappropriate vessels in American waters and to interdict suspicious craft before they enter ports.

The Coast Guard has installed AIS receivers in a land-based network of 55 major ports and nine coastal areas (GAO, 2009). Radar and cameras are also available in some areas to monitor vessel passage and port and coastal activity. Some of the radar and camera feeds come from other maritime stakeholders, such as the U.S. Navy, port authority law enforcement agencies, and private industry. Although the system provides good surveillance for larger ships up to 24 miles from shore, smaller boats that are not covered by the AIS requirements may still operate without surveillance, creating a vulnerability to smuggling and illegal immigration.

The Coast Guard has created relationships with pilots' associations and tugboat operators to assist with intelligence surveillance. The Delaware River Pilots Association was the only source of warning that two small armed boats were traveling at high speed from the Chesapeake and Delaware Canal into the Delaware River. While the threat was in fact a Navy Seals exercise (GAO, 2009), this proved the value of bringing other watermen into the counterterrorism efforts in the maritime domain. America's Waterways Watch, discussed in Chapter 3, extends beyond the professional stakeholders to pleasure boat owners and nonregistered watercraft users, much as "see something, say something" brings commuters into mass transit system surveillance. DHS "considers the small vessel community as the single largest asset in addressing the threat from small boat attacks" (GAO, 2009, p. 11).

HSPD-13

Homeland Security Presidential Directive-13 of 2004 required the development of a national strategy for maritime security. HSPD-13 describes the maritime domain as "all areas and things of, on, under, relating to, adjacent to, or bordering on a sea, ocean, or other navigable waterway, including all maritime-related activities, infrastructure, people, cargo, and vessels and other conveyances" (GAO, 2008, p. 1). After 9/11, various organizations within the federal government recognized the vulnerabilities to terrorism inherent in the maritime trade environment and began developing plans and strategies to lessen the threat. As a result of their work, HDPS-13 was issued to address

> the coordination of U.S. government maritime security programs and initiatives to achieve a comprehensive and cohesive national effort involving appropriate federal, state, local, and private sector entities. HSPD-13 established the Maritime Security Policy Coordination Committee as the primary forum to coordinate U.S. policy. (GAO, 2008, p. 6)

The secretaries of Defense and Homeland Security were mandated to create the *National Strategy for Maritime Security*. The stated goal of the national strategy was the creation of a "secure and efficient global supply chain system that is resilient against catastrophic disruptions." The concern was originally prevention of movement into the United States through the global supply chain of nuclear or radiological materials that could be weaponized. However, Stodder (2011) has suggested that vehicles not in the global supply chain, like a private Lear jet or sailboat, could equally well be used to carry a weapon, or it could be made within the United States using readily available bought or stolen materials. The focus of maritime security is broader than just WMDs and IEDs.

The *National Strategy* was issued in 2005, and eight additional plans were proposed that would guide implementation of the strategy. The suite of plans is intended to protect the global supply chain for economic purposes as well as to prevent the introduction of a bomb. Destruction of the global just-in-time strategy for production could become a national and even international economic bomb. Stodder (2011) points out that after 9/11, cargo was held up in Canada while security at the border was reevaluated and that car parts "stalled at the Canadian border strangled Michigan car plants." The example of the shutdown of the Fremont, California, car plant by the West Coast port strike (discussed in Chapter 8) demonstrates how loss of a port would impact the domestic and global economy.

Piracy

Piracy involves an attack on a merchant ship, taking control of the vessel through violence against the crew, and either holding the crew and cargo for ransom or stealing the cargo. Piracy poses a threat to the global supply chain for its disruptive power. The United States began antipiracy maritime security operations in the Persian Gulf region in 2001, extending into the Indian Ocean trade routes.

More than 25 nations have now joined the Combined Maritime Forces Mission to combat piracy at sea, protecting 2.5 million square miles of international waters. The visible presence of warships is intended as a deterrent to pirates, but the ocean is large and the military assets are relatively limited, so piracy continues. Navy Seals rescued the *Alabama*'s captain in 2009, and in 2010 U.S. marines rescued the crew of a German-owned cargo ship, capturing nine pirates. The military forces captured hundreds of pirates in the Gulf of Aden from 2009 to 2010 (U.S. DOT BTS, 2011, p. 35).

CSI

Starting in 2002 the Customs and Border Patrol developed a system for inspecting cargo containers outside the United States to protect against the introduction of WMDs and improvised explosive devices (IEDs) into the U.S. supply chain. An automated targeting system determines which containers are to be inspected. Customs and Border Patrol agents are stationed overseas and work with law enforcement of the host country to identify and inspect high-risk cargoes before they are placed aboard ships bound for the United States (GAO, 2008).

Cargo in the international corridor provides "unsurpassed access to examining the cargo, because there is no presumption of confidentiality or privacy. Search warrants, probable cause, or specific suspicion are not required for a thorough search" (Edwards & Goodrich, 2010, p. 11). Customs officials of the sending and receiving jurisdictions can inspect cargo randomly or based on signals from the smart containers, although the volume of containers prevents 100% inspection.

By 2010 there were 58 foreign ports collaborating on the Container Security Initiative (CSI), covering 86% of all containerized cargo (U.S. DOT BTS, 2011, p. 37). U.S. and host nation agents use "large scale x-ray and gamma ray machines and radiation detection devices. In addition, smart containers that easily reveal tampering are preferred for U.S. destinations" (Edwards & Goodrich, 2010, p. 11).

C-TPAT

The Customs-Trade Partnership Against Terrorism (C-TPAT) is a partnership between Customs and Border Patrol and private companies, including "importers, customs brokers, terminal operators, transportation companies and foreign manufacturers" (Edwards & Goodrich, 2010, p. 12). The security of the entire production chain is examined, including parts suppliers to the primary contractor. The process ensures that products are made from the components as intended and that the entire supply chain is secure. The precautions enhance security against ordinary crime, as well, and more than half of the C-TPAT members did not have a secure supply chain before joining the partnership. This level of supply chain inspection creates a secure partner whose containers are less likely to be held up in transit for secondary searches. By March 2008, C-TPAT had "8,200 members, or eighty percent of the value of imported goods" (U.S. DOT BTS, 2011, p. 37).

Radiological Shipments Deterrence

The Megaports Initiative was the first of several programs designed to deter terrorists from shipping radiological and nuclear material to the United States. Starting in 2003, the Department of Energy began installing radiation detectors in foreign ports for the use of foreign customs services in inspecting United States-bound cargo. The goal was to ensure that radiological materials, including nuclear bombs, were not shipped covertly to the United States in containers. By October 2007, there were 27 foreign ports with the equipment.

Secure Freight Initiative (SFI), created in 2006, was a program that proposed to scan 100% of United States-bound containers for nuclear and radiological materials at selected ports. The cost of the inspections was high relative to the benefit expected, and they slowed the movement of containers through the shipping process. Although seven ports started the program, by April 2010, there were only five operating ports and two ports that started had dropped out, citing "concerns about the safety of the scanning technology, their inability to allocate port personnel to the SFI program, and negative impacts of scanning on port efficiency" (U.S. DOT BTS, 2011, p. 36).

Domestic Port Radiation was a program to scan all containers arriving in the United States before they left the port of arrival. Starting in 2007, the Department of Homeland Security installed radiation portal monitors for trucks and trains to pass through as they left the ports. This system proved less burdensome, and by April 2009, Customs and Border Patrol had installed 409 monitors at ports accounting for 98% of all arriving containers.

10+2

Importer Security Filing and Additional Carrier Requirements (10+2) is a program begun in 2009 to ensure that Customs and Border Patrol received information on shipments bound for the United States 24 hours before arrival in an American port. Ten "shipping data elements" are provided by the importer, and two more come from the vessel carrying the goods. The data include information on the source and destination of goods and all the elements of the supply chain, including where the container was loaded. The vessel has to show the stowage plan and status messages. The information allows Customs to determine which containers should receive additional searches upon arrival at U.S. ports (DHS BTS, 2011, p. 36).

VIPR Teams in Maritime Security

Implementing the Recommendation of the 9/11 Commission Act of 2007 (Public Law 110-53) authorized the creation of visible intermodal prevention and response (VIPR) teams. In Chapter 3, the creation and operation of VIPR teams was described, and in Chapter 7 their role in mass transit was described. They also have a counterterrorism role in maritime activities. Passenger vessels can benefit from VIPR team participation in surveillance and interdiction.

Just as VIPR teams' presence in land-based mass transit serves as a deterrent to ordinary crime and terrorist activity, their participation in ferry systems' security activities heightens passenger safety. VIPR teams with their highly visible presence will monitor the ferry, dock, passengers, and baggage (TSA, n.d.). Critical transportation links, like the Lewes Ferry linking Delaware and New Jersey and the ferries linking the Boston area and Martha's Vineyard, have been evaluated as potential terrorist targets, and VIPR has helped to enhance the security in such systems.

Cruise ships are also potential terrorist targets. VIPR teams work with the Coast Guard to check passenger terminals for contraband and IEDs and to watch passengers leaving the ship and going through Customs areas. They can also provide extra security in perimeter areas. Their processes can also be low visibility if the cruise lines wish to avoid alarming holiday makers.

Marine cargo operations are another area where VIPR teams have been active. The cargo port, terminal, and multimodal transfer points may offer opportunities for terrorist activity and ordinary crime. This is an area of overlapping jurisdictions where local law enforcement, Customs and Border Patrol, and the Coast Guard all have elements of jurisdiction. VIPR can augment these agencies' surveillance, focus on specific areas of vulnerability, and serve as a "visible presence to discourage threats" (TSA, n.d.).

Case Studies

Cosco Busan Oil Spill

The navigable waterways of the United States are under the control of the Coast Guard. They issue the licenses for merchant marine crew members on U.S. flagships and for pilots certified for U.S. waters. The role of the pilot in entering and exiting U.S. harbors is crucial because the many potential impediments to safe passage require that the person navigating large ships out of the harbors be familiar with their locations. Some impediments are permanent, like bridge structures, piers, and rocks. Other may be seasonal, cyclical, or temporary, like sandbars or floating docks. It is the pilot's responsibility to be aware of all such impediments and to ensure that he charts them regularly. He also has to be familiar with the tides and currents.

The main navigation channel lies between the delta and echo towers of the bridge and is 2,200 feet wide. The centerline of the channel is marked by radar and the bridge is marked with navigation lights. The Coast Guard Vehicle Tracking Service (VTS) uses AIS, radar, VHS-FM radio, and closed circuit television (CCTV) to plot the location of vessels, especially in "regulated navigation areas (RNAs) in areas where maneuvering room is limited" (Coast Guard, 2010). Qualified harbor pilots are also required (NTSB, 2009a).

The *M/V Cosco Busan*, a container ship registered in Hong Kong traveling from the Port of Oakland to Korea, hit the protective bumper of the delta tower of the San Francisco Bay Bridge in the fog on November 7, 2007, at about 8:30 a.m., creating a gash in its 900 feet long hull. The resulting damage was 212 feet long, 10 feet high, and 8 feet deep, puncturing two fuel tanks and a ballast tank on the port side of the ship. The hole caused a spill of 53,500 gallons of bunker fuel into the bay. The damage to the bridge was $1.5 million and the damage to the ship was $2.1 million (NTSB, 2009b).

The ship's master was Chinese and was on his first trip out of San Francisco Bay. The ship's chief officer was also Chinese, and although he had been in San Francisco Bay in 1999, he had never been in the port because his ship stayed at anchorage. The rest of the ship's officers had never been to San Francisco before and some had never before sailed on a ship that large. The pilot was a San Francisco Bay mariner with 26 years' experience (NTSB, 2009a).

The environmental damage to the bay's sensitive ecosystem included the pollution of 26 miles of shoreline and the deaths of 2,500 birds, and closed the bay to fishing for a short time. It also caused the crab season, which is already short, to be postponed until the cleanup was complete. The cost of the environmental cleanup was $70 million (*ABC News,* 2009).

The ship's owner initially used a commercial cleanup firm, and the extent of the damage is blamed on its failure to place absorbent booms properly around the spill. The Coast Guard ultimately took command of the cleanup operation, but Bay Area environmental activists have criticized the speed and efficiency with which the work was done (Gordon & Parker, 2007). The pilot and the ship's owner faced criminal charges for the damage to the eco-system of the bay.

Numerous civil suits were also filed by individuals who were directly damaged by the accident and its environmental impacts (*ABC News,* 2009). The National Transportation Safety Board (NTSB) conducted an extensive investigation that determined that the cause of the crash was human error and pilot impairment. They highlighted "the pilot's degraded cognitive per-formance from his use of impairing prescription medications" and commu-nications failure between the pilot and the ship's master before beginning the voyage out of the port (NTSB, 2009b).

The Coast Guard was also held responsible for failing to provide proper medical oversight of the pilot after he had reported his alcohol addiction in 1999 following a second DUI arrest. NTSB evaluators concluded that because alcohol addiction is a chronic problem, the pilot should have had frequent reevaluations. Although he had undergone treatment for his alco-hol addiction and received a waiver from the Coast Guard Medical Review Board, he was then treated for sleep apnea, including medication use that he did not report, which was deemed to have contributed to his poor perfor-mance during the accident.

The same conclusion had been reached by the NTSB after the ferry acci-dent in New York in 2003 when the assistant captain's medical impairment was the primary cause of the collision with the pier during docking. The NTSB's investigators concluded that the Coast Guard should

> revise regulation 46 CFR 10.709 to require that the results of all physical examinations be reported to the Coast Guard, and provide guidance to mariners, employers, and mariner medical examiners on the specific actions required to comply with these regulations. (NTSB, 2009a, p. 121)

Pirates Attack *Seabourn Spirit*

For 2 years, the waters off the coast of Somalia bristled with pirates, but they did not attack cruise ships. In all of 2004, there were only two pirate attacks in that area, leading mariners to believe that sailing closer to the coast was safe. However, the International Maritime Bureau had issued warnings to stay 150 miles off the coast because pirate attacks had risen to 25 events from March to November of 2005. Somalia, a failed state with Africa's longest coast line, has urged neighboring nations to fight the pirates, while U.S. and NATO forces cannot enter Somalia's territorial waters (Associated Press, 2005).

On November 5, 2005, an early morning attack was repelled by the rapid reaction of two crew members. Using a high-pressure hose and a long-range acoustical device (LRAD) that makes more noise than the Concorde on takeoff, they battled the pirates to prevent their boarding the passenger ship, while the captain first tried to ram the smaller boats and then accelerated to depart the area. One of the crew members, a former Gurkha who activated the LRAD, was injured by the pirates. The crew member handling the high-pressure hose was a former member of the Royal Navy with experience as a police officer (*BBC News*, 2007.)

Threat assessments must be ongoing. Emerging threats, changes in technology, and changes in economies all have significant effects on threats and must be considered on an ongoing basis, lest a target be the victim of a new trend. While this attempted attack was rebuffed by the quickly acting crew, adhering to the suggested 150-mile limit recently suggested by a professional maritime organization might have avoided the confrontation.

Summary

Maritime commerce links America to the world. Cargo ships, container ships, and tankers move the goods of the world into national supply chains through connections to intermodal systems of trucks and trains. Vulnerabilities inherent in ordinary crime, like "shrinkage," as well as those created by the reliance on cyber systems, have joined the dangers of sea travel as challenges to maritime security. Closer observance of goods transfer points through technologies and more thorough screening of the employees in the maritime supply chain have led to improvements in safety and security in the maritime environment.

The last link in the goods chain is air cargo. While more expensive than truck or rail by weight, air cargo carries the high-value and perishable goods that fuel high-tech industries and feed people. In the next chapter, the challenge of working in a system with complex and overlapping security systems will be considered.

Discussion Questions

1. Describe the maritime transportation environment. What are the elements of the infrastructure and how are they regulated?

2. What are the major features of maritime commerce—human, cargo, and vehicles—and who regulates them?

3. Why do maritime security experts discount the importance of piracy to American commerce? What security methods have been applied to prevent or disrupt piracy?

4. Describe the *Cosco Busan* accident in San Francisco harbor. What are the key lessons learned for better management of maritime security?

5. You are the security director for a freight maritime company that is considering adding passenger service to enhance revenues. What safety and security considerations would influence your decision to take passengers?

References

ABC News. (2009, February 16). *Cosco Busan* spill report expected. Accessed April 20, 2011, at http://abclocal.go.com/kgo/story?section=news/local/san_francisco&id=6661157

ABC News. (2011, December 20). Coast Guard changes ferry weight guidelines. Accessed January 2, 2012, at http://abclocal.go.com/kgo/story?section=news/national_world&id=8473827

Anderson, S. K., & Spagnolo, P. N. (n.d.). Case study: The *Achille Lauro* hijacking. Idaho State University. Accessed February 5, 2012, at http://www.isu.edu/~andesean/AchilleLauroCaseStudy.htm

Associated Press. (2005, November 6). Pirates leave grenade on cruise ship. MSNBC. Accessed February 5, 2012, at http://www.msnbc.msn.com/id/9932838/ns/world_news-africa/t/pirates-leave-grenade-cruise-ship/

Associated Press. (2008, August 25). Settlement reached in deadly 2003 Staten Island Ferry crash. Fox News. Accessed April 20, 2011 at http://www.foxnews.com/story/0,2933,409904,00.html

BBC News. (2003, April 16). Italy seeks Abbas extradition. Accessed on February 5, 2012, at http://news.bbc.co.uk/2/hi/middle_east/2952473.stm

BBC News. (2007, May 17). I beat pirates with a hose and sonic cannon. Accessed February 5, 2012, at http://news.bbc.co.uk/2/hi/uk_news/6664677.stm

Blaszak, M. (2006, May 1). Intermodal equipment: Flat cars, well cars; containers and trailers. *Trains: The Magazine of Railroading.* http://trn.trains.com/en/Railroad%20Reference/ABCs%20of%20Railroading/2006/05/Intermodal%20equipment.aspx

BLS (Bureau of Labor Statistics). (2009). *Occupational outlook handbook,* 2010–11 ed. Accessed April 20, 2011, at http://www.bls.gov/oco/ocos247.htm

Carmel, S. (2011, July–August). Maritime security, piracy, and the global supply chain. *TR News.* No. 275. http://trid.trb.org/view.aspx?id=1117282

Cisco-Eagle. (2010). Avoiding cargo threat at the point of loading and unloading. Accessed June 10, 2011, at http://www.cisco-eagle.com/catalog/c-3091-security-at-the-shipping-docks.aspx

Coast Guard. (2010). USCG vessel traffic service San Francisco user's manual. Accessed April 20, 2011, at http://www.uscg.mil/d11/vtssf/vtssfum.asp

Coast Guard. (2012). Maritime stewardship. Accessed January 26, 2012, at http://www.uscg.mil/top/missions/MaritimeStewardship.asp

Copenhagen Post. (2011). Maersk reaps profit and praise by taking it slow. Accessed January 11, 2012, at http://www.denmark.dk/en/servicemenu/News/BusinessNews/MaerskReapsProfitsAndPraiseByTakingItSlow.htm

deBlij, H. (2005). *Why geography matters.* New York, NY: Oxford University Press.

Department of Defense. (2006). *Merchant vessel inspection guide: Vessel and cargo types*, 55–71.

DHS, OPS (Office of the Press Secretary). (2010, May 13). DHS Secretary Napolitano announces nearly $790 million in critical infrastructure & preparedness grants. Accessed June 10, 2011, at www.dhs.gov

DHS, TSA. (2010). TWIC dashboard. Accessed April 1, 2011, at www.tsa.gov/assets/pdf/twic_dashboard.pdf

Edwards, F. L., & Goodrich, D. C. (2010). Supply chain security and the need for continuous assessment. In A. Thomas (Ed.), *Supply chain security.* Santa Barbara, CA: Praeger.

Ensor, D. (2003, April 16). US captures mastermind of *Achille Lauro* hijacking. CNN World. Accessed February 5, 2012, at http://articles.cnn.com/2003-04-15/world/sprj.irq.abbas.arrested_1_hijacking-abu-abbas-hostage-taking-and-conspiracy?_s=PM:WORLD

GAO. (2008). *Maritime security: National strategy and supporting plans were generally well-developed and are being implemented* (GAO 08-672). Washington, DC: GAO.

GAO. (2009). *Maritime security: Vessel tracking systems provide key information, but the need for duplicate data should be reviewed* (GAO-09-337). Report to the Committee on Homeland Security, U.S. House of Representatives.

Gordon, D., & Parker, W. (2007, November 18). *Cosco Busan* spill a wakeup call. *San Francisco Chronicle*, p. E-5.

GPS.gov. (2011). Marine. Accessed January 10, 2012, at http://www.gps.gov/applications/marine/

Hull, P. (2008, March 10). Port relies on high tech cranes to speed flow of cargo. *Post and Courier.* Accessed July 20, 2011, at http://www.postandcourier.com/news/2008/mar/10/cranes33078/

KQED. (2012). The formation of San Francisco Bay. *Saving the Bay.* San Francisco, CA: KQED. Accessed April 10, 2011, at http://education.savingthebay.org/wp-content/guides/The-Formation-of-San-Francisco-Bay.pdf

Lieberman, S. (2012, February 4). Giovanni Massa recalls 1985 hijacking of the *Achille Lauro. Palm Beach Daily News.* Accessed February 5, 2012, at http://www.palmbeachdailynews.com/news/giovanni-massa-recalls-1985giovanni-massa-recalls-1985-hijacking-of-the-achille-2148936.html?cxtype=rss_news

Long Beach Island Foundation. (2008). *The island blue pages.* Loveladies, NJ: The Long Beach Island Foundation.

Mazzetti, M., & Otterman, S. (2009, April 9). U.S. captain is hostage of pirates; U.S. Navy ship arrives. Accessed April 9, 2009, at www.nytimes.com/2009/04/09/world/africa/09pirates.html

MBTA. (2011). Boat map and schedules. Accessed April 10, 2011, at http://www.mbta.com/schedules_and_maps/boats/

NTSB. (2009a, February 18). *Allison of Hong Kong—Registered container ship* M/V Cosco Busan *with the Delta Tower of the San Francisco–Oakland Bay Bridge, San Francisco, CA, November 7, 2007* (Accident Report NTSB/MAR-09/01, PB2009-916401).

NTSB. (2009b). Marine accident report executive summary. Accessed April 20, 2011, at http://www.ntsb.gov/investigations/summary/MAR0901.htm

Oklahoma State University. (2003). NFpA Placard. Accessed March 7, 2003, at http://www.pp.okstate.edu/ehs/TRAINING/Nfpadiam.htm

RITA. (2011). *National transportation statistics.* Washington, DC: BTS.

Ritter, L., Barrett, J. M., & Wilson, R. (2007). *Securing global transportation networks.* New York, NY: McGraw–Hill.

Rocchio, P. (2010, August 19). Prison barge sets sail to Rikers. *New York Post.* Accessed April 20, 2011, at http://www.nypost.com/p/news/local/bronx/prison_barge_sets_sail_to_rikers_p6AjQv1MU1Da5PaD68n7vJ

Schwartz, J. (2010, July). Safe harbor? *Boston Magazine.*

Smith, R. (2005, June 18). Cruise ship sails under American flag. NPR. Accessed April 20, 2011, at http://www.npr.org/templates/story/story.php?storyId=4709434

Stodder, S. (2011). *Supply chain security since 9/11.* A paper presented at the TRB Security Roundtable, Irvine, California, August 24.

TSA. (n.d.). Maritime: Put visible intermodal prevention and response (VIPR) to work for you. Washington, DC: TSA.

UN. (1982). United Nations Convention on the Law of the Sea. Accessed April 10, 2011, at http://www.un.org/Depts/los/convention_agreements/texts/unclos/unclos_e.pdf

U.S. Census Bureau. (2011a). Foreign trade: U.S. exports. Accessed January 20, 2012, at http://www.census.gov/foreign-trade/statistics/product/enduse/exports/c0000.html

U.S. Census Bureau. (2011b). Foreign trade: U.S. imports. Accessed January 20, 2012, at http://www.census.gov/foreign-trade/statistics/product/enduse/imports/c0000.html

U.S. DOT. (2011). *Pocket guide to transportation.* Washington, DC: RITA.

U.S. DOT. (2012). America's Marine Highway Program. Accessed January 7, 2012, at http://www.marad.dot.gov/ships_shipping_landing_page/mhi_home/mhi_home.htm

U.S. DOT. (n.d.). America's marine highway corridors. Accessed April 10, 2011, at http://www.marad.dot.gov/ships_shipping_landing_page/mhi_home/mhi_home.htm

U.S. DOT BTS. (2011). *America's container ports: Linking markets at home and abroad.* Washington, DC: BTS, RITA.

U.S. DOT MARAD. (2010). North American cruise statistical snapshot, 2010. Accessed October 28, 2011, at http://www.marad.dot.gov/documents/North_American_Cruise_Statistics_Quarterly_Snapshot.pdf

Washington State DOT. (2011). Washington state ferries route map. Accessed April 10, 2011, at http://www.wsdot.wa.gov/ferries/info_desk/route-maps/

WCVB. (2006, August 23). LNG storage facility security breached. Accessed April 20, 2011, at http://www.thebostonchannel.com/r/9722000/detail.html

WETA. (2009). *Ferry fast forward.* San Francisco, CA: WETA.

Weinberg, J. (2003). Port security war game: Implications for US supply chains. Accessed June 10, 2011 at http://www.booz.com/media/uploads/Port_Security_War_Game.pdf

White, R. D. (2010, July 31). Ocean shipping lines cut speed to save fuel costs. *LA Times.* Accessed July 31, 2010, at latimes.com/business/la-fi-slow-sailing-20100731,0,3362974.story

Yachtpals. (2008). The world's fastest sailboats: Sailing for speed freaks. Accessed April 20, 2011, at http://yachtpals.com/fastest-sailboats-2079

Yanchunas, D. (2008, August). Coast Guard says new medical rules will simplify medical evaluations but not boost rejections. *Professional Mariner Journal.* Accessed April 20, 2011, at http://www.professionalmariner.com/ME2/dirmod.asp?nm=Archives&type=Publishing&mod=Publications%3A%3AArticle&mid=8F3A7027421841978F18BE895F87F791&tier=4&id=17E72217763E4092960FB78B233EB592

Chapter 10

Air Cargo Operations Security

Keywords: FAA, TSA, air freight, air cargo, unaccompanied baggage, mail, catering supplies, baggage screening, x-ray screening, explosive detection screening, intermodal, surveillance, sabotage, smuggling, safety, security, explosives, IEDs

Learning Objectives

After reading this chapter you should be able to

- Identify potential security vulnerabilities in air cargo transportation
- Understand how air cargo operations generate vulnerabilities
- Understand the role of technology in air cargo operations security
- Understand the strategies used by terrorists to disrupt air cargo transportation systems

Components of the Air Cargo Transportation System

The American air cargo system integrates passenger and cargo carrying systems at the same airport—often in the same terminal. Companies that carry only freight generally have their own terminals on an air cargo part of the ramp, while dual use companies like Delta and Lufthansa integrate passengers, their luggage, mail, and cargo in the same plane. Dual use leads to cross contamination, mixing thoroughly screened passenger baggage with items that may have had screening or not.

Air cargo is defined as "normal freight, consolidations, transshipments, unaccompanied courier items, and unaccompanied baggage" (Aleman, 2010, p. 191). U.S. passenger aircraft "carry about 7.6 billion pounds of cargo per year…including electronics, auto parts, clothes, fresh produce and medical supplies" (Aleman, 2010, p. 197). The volume and variety of goods create a daunting challenge to air cargo security.

The topic of air transportation industry security is beyond the scope of this book. For example, airport management of sterile terminal areas, airport employee vetting and training, and passenger screening are not addressed. The focus of this chapter is on the security systems developed for air cargo and mail, including cargo carried in passenger planes. In fact, two cargo-based disasters, Pan Am 103 and ValuJet, occurred on passenger planes. The September 2010 printer cartridge attack was against two cargo carriers.

History of Air Cargo

The American romance with flying started with Charles Lindbergh's heroic solo flight across the Atlantic to Paris. People had been flying in balloons and small aircraft, but without any practical commercial application. From Lindbergh's successful flight to Europe in 1927 a new confidence in air travel developed. The U.S. Postal Service saw an opportunity to create a faster mail delivery service using airplanes, thus beginning the air cargo industry. While World War II disrupted civil aviation's development to support the war effort, the end of hostilities restored civilian aviation services, and the following economic boom supported the further development of air cargo systems.

Aviation technology had been greatly improved through war-related research and development, and by the 1960s air travel for people and goods was becoming economically competitive with rail transport domestically. Globalization of trade led to air cargo increases through the end of the twentieth century. A failed MBA project known as FedEx changed the way in which packages were delivered inside the United States, using the model of centralized sorting and redelivery for packages and letters to become the world's largest air cargo carrier. United Parcel Service, a truck-based package delivery service, added air delivery service for packages, making it the world's largest package delivery service (Webb, 2012). Both companies successfully competed with the U.S. Postal Service, siphoning off the most lucrative mail elements of the overnight delivery and package delivery business.

FIGURE 10.1   Terminal B, Mineta San Jose International Airport.

After World War II, global businesses adopted just-in-time supply chains to raise return on investment by lessening the investment in stored parts and the cost of warehouse space—but at the expense of a demand for more rapid component delivery. For example, by the 1990s, chips produced in California's Silicon Valley were flying to Tokyo 5 days a week for incorporation into the electronics production of Sanyo and Toshiba and the automobiles of Toyota and Nissan. Ralph Tonseth, San Jose International Airport executive director, was asked how American Airlines could afford to fly half-empty passenger planes to Japan from San Jose five times a week. He replied that American Airlines made more money per flight when there were fewer passengers and luggage, because it then had the weight capacity to fly more air cargo like the chips, which paid by the pound. In 2011, Delta, the second largest U.S. air carrier by passenger traffic, made 50% of its $1.2 billion profit from its cargo business (Figure 10.1) (Webb, 2012).

Categories of Air Cargo Carriers

Commercial aviation uses both passenger and cargo planes to carry air cargo. International shipping companies like FedEx and UPS have their own fleet of cargo planes, while passenger companies operate mixed passenger/cargo flights and cargo-only flights.

FIGURE 10.2 Air cargo being loaded.

Passenger Aircraft and Cargo Interface

About 50,000 tons of goods are shipped by air each day inside the United States. Air cargo is carried on passenger planes as space permits—about 12,500 tons on an average day. Industry experts have noted that as more wide-body planes are put in service, such as the Airbus A-380 and the Boeing 777, and passengers are discouraged from checking much luggage by charges of up to $50 per bag, more cargo capacity is created (Webb, 2012). Cargo on passenger planes includes mail, live animals, bodies in coffins, business goods like chips and components, and any commercial goods in the just-in-time chain (Figure 10.2).

Passenger planes are loaded with passenger luggage, catering supplies, cabin support supplies like toilet paper and paper towels, and clean blanket and toiletry packs for first-class passengers. Containers of mail include letters, publications, and packages. International flights also have duty-free merchandise for sale, including liquor, perfume, and jewelry. While all passenger luggage must be screened before loading, other goods may come from "known shippers" like the contracted catering company and have only cursory examination before loading.

The Act of 2007 (Public Law 110-53), the so-called "100% rule," required TSA to provide 50% screening for air cargo carried on passenger planes by February 3, 2009, and 100% screening by August 3, 2010 (Branch & Hinton, 2009). TSA reported that it had met the mandates of the 50% regulation by early 2010:

One hundred percent of the cargo on 96 percent of the flights originating in the United States is now screened. Eighty-five percent of the passengers flying each day from U.S. airports are on planes where all of the cargo has been fully screened. (TSA, 2010)

Air Cargo Transportation Environment: Components and Operations

Most cargo services have facilities at commercial airports that also have passenger air service. The freight terminal is usually separate from the passenger terminal, and larger companies like FedEx and UPS may have their own terminals. The airport includes an apron immediately adjacent to the terminal building and a ramp next to the building that connects the aircraft stands, or parking spots, to the taxiway. An aircraft is usually pulled down the ramp to the taxiway by a tug, a small wheeled ground vehicle. The plane travels on its own power to the runway, where it gains speed and takes off.

In the air cargo area, the terminal is typically a large warehouse facility where cargo is received from the intermodal system, either from trucks or a railroad siding. This is called the landside and includes receiving facilities that are outside the secure area. The cargo is screened, based on whether it is going on a passenger aircraft or cargo aircraft, and prepared for loading. The goods move through Customs if they are for export. They are then moved to the air side under secure conditions and kept secured until loaded onto the aircraft. A shipment delivered by air arrives on the air side and remains in bond until the receiver arrives to take it through Customs and transport it forward.

Freight may be shipped in shrink-wrapped piles, on pallets, in tubs, or as individual packages in the case of large crates. If the cargo is going into a passenger plane, it must be placed in a "unit load device" (ULD)—a metal container that holds a large quantity of smaller packages or mail. The ULDs are also used in some freight aircraft; they come in dozens of configurations, and each is numbered to identify its type and owner. There are special ULDs for horses or cattle. Some ULDs are refrigerated, while others are pallets that may be flat or with wings, and some are made of Kevlar to be bomb proof. Configurations include shapes for main deck use, lower deck use, and for management by forklift (World Trade Press, 2000).

There are several segments of the air cargo supply chain. The manufacturer creates and ships the goods to the initial purchaser, wholesaler, or a freight forwarder or freight consolidator, either of which will move the goods forward by truck or rail. As will be seen later in the chapter, the forwarder or consolidator may handle the security screening for the goods or deliver them unsecured to the shipment point. A single package may pass through the hands of as many as 18 entities before reaching the final purchaser (Bloom, 2011, p. 36). Thus, the air cargo system is a porous network requiring complex security systems.

Cargo plane movements are monitored by Federal Aviation Administration (FAA) systems, including transponders within the plane and radar. Pilots file flight plans before takeoff, and planes are tracked through the various air traffic control facilities as they fly across the country and even across the ocean.

Air Cargo Commerce

The Bureau of Transportation Statistics estimates that U.S. airports handle more than $700 billion annually in trade goods (U.S. DOT, 2011, p. 33). Air transportation accounts for 26.8% of all U.S. trade by value, with $334 billion in exports and $367 billion in imports in 2009 (U.S. DOT, 2011, p. 33), although air carries less than 1% of total trade by weight (U.S. DOT, 2011, p. 34). As shown in Table 10.1, the top-dollar-value international trade air freight gateway in the United States is Kennedy International Airport, with $127 billion in 2009; Chicago O'Hare is second with $91 billion. Of the top 20 international freight gateways by value of trade goods, eight are air (U.S. DOT, 2011, p. 36).

Air cargo is an important element of the financial structure of airlines. Aleman (2010) notes that "the revenue derived by carriers from carrying air cargo far exceeds the revenue received from passenger travel...many airlines would go bankrupt if they ceased to carry air cargo" (p. 191).

TABLE 10.1 Top U.S.–International Trade Air Freight Gateways by Value

Rank	City/Airport	Exports (Billions)	Imports (Billions)	Total (Billions)
3	NYC/Kennedy	$66	$61	$127
6	Chicago/O'Hare	$31	$60	$91
9	Los Angeles/LAX	$31	$32	$63
13	New Orleans	$19	$26	$45
16	San Francisco/SFO	$21	$19	$40
17	Miami/MIA	$27	$12	$39
18	Dallas/DFW	$15	$21	$36
19	Anchorage	$8	$26	$34

Source: U.S. DOT. (2011). *Pocket guide to transportation.* Washington, DC: RITA, p. 36.

Threats to the Air Cargo Commerce System

Complex System

Aviation operates in the open sky. Once a plane has left the runway, it is in a completely unforgiving environment. The bird strike over New York City demonstrated that an experienced pilot confronted with a sudden compromise to the plane may be able to effect an emergency landing with the right circumstances: a clear day, a relatively empty river, a ready cadre of operating ferries and small boats to rescue the passengers. The 2009 USAirways crash after a bird strike by a flock of geese was, as New York Governor David Paterson said, "A miracle on the Hudson" (CNN US, 2009).

While crashes of commercial passenger liners get wide news coverage, crashes of cargo planes tend to get little media attention. In July 2011, a NATO-chartered cargo plane supplying troops in Afghanistan crashed in the mountains, killing all nine crew member (Salahuddin, 2011), and later that same month a South Korean cargo plane on the way to China crashed in the water off South Korea, killing its two crew members (Kim, 2011). In each case, some combination of topography, turbulence, and aircraft performance resulted in loss of the crew, plane, and cargo. The fatal combination of gravity and physics in the open air denied the pilots a lifesaving solution.

Regardless of the unforgiving environment, air transportation remains the safest mode, with only 0.14% of all transportation-related fatalities occurring on large U.S.-based air carriers, with 52 deaths in 2009 (U.S. DOT, 2011, p. 2). Strict regulation of airport operations and licensing of airmen by the FAA mitigate the inherent danger of flying.

Hijacking

Passengers have proven to be a threat to safe aviation operations. In the 1960s, a spate of hijackings occurred, perpetrated by individuals trying to get to foreign countries and leading to the 1961 Air Piracy Act and the Sky Marshal program. In 1971, D. B. Cooper held an airliner and its passengers for ransom, parachuting into the Pacific Northwest with his cash, never to be seen again. This led the FAA to require "universal screening of passengers and their carry-on luggage" by 1973 (Costello, 2005).

By 1976, the number of hijackings had diminished significantly. Landes (1978) suggests that airport searches begun in 1972, "[i]ncreases in the probability of apprehension, [and] the conditional probability of incarceration…are associated with significant reductions in aircraft hijackings in the 1961 to 1976 time period." The direct cost of the search program was

$194.24 million between 1973 and 1976 alone and focused on commercial passenger flights. Passengers were told to remain calm and cooperate with hijackers because history had shown that they were generally interested in transport to a nation of their choosing, not harming passengers. There have been reports of cargo plane pilots "hijacking" their planes to different countries, such as the Taiwanese pilot who took his plane to Canton, China, in 1986 (Times Wire Service, 1986).

The 9/11 hijacking of four passenger planes by Al Qaeda terrorists changed the attitudes of passengers toward hijackers. Passengers in the fourth plane apparently fought the hijackers for control of the plane and prevented it from reaching a national profile target. It crashed in rural Pennsylvania. The events of 9/11 heightened the levels of security for passenger planes and led to some changes in air cargo search protocols.

In 2003, the FBI and Department of Homeland Security (DHS) suggested that hijacking cargo planes might be the next tactic used by terrorists to obtain a weapon for attacking critical infrastructure. LNG and LPG storage facilities and dams were considered likely targets (*USA Today,* 2003). "The consequences could include high numbers of human casualties, a small number of casualties with high symbolic value, and symbolic, significant and even catastrophic damage to communications, energy and other infrastructure of national and international significance" (Bloom, 2011, p. 35).

Smuggling and Theft

Smuggling of contraband goods inside the cargo supply chain is not new. In 1999, a trial in Miami revealed an ongoing drug and gun smuggling ring operating out of Miami International Airport (MIA) (Korten, 1999). Post-9/11 inspection protocols were designed to lessen the chance of explosives and IEDs being introduced into the air cargo supply chain, but the steady stream of drugs and guns found in shipments suggests that the system is still porous. For example, money has been smuggled in DHL and FedEx packages across the Mexican border. Cash for Columbian drug lords has been found in dolls, cars, and television sets (Naim, 2005).

In 2010 Miami International Airport air cargo workers were arrested for running a cocaine ring that used air cargo as a cover. A 5-year operation at MIA, the 17th largest freight gateway by value, revealed "MIA cargo workers who use their official airport access to divert drugs from the U.S. customs inspection area" (Weaver, 2010). According to the Department of Justice (2010), "24 percent of heroin seizures, 15 percent of MDMA seizures, 6 percent of cocaine seizures, and less than 1 percent each of methamphetamine and marijuana seizures were from commercial air conveyances"; this includes human couriers on passenger planes and material shipped in air cargo.

IATA, the business association for air cargo carriers, focused its 2008 meeting on air cargo security issues because of the pressure for better cargo security and the growing losses in the industry. John Edwards, security chief for IATA, has said, "In addition to theft, smuggling is a problem for air cargo security. Smuggling operations are often linked to organized crime, and may provide support for terrorist activities" (Homeland Security News Wire, 2008).

Contraband can be introduced into the air cargo at any point in the intermodal supply chain. The initial point of packaging is just the first point of vulnerability, which extends through the freight forwarders, courier services, warehouses, and airport operations. While it was ramp workers who were arrested in Miami, there are thousands of employees involved in the management of air cargo along its complex route. Post-9/11 concerns about shipments have led to the development of inspection protocols by both the air cargo industry and government agencies that will be covered in a later section of this chapter.

Mail

Mail was the first cargo carried by airlines. It remains a mainstay of passenger airline operations. The U.S. Postal Service has instituted a strict regime for the acceptance of all packages, requiring that anything over 11 ounces be delivered directly to a clerk for mailing. Clerks will refuse suspicious packages and hazardous materials including explosives (ATF, 2011).

Under the international shipment protocols for passenger airplanes, the postal service is responsible for the screening of all mail sent by air. X-ray and explosives detection protocols are regularly used to limit the risk to passenger airplanes carrying mail. Nevertheless, there is the possibility of a dangerous device being introduced into the mail and carried onto a plane inadvertently. For example, a colleague received a novelty butane lighter from a family member in a small parcel that was shipped through the mail.

Two ounces of detasheet in a greeting card can create a significant explosion. In a 10×10 foot room at the New Mexico Institute of Technology's test site, such a device blew out the window and made a hole in the torso of the mannequin sitting at the desk. Gifted bomb builders could create bombs that looked enough like ordinary cargo items to pass the mail x-ray test. For example, El Al received a piece of luggage that had the base plate of the rolling bag replaced with plastic explosives. The detonator was a calculator that was packed in the bottom of the bag, complete with a timing device, but separate from the explosive material. Such a device would work on the sympathetic detonation principle, where an explosive charge detonated in close proximity to another explosive charge will cause a much larger secondary charge to go off.

While traditional luggage inspection looks for PIES (power supply, initiator, explosives, and switch), the screeners would have to understand that while an explosive device with a very small charge may seem fairly harmless, the items surrounding it require greater scrutiny. Due to the size of the small initiating devices, additional diligence is required in luggage screening to remove any device that appears to be a detonating device.

Fuel Shipments, Pipelines, and Storage

Fuel has to be delivered to airports in large quantities. Some airports, like Los Angeles International Airport (LAX), are served by direct underground pipelines from the refinery to the airport, where it is stored in large tanks in the "fuel farm." Other airports, like Mineta San Jose International Airport, receive their fuel in tanker trucks (about 75 per day). Airport fuel trucks then fill up at the fuel farm and drive onto the apron to fill the waiting planes (Figure 10.3).

The pipeline is vulnerable to tampering along its path to the airport, to create a denial of service at the airport through lack of fuel or to introduce damaging material into the airplane fuel. The fuel tanker trucks may be hijacked and used as weapons, as noted in Chapter 5. The fuel truck driver has access to parts of the airfield to make the deliveries, and that access could be used to introduce explosives, an IED, or other damaging goods into the fuel farm area. The fuel storage tanks can become bombs by attaching explosive devices to sensitive sections of the equipment.

FIGURE 10.3   Refueling truck at Mineta San Jose International Airport.

Cyber Dependencies of Air Cargo Transportation

The air cargo system is dependent on a variety of cyber-based systems. The business side of the operation depends on computers to coordinate the shipments of goods to the right airport and to get them placed on the right flight. Cargo can be diverted to damage the sender or receiver economically, because, as discussed in previous chapters, the just-in-time supply chain creates a vulnerability to diversion and delay of goods. Air cargo tends to be higher value than freight shipped by other methods, and it is often more time sensitive, such as pharmaceuticals and blood products that have short expiration periods.

The air traffic control system is also dependent on GPS, radar, and computer-controlled communications systems. These are operated in common with commercial passenger aviation. Worms and viruses in the computer can lead to system crashes or the delivery of misinformation, which can lead to misrouting, landing at the wrong airport, or running out of fuel. Computers are also used to track maintenance on aircraft, and tampering with that information can lead to damage to equipment and even plane crashes due to deferred maintenance, as will be discussed in the next section.

Loss of power or telephone communications systems can also damage the functionality of the cyber systems on which aviation depends. Power failure in an area could impact air traffic control functions and plane tracking, while loss of telephone service could interfere with the communication of aviation information from one ground location to another. Thus, aviation tracking and navigation rely on ground-based critical infrastructure systems for their safety.

Accidents and Attacks on Air Cargo Planes

ValuJet Accident, 1996

In May 1996, a ValuJet flight crashed in the Everglades not far from Miami International Airport. The passenger plane was also carrying 4,109 pounds of cargo, including baggage, mail, and "company owned material." This category included some tires and wheels, and five boxes called "oxygen canisters—empty" (NTSB, 1997). These were chemical oxygen generators that had been removed from an aircraft at their expiration date and were being shipped back to the headquarters in Atlanta for refurbishing. Protocol required that a safety cap be placed over the primer so that the oxygen generating system did not begin while the generators were in transit.

Due to a mechanic's error, the generators were shipped without the safety caps. They were placed in bin 1 of the Class D forward cargo compartment, along with passenger goods and other cargo. Upon takeoff, the change in pressure in the cargo hold triggered the generators, and at least three of them caught fire. Although the fire was limited to the Class D compartment, there was no smoke detector and no fire suppression system in the compartment, so the fire interfered with the pilot's ability to fly the plane, and it crashed into the Everglades in a remote area, killing everyone aboard (NTSB, 1997).

The tragic crash was the result of a series of bad decisions by ValuJet's ground crew. It demonstrates the danger of introducing flammables, explosives, and other dangerous goods into the cargo hold of a plane without taking the mandated safety steps. Employee training was faulted in this case, but intentional acts of sabotage could have the same result.

Alaska Airlines Crash, 2000

On January 31, 2000, an Alaska Air flight from Mexico to the United States was loaded with vacationers returning home. Couples and whole families were on board. The plane developed problems near San Diego, but the crew was advised by ground control to try a few midair maneuvers to correct the problem with the plane's horizontal stabilizer. When the problem got no better, they were advised to proceed to LAX for an emergency landing. The plane crashed into the ocean off the coast of Ventura County (NTSB, 2002).

The NTSB investigation revealed that the jackscrew had failed due to a lack of maintenance. Failure to lubricate the jackscrew properly caused a functional failure that led to loss of horizontal control of the aircraft and its ultimate crash into the ocean (NTSB, 2002). While the recommended maintenance interval was every 600–900 flight hours, Alaska Airlines had extended the intervals to every 2,550 flight hours, and the FAA failed to monitor this maintenance change and correct it.

In this instance, the change to maintenance interval was a conscious decision by the airline. The loss of airline maintenance records through cyber systems damage or through intentional tampering with maintenance records themselves could result in similar damage to the airplane and loss of life.

IEDs as Aircraft Attack Modes

Improvised explosive devices (IEDs) have been used against airplanes with varied success, as will be shown by two examples here. PETN has become a popular explosive for use in IEDs because it is very difficult to detect with "sniffers," whether dogs or machines. Swabbing the surface of the package is the best way to detect the presence of PETN, but swabbing every package in the global supply chain is not possible. Experts state that "a comprehensive switch to these swabbing devices would create massive delays of everything....Relatively inexpensive cargo transport would become a thing of the past, with draconian implications for world trade" (Katz, 2010).

Unlike the limited number of passenger security lines at the air terminal, cargo comes in from multiple sites in varied streams. Installation of monitoring equipment at every portal for all air freight would be complicated and expensive. As will be shown later in the chapter, the TSA has established a multilocation strategy for air cargo screening for goods going on passenger planes as one way of managing the increased screening required by the 100% rule.

In Europe, the airports have the same security challenges but with multiple nations overseeing the solutions. Security is currently 35% of airport operating cost in Europe, while it was only 8% or less before 9/11. Forty percent of the staff at Europe's 313 airports is security related (Katz, 2010). Even in the environment of this ramped-up security, air cargo has been successfully targeted by terrorists.

UPS, Dubai, 2010

In September 2010, a UPS cargo plane crashed in Dubai, killing its crew of two (BBC News Middle East, 2010). The United Arab Emirates General Civil Aviation Authority's investigation determined that the fire that started in the cargo hold was caused by a shipment of lithium batteries that was not properly marked as a hazardous shipment and therefore not properly handled. The pilot requested an emergency landing, but the fire damaged the landing gear and the smoke in the cockpit obscured the flight instruments, leading the plane to overshoot the runway and crash (Garthwaite, 2011).

A month later, Al Qaeda in the Arabian Peninsula claimed credit for the crash (Reuters, 2010b) after two printers with cartridge bombs intended for Chicago synagogues were discovered in Britain and Dubai in air cargo shipments (Reuters, 2010a). The UAE officials are re-investigating the Dubai crash as a result of the claim and the two printer bombs that were found in October (Reuters, 2010b). Al Qaeda published a special edition of its *Inspire* magazine in November 2010 to describe its October attacks on FedEx and UPS and claim credit for the Dubai crash as the first of three attacks, but provided no specific details on the September attack. The devices for the October attack were thoroughly described (*Inspire,* 2010), calling into question the veracity of their Dubai assertion.

Al Qaeda Attacks on Cargo Planes, October 2010

In 2010 Al Qaeda in the Arabian Peninsula (AQAP) studied the vulnerabilities of air cargo. They discovered that air freight is a multimillion dollar industry. "FedEx alone flies a fleet of 600 aircraft, and ships an average of 4 million packages a day" (*Inspire,* 2010). The leadership of AQAP determined to create an attack on air cargo to cause damage to the American economy. The goal was not maximum casualties, as they were aware that the typical cargo crew was only two people, but to create stress on the air cargo sector and through it on the economy.

AQAP considered that it had a success because they were able to pass an explosive device through airport security, forcing American and international shippers to spend more time and money on cargo inspection. The Saudi security forces warned air cargo companies about the devices, which had been shipped from Yemen through third-party shippers, and they were interdicted in Great Britain and Dubai (Reuters, 2010a). AQAP leadership stated in their newsletter, "You either spend billions of dollars to inspect every package in the world, or you do nothing, and we keep trying again" (*Inspire*, 2010).

Security Strategies for Air Cargo Transportation

In the preceding sections, the threats to air cargo and actual attacks and accidents have been examined. Security strategies have been developed as part of the "lessons learned" from these events. These strategies may provide multiple benefits, such as preventing theft, discouraging smuggling, and revealing the creativity of terrorists.

The cost of security continues to be an economic challenge to airlines, the supply chain, and the global economy that has to absorb the added expenses. Costello (2005) estimated that the cost of aviation security to the federal government exceeds $5 billion per year. Bloom (2011) points out that estimating the existing level of security for a given airport is difficult, so "deciding how much money to appropriate and allocate for airport security is difficult. Terrorists…[have to decide] how much money and what expenditures will yield the greatest effect…attack via passengers, air cargo, both…?" (p. 31).

Ordinary Crime in the Air Cargo Environment

Theft of air cargo is similar to theft in the trucking and maritime transportation sectors. Because the cargo changes hands many times and in several places during its shipment, perfect control of all goods is not possible (Figure 10.4). Although air cargo represents only 0.4% of the weight of all shipped goods, it has been shown to be more valuable per pound (U.S. DOT, 2011, p. 34), with 26.8% of the value (U.S. DOT, 2011, p. 33), so tracking devices like GPS and RFID are used and detailed inventories are checked at intermodal change points. Regardless of this care, "shrinkage" occurs because all security ultimately relies on the human factor for success.

As part of its counterterrorism efforts mandated by the 9/11 act, TSA is doing background checks for 100,000 air cargo employees "who screen

FIGURE 10.4   Air cargo on apron waiting to be loaded.

cargo and/or have knowledge of how it is going to be transported or actually transport the cargo" (TSA, 2010). TSA also boosted the number of air cargo inspectors to 620, including 120 canine teams (TSA, 2010). These steps are expected to lessen the rate of ordinary crime, as well as deter terrorism.

While locks and seals may be effective in preventing theft, they are often removed during the air cargo screening process required for terrorist attack prevention, detection, and interdiction. As will be discussed in a later section, screening air cargo bound for passenger planes can now be accomplished early in the supply chain through several TSA initiatives, allowing for the goods to be sealed, locked, or containerized to discourage theft, tampering, smuggling, or introduction of unwanted items into the shipment. Air cargo shipments do not have the same screening requirements, so goods can be locked, sealed, netted, or containerized earlier to discourage theft; however, the goods change hands as many as 18 times between manufacturer and customer (Bloom, 2011, p. 36), so standard security practices for theft prevention are essential.

Terrorism

U.S. airports are critical infrastructure for America's global economy. As shown before, globalization of the economy has resulted in increased vulnerability to loss in air cargo supply chains, potentially through the destruction of planes, airports, terminals, fuel farms, and adjacent intermodal transfer points.

Screening Cargo

Cargo screening is a complex activity, complicated by the variety of goods to be screened. Items are of differing sizes, densities, weights, and economic value. Weapons vary in size and include weapon parts and explosives. Items are packaged in different materials and configurations. Some items are already on pallets or banded together on arrival at the airport. Some items come in netting or with straps. Some come in containers that are already sealed. "Packaging is associated with tape, locks, seals, tracking technologies, and sequenced methods for opening and closing, which pose strengths as well as vulnerabilities" (Bloom, 2011, p. 35).

Bloom (2011) notes that screening challenges include

> a) possible electrostatic discharge; b) physical damage related to the method of screening; c) levels of specificity and sensitivity related to cargo content; and d) terrorist knowledge of screening methods, which can lead to the development of countermeasures or to other methods of exploitation. (p. 35)

The aircraft itself and its design may contribute to security challenges, such as fire suppression systems in specified areas, the loading characteristics of the plane, fuel load, and structural materials of the aircraft. Because screened international cargo and cargo going on passenger planes must be held in secure areas between screening and loading, rapid loading capability is an economic benefit.

International Standards for Screening Cargo

The International Civil Aviation Organization (ICAO), a United Nations agency, creates "guidelines and directives for member states" related to the security of cargo and mail (Aleman, 2010, p. 190). Standard 4.6.1 requires all member states to apply security controls to cargo carried on passenger planes. Security controls must be applied to any "means by which the introduction of weapons, explosives or other dangerous devices, articles or substances which may be used to commit an act of unlawful interference can be prevented" (Aleman, 2010, p. 190). The rigorous screening of passengers and luggage has made a shift to cargo the next step for terrorists, as shown in the 2010 printer cartridge attack.

Standard 4.6.2 requires that the screened air cargo must be stored securely after the screening and before placement on the aircraft. This means that an area has to be created that cannot be accessed by unauthorized personnel. This secure zone for air cargo has to be large enough to contain all the screened goods until they are placed on the plane. All personnel have to have identification that positively confirms their need to be in the secured area on the air side of the airport.

Protection of air cargo begins at the point of manufacturing and packaging and extends through the entire supply chain until it is loaded onto the plane. Typical screening includes x-ray equipment, explosives detection devices and dogs, "explosive trace detection equipment, hand searches, [and] simulation chambers" (Aleman, 2010, p. 192). The goal is to create a secure package that is kept secure until it is shipped.

Standard 4.6.3 says that countries may approve "regulated agents" who can be responsible for the prescreening of air cargo. This includes any entity that can provide acceptable security systems to permit its air cargo to enter the system without additional searches. "Aircraft operators, freight forwarders, postal authorities and courier companies should be made specifically accountable for the security of all consignments" of air cargo (Aleman, 2010, p. 192). This entails examining and ensuring the security of facilities and vehicles used to handle air cargo and the training of all personnel. These programs are defined by each member state.

Standard 4.6.4 requires that all air cargo to be carried on passenger planes be certified as screened, and Standard 4.6.5 requires that all the food and cabin supplies have to be prepared and maintained in a secure environment. Whether the catering company is part of the airline or independent, it is obligated to provide background checks for all of its employees that are the same as those used for the unaccompanied airline and airport staff who work in secure areas. Company employees also must receive the same security awareness training as the regulated agents' employees (Aleman, 2010, p. 194).

Standard 4.6.6 requires member states to examine air cargo to be carried on cargo aircraft based on a risk assessment. The International Air Transportation Association (IATA), which represents the pilots and crew of cargo aircraft, FedEx, DHL, and UPS, recommended that security screening be extended to air cargo carriers, so Standard 4.6.6 was passed as a recommendation.

In the United States, the TSA is the responsible organization for the implementation of the ICAO regulations. The United States is the "world leader in aviation, with more airlines, airports, air passengers, airline operations, and air cargo miles flown than any other state" (Aleman, 2010, p. 196).

Screening Technologies

Since 9/11 the federal government has invested in research and development by private corporations to advance the creation of efficient and effective screening technologies for air cargo to protect against dangerous goods and terrorist devices. TSA's list of currently approved air cargo screening technology for passenger aircraft includes a variety of methods. The list falls into three categories: "Qualified technology" has undergone TSA testing, "approved technology" has conditional approval and is undergoing field testing, and "grandfathered technology" has current approval with an expiration date. Qualified technology includes noncomputed tomography (non-CT) transmission x-ray devices, explosive trace detection (ETD) devices, and explosive detection systems (EDSs). The approved technology list also includes electronic metal detection devices (EMDs). Grandfathered devices include some ETD and EMD technologies (TSA, 2011).

TSA Compliance Programs

As the regulator for U.S. aviation security involving 300 air carriers at 450 airports (TSA, 2009), TSA has developed a number of programs to comply with the international requirements for cargo screening ad security. For example, the 100% screening requirement for the 13,000 tons of cargo transported on passenger aircraft daily (DHS, OIG, 2009) was achieved with a layered approach to security, encouraging each portion of the air cargo supply chain to take responsibility for pre-airport screening and security.

Known Shipper   One approach is the Known Shipper Program. This allows American companies to be reviewed by TSA for security purposes, leading to the capability to prescreen their own goods. The program begins with a risk assessment of the company and the cargo, and the information is entered into a database—the Known Shipper Management System—that can be accessed by shipping companies to determine the level of secondary screening that will be required of goods carried for the known shipper.

According to the DHS Office of Inspector General:

> A known shipper is a person that has an established business relationship with an indirect air carrier, an aircraft operator or an air carrier based on items such as customer records, shipping contracts, a business history and a site visit, or Dun and Bradstreet vetting. (DHS, OIG, 2009, p. 2)

The designation allows freight forwarders to accept goods from known shippers for transport on passenger airplanes as air cargo. The program was begun by the FAA and turned over to TSA after DHS was created. The manual vetting process was taken over from FAA and is being integrated into a database and management system for ease of operation. The Department of the Treasury maintains a list of entities subject to sanctions based on terrorism or narcotics smuggling, and such entities cannot become known shippers (DHS, OIG, 2009, p. 4). By 2008, TSA had registered 1.4 million known shippers (TSA, 2008).

Certified Cargo Screening Program   A second initiative to comply with the 100% screening requirements for cargo on passenger airplanes is the Certified Cargo Screening Program (CCSP). This program partners TSA with private entities that screen cargo before it arrives at the airport. This is a voluntary program designed to enable vetted entities to speed the air cargo process for their clients.

The 9/11 Act of 2007 requires that all air cargo on passenger planes must be screened at the piece level, including removal from all pallets and packing configurations and repacking when screening is complete. Freight forwarders and shippers who have become part of CCSP can screen the goods at their facilities. "Cargo is screened at the most efficient and effective point. It is done before individual pieces of cargo are consolidated for shipment" (TSA, n.d., a). For example, funeral homes have become CCSP members to ensure that the caskets do not need to be screened in transit. Eligible entities include "manufacturers, warehouses, distribution centers, third party logistics providers, [and] indirect air carriers"—all of whom benefit by speeding the acceptance process at the airport (TSA, 2008).

CCSP is not the same as the Border Patrol's C-TPAT, which was discussed in earlier chapters. CCSP is the certification of an individual facility, while C-TPAT is a supply chain security program for land-based transportation. CCSP recognizes that facilities that are part of C-TPAT may already meet their standards, but each facility has to have its own screening process to participate in the 100% passenger airplane cargo screening program (TSA, n.d., a).

The key features of the CCSP are the need to provide background checks and training for all employees who handle the screened cargo and to maintain a chain of custody of the screened goods between screening and placement on the aircraft. Each facility where screening and postscreening secure storage will be conducted is inspected initially by a TSA employee, with follow-up inspections performed by a validation firm (TSA, 2008).

Bloom (2011) has noted that while "known shipper" and CCSP provide some enhanced security for the air cargo shipped on passenger planes, there are gaps in the process. The Known Shipper Program only addresses the originating company, and the CCSP does not address all the chain-of-custody vulnerabilities (p. 36).

Indirect Air Carrier Program   TSA has created the Indirect Air Carrier Program for freight forwarders, with 4,100 members by 2009 (TSA, 2009). These companies are authorized to handle screened cargo. This means that a CCSP that has done its own screening but does not transport the goods to the airport can use an IAC member and avoid additional piece-based screening at the airport, unless it is required by random-check protocol or risk-based analysis. IACs generally do not screen cargo, but rather safeguard it to retain the secure chain of custody required by the 100% rule for cargo transported on passenger planes (TSA, 2008).

Vulnerability Assessment Program TSA is evaluating the air cargo vulnerabilities at the nation's international airports. "The vulnerability assessment program is designed to identify critical air cargo supply chain nodes and assess the assets and potential loss impacts to these assets" (TSA, 2008). The goal is to provide guidance for all supply chain members to enhance their security.

Air Cargo Watch Modeled on the successful "see something, say something" campaign on mass transit, the Air Cargo Watch is designed to heighten the awareness of workers in the air cargo industry to possible incursions into secure areas, as well as other security threats in the air cargo supply chain. The program is focused on the principles of "detect, deter, and report" any threats to air cargo security. The program includes an educational PowerPoint presentation, a poster, and a guide for use by all entities in the supply chain (Figure 10.5). The guide refers reports to local law enforcement and fire and rescue organizations for response to workplace concerns (TSA, 2008). A website has been established for use by all air cargo shippers

FIGURE 10.5   TSA's air cargo watch poster.

joining or participating in the Air Cargo Watch program (http://www.tsa.gov/what_we_do/layers/aircargo/watch.shtm).

VIPR Teams in Air Cargo Security

VIPR teams assist airport security in cargo areas by enhancing existing security personnel capabilities to detect and interdict security threats on the airfield and in air cargo management areas. Their detectors and dogs can be used to check cargo and personnel for drugs and explosives. VIPR teams can assist with threats from off-airport locations, such as observing potential vantage points along the approaches to the landing zone. Team members can provide specific surveillance of personnel in secure areas for suspicious behavior and augment badge checks for airline and airport personnel (TSA, n.d., b).

VIPR teams at airports are coordinated through existing TSA personnel and the FAA. In addition to working with airport security personnel during high threat periods, they can assist with exercises, including Red Team events where outsiders test the operation of existing airport security by trying to breach it. The security value of VIPR teams is enhanced by their ability to be deployed at random times and in random places, on unpredictable schedules—making surveillance and planning difficult for criminals and terrorists (TSA, n.d., b).

The Challenge of Inbound Cargo

Cargo planes originating in other nations are inspected and loaded based on the rules of the ICAO or of the country where the flight originates. A manifest is prepared listing all the cargo to be delivered to the United States, and this list is delivered to U.S. Customs Service at least 4 hours before the plane is scheduled to land. As the cargo is unloaded, Customs or security forces may screen packages again based on intelligence that has been received about threats.

Customs experts have suggested that security could be improved by having the manifest received and reviewed before the plane leaves the nation of origin, to actually prevent the delivery of suspect goods. However, because manifests are being amended until takeoff under the present system, such a change would result in delayed departures while the last version of the manifest was received by U.S. authorities and cleared for delivery.

Economic Implications of Security

Screening of all baggage going on passenger planes was required by 2010 (Figure 10.6). Regardless of the technologies employed and the availability

FIGURE 10.6   Passenger awaiting luggage at the baggage handling system.

of modern screening devices, two printers with cartridges filled with PETN passed all the safeguards. The cartridge found in Dubai had already flown on two passenger airplanes before they were seized (Katz, 2010). Security experts agree that "screening every piece of air cargo…might bankrupt international shipping companies, hobble already weakened airlines and still not provide full protection" (Katz 2010). The 100% screening rule for cargo carried on passenger planes has already cost $700 million for the first year and required 9,000 employees in the freight forwarding supply chain (Katz, 2010).

Case Studies

Operation Hemorrhage: Printer Cartridge

On October 30, 2010, two bombs were discovered in air cargo consignments in Great Britain and Dubai. One bomb was sent via FedEx and the other via UPS. Thanks to a warning from the Saudi security agency, the companies were able to confiscate the two printers that were sent from Yemen and bound for Chicago synagogues.

The bombs were made from a Hewlett Packard printer. The toner cartridge was filled with 340 grams of PETN, an amount that mimicked the weight of the usual printer toner while having the power to inflict significant damage on an airplane. PETN was selected because it had "a similar molecular density to toner" and also has a low vapor pressure, making it more difficult for explosive detection equipment or dogs to detect (*Inspire,* 2010). Four grams of lead azide, a sensitive primary explosive, was used as the detonator. The wires were connected from the circuit to the toner in a way that would not arouse suspicion. A circuit card from a Nokia mobile phone was attached next to the circuit board of the printer, allowing a cell phone call to trigger the detonation of the bomb.

When x-rayed, both circuit cards would look like they overlapped and not be recognizable as a modification using mobile phone parts. The design of the printer forced the toner to be placed properly in order for the outside printer door to be closed; this ensured proper reassembly after inspection. From previous research, it was known that x-ray scanners would be used to inspect the packages at both UPS and FedEx. The design was created to ensure easy passage through these devices (*Inspire,* 2010).

"The Nokia phones cost $150 each, and the printers cost $300 each. Shipping, transportation and miscellaneous expenses [including explosives] added up to $4,200" (*Inspire,* 2010). The plot took six people 3 months from planning through execution. While no planes blew up and the printers did not reach the Chicago synagogues that were the intended target, AQAP considers it a victory because the successful acceptance of these packages containing bombs will create new security costs for the inspection of future packages (*Inspire,* 2010). The Chicago explosions never occurred, but the economic impact is global.

Pan Am 103, Lockerbie

In 1988, passengers and airliners became targets of terrorism. Pan Am 103, a Boeing 747 wide-body aircraft, left London bound for the United States and exploded over Lockerbie, Scotland, killing all 259 people on the plane and 11 people on the ground (Costello, 2005). The suitcase loaded with 1.5 pounds of explosives was in a UDL container on the left side of the plane near the wing. It was air cargo—unaccompanied baggage (Aleman, 2010).

The CIA at first thought that the bombing was organized by a radical Palestinian group, Popular Front for the Liberation of Palestine, hired by Iran for $1.3 million. It was believed to be retribution for the *USS Vincennes* shooting down an Iranian aircraft in July of 1988 (Ottaway & Parker, 1989). But a later investigation proved that the bomb was created by two Libyan intelligence officers:

> The investigation concluded that Pan Am 103 was blown up by a plastic bomb that had been built into a Toshiba radio-cassette recorder, then put into a suitcase packed with clothing; the suitcase was stored in a forward cargo hold.

A fragment of the timing device tied the bomb to a Swiss manufacturer who had sold 20 of the bomb timers to a Libyan between 1985 and 1986 (Lardner, 1991).

The Libyans worked as airline employees in Malta. They acquired some Air Malta luggage tags and used them "to route the bomb-rigged suitcase as unaccompanied luggage aboard an Air Malta flight to Frankfurt. There, the suitcase was transferred to Pan Am Flight 103A and, on arrival in London, it was put aboard Pan Am Flight 103" (Lardner, 1991). The plane blew up about half an hour after takeoff. The bomb had only a Swiss digital timer, which tied it to the Libyans, while the Palestinian bomb design included a timer and an altimeter to ensure that the bomb did not go off until the plane was actually in the air (Lardner, 1991).

As a result of this disaster, the President's Commission on Aviation Security and Terrorism recommended that passenger and luggage screening be augmented. Passenger carry-on luggage had long been screened for weapons with a magnet and x-ray; now, explosives detection equipment was added to the security chain. The CT scan-based explosive detection system that is still in use dates from that time (Costello, 2005). The big change from this disaster was adding "hold" luggage to the screening process for international travel. The change to the international aviation screening requirements included "the addition of security controls over cargo, courier and express parcels and mail" (Aleman, 2010, p. 196).

Summary

Air cargo is an essential part of the global supply chain and makes a significant contribution to the global economy. Bloom (2011) suggests that even the threat of terrorist attack via air cargo has driven up the cost of goods shipments, so balancing the cost of screening against the cost of attack-based losses becomes problematic. Having taken draconian steps to deter, detect, and interdict terrorist acts by passengers after 9/11—the "shoe bomber" and the "underwear bomber"—TSA has had to institute a thorough screening of air cargo in response to threats and the printer cartridge attacks.

Perfect safety is not possible. Resolution of all Al Qaeda's demands is not reasonable. Fighting terrorism results in the redirection of scarce resources from more socially and economically productive endeavors. Intelligence gathering and analysis offers one method for effective interdiction, as shown in the printer cartridge bomb attack. AQAP classified the Yemen-based printer bombs as a success because they made it past screening and into the air cargo system, but intelligence work led to the Saudi warning that stopped their forward movement beyond Dubai in one case and Britain in the other. Neither made it to Chicago, this time.

The final chapter examines the relationship among transportation security, the global supply chain, and critical infrastructure.

Discussion Questions

1. What is the role of TSA in air cargo security? How do they use technology to enhance air cargo security?

2. Describe the air cargo environment. What are the elements of the infrastructure and how are they regulated?

3. What is the passenger/air cargo interface? How does this interface enhance security challenges for passenger airlines? Why do they continue to carry cargo, given the risks?

4. What vulnerabilities did the ValueJet and FedEx plane events demonstrate? What technologies and strategies can be used to mitigate this kind of hazard?

5. You are the new director of security for a regional commercial airport. A high-tech company has just opened an assembly facility in your community. You have made an appointment to meet with their logistics team to discuss the role of the airport in their global supply chain. What items would you want on the agenda? What questions would you ask?

References

Aleman, M. A. (2010). International aviation security practices relating to the global supply chain. In A. Thomas (Ed.), *Supply chain security.* Santa Barbara, CA: Praeger.

ATF. (n.d.). The ATF law enforcement guide to explosive incident reporting. Accessed April 3, 2011.

BBC News Middle East. (2010, September 3). UPS cargo plane crashes in Dubai, killing two. Accessed April 3, 2011, at http://www.bbc.co.uk/news/world-middle-east-11183476

Bloom, R. W. (2011, July-August). Airport security: Which poses the greater threat—Passengers or cargo? *TR News,* 31–36.

Branch, H., & Hinton, W. H., II. (2009, October 12). TSA finalized cargo screening rule for passenger aircraft. Smith, Gambrell & Russell, LLP. Accessed on April 3, 2011, from http://www.sgrlaw.com/resources/client_alerts/1387/

CNN US. (2009, January 15). Airplane crash-lands into Hudson River; all aboard reported safe. Accessed April 3, 2011, at http://articles.cnn.com/2009-01-15/us/new.york.plane.crash_1_air-traffic-controllers-bird-strike-pilot?_s=PM:US

Costello, F. J. (2005). Post 9-11 challenges for aviation security. In W. C. Nicholson (Ed.), *Homeland security law and policy.* Springfield, IL: Charles C Thomas Publisher, Ltd.

Department of Justice. (2010, February). Drug movement into and within the United States. Accessed April 3, 2011, at http://www.justice.gov/ndic/pubs38/38661/movement.htm

DHS. OIG. (2009). *Transportation security administration's known shipper program.* OIG 09-35. Washington, DC: DHS.

Garthwaite, J. (2011, April 4). Lithium ion batteries faulted for jet crash. Earth2Tech. Accessed February 10, 2012, at http://gigaom.com/cleantech/lithium-ion-batteries-faulted-for-jet-crash/

Homeland Security News Wire. (2008, June 23). Cargo security front and center at coming IATA meeting. Accessed April 3, 2011, at http://www.homelandsecuritynewswire.com/cargo-security-front-and-center-coming-iata-meeting

Inspire. (2010, November). Special issue: The objectives of Operation Hemorrhage.

Katz, G. (2010, November 1). Fixing cargo security system would cost billions. Associated Press. http://seattletimes.nwsource.com/html/businesstechnology/2013320827_mailbombcosts02.html

Kim, S. (2011, July 27). South Korean cargo plane carrying 2 crashes. Associated Press. Accessed April 3, 2011, at http://news.yahoo.com/south-korean-cargo-plane-carrying-2-crashes-023232992.html

Korten, T. (1999, November 4). Deadly cargo: Big payoffs. Gruesome murders. Nosy feds. Life as a cargo handler at MIA just ain't what it used to be. Accessed April 3, 2011, from http://www.miaminewtimes.com/content/printVersion/240535/

Landes, W. M. (1978, April). An economic study of U.S. aircraft hijacking, 1961–1976. *Journal of Law and Economics, 21*(1), 1–31.

Lardner, G., Jr. (1991, November 15). 2 Libyans indicted in Pan Am blast. *Washington Post,* p. A01.

Naim, M. (2005). *Illicit.* New York, NY: Anchor Books.

NTSB (National Transportation Safety Board). (1997). *Aircraft accident report: In-flight fire and impact with terrain, ValuJet Airlines, Flight 592* (NTSB/AAR-97/06). Accessed April 3, 2011, at http://www.ntsb.gov/investigations/summary/AAR9706.html

NTSB (National Transportation Safety Board). (2002). *Aircraft accident report: Loss of control and impact with Pacific Ocean Alaska Airlines flight 261* (NTSB/AAR-02/01). Accessed April 3, 2011, http://libraryonline.erau.edu/online-full-text/ntsb/aircraft-accident-reports/AAR02-01.pdf

Ottaway, D. B., & Parker, L. (1989, May 11). CIA confident Iran behind jet bombing. *Washington Post,* p. A01.

Reuters. (2010a, November 5). Al Qaeda Yemen wing claims parcel plot, UPS crash. Accessed April 3, 2011, at http://www.reuters.com/article/2010/11/05/us-usa-yemen-bomb-idUSTRE6A44PU20101105

Reuters. (2010b, November 6). UAE says investigating Qaeda claim for UPS plane crash. Accessed April 3, 2011, at http://www.reuters.com/article/2010/11/06/us-uae-qaeda-ups-idUSTRE6A50CA20101106.

Salahuddin, S. (2011, July 6). NATO cargo plane crashes, 9 killed. *Washington Post.* Accessed April 3, 2011, at http://www.washingtonpost.com/world/war-zones/nato-cargo-plane-crashes-9-killed/2011/07/06/gIQAqWKV0H_story.html

Times Wire Service. (1986, May 13). Hijacked plane will end 2 China's 40-year silence: Taiwan to negotiate on aircraft. *LA Times.* Accessed April 3, 2011, at http://articles.latimes.com/1986-05-13/news/mn-5861_1_kuomintang

TSA. (2008). Programs and initiatives. Accessed April 3, 2011, at http://www.tsa.gov/what_we_do/tsnm/air_cargo/programs.shtm

TSA. (2009). Air cargo: Transportation sector network management. Accessed April 3, 2011, at http://www.tsa.gov/what_we_do/tsnm/air_cargo/index.shtm

TSA. (2010). Air cargo: Security programs. Accessed April 3, 2011, at http://www.tsa.gov/what_we_do/layers/aircargo/index.shtm

TSA. (2011). *Air cargo screening technology list for passenger aircraft.* Washington, DC: DHS/TSA.

TSA. (n.d., a). Certified cargo screening program. Accessed April 3, 2011, at http://www.tsa.gov/what_we_do/layers/aircargo/certified_screening.shtm

TSA. (n.d., b). *Commercial and general aviation.* Washington, DC: TSA.

USA Today. (2003, November 22). Government warns of increased terrorist threat. Accessed April 3, 2011, at http://www.usatoday.com/news/washington/2003-11-21-terror_x.htm

U.S. DOT. (2011). *Pocket guide to transportation.* Washington, DC: RITA.

Weaver, J. (2010, August 13). Cocaine, heroin seized in latest drug-smuggling bust of Miami airport workers. Accessed April 3, 2011, at http://articles.sun-sentinel.com/2010-08-13/news/fl-miami-airport-drug-bust-20100813_1_operation-ramp-rats-miami-airport-workers-cargo-workers

Webb, A. (2012, February 10). Airlines ponder careful what's wished for in A380 glut: Freight. Accessed February 11, 2012, at http://www.businessweek.com/news/2012-02-10/airlines-ponder-careful-what-s-wished-for-in-a380-glut-freight.html

World Trade Press. (2000). Guide to air freight containers (ULDs). Accessed April 3, 2011, at http://www.fredoniainc.com/glossary/air.html

Section III

Putting It All Together

Chapter 11

Transportation Security, Supply Chain, and Critical Infrastructure

Keywords: Critical infrastructure, supply chain, business continuity, continuity of operations, cascading events, TMC, EOC, fusion center, recovery, EMAC, public–private partnerships

Learning Objectives

After reading this chapter you should be able to

- Identify critical infrastructure interdependencies
- Understand the evolution of emergency management after 9/11 and Hurricane Katrina
- Understand the role of continuity of operations/business continuity
- Understand the role of the TMC, EOC, and fusion center in transportation security
- Understand the role of public–private partnerships in transportation security and support of disaster response

9/11: A Failure of Imagination

Recent disasters have changed the way the American federal system manages disasters. Surprises and failures resulted in new structures that have evolved to finally recognize the key role of the private sector in the management of disaster response and recovery.

On September 11, 2001, the U.S. mainland was attacked by a foreign enemy for the first time since the War of 1812. This tragedy was the result of terrorist activity, the end of a well planned and executed approach to taking down the World Trade Center—the symbol of Western wealth and economic dominance—and attacking the nation's capital. While various exercises had postulated some elements of the 9/11 attacks, the missing link was organized intelligence sharing among federal agencies. After rating the attacks of 9/11 as a "failure of imagination," the Congress and Executive Branch created new systems to enhance nationwide preparedness for future terrorist attacks, including the creation of an "intelligence czar." The National Intelligence Program coordinates "foreign, military and domestic intelligence in defense of the homeland and of United States interests abroad" (ODNI, n.d.).

A series of Homeland Security presidential directives shaped a new national approach to disaster preparedness. The National Incident Management System (NIMS) was mandated by HSPD-5. Concern for the safety of critical infrastructure was exemplified in HSPD-7. A coordinated preparedness program was mandated by HSPD-8. Legislation created the Department of Homeland Security (DHS), the State Homeland Security Grant Program (consolidating previous antiterrorism grant programs), the Urban Area Security Initiative (USAI) Program for developing protection of the nation's large cities, and enhanced the Metropolitan Medical Response System's (MMRS) funding and mission.

In every case, the focus was on government's response to terrorism. The four phases of emergency management were supplanted by the five phases of homeland security: prevention, protection, preparedness, response, and recovery. The Federal Emergency Management Agency (FEMA) was subsumed under the DHS organization chart, and the FEMA director became just one more bureau chief in the largest federal department, without access to the president or even to his own cabinet secretary.

Katrina and New Orleans: A Failure of Initiative

FEMA's response to Hurricane Katrina in New Orleans was rated a "failure of initiative" by Congress, as the organization struggled under DHS control. FEMA's director, Michael Brown, could not get the National Coordination Center to provide busses until a DHS analyst determined whether 500 busses were actually needed. Secretary Michael Chertoff did not want to provide federal assets until he was sure whether the levees had been breached or were overtopped. Unlike James Witt, former director of FEMA who had had cabinet rank, Director Brown was denied access to the president (Cooper & Block, 2006).

New mandates changed FEMA's status under DHS, and it was brought back as the lead agency for all-hazards disaster preparedness. New legislation changed the focus of funding to a more balanced view of hazards, gave the FEMA director access to the president during presidential disaster declaration events, and enhanced support for the community emergency response team program. S. 3721 (109th Congress), the Post-Katrina Emergency Reform Act of 2006, transferred the old DHS preparedness directorate functions back to FEMA, including oversight of NIMS and the National Response Framework (DHS, 2008), to replace the famously failed National Response Plan (Cooper & Block, 2006).

Two new elements came from the 2006 reforms. The first was the National Protection and Programs Directorate, bringing together infrastructure protection and cyber security. The new Office of Health Affairs oversees the MMRS, Biowatch, Bioshield, and medical readiness (DHS, 2008). Both infrastructure and cyber protection and medical affairs require close coordination with the private sector, which owns 85% of the critical infrastructure (Jackson, 2007) and most of the medical assets of the nation.

The role of the private sector in disaster response and recovery was emphasized in the failures and outcomes of Hurricane Katrina. For example, while FEMA struggled to coordinate logistics support for victims with the state government, private entities like Wal-Mart and Home Depot responded to disaster victims' needs. Operating from its center in Bentonville, Arkansas, Wal-Mart executives monitored the community conditions and used their state-of-the-art logistics system to rapidly resupply communities devastated by disasters (*ABC News*, 2005).

Political economist Steven Horowitz suggests that the successful response to Hurricane Katrina victims' needs by Wal-Mart, Home Depot, and other private sector actors "seems to confirm the more general conclusion of modern political economy that private institutions better mobilize resources than do public agencies" (Horowitz, 2009, p. 512). Jason Jackson, of Wal-Mart, told an audience of emergency managers that the private sector is a good partner for disaster response because they "play to their strengths. For example, we do logistics, not shelters" (Jackson, 2007). During the Hurricane Katrina response in 2005 and the Hurricane Ike response in 2008, Wal-Mart assisted with trucks and drivers (BENS, 2007; Raths, 2010).

Transportation and Critical Infrastructure

Transportation assets are part of the nation's critical infrastructure. As has been seen in Chapters 5 through 10, transportation is a key to the nation's security

FIGURE 11.1 Critical infrastructure in the Port of San Francisco.

and economic survival. Goods have to be moved efficiently through the supply chain from raw materials providers to final consumers. Pilferage, spoilage, and economic damage can result from a disrupted transportation chain.

Transportation in turn relies on a variety of other critical infrastructures (Figure 11.1). Descriptions in earlier chapters have shown that transportation is reliant on cyber elements, from SCADA systems to surveillance video monitoring. Cyber systems are dependent on electrical power systems and often on phone lines to carry signals. The transportation mode itself may be dependent on electricity, like subways, light rail, and commuter rail. The transportation system relies on electricity and radio or telephone to operate signals and switches on tracked systems, traffic lights, communications systems, and ticketing systems, and for security elements like surveillance cameras, card readers, and sensors.

The interdependence of much of the nation's critical infrastructure can lead to a cascading disaster event. The initial point of failure might be manageable, but as it cascades into ever more elements, its impact—first on service and then on the community—becomes unstoppable and unmanageable, and ultimately a disaster. Larry Babbio, vice chairman and president of Verizon Communications, Inc., commented,

> The telephone companies can only do so much on their own, because eventually they rely on the power companies, who in turn rely on some other industry such as the transportation industry...Working together on a cross-industry basis is the only truly complete solution. (BENS, 2007, p. 15)

The Northeast Power Outage of 2003

On August 14, 2003, in the late afternoon, the northeastern United States and portions of Canada were hit by the largest blackout in history. The loss of 61,800 MW of electricity directly impacted 50 million people (ELCON, 2004), causing 11 deaths. "Streetlights went out, subway trains stopped, mid-tunnel and refrigeration equipment went dead" (Minkel, 2008). Some consumers had service restored by the morning of August 15, although many remained without power until the following day, and some even as late as August 17 (*CBC News*, 2003).

What first started with a FirstEnergy Corp of Ohio unexpected plant shutdown because of a SCADA system bug led to a series of problems on the Midwest Independent Transmission System Operator's (MISO) transmission line, because its power monitoring tool was not functioning. Therefore, the first shutdown was unknown to the operators, so no action was taken to restore that part of the system. During this period, a transmission line contacted trees and shorted out, further stressing the system. The increased demand on the remaining portions of the grid cascaded to other power suppliers and caused a cross-border blackout (*CBC News*, 2003).

The U.S. Department of Energy estimated the economic losses at $6 billion. Almost half of Ohio's manufacturing companies were closed for 36 hours. A multistate survey of manufacturers indicated that losses were $50,000 per hour of downtime, with some up to $1 million per hour. An indirect loss was to manufacturers outside the blackout area who relied on just-in-time delivery of components for scheduled production (ELCON, 2004).

The loss of electricity impacted every industry in the metropolitan region:

- The automotive industry, including General Motors, Ford, and Honda and their suppliers, had at least 70 auto and parts plants shut down by the loss of power, putting over 100,000 people out of work.
- At least eight oil refineries were impacted, with the loss of production threatening a gasoline shortage in the Detroit metropolitan area.
- The main pipeline network for oil shipments from Canada to the Midwest, carrying 2 million barrels per day, was crippled.
- The second largest U.S. Steel plant was shut down for 4 days. Republic Engineered Products in Lorraine, Ohio, had an explosion and fire in its blast furnace because it lost cooling capacity for the iron ore.
- Nova Chemicals Corporation lost 150 million pounds of ethylene and coproducts as a result of the electricity shutdown.
- New York City businesses experienced losses from the power outage when $250 million in frozen and perishable food had to be dumped. The city of New York spent $10 million in overtime expenses for public employees (ELCON, 2004).

Loss of electricity stopped water purification processes, demonstrating "the interconnectedness and fragility of public service infrastructures" (*Water & Health,* 2012). The loss of electricity impacted medical systems, air conditioning cooling units, and public water system management, including the possible introduction of bacteria into the system. Residents received boil-water orders in many communities, and restaurants were closed in the Detroit area until the water system was recertified (*Water & Health,* 2012).

Electricity's impact on transportation was wide ranging. The New York City subway system stopped, stranding 350,000 passengers. Emergency power kept the lights on briefly, and when they went out, employees with flashlights led passengers from stations up to daylight. Eight trains were on bridges and 19 were under water (Kennedy, 2003). The evacuation of the subway system started within 15 minutes of the blackout, as ConEd notified New York City Transit that the outage was likely to be for a long time (DiBlasio, Regan, Zirker, Lovejoy, & Fichter 2004). For almost 3 hours, employees led passengers down tracks and out hatches to safety. The system remained closed for 8 hours after power was restored so that workers could check the system's 12,000 signals (Kennedy, 2003).

The streets were gridlocked because all of the 11,600 signals were dark, with police and pedestrians trying to manage traffic with cardboard stop signs. Busses were traveling 2 miles an hour due to the congestion. People were renting bicycles, lining up for ferries, and walking across the Brooklyn and Manhattan Bridges. The Port Authority Bus Terminal was a scene of chaos as commuters arrived only to be told they had to get out of the darkened building (Kennedy, 2003). New Jersey Transit had "load and go" bus service to the Meadowlands station. Drivers often could not retrieve their cars from garages because the car elevators had no power (Scott, 2003). The MTA suspended outbound tolls and created a bus lane for returns to Manhattan. New York City Transit provided a bus bridge from Penn Station to the Long Island Railroad Station in Jamaica, Queens, and sent busses to the largest subway stations. The Lincoln and Holland Tunnels were closed, but the George Washington Bridge remained open (DiBlasio et al., 2004).

Three quarters of all work trips into New York are made using transit (DiBlasio et al., 2004). The commuter rail network was stopped, with a Long Island railroad train with 1,000 passengers trapped beneath the East River for over 2 hours in a tunnel without air conditioning until a diesel engine was able to pull it back to Penn Station (Kennedy, 2003). Amtrak had 18,000 stranded riders who could go no further north than Newark, and New Jersey Transit and Amtrak still had limited service hours after power was restored (Kocieniewski, 2003).

In Detroit the mass transit system and road system were equally impacted. The Detroit–Windsor Tunnel that crosses the international border was closed, evacuated within 15 minutes of the power failure. It receives electricity from four separate sources, a redundancy that had kept it open during previous power problems, but this time all four sources failed. Although the power to the Detroit metropolitan area was restored after less than 10 hours, the feeds were unstable, leading to rolling outages, and equipment that had to be reset frequently (DiBlasio et al., 2004).

Transportation infrastructure depends on electricity in even more subtle ways. "[T]unnel lights and ventilation; intelligent transportation systems (ITS) equipment such as cameras, loop detectors, variable message signs, and electronic toll collection equipment; and pumps to control flooding in depressed roadways" all rely on electricity to function. Even New York's vaunted security camera system was a victim of the outage. The day after the power outage began, the depressed sections of freeway in Detroit were flooded because there was no power for the sump pumps, and the public could not be effectively warned or redirected because the ITS was also without power (DiBlasio et al., 2004).

Although the FAA operations remained functional due to backup power supplies, numerous airports were closed by the loss of power, including New York, Newark, Detroit, Cleveland, Toronto, Montreal, Ottawa, Islip, Syracuse, Buffalo, Rochester, and Erie. The security check systems cannot operate without power, and the airlines lost the electronic ticket system, so passengers could not be cleared for flights. The closures of these airports created nationwide impacts, with flights cancelled in San Francisco and Los Angeles and stranded passengers in Chicago O'Hare Airport (Zernike, 2003). Power outages deprived the terminals of air conditioning and even toilet flushing (Scott, 2003).

The electric grid failure is just one clear example of the interconnectedness of infrastructure systems. Transportation, communications, and cyber systems all are part of the architecture of modern economies, and each sector has to be prepared for failures from within and outside. According to Arshad Mansoor of the Electric Power Research Institute, "[Y]ou can't just look at your system. You've got to look at how your system affects your neighbors and vice versa" (Minkel, 2008).

Information Coordination Across Sectors

These cascading events demonstrate that critical infrastructure organizations depend on each other and on government agencies for response and recovery. Coordinating information during the cascading event is essential for the development of a comprehensive approach to assisting the victims and restarting the damaged local economy.

TMC

A transportation management center (TMC) operates day to day to collect and disseminate information about the road network within a given jurisdiction (Figure 11.2). Collaborators within a typical regional TMC include the state highway system manager (usually the state department of transportation), the law enforcement agency for the state highway system, and often representatives of mass transit organizations. Elements of the ITS, such as sensors, cameras, signal control systems, computers linked to dispatch systems, and patrol and maintenance personnel, provide information on the operation of the road network, including congestion, accidents, and maintenance work. This information is used to manage roadway operations, including the creation of detours and dispatch of highway assistance personnel, which is disseminated to the public through 5-1-1 road information systems, the media, and electronic sign boards—both permanent and portable.

In a disaster, the TMC is the central point for the collection of transportation operations intelligence. Communication of this intelligence to transit and transportation partners is essential for rerouting road-based assets and creating "bus bridges" for rail-based assets around disaster damage. The information can be used to advise first responders on safe routes to victims and to interact with transportation department headquarters to set priorities for debris removal, road repair, and road reopening based on community needs.

FIGURE 11.2 Caltrans' Los Angeles District transportation management center.

TMCs may be located in state-level transportation organization regional headquarters, in county and city transportation departments, and even in rural areas to coordinate rural bus transit and road operations. They manage day-to-day road operations based on normal traffic patterns, special events based on the nodes that will be impacted, and disasters based on reported damage.

EOC

An emergency operations center (EOC) is a place where leaders can gather to make decisions regarding the response to and management of an emergency or disaster. The scope of the organization's work will dictate the size and composition of the EOC. Public transportation organizations are mandated by NIMS to use ICS in the field (HSPD-5), but the style of organization within the EOC should be selected to best meet the needs of the organization. While an "ICS indoors" model has proven successful in California and is one of the styles recommended by FEMA (called the ESF model), smaller transportation organizations may find another model better suited to their responsibilities and available staffing (Edwards & Goodrich, 2011).

Wal-Mart's EOC uses what Jackson (2007) calls "private sector ICS that maps back to ESFs." Using this approach daily for crime, food-borne illnesses, and medical emergencies, Wal-Mart is ready to use it when disaster looms. Its 40-seat EOC focuses daily on supporting the truck-based delivery to its nationwide chain of stores, monitoring threats like interstate closures and snowstorms. Its technology supports decision making for rapid supply chain management (Raths, 2010).

While TMCs are open every day, usually on a 24-hour schedule, the EOC is generally opened in anticipation of a planned event, like a parade, presidential visit, or major sporting event; of a pending disaster, like a predicted hurricane or severe storm; or in response to an actual emergency or disaster. EOCs manage community evacuations, emergency responder support operations, and disaster relief during response and recovery. Some EOCs, like the U.S. DOT Crisis Management Center, are staffed continuously to monitor conditions, notify senior officials of developing events, and provide immediate response planning for disasters.

Large, state-level transportation organizations will generally have their own EOCs (Figure 11.3), as will large corporations that manage fleets of trucks, like Wal-Mart. Transportation departments in cities, counties, and states will generally have a representative in the organizational EOC, generally in the Logistics Section, focusing on the movement of goods and relief supplies, and often in the Operations Section, focusing on the support of first responders through road debris removal, road and bridge inspection, and road reopening through rapid repairs.

FIGURE 11.3 State of California operations center.

EOCs collect information through computer systems connected to dispatch systems, media monitoring, and ITS elements, either through the TMC or through information delivered directly to the EOC. For example, in San Jose, California, the EOC video system can view all the traffic cameras in the city, and can change their focus and direction to enhance disaster information. In the floods of 1997, the cameras provided crucial information regarding street flooding and traffic movement. Regular meetings, called action planning meetings, provide an opportunity for the section chiefs to share information they have acquired through field staff, contractors, or other reliable sources, with the goal of shaping the action plan for the next action planning period. The outcome of the meeting is an action plan that guides the work of the EOC and leads to the creation of reports for higher levels of the organization or the state emergency management organization.

FCs

In the aftermath of 9/11 the federal government focused on the importance of information gathering, evaluating, and sharing; however, the information was seldom shared with state or local governments or the private sector (DOJ, 2008). Under the State Homeland Security Grant Program, many substate fusion centers (FCs) were formed to combat crime and terrorism on a regional basis, but there was little consistency in the technologies or systems used to gather and disseminate information.

After Hurricane Katrina, the federal government recognized the need for two changes. First, there should be some consistency in how information was gathered and analyzed to make it more universally useful across levels of government. Second, all-hazards information was recognized as an important element in fusion center activities. Better sharing of hurricane disaster information in the earliest hours might have triggered a faster federal response to the victims of the flooding of New Orleans.

In addition, the fusion centers had to go beyond law enforcement and include other first responders, like fire departments and emergency medical services providers, whose work could be directly impacted by information like stolen hazardous materials tankers in their areas or bombers using ambulances for cover, as described in Chapters 5 and 6. Although transportation is the key to all disaster response—evacuating populations, transporting first responders, moving emergency supplies—few fusion centers included transportation personnel, who could be both consumers and providers of crucial disaster-related intelligence. Furthermore, the private sector had not been part of the fusion center process, as intelligence was viewed as "need to know" and "law enforcement sensitive."

In 2008, the Department of Justice developed new guidance for fusion centers aimed at creating consistent models for information sharing and intelligence creation. It also advised fusion center organizers to include a broader range of public agencies, including transportation, fire, and public health, and private sector partners, stating as the goal: "Fusion centers bring all the relevant partners together to maximize the ability to prevent and respond to terrorism and criminal acts" and natural hazards (DOJ, 2008, p. 1).

"The primary function of an FC is to gather and analyze data, resulting in a finished, timely, credible and actionable product that is useable in the decision-making process" (FHWA, 2010, p. 18). Federal FCs have been providing intelligence bulletins and reports that address sector-specific issues, such as trends or concerns in transportation (FHWA, 2010, pp. 32–33). FCs are expected to coordinate with EOCs "during crisis management and recovery operations in coordination with the ICS, NIMS and NRF" (FHWA, 2010, p. 36).

The TMC, EOC, and FC share a common focus on timely understanding of threats, and activation of appropriate response to save lives and protect the environment and property. The TMC focuses on the transportation network, the EOC on multiple infrastructures, and the FC on "multiple public safety and security threats and critical infrastructures" (FHWA, 2010, p. 38).

Information collected by each entity may be useful to the others. For example, the TMC has information on transit operations and ridership, public parking capacity, and bridge traffic loads. The EOC might use that information to develop incident deployment and evacuation management plans. The FCs know the location of sensitive infrastructure and buildings and would benefit from knowing their relationship to bus and rail routes (FHWA, 2010, p. 41).

Continuity of Operations/ Business Continuity

Horowitz has noted that Wal-Mart's corporate intelligence system is part of its larger continuity of operations, or business continuity, plan. Developed to respond to a blackout, fire, or something else affecting the company's ability to do business (Horowitz, 2009, p. 513), these systems enabled Wal-Mart to evaluate the status of its buildings, the supplies that customers would need, and the routes open for its trucks to make deliveries after Hurricane Katrina.

Business continuity operations planning began with the information technology community in the late 1970s because businesses were becoming so dependent on computers. Early computers were susceptible to hardware failures and software problems, so redundant servers, RAID (redundant array of inexpensive disks/independent drives), and hot site/cold site plans were created to minimize loss of data. As computer systems became more elaborate, the maintenance became more complex, and therefore more comprehensive plans needed to be developed to ensure their continued operations. The fire in the Interstate Bank Building in Los Angeles in the early 1980s, on the day following the annual earthquake exercise, proved the value of business continuity planning for rapid business recovery.

The Disaster Recovery Institute (now DRII) began offering certification in business continuity management in 1988 (DRII, 2010). Its focus was on business recovery, leaving emergency response to the public sector. Certified business continuity professionals are responsible for the overall business continuity plan, including the safety of vital records and business processes. Recently, the DRII has collaborated with FEMA in the development of private sector interaction with government during disasters (DRII, 2010).

The federal government has an obligation to ensure "enduring constitutional government" at the local, state, and federal levels, regardless of the disaster. Continuity of government (COG) was the original focus of civil defense at the federal level. National Security Presidential Directive-51/ Homeland Security Presidential Directive-20 defines continuity of operations for individual executive departments "to ensure that Primary Mission Essential Functions (PMEFs) continue to be performed during a wide range of emergencies including localized acts of nature, accidents and technological or attack-related emergencies" (FEMA, 2010a). Continuity capability is the ability to provide the organization's identified essential functions continuously, regardless of the emergency.

Essential functions are those activities that define an organization. They are the activities that the organization is primarily responsible for within the larger government structure. At the national level, there are national essential functions that are required to maintain enduring constitutional government. Next are the primary mission essential functions (PMEFs) that each department performs. Finally, there are mission essential functions (MEFs) that further support the department's work. Local and state government agencies define their essential functions in support of the PMEFs and MEFs and for their role within the larger organization.

The continuity plan will encompass a number of elements. First, the organization must identify its essential functions. For example, a state transportation agency might define its essential functions as maintaining the state highway system, including rapid repair of disaster damage (Figure 11.4), supporting first responders' need for access to disaster sites, providing transportation-related information to the governor, and supporting federal PMEFs in Category A. Category B might include ensuring that employees are paid, that cyber systems are functioning, and that documentation for reimbursement is being accumulated. Category C might include oversight of ongoing maintenance, repair, and construction projects outside the disaster area.

Second, the organization has to maintain itself. Orders of succession have to be in place for all key personnel to ensure that lawful decisions can be made when the incumbents are unavailable or incapacitated. Delegation of authority gives contracting and decision-making authority to specific positions during a continuity situation. Should the normal headquarters be

FIGURE 11.4 **Rapid repair of flood damage to the road.**

FIGURE 11.5   **Caltrans' OASIS emergency communications trailer.**

unavailable, a continuity facility from which the essential functions can be performed, coordinated, or overseen has to be designated and prepared (Figure 11.5). An alternate communications system has to be created to support internal and external connectivity during a continuity situation that encompasses the organization, its customers, and the public. Vital records must be identified that are needed to perform the essential functions, and these must be safeguarded and available at the continuity site.

Third, the personnel of the organization must be organized for the continuity response. A human capital management system must be in place to call out the emergency relocation group members who will go to the continuity site to carry out the essential functions. The human capital unit must also maintain communications with the rest of the employees, organize telework, coordinate vacation and pay issues with those not assigned continuity duties, and prepare employees for resumption of normal work.

Fourth, a plan must be in place for the devolution of essential functions to another agency, to a group of employees in a different location, or to a different organizational level if the continuity plan cannot be activated as planned. Devolution may include just some or all of the essential functions.

Next, the continuity organization must oversee the return to normal—or a new normal—for the organization. This could include repairing and restarting the headquarters or obtaining a new rental or permanent facility for the organization.

Finally, the plan must be maintained, staff must be trained, and exercises must be conducted to ensure that the plan is up to date and the employees are able to perform their assigned tasks. Ideally, the exercises would be conducted with other parts of the organization to test compatibility of communications, equipment, and training.

The continuity plan addresses four phases. The first is preparedness, when plans, equipment, and facilities are prepared and employees are trained. Second is the activation and relocation phase, when essential equipment, vital records, and personnel relocate to the continuity location with their personnel support kits. The third phase is the full operation of the agency's essential functions from the continuity location. Finally, in reconstitution, the essential functions are transferred in an orderly fashion back to the headquarters and normal operations are resumed.

A continuity plan would be activated any time that the headquarters or other normal operational facility is unable to conduct the essential functions. This could include evacuation of a building due to mold or fire, inability to access the building due to flooding, or community-wide disruption like an earthquake or hurricane.

Designation of essential functions is a key activity for all transit and transportation agencies, the linchpin of emergency response capabilities. Even when the whole community is a victim, the essential functions of transportation must continue to support first responders and remove victims from a disaster environment, to bring in essential relief supplies, and to support the federal PMEFs. In addition to debris removal, bridge inspection, and expedient road repairs, transportation departments may need to advise on appropriate routes and give overweight permits for disaster relief equipment and goods. They may need to collaborate with law enforcement regarding evacuation routes or security perimeters that impact roadway usage.

Continuity of operations requires coordination with private sector partners. Contractors and suppliers of essential repair materials are most likely to be private sector organizations. In advance of need, it is important to share continuity plans to ensure that expectations of all partners are reasonable as to ability to perform, access to resources, and willingness of private sector personnel to engage in disaster work.

New Standards for Private Sector Preparedness

Following Hurricane Katrina, it was recognized that the private sector was an integral partner in emergency response and recovery operations. Wal-Mart and Home Depot were the models for private sector partnership with local governments. For example, the manager of the Wal-Mart in Waveland, Mississippi, was authorized to allow the community access to the disaster-damaged goods that had been washed out of the store. People with bare and bloody feet found shoes, and broken cases of water provided relief for residents. When Wal-Mart realized that goods were being donated to the televised disaster locations, it coordinated with state and local government to deliver goods to locations that needed assistance. Using GIS, it coordinated with FEMA for the relocation of federal disaster supply distribution to areas with an open store more than 5 miles away. This ensured that victims had access to resources (Jackson, 2007).

Wal-Mart's success led some states to add private sector representatives to their emergency management function. For example, the California Emergency Management Agency (CalEMA) invited private sector representatives to the state operations center as early as 2006, when the governor signed executive order S-05-06 directing CalEMA to bring the private sector into state disaster planning. After signing agreements with the grocers' and utility owners' associations, and big companies like Wal-Mart and Target, CalEMA created the business and utilities operations center within the state operations center. The goal is to help businesses with statewide locations to have better situational awareness, while also enhancing the speed of coordination between the public and private sectors for disaster response.

The 2007 wildland urban interface fires in San Diego County proved the benefits of this coordination, as Wal-Mart sent logistics employees to manage the donations pouring into QualComm stadium after television coverage of the shelter. The donations got to the victims efficiently (Raths, 2010).

After the 9/11 attacks, the importance of the private sector in economic recovery was recognized. Implementing the Recommendations of the 9/11 Commission Act of 2007 was passed, including a provision for the development of voluntary emergency preparedness standards for private organizations. The 9/11 Commission report and the 2007 law recognized that businesses in the area of the World Trade Center attacks had little planning for business continuity, and most small businesses in the area failed. Title IX of the Act of 2007 required FEMA to work with the private sector to create criteria for disaster preparedness and business continuity.

FEMA created the PS-Prep Program and designated an accreditation body for companies wanting to join the program (FEMA, 2008). DRII represented business in the deliberations. One private sector analyst suggested that "the PS Prep program is designed to build awareness and give businesses of all sizes the ability to plan, test and recover by having disaster management, emergency management and business continuity programs" (Continuity Compliance, 2011).

In June of 2010 the secretary of DHS announced the adoption of standards for PS-Prep, the voluntary private sector preparedness program (FEMA, 2010b). While mass transit and road systems are generally public agencies whose disaster preparedness requirements are covered under the various Homeland Security presidential directives and related laws, maritime, aviation, and trucking are private sector entities that are integral to global supply chain management and generally operating without disaster preparedness guidelines.

FEMA partnered with the American Society of Industrial Security to develop the first standard, Organizational Resilience: Security Preparedness, and Continuity Management System (ASIS, 2009). The second standard, developed by the British Standards Institution, is Business Continuity Management, and the third, developed by the National Fire Protection Association, is Standard on Disaster/Emergency Management and Business Continuity Programs (FEMA, 2010c). Private sector organizations may voluntarily adopt the programs attached to the standards and choose to work toward accreditation under the PS-Prep Program. The standards are focused on organizational resilience across all phases of emergency management and homeland security, based on regular assessment of the systems in place. Businesses attaining accreditation have greater assurance of resilience in a disaster.

The Private Sector Preparedness Council, chaired by the FEMA administrator, is developing the business case for private sector entities to become accredited under the PS-Prep standards (FEMA 2010d). For years small businesses have considered disaster preparedness an expensive luxury, while growing businesses have balked at the impact of planning, training, and exercises on profits. However, insurance companies have included an evaluation of disaster preparedness in the risk analysis of their customers and adjusted policy coverages and premiums accordingly.

The PS-Prep program may reframe business's approach to emergency preparedness. Customers in a just-in-time supply chain might evaluate the benefit of PS-Prep certification for a potential supplier as enhanced reliability. One private sector analyst suggested that companies in the supply chain might find themselves at a competitive disadvantage if having PS-Prep certification becomes an expectation of large enterprise and government customers (Continuity Compliance, 2011).

Case Studies

2006 European Power Blackout

In 28 seconds, 15 million European households lost power late on the evening of November 4, 2006, due to a change in power management plans (UCTE, n.d.). The E.ON Netz electric utility had planned to turn off a 380-kilovolt electric power transmission line to allow a new ship, the *Norwegian Pearl*, to be moved from the shipyard in Germany to the North Sea through the Ems River from 0100 to 0500 on November 5 (UCTE, n.d., p. 6). Safety procedures require that ships not pass under working power lines with a clearance of less than 5 meters.

Because the ship was taller than 60 meters, the power line over the river had to be turned off. The shipyard had coordinated such passages with the power company often in the past (Reuters, 2006). At the last minute, the timing of the ship's movement was changed to the late evening of November 4, apparently without adequately coordinating the power change with related transmission system operators (TSOs).

Europe's 50-year-old power grid had become increasingly integrated as power demand throughout the continent increased. The continent was divided into three generation units that interchanged power across the grid: west, northeast, and southeast. Each unit had a different balance between generation and consumption. When the power line shutoff was changed from the middle of the night to the late evening, the system operators were unable to compensate for the loss of the 380-kilovolt line (UCTE, n.d., p. 7). Transmission stations across the continent were tripped by the load change (Castle, 2006).

In addition, Europe had integrated alternate power supplies into its system. "Generally, the uncontrolled operation of dispersed generation (mainly wind and combined heat and power) during the disturbance complicated the process of re-establishing normal system conditions" (UCTE, n.d., p. 6). Resynchronization of the system was completed within 38 minutes, and power was restored to all consumers within two hours (UCTE, n.d., p. 6).

The power outage had significant social impacts. One hundred trains in Germany and several more in Belgium experienced delays of up to 2 hours. In France five million people were affected in Paris and Leon. In Paris firefighters rescued people stuck in more than 40 elevators, but the Paris Metro continued to operate (Castle, 2006). In Spain the power losses extended to Madrid, Barcelona, Zaragosa, and Andalucia, while in Italy the problems were concentrated in the northwest, but extended to Puglia in the southeast (BBC, 2006).

There were two main causes identified for the failure. First, the interconnectedness of Europe's power grid caused the cascade of power outages across the continent, as the German network became overloaded through the loss of the 380-kilovolt line. Italy's prime minister said that this indicated a need for better coordination of power supplies through a central authority instead of several large private sector generators (Castle, 2006).

Second, staff training for major power interruptions seemed to be inadequate to manage the sudden power shift. The UCTE report noted:

> Although training of dispatchers has been well developed for a couple of years for situations related to TSOs internal control area conditions, incidents originating from external networks and affecting a TSO's own grid are not always trained. Joint simulation training with neighboring TSOs is not yet a common practice. (n.d., p. 7)

The more interdependent that the systems become, the less is the variance between generation and consumption that can be tolerated and the more common training and exercises are required.

European Union Energy Commissioner Andris Piebalgs stated, "Europe should draw lessons from this blackout that left millions of Europeans in various Member States without electricity and develop stronger network [operating] security standards" (Continuity Central, 2007).

> All this, also on November 4, led TSOs to operate the system closer and closer to its limits according to current security criteria based on system physics that will therefore remain of decisive relevance for a secure operation of the electricity transmission infrastructure. (UTCE, n.d., p. 5)

Impact of Great East Japan Earthquake's Radiation Leak on Global Trade

The great East Japan earthquake is the worst natural disaster in Japanese history. The earthquake registered 9.0 at the epicenter, and the tsunami wave was more than 31 feet high. More than 19,000 people were dead or missing, and 700 people were still in evacuation centers on December 20, 2011. There were 500 square kilometers of northeastern Japan devastated, with many small cities and villages destroyed. The estimate of direct damage to facilities and infrastructure is 16–25 trillion yen, which is $205 billion–$321 billion (Tanemura, 2012).

This event did not stop in Japan, but traveled across the Pacific Ocean. In Hawaii the emergency operations plan was activated, and civilians were evacuated inland. One person in California died, swept away by the tsunami wave, and there was a great deal of damage caused to the fishing fleets in Santa Cruz and Crescent City. It also required an evacuation of low-lying areas (Goldman & Little, 2011).

The Fukushima nuclear power plant was inundated by the tsunami. Some facilities exploded and released radiation. There is now an "entry prohibited" zone of 20 kilometers around the plant. People had to evacuate because the cumulative radiation exposure was too high (Tanemura, 2012).

The radiation emanating from the Japanese power plant had an international trade impact. Hong Kong banned food imports from Japan after discovering elevated radiation levels in turnips and spinach. Taiwan's Fisheries Agency banned its boats from fishing near the power plant (Reuters, 2011b). An All Nippon Airways cargo plane that arrived at Dalian, China, was turned away on March 16 because of the high radioactivity readings for its cargo, while a later plane was allowed to land with elevated radiation levels (Reuters, 2011a).

On March 17, 2011, the U.S. Maritime Administration (MARAD) issued an advisory to all ships to avoid transiting within 80 kilometers of the Fukushima Nuclear Power Plant and that tracking line planning should include current wind and weather conditions. It led chemical biological radiation defense training (CBRD) for U.S. mariners in response to potential contamination as the winds blew the radiation eastward. On March 21, a container ship owned by MOL that originated in California and had spent only a few hours in the Port of Tokyo was turned back from China due to high levels of radiation. Although international monitoring agencies have not recommended any protective measures, the Chinese government declared the ship to be too contaminated to enter port.

Concerned about impacts on international trade, the Japanese government asked the Chinese government

> to carry out a radiation check on ships and airplanes arriving from Japan in a "rational manner," an official at the Ministry of Land, Infrastructure, Transport and Tourism said. "We have also asked the Chinese government to provide specific figures, such as radiation levels found in tests and standard levels. Unless we have such figures, we cannot cope with (the situation)." (Masaki, 2011)

By December 2011, the reactors had "reached a state of cold shutdown." This is a step toward allowing the evacuated residents to return to their homes (Reuters, 2012).

Public–Private Partnerships: Mid-Atlantic and Northeast Initiatives

The All-Hazards Consortium has developed a series of regional integrated planning initiatives for its partner agencies in the mid-Atlantic and Northeast regions, all of which include transportation sector activities. These initiatives "promote coordination and integration of planning efforts on specific projects and investments between state/local governments and the private sector 'life line sector' owner/operators of the critical infrastructure" (All-Hazards Consortium, 2012).

Regional Rail Security Integrated Planning Initiative

The Washington Metropolitan Area Transit Authority (WMATA) and the New Jersey Urban Area Security Initiative (UASI) formed an alliance among passenger and freight railroads, UASI, and state representatives and the Transportation Security Administration (TSA) to develop emergency planning guidance. One product being created is a "public/private rail owners/operators framework for critical decision making built on the existing interdependencies between these public/private organizations with an emphasis on state and local integration" (All-Hazards Consortium, 2012, p. 1). As mentioned in earlier chapters, the Northeast corridor track is mostly owned by Amtrak, a public corporation, but is used extensively by private freight rail operators.

All the partners in the consortium have some security practices in use, but this new initiative will try to better coordinate their use and protocols to enhance future responses to emergencies. They are also including research on security that is available from public and private entities. The first product focused on operational readiness of the regional rail system as a whole and studied the "plans, prevention considerations and identified technologies" already in use. The goal is to create a "consistent regional response" to future events.

Regional Rapid Critical Infrastructure (CI)/ Key Resources (KR) Restoration Initiative

This initiative integrates representatives from New Jersey and Pennsylvania energy, communications, IT, transportation, emergency management, homeland security, public safety, finance, retail, and chemical sectors and local government officials into a collaborative effort to create plans for mutual aid after disasters. With the goal of speeding restoration of critical services, this plan integrates public and private resources to examine existing impediments to rapid restoration. A study of past disasters has revealed that critical repair equipment is delayed through interstate requirements for stopping at truck scales and adhering to a variety of legal operating requirements. The purpose of this project is to identify those impediments in advance and determine how to eliminate or overcome them during disaster response (All-Hazards Consortium, 2012, p. 2).

Regional Disaster Food Distribution Project

Delivering food and water to disaster victims is a key response action, but it is often held up by impediments to transportation and distribution. This initiative includes New York City, Pennsylvania, Maryland, Virginia, and West Virginia working together to develop a Food Sector Resiliency Plan.

The food resilience plan's elements fall into several categories. The first is mapping out the logistics of moving food within the AHC states and their partner states. The second is the development of interstate coordination of activities to match requests for food with available resources through existing systems like AID Matrix (supply chain management for humanitarian relief) and EMAC (emergency management assistance compact). The third is to include food sector representatives in the state emergency operations center within the emergency support function activities.

Summary

The constantly changing nature of society and the economy also impact transportation security across the global supply chain. For example, the challenge of copper thefts from transportation infrastructure is directly tied to the global demand for raw materials, currently including copper. Consumers continue to demand greater access to a larger variety of electronic consumer goods, which poses another threat to transportation security because of the multiple uses to which a remote control or communication device may be put. In addition, new communications systems have changed the way in which information is stolen. While 50 years ago a spy had to smuggle out sensitive information on microfilm using mail or a courier, today the same information can be sent instantly and anonymously by e-mail.

Perfect security is neither affordable nor possible in an open democracy. As was discussed in the modal chapters, technological capabilities exist to screen packages more thoroughly, but the time and cost involved would change the transportation profile for the world. Higher costs of goods engendered by the added security would price many current consumers out of the market for elastic goods like exotic fruits and fashionable shoes. With a new security charge in every element of the supply chain, the global commerce in raw materials and merchandise would change. Rising prices and falling consumer demand would upset economies everywhere. Furthermore, Magnus Ranstorp of the Swedish National Defense College points out that "it would be too expensive to try to establish a foolproof system because of the constantly changing tactics used by terrorist groups" (Katz, 2010) and the ever-evolving nature of commerce.

Regardless of the terror attack, grid failure, or natural disaster, transportation is the linchpin that makes recovery possible. Vince Pearce of FHWY said,

> The more we look at large scale situations, the more we see that if transportation does not work right, it's too hard for other responders to do their jobs. If we can't get the fire trucks and ambulances to the scene, we can't put the fires out or help the injured. Transportation must work at its absolute best in these kinds of situations. (DiBlasio et al., 2004)

Discussion Questions

1. Security for any transit or transportation agency addresses a large number of assets and infrastructure for any organization. How do you set a priority on which assets to protect?

2. There is an inherent conflict between access and security. How do you balance the two aspects of transportation systems?

3. Transportation is a critical part not only of the economy of the host nation, but also of the global supply chain. How do you balance risk, mitigation, prevention, and cost? Who are your customers, and how do you balance their conflicting demands?

4. Transportation security depends on the development of intelligence. What is the role of the TMC, EOC, and FC in developing, confirming, and disseminating intelligence?

5. What is the balance of public and private ownership in the transportation sector? What infrastructure is usually public and what is usually private? How do you evaluate the appropriate balance of benefit and cost for security programs between public and private entities?

References

ABC News. (2005, September 29). What can Wal-Mart teach FEMA about disaster response? Retrieved April 12, 2011, from http://abcnews.go.com/WNT/HurricaneRita/story?id=1171087&page=1

All-Hazards Consortium. (2012, February 23). *2012 AHC February Integrated Planning Newsletter*.

ASIS. (2009). Organizational resilience: Security, preparedness, and continuity management systems—Requirements with guidance for use. Accessed May 31, 2011, at http://www.asisonline.org/guidelines/ASIS_SPC.1-2009_Item_No._1842.pdf

BBC. (2006, November 5). Bid to overhaul Europe power grid. *BBC News*. Accessed April 12, 2011, at http://news.bbc.co.uk/2/hi/6117880.stm

BENS. (2007). Getting down to business: An action plan for public–private disaster response coordination. Accessed on April 30, 2011, at http://www.caresiliency.org/page/about-us

Castle, S. (2006, November 6). Europe suffers worst blackout for three decades. *The Independent*. Accessed April 12, 2011, at http://www.independent.co.uk/news/world/europe/europe-suffers-worst-blackout-for-three-decades-423144.html

CBC News. (2003, November 19). The blackout explained. Accessed on May 31, 2011, at http://www.cbc.ca/news/background/poweroutage/explained.html

Continuity Central. (February 1, 2007). European blackout of 2006: Important lessons to be drawn. Accessed April 12, 2011, at http://www.continuitycentral.com/news03043.htm

Continuity Compliance. (2011). PS-Prep. Accessed May 31, 2011, at http://www.continuitycompliance.org/ps-prep-overview-complete/

Cooper, C., & Block, R. (2006). *Disaster! Hurricane Katrina and the failure of Homeland Security*. New York, NY: Henry Holt & Co., Inc.

DHS. (2008). Implementation of the post-Katrina Emergency Management Reform Act and other organizational changes. Accessed April 12, 2011, at http://www.dhs.gov/xabout/structure/gc_1169243598416.shtm

DiBlasio, A. J., Regan, T. J., Zirker, M. E., Lovejoy, K., & Fichter, K. (2004). Learning from the blackout. *Public Roads, 68,* 2. Accessed February 20, 2012, from http://www.fhwa.dot.gov/publications/publicroads/04sep/04.cfm

DOJ. (2008). Fusion center guidelines: Developing and sharing information and intelligence in a new era. Accessed May 31, 2011, at http://it.ojp.gov/documents/fusion_center_guidelines_law_enforcement.pdf

DRII. (2010). Fact sheet. https://www.drii.org/docs/DRII%20Factsheet.pdf

Edwards, F. L., & Goodrich, D. C. (2011). *Continuity of operations/continuity of government for state-level transportation organizations.* Report 11-02. San Jose, CA: Mineta Transportation Institute.

Elegant, S. (2004, August 23). The return of Abu Sayyaf. *Time Magazine.* Retrieved April 19, 2012 from http://www.time.com/time/printout/0,8816,686107,00.html

ELCON. (2004). The economic impacts of the August 2003 blackout. Electricity Consumers Resource Council. http://www.elcon.org/Documents/EconomicImpactsofAugust2003Blackout.pdf

FEMA. (2008). DHS selects ANSI-ASQ National Accreditation Board to support voluntary private sector preparedness certification program. Accessed May 31, 2011, at http://www.fema.gov/news/newsrelease.fema?id=45280

FEMA. (2010a). Continuity of operations overview. Accessed May 31, 2011, at http://www.fema.gov/about/org/ncp/coop/index.shtm

FEMA. (2010b). Secretary Napolitano announces new standards for private sector preparedness. Accessed May 31, 2011, at http://www.dhs.gov/ynews/releases/pr_1276616888003.shtm

FEMA. (2010c). Voluntary private sector preparedness accreditation and certification program (PS-Prep) resource center. Accessed May 31, 2011, at http://www.fema.gov/privatesector/preparedness/adoption_standards.shtm

FEMA. (2010d). Voluntary private sector preparedness accreditation and certification program. Accessed May 31, 2011, at http://www.fema.gov/media/fact_sheets/vpsp.shtm

FHWA. (2010). *Federal Highway Administration information sharing guidebook for transportation management centers, emergency operations centers and fusion centers.* Washington, DC: FHWA, HOTO-1.

Goldman, R., & Little, L. (2011, March 11). Search suspended for California man swept into the sea by tsunami. *ABC News.* Accessed April 12, 2011, at http://abcnews.go.com/US/california-man-swept-sea-tsunami/story?id=13112901

Horowitz, S. (2009). Wal-Mart to the rescue: Private enterprise's response to Hurricane Katrina. *Independent Review, 13*(4), 511–528.

Jackson, J. (2007, November). *Emergency management: Evolution of the private sector: WalMart and Katrina.* A paper presented at the International Association of Emergency Managers Annual Conference, Orlando, FL.

Katz, G. (2010, November 1). Fixing cargo security system would cost billions. Associated Press. http://seattletimes.nwsource.com/html/businesstechnology/2013320827_mailbombcosts02.html

Kennedy, R. (2003, August 15). Thousands stranded on foot by crippled trains, crawling buses and traffic gridlock. *New York Times.* Accessed May 31, 2011 at http://www.nytimes.com/2003/08/15/nyregion/15TRAN.html?ref=newyorkcityblackoutof2003

Kocieniewski, D. (2003, April 16). Economic toll "devastating," a troubled McGreevey says. *New York Times.* Accessed May 31, 2011, at http://www.nytimes.com/2003/08/16/nyregion/16JERS.html?ref=newyorkcityblackoutof2003

Lipton, E. (2005, March 20). Trying to keep nation's ferries safe from terrorists: Coast Guard studies security threats. Retrieved April 19, 2012 from ProQuest Historical Newspapers: *The New York Times* (1851–2007).

Masaki, H. (2011, March 29). China turns away MOL ship for radiation. *Journal of Commerce.* Accessed April 12, 2011, at http://www.joc.com/maritime/china-turns-away-mol-ship-radiation

Minkel, J. R. (2008). The 2003 Northeast blackout—five years later. *Scientific American*. August 13. http://www.scientificamerican.com/article.cfm?id=2003-blackout-five-years-later

ODNI. (n.d.). Office of the Director of National Intelligence: About. Accessed April 12, 2011, at http://www.dni.gov/who.htm

Raths, D. (2010, May-June). Working together. *Emergency Management.*

Reuters. (2006, November 6). European blackout: German power firm to risk another switch-off. *Spiegel On-Line International.* Accessed April 12, 2011, at http://www.spiegel.de/international/0,1518,446770,00.html

Reuters. (2011a, March 23). China province detects radiation from Japan plane: Report. Accessed April 12, 2011, at http://www.reuters.com/article/2011/03/24/us-japan-quake-china-radiation-idUSTRE72N03V20110324

Reuters. (2011b, March 23). Restrictions on Japanese food imports. Accessed April 12, 2011, at http://www.reuters.com/article/2011/03/23/us-japan-food-idUSTRE72L88X20110323

Reuters. (2012, February 2). Fukushima reactor leaks, radiation tiny—Tepco. Accessed February 12, 2012, at http://in.reuters.com/article/2012/02/02/japan-nuclear-leak-idINDEE81105520120202

Scott, J. (2003, August 15). In subways, in traffic, in elevators: All stuck. *New York Times*. Accessed May 11, 2011, at http://www.nytimes.com/2003/08/15/nyregion/15STUC.html?ref=newyorkcityblackoutof2003

Tanemura, M. (2012, January 9). *Japanese transportation systems after the great East Japan earthquake.* A paper delivered at the U.S.–China Disaster Assistance Working Group, San Jose, CA.

UCTE (Union for the Coordination of Transmission of Electricity). (n.d.). *Final report: System disturbance on 4 November 2006.* Accessed April 12, 2011, at http://www.cigre-uk.org/Memberssection_files/ucte_final_report_nov_06_disturbances.pdf

Water and Health. (2012). Water on the balance—a boiling crisis for the nation's water supply. http://www.waterandhealth.org/newsletter/new/winter_2004/water_balance.html

Zernike, K. (2003, August 15). The blackout of 2003: Travel woes; rippling across continent, chaos strands thousands. *New York Times.* Accessed May 31, 2011, at http://www.nytimes.com/2003/08/15/us/blackout-2003-travel-woes-rippling-across-continent-chaos-strands-thousands.html

Glossary

Action Plan	Written plan created from the action planning briefing that includes goals and objectives, operational period, maps, organization charts, and any auxiliary plans to be used during the covered operational period.
Action Planning Briefing	A meeting held as needed throughout the duration of an incident to select specific strategies and tactics for event control operations and for service and support planning. The action planning briefing allows all general staff to collaborate with each other and the management section chief to develop the action plan.
Agency	An agency is a division of government with a specific function or a nongovernmental organization (e.g., private contractor, business, etc.) that offers a particular kind of assistance. In ICS, agencies are defined as jurisdictional (having statutory responsibility for incident mitigation) or assisting and/or cooperating (providing resources and/or assistance).

Agency Representative	An individual assigned to an incident from an assisting or cooperating agency who has been delegated authority to make decisions on matters affecting that agency's participation at the incident. Agency representatives report to the Liaison Office.
Automated Information System	An information sharing system designed to chart the locations of ships at sea to prevent collisions; also used for coast and port security.
Branch	The ICS organizational level having functional responsibility for major operations. The branch level is, organizationally, between the section and the group or unit.
Buffer Zone Protection Plan	A plan to provide standoff and perimeter protection to critical infrastructure elements. Federal funding was available to assist with the creation and implementation of the plan.
Business Continuity	Plans for business to continue after a disaster or emergency, including plans for alternate locations and data recovery.
Cascading Event	An emergency or disaster that starts by impacting a discrete area or single sector and then causes additional follow-on damage in other areas or sectors.
Catastrophe	A natural, technological, or human-caused event that overwhelms existing plans for disasters and emergencies, causes widespread or economically significant damage across multiple jurisdictions, and requires significant outside assistance, including federal response.
Chiefs	The ICS title for the general staff individuals responsible for supervision of functional sections: Operations, Planning, Logistics, and Finance/Administration.
Command Staff	The EOC command staff consists of the information officer, safety officer, security officer, emergency management coordinator, and liaison officer. They report directly to the management section chief. They may have an assistant or assistants, as needed.
Continuity of Operations	Plans for a government entity to continue providing essential services after a catastrophic event, including alternate locations, vital records preservation, and communications systems.

Critical Infrastructure	Public and private assets that are essential to the operation of society's public health and safety, security, and economy.
Deputy	A fully qualified individual who, in the absence of a superior, could be delegated the authority to manage a functional operation or perform a specific task. In some cases, a deputy could act as relief for a supervisor and therefore must be fully qualified in the position. Deputies can be assigned to the incident commander, general staff, and branch directors.
Director	The ICS title for individuals responsible for supervision of a branch.
Disaster	A natural, technological, or human-caused event that overwhelms the usual systems of emergency response and requires outside assistance.
Emergency Management	A system for organizing resources to mitigate against, prepare and plan for, respond to, and recover from emergencies and disasters.
Emergency Medical Technician	A healthcare specialist with particular skills and knowledge in prehospital emergency medicine.
Emergency Operations Center (EOC)	A predesignated facility established by an agency or jurisdiction to coordinate the overall agency, or jurisdictional, response to an emergency or disaster event.
Emergency Services Coordinator	The individual within each political subdivision that has coordination responsibility for jurisdictional emergency management.
Finance/ Administration	The section responsible for all event costs, reimbursements, and financial considerations; includes the Time Unit, Procurement Unit, Compensation/ Claims Unit, and Cost Unit.
Fusion Center	A location where law enforcement and federal Homeland Security entities meet to evaluate streams of information and convert it to actionable intelligence to enhance safety and security.
General Staff	The group of personnel reporting to the management section chief: operations section chief, planning section chief, logistics section chief, and finance/administration section chief.

Hazardous Material	Any material so categorized by federal or state law that is capable of doing harm to humans or the environment through routine or accidental exposure.
High Threat Urban Area	An urban area in the United States that has been evaluated using risk analysis techniques and determined to have many hazards and vulnerable populations and facilities that, if damaged, would have significant security or economic consequences.
Homeland Security	A concept developed after the terrorist attacks of 9/11/01 to enhance the safety, security, and emergency management of domestic communities and resources, including critical infrastructure.
Homeland Security Presidential Directive 7	A directive issued by President George W. Bush that required identification, prioritization, and protection of the nation's critical infrastructure.
Improvised Explosive Device	An explosive device made by an individual using components and explosive materials gathered from the normal commercial supply chain—not commercial or military explosive devices.
Incident Action Plan	Created by the incident commander in the field during an ICS event. Contains objectives reflecting the overall incident strategy and specific tactical actions and supporting information for the next operational period. The IAP may be oral or written.
Incident Commander	The individual responsible for the management of all incident operations at the incident site in the field.
Incident Command System	A standardized emergency management concept specifically designed to allow its users to adopt an integrated organizational structure equal to the complexity and demands of single or multiple incidents without being hindered by jurisdictional boundaries.
Incident Objectives	In the field, statements of guidance and direction necessary for the selection of appropriate strategies and the tactical direction of resources. Incident objectives are based on realistic expectations of what can be accomplished when all allocated resources have been effectively deployed. Incident objectives must be achievable and measurable, yet flexible enough to allow for strategic and tactical alternatives.

Liaison Officer	A member of the command staff responsible for coordinating with representatives from cooperating and assisting agencies.
Logistics Section	The section responsible for providing facilities, services, and materials for the incident or in the EOC.
Management by Objective	In ICS, this is a top-down management activity that involves three steps to achieve the incident or EOC goal: establishing the objectives, selection of appropriate strategies to achieve the objectives, and the tactical (in the field) or strategic (in the EOC) direction associated with the selected strategy. Tactical direction includes selection of tactics, selection of resources, resource assignments, and performance monitoring.
Mitigation	Steps taken in advance of a disaster to protect populations and critical infrastructure, or to lessen the damage they incur.
Multiagency Coordination System (MACS)	The combination of personnel, facilities, equipment, procedures, and communications integrated into a common system. When activated, MACS has the responsibility for coordination of assisting agency resources and support in a multiagency or multi-jurisdictional environment.
Mutual Aid Agreement	Written agreement between agencies and/or jurisdictions in which they agree to assist one another upon request by furnishing personnel and equipment.
National Incident Management System (NIMS)	Developed by the secretary of Homeland Security at the request of the president, the National Incident Management System (NIMS) integrates effective practices in emergency preparedness and response into a comprehensive national framework for incident management. Based on ICS, the NIMS will enable responders at all levels to work together more effectively to manage domestic incidents no matter what the cause, size, or complexity.
National Infrastructure Protection Plan	A national plan for protecting locations and resources in specified sectors within the United States, including transportation and utilities.

Officer	The ICS title for the person responsible for the command staff positions of safety, liaison, and information.
Operational Period	In the field, the period scheduled for execution of a given set of operation actions as specified in the incident action plan. Operational periods can be of various lengths.
Operations Section	The section responsible for all tactical operations at the incident or, in the EOC, for supporting field operations. Includes branches, divisions and/or groups, task forces, strike teams, single resources, and staging areas in the field; and branches, groups, and units in the EOC.
Planning Section	Responsible for the collection, evaluation, and dissemination of information related to an event, and for the preparation and documentation of action plans. The Planning Section also maintains information on the current and forecasted situation and on the status of resources assigned to the incident. Includes the Situation, Resource, Documentation, and Demobilization Units, as well as technical specialists.
Preparedness	Steps taken in advance of an emergency or disaster to organize resources to enhance safety; includes planning, training, exercising, and stockpiling.
Public Information Officer	A member of the command staff responsible for interfacing with the public, media, or other agencies requiring information directly from the incident or the EOC. There is only one public information officer (PIO) per incident in the field. There is a PIO in the EOC whenever it is opened.
Recovery	Steps taken after a disaster to repair damaged property, restart the economy, and repair critical infrastructure functionality.
Response	Steps taken during a disaster or emergency to save lives, protect the environment, and protect property, including critical infrastructure.
Risk Assessment	A systematic review of potential hazards, vulnerabilities, and consequences focused on a specific location, community, or economic sector.

Safety Officer	A member of the command staff responsible for monitoring and assessing safety hazards or unsafe situations and for developing measures for ensuring personnel safety. In the EOC, this includes ensuring the psychological safety of the EOC staff by ensuring that regular shift changes are planned for and that appropriate food is delivered in a timely fashion during prolonged activations.
SCADA	A computer system that controls and monitors a process. This process can be infrastructure, facility, or industry based.
Section	The organizational level with responsibility for a major functional area of the event (e.g., Operations, Planning, Logistics, Finance/Administration). The section chief works directly for the management section chief and oversees branches, groups, and units.
Span of Control	The supervisory ratio: in the field, ranges from three to seven individuals per supervisor, with five workers to one supervisor being optimum. In the EOC, there is no minimum, and up to 10 personnel may report to one supervisor.
Staging Areas	Staging areas are locations set up at an incident where resources can be placed while awaiting a tactical assignment.
The Operations	The section that manages staging areas.
Toxic Inhalation Hazard	A material that causes distress, injury, or death to humans or animals through inhalation.
Transportation Management Center	A location at which the transportation agency collects and analyzes information about the operation of the transportation and transit systems in the community, integrating information from the Intelligent Transportation System technology, such as road sensors and traffic cameras.
Unity of Command	The concept by which each person within an organization reports to only one designated person.
Urban Area Security Initiative	A federal program that provides terrorism preparedness, response, and mitigation funding to the nation's largest cities and their adjacent communities.

Vehicle-Borne Improvised Explosive Device	An explosive device carried by a car, truck, or other vehicle that is made by an individual using components and explosive materials gathered from the normal commercial supply chain—not commercial or military explosive devices.
Weapons of Mass Destruction	Generally, a characterization of large bombs, especially biological weapons, nuclear bombs, or fire bombs, capable of destroying large areas and large numbers of people at the same time.
Weapons of Mass Disruption	Any explosive, chemical, biological, radiological, or incendiary device capable of causing significant localized loss of life and property damage.
Weapons of Mass Killing	Any device capable of killing multiple people in a brief period.

Acronyms

AIS	Automated information system
BZPP	Buffer zone protection plan
COOP	Continuity of operations
C-TPAT	Customs Trade Partnership Against Terrorism
DHHS	Department of Health and Human Services
DHS	Department of Homeland Security
DOE	Department of Energy
DOT	Department of Transportation
EMAP	Emergency Management Assistance Program
EMS	Emergency medical services
EMT	Emergency medical technician
EOC	Emergency operations center
EOP	Emergency operations plan
FAA	Federal Aviation Administration
FEMA	Federal Emergency Management Act
FHWA	Federal Highway Administration
FIRM	Flood insurance rate map

FTA	Federal Transit Administration
GIS	Geographical information system
GPS	Global positioning system
HAZMAT	Hazardous material
HSPD-7	Homeland Security Presidential Directive 7
HTUA	High threat urban area
ICS	Incident Command System
IED	Improvised explosive device
LNG	Liquefied natural gas
MACS	Multiagency coordination system
MDA	Maritime domain awareness
MOU	Memorandum of understanding
MTSA	Maritime Transportation Security Act
NAFTA	North American Free Trade Agreement
NFPA	National Fire Protection Association
NIMS	National Incident Management System
NIPP	National Infrastructure Protection Plan
NGO	Non Governmental Organization
PIO	Public information officer
SCADA	Supervisory control and data acquisition
SOC	State operations center (the state's EOC)
TIH	Toxic inhalation hazard
TMC	Transportation management center
TRB	Transportation Research Board (part of the National Academy of Sciences)
TSA	Transportation Security Administration
VBIED	Vehicle-borne improvised explosive device
WMD	Weapon of mass destruction

Index